Reinventing Cotton Mather
in the American
Renaissance

✛

Reinventing Cotton Mather
in the American Renaissance

+

Magnalia Christi Americana
in Hawthorne, Stowe, and Stoddard

CHRISTOPHER D. FELKER

Northeastern University Press

Boston

Northeastern University Press

Library of Congress Cataloging-in-Publication Data

Felker, Christopher, 1963–
    Reinventing Cotton Mather in the American renaissance : Magnalia Christi
Americana in Hawthorne, Stowe, and Stoddard / Christopher Felker.
        p.   cm.
    Includes bibliographical references and index.
    ISBN 1-55553-187-3
    1. Political fiction, American—New England—History and
criticism.   2. Politics and literature—New England—History—19th
century.   3. Mather, Cotton, 1663–1728.   Magnalia Christi Americana.
4. Hawthorne, Nathaniel, 1804–1864.   Grandfather's chair.   5. Stowe,
Harriet Beecher, 1811–1896.   Minister's wooing.   6. Stoddard,
Elizabeth, 1823–1902.   Morgesons.   7. American fiction—19th
century—History and criticism.   8. New England—Politics and
government—Historiography.   9. Democracy in literature.
10. Puritans in literature.   I. Title.
PS374.P6F45   1994
813'.309358—dc20   93-42071

FTW
AFD 1295

Designed by Nighthawk Design

Composed in Stempel Garamond by Coghill Composition in Richmond, Virginia. Printed and bound by McNaughton & Gunn, Inc., in Saline, Michigan. The paper is Natural Offset, an acid-free sheet.

MANUFACTURED IN THE UNITED STATES OF AMERICA

98   97   96   95   94   5   4   3   2   1

TO MY FATHER
Daniel B. Felker

Contents

+

Illustrations

✠

Preface

✛

My aim in this work is to show the importance of a Puritan political sentiment that advanced the desire of several American Renaissance writers to address the implications of democracy. Nathaniel Hawthorne, Elizabeth Drew Stoddard, Harriet Beecher Stowe, and others depended on Cotton Mather's *Magnalia Christi Americana* to discover, in their own times, the importance of democratic concepts and categories.

In my study of the importance of Thomas Robbins's 1820 edition of *Magnalia*,[1] I have tried to responsibly reinterpret a canonical work as an important moment in the history of the book in America. Mather's sense of history was, first and foremost, a strategy intended to create in his audiences a profound sense of the "constructedness" inherent in self and history. After the American publication of *Magnalia* in 1820, Mather's strategy took on a new force and importance as a number of New England writers sought to anchor their examinations of liberal democracy in the "authenticity" of Mather's writing. The group of writers whom I discuss knew, as Mather did, that histories are written less to glorify God than to transform an audience's conception of their social world. As Stephen Arch has noted in a recent study, Mather revised the whole of New England's history as he had received it from his father and grandfather. He did so for two reasons: to accommodate radical cultural, social, political, and religious change; and to alter his readers' conception of the meaning of New England, directing them to act and think and see in such a way that their reconstructed vision of New England's critical mission would, through the audience's reception of the text, duplicate many of the insights Mather himself held to be essential to the expression of progressive government. This historical revisionism insinuated itself into several popular nineteenth-century cultural forms: children's tales, wonder-cabinets, historical romances, and the feminist discourse of spiritualism.

These forms (and others) explored the problems and possibilities in literary treatments of historical conditions within and among newly emergent classes of print consumers. Antebellum writers excited by the politics that Mather revealed in *Magnalia* produced a literature that was simultaneously self-sufficient and historically shaped by issues of authorial identity and political authority.

For Sacvan Bercovitch, the fundamental substructure underlying the "Puritan Imagination" is a "typological imperative" that is the critical and defining element of American ideology. In *The Puritan Origins of the American Self*, Bercovitch used Mather's nineteen-page biography of John Winthrop to extend the notion of a typological imperative into a "miniaturized edition of our civil theology" that transforms every opposition and contradiction into implicit assent.[2] Over the course of his career, Bercovitch has been engaged in the process of releasing Perry Miller's stranglehold on Puritan studies.[3] As David Harlan has observed, Bercovitch's New Americanist criticism has given us readings of classic American texts that are "always complex, intricate, well informed"; however, in his adherence to a firm notion of consensual culture, "those readings are always made to demonstrate the same monotonous and desolate lesson: how a monolithic and hegemonic American culture has absorbed all challenges and repressed every possibility" (965). Perhaps my counter-reading bears a similarly desolate conclusion; yet I argue that when Robbins's edition of *Magnalia* is fully historicized, so that what initially seems "background" is recast as a complex network of institutions, practices, and beliefs that arrange Puritanism, literary consensus is not, in fact, a reality but an invention that responds to the shifting market demands for "authenticated" culture. Sacvan Bercovitch has provided us with important readings of Mather's text that move us away from the unwieldy notion of "Puritan Mind" to "Puritan Imagination." This study, however, addresses an important question posed by Michael Colacurcio: "What exactly *is* our interest in writing about (or merely in teaching) writers in aggregates rather than as unique instances?" ("American-Renaissance Renaissance" 493). By retracting the political understanding of Mather within the texts of an exceptionally ambitious and experimental group of New England writers closely associated by critics today with the American Renaissance, we can better understand the notion of *Magnalia* as a "corporate intertextual enterprise." As an (or perhaps *the*) informing event of literary nationalism, Robbins's *Magnalia* showed that writers anticipated the bundling of their texts around the failure of nationalistic projects that would control the expression of authorship within socially contested limits.[4]

The three works that I have chosen to discuss in this study were published in 1839, 1859, and 1862 and therefore provide a good comparison of how Mather's history was translated by representatives of two generations of New England writers supremely interested in authentic source material about seventeenth-century social history. The fact that Stoddard and Stowe are often grouped by critics like Lawrence Buell intensifies in my mind the ironic uses of Mather's history that all three employed. Besides specific textual references to the American edition of *Magnalia* (and in Stoddard's case to Thomas Robbins himself), all three of the works I discuss attempt to decipher a "distinctive" New England literary tradition based on a purposeful apprehension (or invention) of Puritan social and political history. I mention this fact here, because this study is not an influence study in the manner of F. O. Matthiessen. Instead, I propose to offer the thesis that the primary efforts of New England writers during the American Renaissance were directed at creating an audience of democratic readers capable of modeling their individual gestures as readers on the contingent realities of American Puritanism. Each of the three writers I discuss learned of the importance of democratic concepts and categories from a variety of influences and sources. However, these writers depended on the Robbins edition for something more far reaching: the interpretation and appropriation of the variety of democratic conditions that were made available for appropriation because of the "tutor text" potential of *Magnalia*.

I hesitate to call the works I discuss here "minor works," although I am aware that many of my readers will be more familiar with the authors than with the works I have chosen. Many of these works have only recently been incorporated into critical discussions of American literature; however, the fact remains that texts such as the ones I examine here describe the peculiarly "democratic" transactions between readers and books far better than do many "classics." The editorial strategies that shaped *The Scarlet Letter* and *Uncle Tom's Cabin* (or bestsellers in general) are markedly different from those used to produce popularly subversive literature. The works examined here are not impressive because they exhibit a high degree of aesthetic virtuosity; instead, these texts are crisscrossed by political concerns about the definition of a specific relationship between print culture and the varying cultural uses of historical information among different classes of readers. Each of the individual texts I discuss foregrounds this issue both conceptually and historically; each has its origins in the 1820 *Magnalia* and ends in what Roger Chartier calls the intimate and secret relationship between the reader and his or her book (*Cultural Uses* 183–84, 219–25).

In Chapter 1 I argue that Mather's attempt to record the Puritan experience in New England did not form a coherent "system" for telling that story. What Mather did do was record his political inflections in such a way as to cluster his public life and commitments around key interests that he had as a historical writer: which "genre" conventions to uphold and modify when narrating a politically aware narrative; how to depict the "constructedness" of representative personalities; how to cope with the reality of aliases in writing and political life; and how to translate political knowledge into cultural forms that can be useful to those who want to shape the opinions of others. The issues Mather brings to light become sites of negotiation that (through form and theme) record the archive of the past and remain open to invention. Further, Mather's political awareness is coded in markers, or textual traces, that Mather used to narrate the identity of the colony of Massachusetts for an eager reading public in England. The initial euphoria of the 1689 rebellion in Boston held forth the promise of popular rule, rapid economic growth, the redistribution of social importance, cultural regeneration, and the specter of regional greatness. It was these considerations, certainly dimly perceived at the moment the *Declaration of the Gentlemen* was read from the balcony of the Town House, that fed Cotton Mather's sense that he was near the center of a valuable undertaking. In his several acts of reading and remembering the sequence of events leading to the suspension of the colony's charter, Mather knew that the desperation to reconstruct a secure regularity was impossible under the Dominion. The empty notion that the "city on a hill" held relevance for a rapidly modernizing international state was part and parcel of the regional consciousness. As the days and weeks after the initial uprising made clear, the agenda undergirding the revolution became increasingly attenuated.

When Thomas Robbins published *Magnalia* at Hartford in 1820, the political markers of the text became important for other writers looking for authoritative sources to work from in their attempt to reconcile antiquarianism with political issues in Jacksonian America. In Chapter 2, Mather's markers become accents of the struggles that nineteenth-century writers faced in their gathering together the representations of the past with material designed to enhance participatory democracy. As Robbins knew, the great theme of his own time was the extension of democracy and its effects on

American desires on the one hand for the re-establishment of true community and on the other hand for the competing attractions of competitive individualism. Robbins surmised that readers were drawn not to the church history aspects of the work but rather to its grasp of political and historical realities. The fascination of the book for many came from the manner in which it spoke to the enormous growth of the nation. The period beginning around 1820 has been commonly viewed as a *locus classicus* in American literary history. As applied by critics like Douglas, Matthiessen, Pease, and Tompkins, the term *American Renaissance* designates a moment in America's history when "original" works laid claim to an "authentic" cultural achievement. Mather's *Magnalia* was an important touchstone for this revival of culture, and it may represent the key to understanding the rise of democratic readership before the Civil War.

Chapter 3 engages the concept of the *wunderkammer* (wonder-cabinet) by linking Charles Willson Peale's museum, Mather, and Hawthorne. Hawthorne's use of cultural artifacts forges an analogical/causal link between his own times and the Puritan settlement. Invariably, once Hawthorne establishes this relationship, his prose communicates a sense of estrangement that capitalizes on and complicates historical judgments. Because Hawthorne intends to use his material to bring himself and his readers into a communication with the past, his evocation of cultural resonance depends on the production of "wounded artifacts" —objects that are overdetermined and made to stand for an array of culturally significant discourses. In Hawthorne's arrangement of these artifacts, his roles as collector and author merge. Like Mather in his desire to heap treasures on the great dining table of North American history, and like Peale in his attempt to bring the world into the confines of a single room, Hawthorne practices a cultural poetics in which the presence of wounded artifacts ensures the continued circulation of the discourses they express. This process directly links Hawthorne's project to Mather's *Magnalia*. In both cases, the presence of unexpected survivals is brought to light by the labors of the collector's touch.

Chapter 4 suggests that viewing *The Minister's Wooing* as a sophisticated act of historical criticism explains Stowe's continuing interest in Puritanism. Stowe was suspicious of the nineteenth-century belief that all history had to be rewritten in forms that testified to a retrospective and evolutionary sense of progress. This suspicion guided her forays into Mather's historicism. By depicting the boredom of domestic life, Stowe paradoxically animates pressing political and social concerns relating to the New Politics of U.S. president Zachary Taylor. Her romantic antiquarianism was not harmless or trivial, however, for she endeavored to write fiction that seemed to flow naturally out of democratic ideals of domesticity. *The Minister's Wooing* is about two things: (1) the construction of a representative figure for Puritanism and (2) a concern for historical knowledge, which becomes the basis of a radical literary realism. Stowe's reading of *Magnalia* was an act of preterition that was both self-protective and opportune: self-protective, because Stowe's exploitation of the sentimental romance allows her to put forward radically counterfactual examples of Puritan ideology; opportune, because Stowe was able to construct a notion of society and culture that challenged her readers' common assumptions about the democratic enterprise in the early republic.

Chapter 5 traces Stoddard's creation of an authorial stance that (in its appropriation of the significance of witchcraft and spiritualism) helps her to accommodate her work as a historical critic with other, competitive antiquarian strategies. Stoddard's *The Morgesons*, an innovative restructuring of Puritanism, effectively explains the need for her contemporary culture to attend to voices excluded from a liberal Christian magnanimity. Stoddard's novel participated in democracy by tapping into the energies and sympathies of "fantastic" religious movements that endowed their adherents with a strong capacity for cultural criticism. Against the consolidating forces of Jacksonian democracy, Stoddard offers a view that vaunts the intrinsic values of difference and thereby increases the likelihood that occult memories will survive. Her ability to produce these effects comes from a rigorous teleological labor of applying her narrative strategies to *Magnalia*. Stoddard's convoluted text poses several challenges for her readers. Her description of radical historicism, in the shifting domains of her family's connection to New England geography and Puritan ancestors, is warped by an extreme polymorphism. The intelligibility of the narrative is a function of the story's attempt to bring elements, relations, and domains of reference separated by time into conversation with each other. Therefore, her readers' incomplete comprehension of the significance of these factors sounds out a general appeal shared by author and readers for a meaningful (and popular) historical conscience and consciousness. Her sense of culture is derived from Mather's discussion in *Magnalia* of aliases and specters representing more familiar personalities. Stoddard uses Mather's "multiaccentual" understanding of enacted (and enacting) selves to prove the democratic potential of her audience. It would be wrong to suggest that Stoddard's readers longed for witch trials and pneumatic events. Nevertheless, Stoddard's appropriation of Mather's "darker" side engaged the grainy (and sometimes secret) spaces in her readers' experience of culture.

Acknowledgments

✛

Many people helped me write this book, both directly and indirectly. Rick Cannon, Dave Civali, and Michael O'Carolan at Gonzaga College High School first had me write about American literature, post-structuralist theory, and history. Christopher Wilson, Cecil Tate, Alan Lawson, and John McAleer guided my forays into American studies and, after a false start on my part, lent much needed encouragement and support. At the College of William and Mary, Scott Donaldson, Bruce McConachie, and Robert Scholnick all offered valuable guidance in a most appropriate setting for early American studies. At the University of New Hampshire, David Watters started me on this particular study with his seminar on early American culture. Lisa MacFarlane, Patrocino Schweickert, Sarah Way Sherman, Laurel Thatcher Ulrich, and Watters then guided my research and patiently helped me to find a voice in the wilderness that is *Magnalia*. My students and colleagues were most kind as were Michael DePorte, Melody Graulich, Charles Shepardson, Dean Raymond Erickson, Sabina Foote, Tory Poulin, Kim Bousquin, Michael Pugh, and the staff of the Dimond Library. I am grateful to the College of Liberal Arts and the Graduate School, which provided me with two fellowships that came at crucial moments. Leo Marx, Peter Donaldson, and Pauline Maier, all of the Massachusetts Institute of Technology, donated time and assistance.

The Interdisciplinary Group for the Historical Study of Literature at Texas A&M, and especially Larry Reynolds, provided a model of the lively, engaged, and focused audience I hope to engage with this book. Participants in the Boston Area Early American History Seminar, especially Lawrence Buell, David Hall, and Robert Gross, were kind exemplars of Americanist scholarship. I appreciated sharing in their ideas. James Hoopes and Philip Gura generously read parts of the manuscript and made helpful suggestions.

When the need was greatest, Patrick Murphy, whose steady friendship has been much appreciated, helped bring this project to a satisfying conclusion. In Patrick, I experienced the marks and works of a studious mind; I am only sorry that, as happened to Nathaniel Mather, while he devoured books, it came to pass that my book devoured Patrick.

I would like to thank the American Antiquarian Society, the Massachusetts Historical Society, the Detroit Institute of the Arts, the Pennsylvania Academy of the Fine Arts, the Connecticut Historical Society, the Boston Public Library, the Houghton Library at Harvard University, the Hayden Library at Massachusetts Institute of Technology, and the O'Neill Library at Boston College for permission to reproduce materials in their collections and for their help in obtaining sources. I would also like to acknowledge The L. J. Skaggs and Mary C. Skaggs Foundation for their generous financial assistance.

I am especially grateful to the Northeastern University Press. Kristen Hatch saw the manuscript through several stages of review, and Emily McKeigue guided it through production. The Press's outside academic readers gave me fine readings and probing criticism that served the book well. If the book is not better for their help, the responsibility is mine, not theirs. Finally, in my friends and family, my wife Aimee Marie and our son William Christopher, I have found persons whose thoughtfulness and sensibilities give the granite rocks on which New England is founded a private and familiar existence. This book could not have been written without them.

July 1993
Boston, Massachusetts

Part One

Identity Politics and Positional Strategies: *Magnalia Christi Americana* in the Period Between Charters, 1684–91

Introduction

✤

1690. An uncomfortable September evening at the Boston Town House. Cotton Mather stands at the margins of the assembled audience as Simon Bradstreet reads a harsh proclamation against recent publications that have appeared criticizing the progress of King William's War. Cotton Mather is not named, in deference to his family, but his authorship of *Publick Occurrences* was the latest in a series of performances calculated to reveal his ambition, ironic amusement, curiosity, and revulsion regarding the political situation in Massachusetts. A month later, in a letter to his uncle John Cotton, Mather remembered the event and fashioned it as "the occasion of much discourse . . . about the country; and some of that might well have been spared" (*Selected Letters* 27–28).

After the departure of his father Increase to England in April 1688 to negotiate a new charter for the New England colonies, Cotton Mather had asserted a new boldness and authority in his politics. Forever linked to the heritage of his first- and second-generation ancestors who had labored patiently for the establishment of a "rational millennium" in America, he sought new opportunities in the emerging print culture of the colonies for advancing novel political identities that conflated his image with the fluctuating legacy of political authority in New England. In September 1690, Cotton Mather had authored *Publick Occurrences*, and the paper instantly drew the attention of the Massachusetts Council. It contained a report of William Phips's failed Canadian expedition, which the Bradstreet administration had authorized as testimonial to the authority of William of Orange and the new charter, and was ordered suppressed. *Publick Occurrences* was unlicensed, contained doubtful reports that were not based on actual observation, and offered its readers profound criticisms of the Bradstreet government. In censoring Mather, the Council had issued a severe proclamation that "thunders against some that had published that scandalous thing."

Considering the newspaper "noble, useful, and laudable," Cotton Mather explained to his uncle John Cotton: "the publisher had not one line of it from me, only as accidentally meeting him in the highway, on his request, I showed him how to contract and express the report of the expedition." Vexatiously, Cotton Mather stated, "a few such tricks will render me uncapable of serving either God or man in New England" (*Selected Letters* 27–28).

Mather's letter recalls the recent past, a time of anxious gossip, shifting alliances, external and internal threats. That past, beginning in 1684 with the suspension of the original charter granted to John Winthrop, figured in Mather's mind as providential. It heralded new opportunities for him as a historian and political insider, and it provided him with strategies of persuasion that exceeded the shadow of his tarnished pulpit. There was a peculiar atmosphere in Boston when the new royal government supplanted the old charter government. Sir Edmund Andros's administration, with its powerful and well-crafted spectacles of government emphasizing efficiency while minimizing difficulty, suggested a new configuration for the Puritan mission in America. The context of failed administrations, stifled communication, and relentless urgency informed Mather's political ambitions and his prose writings. Importantly, Mather's impeccable Puritan origins were transformed in the light of new print technologies and ideologies. Mather's insistence on linking the generational experience of his father and grandfather produces a fictional spectacle of self-love and self-cancellation. After recounting the Council's proclamation against him, Mather recalls,

> This accident gave a mighty assistance to the calumnies of the people against poor me, who have deserved so very ill of the country. The reason why I sent you not one of the papers, was because I did myself at first agree in my opinion . . . ; but I have since changed my mind. I now find, there is not a word said of the Maquas but what we ought to say to them, or else we bring guilt upon ourselves. (*Selected Letters* 27–28)

An ambitious, clever, young man eager to take his appointed role at the head of a fractious Massachusetts colony, Mather distills his several-stranded career at the heart of dangerous, ambiguous postcharter politics. Conflicts that had not been thought appropriate to print were suddenly being waged in a public realm of proclamations, anonymous authorship, and several competing identities. Cotton Mather, in presenting himself as a weeping prophet and as an angel of light, used some traditional roles common to earlier Puritan preaching to criticize the Council's decision, but he also conveyed the novel ethic of a preacher who, far from hiding his personality, displays it freely and places himself at the center of his preaching.[1]

The political discourse Cotton Mather brought to bear on New England did not just represent a new way of carrying on the definition of Puritan theocracy: it marked a critical shift in the arena of power. Mather's New England fully became a culture of its own when he made plain to readers that he would be not simply a commentator on his times but an active participant in the interpretation of events. In 1820, when the Robbins edition was published, the issues that *Magnalia* raised about New England's status were unresolved, "at the interstices between public rhetoric and private expression" (Davidson 260). Like the historical novels it anticipates, *Magnalia* brought the social formlessness to expression within new rhetorical and textual forms, a fact that led Kenneth Silverman to remark that "in August 1697 . . . [Mather] gave thanks for having been allowed to complete his *Magnalia Christi Americana.* . . . Pride and vanity [were] swallowed up in a merging of self with divine intentions to use the author's learning, pride, and vanity in an extension of divine glory. . . . The family name, moreover, enabled him to achieve an [extraordinary] union on a more earthly plane" (283–84). Mather's book is the most persuasive account of doubt and uncertainty in the life of a Puritan minister. The product of an experimental process, *Magnalia* is resistant to singular readings, and it served as a catalyst for new explications and forays into alternative possibilities of meaning (Davidson 260).

The remarkable nature of the American edition of *Magnalia* and its appropriation by Nathaniel Hawthorne, Elizabeth Drew Stoddard, and Harriet Beecher Stowe lies in the fact that the text, capitalizing on alternative possibilities of meaning, was ideally positioned to attract the interest of three fundamental groups of nineteenth-century print consumers: children (Hawthorne), women (Stoddard and Stowe), and democratic readers (Thomas Robbins's 1820 edition of *Magnalia*). One of the keys to the period that literary critics call the American Renaissance is that the books written from roughly 1820 to 1865 heavily exploited new categories of readers whose demand for authentic texts dramatically expanded the book market as a whole. This general phenomenon has been well documented in Michael Gilmore's *American Romanticism and the Marketplace*, but my study examines those specific instances where literature destined for a particular audience re-

hearses a way of reading New England's past that was developed and anticipated by contradictions in Mather's text.

My study reflects the revisionist scholarship within American Studies on
literary vocation and the reconstruction of literary genealogies. It shares with
other studies—Mitchell Breitwieser's *American Puritanism and the Defense
of Mourning* and *Cotton Mather and Benjamin Franklin*, Michael Denning's
Mechanic Accents, Walter Benn Michael's *The Gold Standard and the Logic
of Naturalism*, Janice Radway's *Reading the Romance*, Cathy Davidson's
Revolution and the Word, and Lawrence Buell's *New England Literary Culture*—a guiding spirit that reads texts as local, miniaturist, and "dialogic."
Drawing on the work of Clifford Geertz, these critics urge such readings to
heighten our sense of mediating between a sociocultural system in its own
terms and the critic's own fiction making. Textual significance is not found
so much as it is (re)created through acts of interpretation. For Greenblatt
and the new historicists, literature "depends upon an irregular chain of historical transactions . . . and the circumstances in which it was originally
embedded have been continuously, often radically, refigured. But these refi-
gurations do not cancel history, locking us into a perpetual present; on the
contrary, they are signs of the inescapability of a historical process, a structured negotiation and exchange, already evident in the initial moments of
empowerment" (*Shakespearean Negotiations* 6). *Magnalia* is one work that
fits Greenblatt's description exceptionally well. Certain features of the texts
I discuss are usefully illuminated by his "cultural poetics."[2]

My book is a new-historicist account of the "embedding," within nineteenth-century texts whose aims were to properly express American governmentality, of Mather's explicit thematic concern in *Magnalia* with the historical consequences of Puritanism. Joel Fineman sensed the antagonism of
certain academic historians and literary critics when he wrote of new historicism as "one merchandisable rubric amongst others in the not so free marketplace of academic ideas" (51); but, in fact, no study of the American
Renaissance has succeeded in viewing the period as being profoundly based
on "events." Historians and literary critics have frequently abandoned discussions of events as principles of their interpretations in favor of demo-
graphic processes, anthropological structures, and a variety of "mechanisms." Too often, the American Renaissance has been invoked as an
obvious historical constant in the history of American ideas and publishing.
In making visible the singularity of Thomas Robbins's reappropriation and
republication of *Magnalia*, my study exposes a significant breach between

the history of Mather's book and the self-evident assertions of literary nationalism that typically inform discussions of the American Renaissance. In my first two chapters I restore some of the breaches in self-evidence involved in Mather's role as historian and in Robbins's role as publisher. Their human roles, which define the theoretico-political function of "eventalization," are supplemented by the causal multiplication that accompanies book publication.[3] The printing and distribution (and reception) of Mather's work in the nineteenth century lent itself to the projects of Hawthorne, Stowe, and Stoddard, who, in crafting sophisticated works of historical fiction, transferred the notion of Puritan cultural inheritance to the polymorphic domain of democratic government. The "eventalization" of *Magnalia*'s American publication recenters discussions of American exceptionalism—which have often treated the nexus of fiction and democracy as self-evident, universal, and necessary—to a new ground where connections, encounters, plays of forces, strategies, and discontinuities constitute the specific reality of the politics tested by nineteenth-century writers.

What could be termed Mather's "novelistic realism" in *Magnalia* depends on a definition offered by Lukács, who claims that the realistic work is to be known by the human and historical complexities that cross the grain of its author's explicit view of his society:

A great realist such as Balzac, if the intrinsic artistic development of situations and characters he has created comes into conflict with his most cherished prejudices or even his most sacred convictions, will . . . set aside his own prejudices . . . and describe what he really sees, not what he would prefer to see. This ruthlessness towards their own subjective world-picture is the hall-mark of all the great realists, in sharp contrast to the second-raters, who nearly always succeed in bringing their own *Weltanschauung* into "harmony" with reality, that is forcing a falsified or distorted picture of reality into the shape of their own world view. . . . It is precisely this discrepancy between intention and performance, between Balzac the political thinker and Balzac the author of *La Comédie Humaine*, that constitutes Balzac's historical greatness. . . . Had he succeeded in deceiving himself, had he been able to take his own Utopian fantasies for facts, had he presented as reality what was merely his wishful thinking, he would now be of interest to none and would be as deservedly forgotten as the innumerable legitimatist pamphleteers and glorifiers of feudalism who had been his contemporaries. (*Studies in European Realism* 11, 22)

Mather's writing corresponds well with Lukács's perception of realism, because Mather's "deceptions" are designed to trigger in his readers the "discrepancies between intentions and performance." Mather's discursive strategies may appear counterintuitive at first; he makes us see that the "reality" behind his apprehension of politics depends on the "illusions" he puts forward as an author. "Fascination is a thing whereof mankind has more experience than comprehension," Mather wrote (*Magnalia* 2.544). Illusions that hearkened to an undeniably genuine experience of unrest prevailed in Boston during the years following the revolution of April 1689. Kenneth Silverman in *Life and Times* records that letters written in the summer after the revolt "abound in such comments as 'All is confusion here' or 'Every man is a Governor' " (74). In the several of the passages of *Magnalia* that I discuss, Mather admits that illusions of great sophistication characterize the rhetoric of competing religious and political groups in the years between the charters (1684–91). For Mather, authorial power is equated with the imaginative grasp of complex situations.

In the second half of my study, I consider *Magnalia* in its early-nineteenth-century contexts and attempt to show how Mather's text encapsulated a diverse body of representations that stand in for unsettled Jacksonian politics. Mather's text speaks to the political interests of nineteenth-century audiences through accents.[4] Some of Mather's political accents are derived from the dominant codes of Puritan culture as, for instance, when Mather places in *Magnalia* a map that marks each town with the symbol of the meetinghouse. Other examples of political accents derive from residual or emergent alternative or oppositional cultures as, for instance, when Mather describes "prodigious and astonishing scandals given by the extraordinary miscarriages of some" in the colony.[5] The markers of social disruption that Mather placed in his original text are signs that are, according to Voloshinov, "multiaccentual":

> The social *multiaccentuality* of the ideological sign is a very crucial aspect [of an arena for class struggle]. . . . The very same thing that makes the ideological sign vital and mutable is also that which makes it a refracting and distorting medium. . . . In actual fact, each ideological sign has two faces, like Janus. Any current curse word can become a word of praise, any current truth must inevitably sound to many other people as the greatest lie. This inner dialectic quality of the sign comes out fully in the open only in times of social crises or revolutionary changes. (23)

If Mather's history of New England functioned in some capacity as a master text controlling and organizing the cultural archive of the period between the charters, nineteenth-century writers were able to incorporate political accents into narrative centers, keywords, and plot formulas. The presence of these accents argues that we see them not as one-to-one correspondences between characters or thematic opposition but rather as the means by which authors manage the legacy of the past.[6] In the nineteenth-century context, this task of management was a contest that extended to issues of publication and preservation, the reform of reading habits, and the act of reading itself. The deep structures embedded in Puritan history give rise to the phenomenon that Sacvan Bercovitch brilliantly isolates in *The Rites of Assent*: "Ideology . . . arises out of historical circumstances, and then re-presents these, rhetorically and conceptually, as though they were natural, universal, inevitable, and right. . . . The act of representation thus serves to consecrate a set of cultural limitations. . . . In this double capacity, restrictive and enabling, ideology stands at the crossroads between the terms *literary* and history, mediating between canon and context" (356). If we concentrate on these issues at the point of their recovery—that is, at the time Thomas Robbins prepared *Magnalia* for re-release in order to influence a forming nationalism—then it becomes clear how utterly significant were Mather's words (in the specific sense of Voloshinov) in generating now-familiar material for the pantheon of writers connected to the American Renaissance. Again, by staying on the issue of the Robbins edition, as Bercovitch first did in *Puritan Origins*, it becomes plain how essential it was that *Magnalia* framed for early American critics the notions of allegory, symbolism, and the potential of a literature inspired by political ideology.

Magnalia held a special relevance for the historical literature of New England. It prompted regional writers to conclude that an intervening text always comes between the observer and the origins he or she would observe, making the historian's own tale twice told. What began as accentual signs of political upheaval in Mather's time is transformed by antebellum literary writers and audiences. The prefatory attestations appended to Mather's text show that most who read *Magnalia* in the seventeenth century interpreted it primarily as a realistic portrayal of the political challenges facing a native Puritanism from external and internal sources. By the time nineteenth-century writers like Stowe, Stoddard, and Hawthorne employ Mather's codes for understanding political meaning, the markers in Mather's text are read as microcosmic allegories of political consequences existing in Jacksonian

America. The accentual significance of the past mediates symbolic resolutions to the antebellum ideological antimonies they illustrate.

Cotton Mather framed in *Magnalia* four incidents (among others) relating to his political involvements from 1686 to 1691, thereby providing nineteenth-century writers with strategies for addressing in fiction the political and historical issues of their day. After Thomas Robbins printed the first American edition of Mather's *Magnalia Christi Americana* in 1820, Hawthorne, Stoddard, Stowe, and other writers recognized the significance of that text for their own writing of historical romances attuned to political concerns. In the course of seven years, Mather either participated in or stood very close to the most dramatic public events of this period. Four pivotal events constitute the historical context of the first chapter: (1) the formation of the Dominion of New England, (2) the arrival of Sir Edmund Andros as autocratic governor general of the federation, (3) the uprising in 1689 and the arrest of the principals of the Andros regime, (4) the outbreak of King William's War and the installation of William Phips as royal governor. Readers and writers during the American Renaissance returned to Mather's activities as a political commentator in the seventeenth century to create meaning in the uncertain democratic political contexts before the Civil War.[7] There is a correspondence between Mather's rhetorical portrayal of himself in *Magnalia* as a marginal, indeterminate, decentered identity and the ironic dissemination of democratic values by writers interested in capitalizing on a Puritan legacy in historical fiction.

In Chapter 1 I describe Mather's involvement in four significant political contexts in Massachusetts between 1686 and 1691: his role in drafting the *Declaration of the Gentlemen* and his high-profile activities at the Boston Town House on April 16, 1689; his open criticisms of the Dominion government from the pulpit and in several documents; his arrests and the attempts to prosecute him for sedition; and his attempts to win acceptance of the new charter in two "political fables." These overt political events are viewed for their importance in Mather's construction of key passages of *Magnalia*. These passages incorporate his experience of instability and cultural transformation in the epic pattern of *Magnalia*, and they show his awareness of his roles as actor and author.

These passages also illuminate Mather's attention to political circumstances. He records in the text his understanding of rapidly unfolding events in narrative formulas, keywords, and allegorical sequences. His narrative strategies, and changes within them, mark shifts in his culture's view of political conflict and rhetoric. These key moments, scattered within a larger narrative dedicated to a full appraisal of Puritanism in New England, are "extrinsic" to that story in that they suggest a reading of events that exceeds the stated intentions of the author and work. Political concerns interrupt the flow of the larger narrative design. This periodic "overreaching" of the boundaries of the work's stated intentions—"I WRITE the WONDERS of the CHRISTIAN RELIGION, flying from the deprivations of Europe, to the American Strand"—forms an interesting structural aspect of the book (1.25). However, this overreaching is most important because it registers the range of Mather's political experience.

The "politicized" Mather, recorded in these textual moments, has consequences for our understanding of a writer's relationship to his cultural context. The passages are accents (or signs) that describe the relationship between Mather's political activities within his culture and his practice of authorship. By reading Mather's text within the context of shifting social circumstances of the period between charters (1684–91), we can understand the implication in *Magnalia* that Mather's literary personality is equivalent to his political investments. Mather is a part of the events he labored to explain. Although it is not uncommon for critics to view *Magnalia* as a transitional document that reflects the evolutionary progress of Puritan ideology, my reading suggests that the form of the work reflects Mather's interest in addressing the social aspects of his involvement with history as it condenses and displaces the wishes, anxieties, and intractable antimonies of political life in New England.[8] In other words, *Magnalia* advances an exaggerated political "realism" that depends on the degree to which discrepancies, or alternative interpretations, are allowed to emerge from the historical narrative.[9] Mather's involvement in the Glorious Revolution and its consequences continues into the composition of *Magnalia*. The overall religious design of *Magnalia* fails to annul the power of Mather's anomalous political observation. As a result of his emphatic engagement with the ambiguities and uncertainties inherent in the colonial enterprise after the suspension of the first charter, Mather's focus on political anomaly uncouples his narrative from more abstract religious or mythic frames of representation, which cannot adequately account for the depth of his political experience.[10] These accents in Mather's text command the attention of later New England readers who were in a period of social self-examination and change.[11] Consequently, after Thomas Robbins's decision that the debates of his time needed the "authority" provided by Mather's text, writers in the nineteenth century responded to the opportunities that *Magnalia* made available for employing these political accents in fiction.

The decade 1820 to 1830 is a time recognized by many as a cultural moment when a truly "national" identity and its probable origins focused the attention of intellectuals. *Magnalia*'s reappearance in 1820 (the first American edition, published in Hartford, Connecticut) gave some direction to the effort of cultural definition. It offered a persuasive text for considering New England's role in shaping democratic culture. Protestantism itself owed its rapid rise to the book and to the technologies of publishing. *Magnalia*, Robbins knew, would act as a touchstone for examining the tangled webs of controversy surrounding New England's regional identity and its political significance. The Robbins edition, like few other American books, frames the ways in which the democratic social order can maintain itself or be subverted. The ability of *Magnalia* to bridge two distinct historical periods is the subject of later chapters. Sacvan Bercovitch framed the basic issue when he wrote, "Mather's rhetorical strategies [bespeak] a fundamental cultural polarity between prophet and people . . . while in their aesthetic implications, as a symbolic method which fuses objective and subjective, plural and singular, internalizing history as a defense against time, they may be seen to have found their highest creative expression in the American Renaissance" (*Rites of Assent* 145–46). To be clear from the outset, my interest in *Magnalia* has been profoundly historicist. Although Mather's text undoubtedly carries with it a great deal of "mimetic capital" that serves the purposes of New Americanist critics well, that form of criticism has blundered by "collapsing the distinction between representation and reality" in a condition Greenblatt has equated to an uneasy marriage without ecstatic union or divorce (*Marvelous Possessions* 135).

My own view in these matters has been to place my arguments in such a way that the text, as object and opportunity, becomes the point at which it becomes possible to see that our desires to establish origins have been inevitably a failure to escape our own assumptions. For this reason, my analysis depends on historical contingency, the subversion of meaning by the processes of invention and arrangement, because the reality that undergirds *Magnalia* in the nineteenth century depends on reading the text as more implicated in the culture rather than reading the text as delineating a continuity in either literature or history. The story within the story here is that *Magnalia* looks so attractive as an artifact that participates in a wonderful transformation that appears to allow each reader to move from identification to estrangement. Such a movement is typical of many artifacts and shares with them the innate ability to entice by arousal and frustrate by complication. Ultimately, *Magnalia*'s studied opportunism becomes, in my analysis, an elaborate form of repetition and invention that reiterates certain narrative possibilities only to expose them as another failed attempt to link anecdotal experience with human agency. Flirting with a democratic desire to see New England culture rendered as an intricate, repetitive musicality that periodically surfaces a "pure" passage, *Magnalia* as text bribes those who would see it as the basis for continuity and exceptionalism. As cultural "invention" directed at the expression of authorship and the potentiality of reading acts, *Magnalia* censures the desire of persons to secure guarantees in self-appointed undertakings. Nathaniel Hawthorne, Elizabeth Drew Stoddard, and Harriet Beecher Stowe were drawn to Mather's text because it suggested, in its portrayal of Mather as a politically aware and historically contingent figure, a means for elaborating democratic problems and potentials that resonated with the later authors and their audiences. In each case, the sanction implied by *Magnalia* gave writers and readers cause to demonstrate the impossibility of reproducing completely the "logic" of a Puritan significance in attitudes, cultural givens, or a speaking subject, or in sponsoring a democratic reality.[12] In my opinion, these conclusions are registered at the level of *Magnalia* as book (a point incorporating a larger structure of economic, institutional, and ideological forces that govern its composition, its publication, its circulation, its reading, and the end—canonization or obscurity—to which it is read), for it is there that the reader's recurrent conflicts surface in acts of complicit reading.

I consider three works written after the publication of the Robbins edition: Nathaniel Hawthorne's *Grandfather's Chair* (1839), Harriet Beecher Stowe's *The Minister's Wooing* (1859), and Elizabeth Drew Stoddard's *The Morgesons* (1862). These works best illustrate *Magnalia*'s politically astute display of the equivalence of a writer's public involvements and literary practices. The individual readings that each of these antebellum writers offers of *Magnalia* differ in emphasis and execution, but their texts all share awareness of how Mather's rhetorical stances record political meanings. Of course, the "meanings" of Mather's text have always been viewed as multiple and somewhat ambiguous. The political meanings are important because they function as units of significance within a system of literary genres and formulas that converge on the simulacra between the narratives of Mather and several key texts of the American Renaissance. The rhetorical politics of Cotton Mather can be understood as enactments of social conflicts and political cleavages in New England culture. What originated in Mather's own colonial context became transformed in the postcolonial themes and subjects of the American Renaissance.

The Robbins edition appeared at the historical moment when the heterogeneous, the contingent, and the conjectural aspects of New England's "usable past" were being tested by the region's declining influence in national politics and the increasing competition of the literary marketplace. The historical romances of Hawthorne, Stoddard, and Stowe capitalize on the variety of expression offered by Mather's original text, using it to argue for a social multiaccentuality that accords well with the broad political experience of revolutionary changes in New England society of the antebellum period. Mather's text provided these regional writers with an "original" record from which they could undertake a "transvaluation" of paradigms for understanding the Puritan past in general and political/literary agendas in particular. Hawthorne draws on the representational logic of *Magnalia* and that of Charles Willson Peale's museum to explain New England history in terms of cultural resonance and wonder. Stowe uses Mather's political contributions to find ways of narrating republican conspiracies and the appropriate bases for cultural authority. Stoddard uses Mather to write a female *bildungsroman* that draws on the radical narrative capacities of spiritualism and witchcraft to contextualize political notions of individual autonomy.

In particular, *Magnalia* becomes important to antebellum writers like Stowe, Stoddard, and Hawthorne who associated the form of Mather's text with an artisanal republicanism.[13] Mather's familiar plots, these writers knew, actually disguised, condensed, or displaced thoughts and feelings that were central to their own and many of their readers' understandings of political life in New England. These writers attempted to weave together Mather's unstable economy of narrative formulas with their own literary practices for writing historical romance. Hawthorne, Stowe, and Stoddard generate for their readers an instability that bears the traces of political dissension. A control of the hermeneutic opportunities for grasping New England's Puritan legacy gave these writers public legitimacy in a society in which the place of the arts was insecure.[14]

These writers "rehearsed" *Magnalia* in a variety of idiosyncratic forms. Hawthorne's, Stoddard's, and Stowe's works have as a common motivation the need to show to a postcolonial and democratic readership the signs of intentionality behind a historian's craft.[15] By deploying "spectacular" versions of Mather's Puritan historiography in a postcolonial context, these writers advanced specially prepared and arranged displays of New England history and politics for the entertainment of their audiences. The cultural inquiry that these writers put forward in literature turns on what the sociologist Erving Goffman calls the "focused gathering" surrounding a cultural reading event or moment of reception. Each of these writers and their readers explored the designs of a newly emergent (and evolving) democracy. Readers and writers became what Lawrence Levine calls a set of people who related to one another through the medium of a common activity. In Mather's troubled historiography, fiction writers found ways to address their uncertainties about New England's history and its place in antebellum America.

Behind the spectacle of historical narratives like *Grandfather's Chair, The Minister's Wooing,* and *The Morgesons* was a serious consideration of history's capacity to make lies manifest.[16] My concentration on Mather's *Magnalia* allows me to continue a line of inquiry I started with Roger Williams's *A Key into the Language of America.* In an article devoted to reconsidering the politicized reading situations that John Winthrop and Roger Williams thrust on each other, I considered how both men attempted to validate a political position in discursive arenas.[17] The rhetorical passages that Williams later incorporated into his *Key into the Language of America* embedded his specific criticisms of Puritan hypocrisy in a work disguised as an examination of Native Americans in the New World. Williams, in my view, exemplified Michel Foucault's notion that public "statements circulate, are used, disappear, allow or prevent the realization of a desire, serve or resist various interests, participate in challenge and struggle, and become a theme of appropriation or rivalry" (*Archaeology of Knowledge* 105). In a similar way, Mather's rhetorical politics and their rehearsal in the work of other writers make available to audiences dramatic reading situations that invite participatory democracy.[18]

By inviting the readers of belletristic fiction to question the significance of Aaron Burr's courting of a Puritan maiden, or to wonder whether Cassandra Morgeson is committing crimes under the influence of Ben Somers, or to consider the fantasy of a chair narrating key moments of American political life, authors of these works intended to guide a New England readership to a recovery of the proper readings necessary to invent themselves in the face of competitive democratic circumstances. As historically constructed, these books prepared readers for responsible democratic action by initiating a more careful consideration of how culture is constituted through a multiplicity of contesting and overlapping layers of discourse. Literature functions in a highly social way. Christopher Wilson has suggested that some of this social operation may be seen as part of an extended cultural machinery that prepared reading audiences for democracy's technical operations ("Containing Multitudes" 494–95). The reader's attention is diverted in the work of Hawthorne, Stowe, and Stoddard toward those who ventriloquize—not just in narrative but in government itself.

Chapter One

Poet's Paper

✛

Magnalia Christi Americana

To all those who still wish to talk about man, about his reign or liberation, to all those who still ask themselves questions about what
man is in his essence, to all those who wish to take him as their
starting point in their attempts to reach the truth, to all those who,
on the other hand, refer all knowledge back to the truths of man
himself, to all those who refuse to formalize without anthropologiz-
ing, who refuse to mythologize without demystifying, who refuse to
think without immediately thinking that it is man who is thinking, to
all these warped and twisted forms of reflection we can only answer
with a philosophical laugh—which means, to a certain extent, a silent
one.

> —Michel Foucault, *The Order of Things* (342–43)

Nemo Historicus non aliquid mentitus, et habiturus sum menda-
ciorum comites, quos Historiæ et eloquentiæ miramur authores.
[There is no historian who has not told some falsehoods, and I shall
have as my companions in mendacity those whom all admire as models of historic truth and eloquence.]

> —Cotton Mather, *Magnalia Christi Americana* (2.583)

This chapter considers Cotton Mather's political and rhetorical involvements
in New England during the period between charters (1684–91). Certain biographical details that trace Mather's activities in key political moments constitute a "lived history" that insinuates itself into rhetorical strategies that
Mather used in writing *Magnalia*. Cotton Mather's political involvements in

New England between the charters demonstrated to him that an adequate grasp of the past under the Dominion would inevitably modify what, in earlier times, may have seemed a convincing Puritan hortatory based on scriptural precedent. The Mather who wrote *Magnalia* is quite different from and more political than the "filiopietistic" Mather who has been the cornerstone of criticism by David Levin, Sacvan Bercovitch, and Kenneth Silverman. The Cotton Mather in *Magnalia* is more political, more evasive, and more vexed by historical circumstances than is the man who initially appears dedicated only to memorializing the acts of the dead. In recent criticism much has been made of the need to understand Mather in the correct context. A political focus on Mather's history writing goes a long way toward fixing the proper intonation for his most important work.[1] Biographical and narrative aspects of Mather's politics illuminate what I call, after Mitchell Breitwieser, his manipulation of "exaggerated realism" (*American Puritanism* 10–16). During specific moments in *Magnalia*, Mather's political sensibility is used to create meaningful intrusions on his narrative designs and his readers' attention. Mather uses politics "realistically" to direct his readers to an understanding of a writer's public commitments. Politics, and the rhetorical machinery it mobilizes, form a valuable resource for projecting a cultural identity.

Mather's desire to tell "truthfully" the story of the New England enterprise required that he take into account political realities that, after the suspension of the original charter, gave voice to anomalous experiences that were not explained by explications based on the traditional belief in God's providential historical design. Mather encountered a period of political affliction in New England. In his effort to depict the shifts in authority affecting his culture, Mather used political reasoning to create displays reflecting the "inexorable veracity" of contested meanings. He was, in other words, moved to draw his readers' attention to political constraints that simultaneously sheltered and exposed an author's connection to duplicitous meanings in culture.

This point can be illustrated by comparing Mather's map, which he made to accompany the text of *Magnalia*, to a map made by Phillip Wells (Governor Andros's surveyor) just before the Boston rebellion of 1689. The two maps (see pages 24–25) are a coda for understanding Mather's complex political posture. Mather's map balances a nostalgic veneration for the New England Way against the detailed sophistication of Wells's map. The map sanctioned by the Andros regime is forward-looking, utilitarian, and anxiously asserts an imperial prerogative that seriously undermines a specifically "Puritan" paradigm.

The maps reflect a split in ways of viewing New England's purposes and designs. The Mather family was similarly split in its approach to the crisis brought about by Edward Randolph's arrival in New England in 1686. In order to better understand the context that shaped Increase and Cotton Mather's political activity, it is helpful to review the major events of this period. Attempting to localize Cotton Mather's roles of historical actor and historical writer, I look closely at four situations and their rhetorical assimilation in *Magnalia*:

1. The problems and opportunities inherent in politicized narratives like the *Declaration of the Gentlemen* and *Magnalia*'s "General Introduction."

2. Mather's display of political personality at the Boston Town House and in *Magnalia*'s *Pietas in Patriam*.

3. Mather's anxious admission that aliases inhabit political and literary contexts and "Wolves in Sheeps' Clothing" (Book Two, Chapter 5). These anxieties were borne out in Mather's arrest and in the several accusations brought against him by the Andros administration. These anecdotes are found in a chapter in *Magnalia* devoted to counterfeit ministers.

4. Mather's claim that political fiction is useful for "bargaining" a culture's relative worth. I argue this point by using the four political fables that Mather wrote in support of the 1691 charter and his discussion of Massachusetts's public debt.

Concluding Chapter 1 is a brief discussion of the linkage between political activity and literary intentions. Mather uses political realism to "mark" his contingent positions as a historical actor and writer. These textual traces of the writer's involvements become useful to a generation of nineteenth-century writers. Hawthorne, Stowe, and Stoddard use the 1820 Robbins edition of *Magnalia* as the basis for reconsidering, through political commentary, democratic culture.

Cotton Mather's "ecclesiastical" history of New England has been viewed as a summary of the experience of Puritanism from the first settlement to the turbulent decade of the 1690s. *Magnalia* has invoked critical responses that consider the church history to be the supreme statement of third-generation nostalgia and anxiety. Other critics, interested in early displays of corporate identity, have seen *Magnalia* as participating in an elaborate project of nationalism. For critics interested in ministerial practices, *Magnalia* does serve as an important document recording the ministerial successes of first- and second-generation Puritans. Few critics notice the political inflections in *Magnalia*.

Mather's text brings forward more "local" and "miniature" aspects of the Puritan legacy in New England. After the suspension of the original charter, Cotton Mather's political activities in New England coincided with rhetorical conventions used to signal an author's involvement in acts of interpretation (both cultural and literary). Mather used his public role to reread his relationship to New England. His public and private selves produced a contingent awareness that was echoed in several significant passages in *Magnalia*. Mather's political sensibility intruded on the larger design of the book as a sacred history. Further, these intrusions enlarged Mather's social role as an author. Mather cut loose Puritan history from its theological, aristocratic, and typological moorings and placed historical debates at the service of a larger citizenry. Throughout his works, even those more narrowly theological, Cotton Mather presents New England saints as citizens simultaneously of heaven and of the colonies. Mather, though appearing thoroughly traditional, molded his eulogies into fully developed responses to contemporary issues.[2]

Politics marks *Magnalia* with an exaggerated realism. Mather wrote less out of a tradition of divine inspiration than he wrote in response to a careful sounding of a political culture. Few critics, except indirectly, acknowledge the primacy of political inflection in *Magnalia*. Stephen Foster, author of *The Long Argument*, persists in seeing Mather as oddly "out of tune" rather than deeply involved in the social changes he writes about:

> The work was hardly a tract for the times in which it finally appeared, dominated by the fierce rivalries between political camps headed by Elisha Cooke and Joseph Dudley, and, appropriately, the longest single section in *Magnalia* is . . . Cotton's pointless hagiography of Sir William Phips, long dead by 1702 and by the universal verdict of everyone but the Mathers a dismal failure removed from the royal governorship in well-earned disgrace. (286)

Foster's acerbic criticism is directed at a Mather longing for the representative stature of his father and not at a man who capitalized on the exceptional political realities in a Boston his father never encountered. Mather's engage-

ment with history enlarged his vocation as a writer. He could overcome certain cultural limitations as a specifically "Puritan" voice, and, at the same
time, he could invest Puritanism with a new social agenda. The difficulties
presented by Mather's political vocation encouraged his readers to see the
connection between his efforts and a cultural situation that caused him to
experiment with rhetorical notions.

The four passages discussed below allow Mather to assert what Breitwieser calls an exaggerated realism for treating the course of events in New
England after the Glorious Revolution. Breitwieser, who is interested in
Mary Rowlandson's captivity narrative and her departure from Puritan conventions regarding emotional experience, claims "realism is a function of a
text's meaning exceeding the specific coherence intended by the writer. . . .
The real 'marks' a text through contortions it enacts within the writer's best
intentions" (*American Puritanism* 12). Breitwieser's use of the term *realism*
is important for discussing Mather's text because, in the overlapping of public activity and cultural poetics, the four portions of *Magnalia* that I examine
signal the degree to which authorship and political commitment emerge
from similar vocational pressures. The political climate of 1684 to 1691 suggested the boundaries (and the means to escape those boundaries) for the
composition, publication, and promotion of New England's significance in
Magnalia.

The claim that realism has an ability to "contort" an author's stated designs has a special significance for *Magnalia*. Structural features of the book
(like Mather's conceit that he is relating the seven pillars that support the
church of New England) and numerous prefatory attestations draw attention
to the author's stated claims. But inventive descriptions of political events
and Mather's involvement in them contort these more exaggerated claims.
Mather's political commitments made him attentive to new details that outdistance earlier treatments of New England's significance. When describing
vivid political activities, he found himself caught between a rhetoric that
encouraged his direct involvement (popular politics) and a system (Puritan
exceptionalism) that closed real opportunities for initiative.

Critics of early American literature have long been comfortable with the
notion that several typologies operated within "Puritan" ideology. William
Bradford's *History of Plimouth Plantation* advances a form of biblical typology. Mary Rowlandson's narrative, "coached" by Increase Mather, reflects a
concern for exemplaristic typology. As Emory Elliott has written, "biblical
reference was the jewel of Puritan literature" (15). Most critics, following

Bercovitch, have claimed that historical prophecy and narrative in Puritan typology were fundamentally symbolist as well as figural.[3] But typology still held the historical attention of Mather, a third-generation Puritan intellectual, but primarily in a pejorative way. Mather used the tropes of typology in order to construct a revisionary mythopoesis of New England's origins and worth. Mather saw real limitations in the concept of New England as a "New Israel." New England's continued success depended more on the assertion of rights as English citizens than saintly divines. Countering the hegemony of narrow typological justifications for nationhood, Mather periodically used typology in *Magnalia* to create disjunctions between Puritanism's dominant rhetorical mode and the narrative resolutions that typology could provide.

Identifying the exact points where *Magnalia* departs from some or all varieties of typology is less important than understanding that Mather's rhetorical strategies outdistance even the most elastic powers of typology based on scriptural precedent. Mather reconciled his political expectations with actual experience by remaining attentive to the chaotic and intrusive nature of colonial politics. Mather's insistence on an exaggerated political sophistication created spectacles that "arrange" human inventiveness in such a way that typology's significance was no longer clear. Typology became hieroglyphic and unmanageably complex. Mather shared illusions with his readers so his audiences might better anticipate the "spectral" difficulties that politics posed for their own civic activity. Mather's focus on illusions and spectacles answered to a genuinely revolutionary context that eroded the original prophetic intent of the typological tradition. If Protestant typology seemed to respond to future events consummated in prophecy, then Mather's experience showed a need to decipher present complexities that had few, if any, reliable precedents. Mather, a Calvinist in theology, demoted the importance of Scripture for understanding his political role. It is perhaps characteristic of Mather's intelligence that he could shift so easily (and without apparent contradiction) between secular and theological contexts. At the same time that Mather was using *Magnalia* as a kind of barometer of the changing cultural climate, he also was writing the "Biblia Americana." This enormous manuscript on orthodox Protestant belief Mather designed to be acceptable to men of all persuasions. Mather capitalized on the contingencies of authorship in order to bridge the imagined spaces between New English culture and his projected identity. Jeffrey Richards calls his work an example of *theatrou mestoi*:

Mather's own life, told by himself, tells another story. *Magnalia* documents a corporate design for the lives of each of the individuals in the episodes contained therein; yet the overtly theatrical elements, especially the high-lighting of the saints' lives, redirect the design from separate stories to a history of selves fulfilled on the geographically defined stage of America. . . . Mather makes it quite clear that the locus of revelation in New England, not simply the earth, and thus the lives of those who prepare the place take on special significance. . . . [Mather] not only *represents* the federal mission but also *embodies* it. To that end, *Magnalia* is also about someone else whose biography is missing but whose traces are everywhere. It has as its subject the one person who could both absorb and express the totality of New England church history and at the same time stand before the world to take its spite. (169)

Mather's participation in revolutionary politics formed a fundamental part of his own consciousness.

If one attributes Mather's sensibilities to a "Renaissance" notion of man, then his political strategies allowed him to consider a variety of cultural needs and alternative identities. Political writing, in turn, set the tone for *Magnalia*'s historical content, which entertained possibilities not available to previous Puritan historians. Although Mather remains on the surface a pious Calvinist, "he internalizes the social and political conflicts of his native land and subjugates them to his will" (Richards 169). Mather never denies that he is a historical actor. That realistic sentiment weds him to the cultural circumstances he describes. *Magnalia* allows him to mark a "Puritan" text with reminders of his ability to manipulate appearances. As such, the book forecasts new attractions for writing history. It makes New England history a cultural crucible reflecting pressurized and unstable aspects of American interests and ideology. Puritanism was no longer an objective laboratory for civil government (and probably never was). Instead, it had become (after the suspension of the first charter) an ideology dependent on preplanned, promoted, and, in some cases, fabricated events. The effects of the Glorious Revolution on the definition of Puritanism, as it is recorded by the contrast between Mather and Wells in each of their carefully constructed maps, shows a divergence of opinion on what properly constitutes government in New England.

Mather's 1702 map suggests that civil authority is often an exercise of popular (and nostalgic) will. It is a carefully considered display of regional

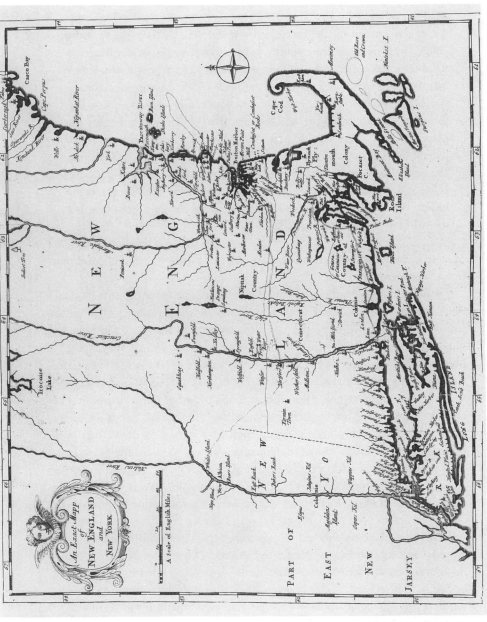

Map of New England and New York from *Magnalia Christi Americana* (1702). (Massachusetts Historical Society, Boston)

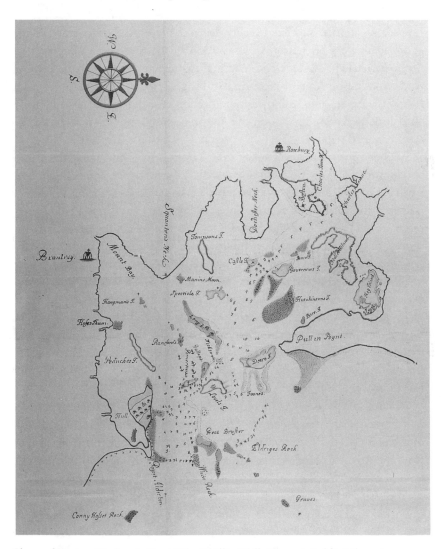

Chart of Boston Harbor (1687–88) by Phillip Wells (Boston Public Library)

knowledge. The map is a late appreciation of the Puritan mission in America. The title is surmounted by the frontal aspect of a human head surrounded by a pair of feathered wings, suggesting that in his attempt to "organize" his culture, Mather was prepared to "fly" from the difficulties of his time. There are only two roads on the map: the post road from Boston to Lime, Connecticut, and the road from Medfield to Hartford. New England's significance is an internal and fixed reality drawn between these two lines. Mather's map mirrors his narrative description in the first book, chapter 7, of *Magnalia*, called "*Hecatompolis*; or, a Field which the Lord hath Blessed. And ecclesiastical MAP of New-England" (1.xxv). The 1702 map preserves Plymouth as a separate colony despite the union with the Bay Colony, and it aims at perpetuating the notion that the fractious Dominion is in fact a culturally unified region.

Mather's map indexes a specifically "Puritan" origin, fixing the names and locations of New England towns with the symbol of the meetinghouse.[4] The map is counterintuitive in that it projects a stable and "primitive" region unified by a prominent Congregational polity. The map is not a clumsy representation of New England because it does not reflect the actual circumstances of the 1680s. Instead, it fulfills a wickedly propagandistic role. The map introduces—by a backward glance, a political reality that (if it existed at all) was located in the 1630s and not in the 1690s—a text that many readers considered to be an "enlightened" treatment of Puritanism. Mather's map exemplifies his "necromantic" capacity for arguing a radical politics through an outmoded system of representation. Mather's map connects with the ideology of the popular faction in Massachusetts politics, which viewed the resurrected government of Simon Bradstreet as supporting self-determination.

By contrast, Wells's map, depicting Boston Harbor, is predictably detailed in its imperialistic apprehension of the native population. This map displays in excessive detail the numerous hazards (literal and political) that voyagers from the Atlantic could readily expect when approaching Boston. Mapping not just the water's passage, Wells illustrated the political nuances of a colony on the eve of rebellion against the Crown. The Wells map anticipates the evolution of the colony into a utilitarian port of international commerce, and, in the process, the map reflects the official uneasiness of the Andros government about the safety of English citizens.

The juxtapositions of the Old World re-enacted and the New World still being rehearsed both claim to be authoritative visions. Each is based on direct observation of cultural circumstances and a little imagination. Wells's map views government as an oligopoly framing a new, shadowy, and unregulated polity where the exercise of public authority is linked to private agendas. Wells connects his map to those in the moderate faction who conceived of the New England enterprise as fundamentally corporate and economic. The places these maps would lead us are not linked by a single idea of progress; instead, they attest to the way chance happenings are inscribed one after another in political experience. Taken together, they do not homogenize the discourse on New England; they bring forward its irrepressible discontinuity.[5]

The diversity in the two maps reveals just how much potential there was during the last decade of the seventeenth century for grafting a persuasive identity onto a region that supported (ironically) both versions and none at all. Here then is my point: Mather's map is a graphic invention of a problematic locus. The map extends the problematic locus within the narratives of *Magnalia*. Mather offers a hitherto undrawn map of New England's destiny, which, though it does not exactly square with the facts, nonetheless offers an alternative teleology.

Between themselves, these two maps do not form a "system"; they have more to do with curiosity and astonishment than with logical truths. Instead, they organize a plurality of options about the New English mission in America. Thomas Robbins found Mather's map to be essential not just for comprehending the text but for grasping the cultural poetics offered in *Magnalia*. The 1820 edition was originally printed without the map, but Robbins convinced George Emery Littlefield to issue it as a facsimile. There is heterogeneity not only in the regions described by these maps but also in Mather's rhetorical treatment of political knowledge within Puritanism.

Mather suggests, quite radically, that history as it is written may owe more of its character to the conditions of its production than to the specific "factual" situation it describes. The power of his historical narrative, among readers at least, depends on *Magnalia*'s ability to address the problematic politics that emerge from his treatment of his own troubled involvements on behalf of a Puritan authority. What causes such divergent views? What is the silent logic underlying the techniques used to make these maps? Whose vision is more plausible and best accords with the views the inhabitants themselves hold?

The answers to these questions, Mather suggests, must account for the fact that the rhetoric of colonial politics consists primarily of expressive actions. While the true social, economic, or political changes happen somewhere offstage, Mather implies that rhetorical contrivances were clear signs that individual inspiration was at work obscuring agendas known by few who were not actual participants. As these maps show, old ideas about authority and self-governance encourage new modes of explanation. New England's incomplete definition, accentuated by the removal of the original charter and the conflict over the new one, is useful to Mather because it frames his recognition of multiple criteria for authority. What Mather would consider an "acceptable" authority is a version of events showing politics not as a prescribed pattern of activity but as an array of possibilities awaiting animation by the politically competent. The appeal of political rhetoric was its apparent ability to manage a reality that far exceeded any individual's capacity. This note is sounded in an anonymous tract that Mather probably helped author in 1689: *An Appeal to the Men in New England.* Mather did not sign but probably wrote the following:

> whether a strict eye ought not to be kept on those *ridiculous Blades at Charlestown,* and those *Mischievous ones* in *Prison* [Palmer] who are scattering about the country their scandalous *Pamphlets.* . . . Whether such empty trifling *Pamphlets* can *Proselyte* any but the villiest *Buzzards* in the world, and whether we have reason to fear we have *many* such among us? (*Andros Tracts* 3:204)

This anxiety was an admission that an author's relationship to the mechanisms by which his work is brought before the public determines the status of that work in the world's eyes. Consequently, Mather labored so that his *Magnalia* would promote a version of political contexts that anticipated their favorable reception by readers.

The Wells and Mather maps illustrate a divergence of opinion on the appropriate representation of New England's political geography. That split was also present in the Mather family. Cotton and Increase Mather were divided in their opinions of how best to deal with the original charter's suspension. Increase considered a direct route, appealing to the prejudices of King James II in person, to be the best means available for countering the reversal of New England's fortunes under the Dominion government. Cotton took a more indirect route by remaining at the center of Boston politics. Cotton tried to foster a persistent ambivalence in Massachusetts politics by creating a disturbing discrepancy between acts and intention. Cotton eschewed the face-to-face style of his father and instead relied on the anticipatory production of roles for his writing and his politics. Cotton's well-studied posture, what Kenneth Silverman describes as a mixture of "belligerent courtesy, self-flattering modesty, fretful calm, and denigrating compliments," was a political stance based on deflected provocations (255).

Further, where Increase had decided to circumvent the Andros regime in New England in order to address the central imperial authorities, Cotton decided to take an ambidextrous approach to the colonial apparatus. From firsthand reportage from his father in London and sources in Boston, Cotton had a sophisticated grasp of how New England's identity was being suffused into a larger political situation quite different from that encountered by any of his ancestors. He used some of this knowledge to undercut the apparent authority of Andros and Randolph, whose constant competition with the Puritan ministry tended to obscure the actual profile of English policies in New England.

By the time Edward Randolph arrived in New England with news of the charter's suspension, both Cotton and Increase Mather had carefully considered their individual responses to the political opportunities and limitations that were to come. Moves against the original charter had been a more or less constant feature of Cotton's adolescence, college preparation, and candidacy for the ministry. At seventeen, six years prior to Andros's arrival in Boston, Cotton took extensive notes on John Eliot's preaching, which claimed that civil and religious liberties secured by the first generation might have to be defended from future encroachments. Periodically, he recorded threats to the stability of the old charter's order. He scorned Edward Randolph as a "man born to do mischief" and reported to his uncle John Cotton that he was praying mightily for the "Deliverance of this poor country" of New Hampshire (*Mather Papers*). When the Catholic king, James II, ascended the throne of England, Cotton withdrew for a day of private humiliation to concentrate on the dangers to Protestantism that James presented.

In 1685, with the news that Massachusetts was to have a new governor, Cotton underlined a passage in one of his father's sermons discussing times of persecution: "*The Ministers of God must then stand in the forefront of the battle, and be the first that shall be shot down*" (*Mather Papers*). Less than five months after his father's departure, Cotton was called upon by Andros to read publicly in the North Church a proclamation for a day of thanksgiving honoring the birth of a son, to be reared as a Catholic, to James II (thus supplanting the Protestant line of ascent represented by James's daughter Mary). Andros's attempt to assert his superior authority over Cotton Mather signaled the governor's awareness that Cotton was an important conduit of information from his father.

Indeed, Increase was consistently relaying letters to his son describing his successes at Whitehall. Additionally, Cotton gained access to (and copied) letters written by Randolph that betrayed his bias against New England. In letters to the English hierarchy, Randolph described New Englanders as "perverse people" amenable only to force, and he said that he considered it no crime "being the occasion of subverting their old Arbitrary government" (*Mather Papers*). Given the level of preparation both Increase and Cotton showed in advance of Randolph's arrival in Boston, it is useful to review the sequence of events leading to the Boston rebellion. Cotton Mather's active participation in politics was informed by his concern for situating his anxiously emerging identity against the role of his father in New England's political drama. I have argued that the Robbins edition of *Magnalia* influenced the politics of the nineteenth century and that the 1702 edition was "rehearsed" as well.

In 1675, Charles II reorganized the oversight of colonial affairs. He claimed that the disposition of American lands was the king's prerogative. The previous Council for Foreign Plantations was replaced in London by a Committee of the Privy Council for Trade and Plantations, known as the Lords of Trade.

In 1676, the Lords of Trade appointed Edward Randolph to handle the New Hampshire rent claims of Robert Mason. Randolph arrived in Boston in 1676 toward the end of King Philip's War. He probed into the political situation in Massachusetts and discovered the split between moderates and the popular parties. He reported to London that the colony was harboring the regicides William Goffe and Edward Whalley, routinely denied Anglicans and Quakers religious opportunity, evaded the Parliament's laws of trade, coined its own money, employed its own oath of fidelity instead of the sanctioned oath of allegiance to the king, and extended voting privileges exclusively to church members. Many in England concluded that Massachusetts had formed a commonwealth and was governing itself according to laws contrary to the laws of England. Randolph suggested royal intervention into the affairs of Massachusetts. He told the king's advisers that many influential citizens of New England would support such interference. The Massachusetts General Court sent William Stoughton and Peter Bulkeley to London late in 1676, and they were confronted with Randolph's charges.

The Massachusetts agents returned home in 1679 with instructions that the colony send agents better prepared to authorize changes in the charter. On December 5, 1683, a vote was taken in the General Court. Reflecting the position of the popular faction, Massachusetts decided to defend its charter in the courts of England. That same December, Edward Cranfield, the royally appointed governor of New Hampshire, declared that all ministers must celebrate the Lord's Supper according to the Anglican Prayer Book. During a town meeting held in Boston to select jury members, Samuel Nowell modified the agenda to consider the General Court's recent decision. In a short speech, Increase Mather made use of Old Testament precedents and the news of Cranfield's actions in New Hampshire to argue against the regulation of the charter in London. Increase Mather's political involvements were greeted warmly by those attending the town meeting; when the vote was cast, no one in the room voted for the charter's submission to London.

Cotton, always ready to be impressed by evidence of his father's acuity at handling a crowd, no doubt saw that his own future importance would hinge on his association with his father. Increase's remarkable foresight had already presaged the coming of King Philip's War and the smallpox epidemics that struck several of his own children.

In 1684, following the initiative of Thomas Osborne, the Tory Lord Treasurer, the Lords of Trade revoked Massachusetts's charter and replaced the independent Puritan colony with a royal Dominion. Economic reasons and not religious reasons inspired England's redefinition of New England's colonial enterprise. The desire for the Narragansett Lands, bounded on the east by the Narragansett Bay and on the west by the ill-defined border of Connecticut, drove a consortium of speculators—the Atherton Associates— to lobby London for an end to conflicting titles and land claims. Conflicting land claims to areas between the Merrimack and Piscataqua rivers had fueled a hunger for land.[6]

Commercial enterprises, because of their close contact with government entities in London, encouraged an ambiguous division of authority in New England. For a small faction of commercial people who were mindful of affairs in London, the larger European context organized political choices. Most New Englanders, however, lived in relative independence from English authority. Geographically, seaports like Boston, Ipswich, and Salem had numerous strong overseas connections. Interior towns like Sudbury, Lancaster, and Billerica seemed a world apart and were isolated from English control. As might be expected, this division was evident in class and regional differences: land speculators and merchants were wealthy and cosmopolitan; farmers and those operating limited commercial enterprises tended to be poorer and less well educated.

The dividing lines converged at Boston, the most prosperous seaport, the center of wealth, and the locus of Puritan authority. There emerged a "moderate" party—favoring compromise and moderation in disputes involving Massachusetts and London—and a "popular" faction representing the majority of people.

The annual elections in 1684 were extraordinary. Anonymous pamphlets circulated widely criticizing Governor Bradstreet and other moderates. This direct, populist criticism of standing authority was rarely heard-of in the earlier days of the colony. To many, it seemed a telltale sign of political decay. Simon Bradstreet was re-elected, and Thomas Danforth returned as deputy governor, but Joseph Dudley and other moderate magistrates lost their places.

On the initiative of the Committee for Trade and Plantations, a writ of *Saicre Fascias* extinguished Massachusetts's original charter. The committee recommended the merger of New Hampshire, Maine, Plymouth, and Massachusetts. The region was to be presided over by a royally appointed governor advised by an appointed council. Months passed before an official notification could reach Massachusetts. Without official decrees, New Englanders thrived on rumors brought by ships calling to port. Boston became progressively more stratified. The city was divided between those who anxiously looked forward to a new government and those sympathetic to a Puritan desire to preserve the prerogatives in the existing order.

While these political postures were being debated in Massachusetts at all levels, news came of England's brutal repression of Monmouth's Rebellion. When Charles II's bastard son James Scott arrived on England's shores with six thousand men after the king's death in 1685, he was soundly defeated at the battle of Sedgemoor (July 6, 1685). Rebels were hunted down, hundreds of prisoners were hanged at perfunctory criminal proceedings, and hundreds more were transported to forced labor in the sugar plantations of the West Indies. To those in Massachusetts considering their own revisionist position to royal authority, Monmouth's Rebellion sent a clear warning.

On May 12, 1686, elections were held for another year under the old charter. Those who had long advocated resistance to the revision of the old charter—Samuel Nowell, Elisha Cooke, and James Pynchon—defeated more moderate assistants by a two-to-one margin. Two days later, the frigate *Rose* delivered Edward Randolph to Boston.

Randolph's arrival ushered in the Dominion of New England. Occurring a mere ten days after Cotton's marriage, the reorganization of government seemed to echo in Mather's private affairs. On May 17, Dudley met members of the General Court at the Boston Town House. At that meeting were representatives of the new governor's council: Dudley, Major Pynchon, Captain Gedney, Robert Mason (of New Hampshire), Randolph, and Wait Winthrop. At this meeting, the judgment against the charter and Randolph's commission were presented. On May 21, the old General Court met for the last time.

When Dudley boarded the *Rose* and departed for England, a grim reversal in New England's providential history had been accomplished. The Puritan millennial belief that New England had been chosen as the place of Christ's Second Coming seemed more and more unlikely. The old English calendar with Christmas, Shrove Tuesday, Easter, and saints' days returned along with public celebrations of royal birthdays and coronations. Increase Mather wrote several tracts in opposition to the social revolution in Massachusetts: *A Testimony Against Several Prophane and Superstitious Customs* (1687) argued against the practices of public dancing and maypole festivities; *A Brief Discourse Concerning the Unlawfulness of the Common Prayer Worship* reviewed Puritan arguments against Anglican church services. In December 1686, Sir Edmund Andros arrived with two companies of soldiers to take over the government of the Dominion of New England. The Dominion was intended to encompass all the colonies from Maine to Delaware. It was to be headed by an army officer responsible directly to London, and he was to be assisted by a council appointed by the royal authorities. There was no legislature. Edmund Andros, the new governor, moved to reorganize life in the colony. He started proceedings against all existing land titles issued by towns, and he levied taxes with the sole advice of his council. On May 27, 1687, James II ordered the Declaration of Indulgence published and enforced in all the colonies. To Puritans in New England, James's proclamation suggested a means for asserting a limited self-determination based on religion. Increase Mather suggested that all the ministers write the king an expression of their gratitude. Mather had managed to get ten churches to agree to send a letter also thanking James. This letter was to be hand-delivered by a direct representative, and the congregation of the North Church bestowed the duty on Increase.

On December 24, 1687, Mather made plans to depart, but Andros had him detained on a charge of defamation. The charge was based on Randolph's forged letter of 1684 to Abraham Kirk. Edward Randolph sued for £500 in damages. The trial, held on December 31, was presided over by members of the North Church, and a verdict of innocent was handed down. At the end of March 1688, Increase again made plans to depart. He told

Andros about these plans in a private meeting, and he preached a farewell sermon to his congregation at the North Church. Randolph tried to prevent his leaving by swearing out another warrant.

Increase avoided the sheriff bearing the warrant, took a variety of evasive moves over the course of several days, and finally sailed out of Boston Harbor on the *President*. Increase's mission to Whitehall put Cotton in exclusive control of his father's congregation. Increase Mather had earlier delayed Cotton's ordination for several years. The uneasiness of that situation reverberated in the political interactions between father and son. It occurred to Cotton that "my Father had now left me, alone, in a great *Place* and in a great *Work*."[7] Though Cotton found himself newly centered in the midst of political affairs, it was a role he had prepared himself for in advance.

On January 10, 1689, Cotton learned of a letter written by his father that declared that the attorney general, Sir Thomas Powys, had ruled that New England's charter had been illegally annulled. In that letter, Increase advised Puritan leaders, including his son, to "prepare the minds of the people for a change."[8] All during the winter of 1688 and early in 1689 there was said to be a great deal of insurrection in the colonies.

In Cotton Mather's Boston, public tension reached a new height when John Winslow, on April 4, 1689, brought a copy of William of Orange's *Declarations of the Hague*, which announced his successful invasion of England. On the streets of Boston, popular rumors surfaced that Andros sympathized with King James and would turn the colonies over to the French. These suspicions were exaggerated by a popular fear that Andros had instigated the present Indian war against Massachusetts. Such charges were bolstered by the large numbers of militiamen present on the frontier under the command of "Popish" officers. It was suggested that Andros was conspiring against New England with the French. On April 16, 1689, a rebellion against the Andros government erupted in Boston.

The *Declaration* and the "General Introduction": The Nature of Politicized Narratives

In April 1689, when news arrived that a company of soldiers serving on the Maine frontier had mutinied and was heading for Boston, a window of opportunity opened for Cotton Mather to take a lead in revolutionary affairs. In the weeks prior to Winslow's news of William's ascent, Mather had been publicly against open revolt. Nevertheless, he met with Elisha Cooke, Wait Winthrop, Simon Bradstreet, and others to draft a "declaration" justifying the expected rebellion against Andros. This document intended to make what might appear as a local insurrection against English authority actually seem part of the English movement to overthrow James II and restore Protestant orthodoxy in the realm. In helping to draft the *Declaration of the Gentlemen* (reprinted as an appendix to this book), Mather asserted himself in matters of civil authority during a time when such activities might appear treasonable. As Silverman records, Mather initially seemed drawn to its pacific sentiments and the opportunity to "act the part of the meek conciliator" (70). As a principal figure behind the *Declaration* (he did not sign the document when it was committed to paper), Mather placed himself between two popular beliefs: that news would arrive restoring the charters (making overt rebellion unnecessary) and that Andros might surrender the Dominion to Louis XIV of France (making rebellion the only honorable choice for loyal English subjects).

The principals decided among themselves that if there was an uprising started by soldiers, they (the principals) would appear to make the attempt at "extinguishing the desire for revolt." But if the mob prevailed in insurrection, they would appear at the Town House and assume leadership in order to prevent the mob from excessive actions that might trigger harsh retaliation from the Crown.

It is unclear whether the *Declaration of the Gentlemen* was prepared a few days before the rebellion or during the heat of the conflict. The document consists of twelve brief articles that claim the Andros administration was part of a sustained effort by Catholics to frustrate Protestantism. Some of the articles rehearse familiar colonial grievances against the Dominion government: imprisonment for refusing to swear by the Bible, revocation of land titles, interference with trade, potential treason in Andros's command of soldiers. The "gentlemen" who wrote the document used these grievances as justification for seizing government officials: "Quiet still . . . we should have been, had not the Great God at this time laid us under a double engagement to do something for our security: besides, what we have in the strangely unanimous inclination which our Countrymen by extreamest necessities are driven unto" (*Andros Tracts* 1:18). The actions of the "gentlemen," who did not claim to adjudicate these controversies, were described in such a way that they could be seen from England as an attempt to contain the revolt, avoid bloodshed, and safeguard the political prisoners until England provided further instructions: "We do therefore seize upon the Persons of those few Ill Men which have been (next to our sins) the grand Authors of our Miseries; resolving to secure them, for what Justice, Orders from his highness, with the English Parliament shall direct" (*Andros Tracts* 1:18–19).

The *Declaration* is remarkable because it carefully frames illegal actions within the rhetoric of colonial obedience. It marks a secular drift in political reasoning. *Declaration* departs substantially from a theological and providential justification of New England politics:

> The people in New-England were all slaves, and the only difference between them and slaves is their not being bought and sold; and it was a maxim delivered in open court unto us by one of the council, *that we must not think the priviledges of English men would follow us to the end of the World*: Accordingly we have been treated with multiplied contradictions to *Magna Carta*. . . . How [our Civil Concerns] have been Discountenanced, has had a room in the reflections of every man, that is not a stranger in our Israel. (*Andros Tracts* 1:14, 17)

The *Declaration* has a constitutional and legalistic logic that asserts rights on the basis of English citizenship rather than the communal context of Protestant belief.

The historical significance of *Declaration* was its ambiguous registering of agency within Massachusetts politics.[9] Up to this point, the convention had been to attach an elaborate preamble to public declarations so that those in the audience who may have been unable to read would know the origin of the statements. The preamble convention in large measure dictated not only the force of the proclamation but the manner in which the statement was meant to be received by the auditors. Consequently, legal directives were usually accompanied by the most authoritative language available (usually with a prominent display of armed soldiers or other high-ranking individuals near the speaker). In this context, then, one can imagine the problems that confronted the auditors at the Town House, for the *Declaration* was delivered while a number of the most respected figures stood on the balcony. Because the "gentlemen" were often present on the balcony of the Town House during public readings affecting the community as a whole, their presence at the reading of the *Declaration* was both reassuring and defamiliarizing. Without the preamble, the notion of agency and "authorship" was completely undermined because no one within hearing distance could associate with certainty the figures on the balcony with the statements being made. On the one hand, the *Declaration* could be used to prove the loyalty of the colony against French aggression. On the other, it seemed a seditious document underscoring American Puritanism's general disdain for the Crown's authority. A "public" declaration unsigned by one of its principal architects, *Declaration* is an autarkic document that insinuates indirectly the personal liberties of its authors.[10] Mather's involvement with *Declaration* helped him to shape rhetorical and thematic structures in *Magnalia*.

Magnalia opens with an introduction that censures the professional ambitions of the author, but the details of the narrative work to sanction Mather's involvement with the history he describes. The *Declaration* was marked by a paradox that is enacted in Mather's concerns in *Magnalia* of authorial predetermination. Both texts are connected by their exploratory rhetorical strategies, which describe political authorship as a multiple, multivalenced, and sometimes unpredictable activity that sometimes produces unintentional interpretations.

Mather brought this sense of ambiguous responsibility for the written word to his church history. As Stephen Foster explains, *Magnalia* was "fitting of the clergy's attainment of supremacy within the Puritan movement and of their ingenious camouflaging of their ascent to power. . . . [The book] is a representative statement of American Puritanism at maturity: evasive and contradictory but entirely successful in disguising the actual achievements of its subjects" (287). *Declaration*, which anticipated the turbulence of rebellion, provided Mather with a text he could use to frame the "General Introduction" to *Magnalia*.

The opening passage of the "General Introduction" begins with the premise that *Magnalia* is a deeply political work:

> I WRITE the WONDERS of the CHRISTIAN RELIGION, flying from the depravations of Europe, to the American Strand; and, assisted by the Holy Author of that Religion, I do with all conscience of Truth, required therein by Him, who is Truth itself, report the wonderful displays of His infinite Power, Wisdom, Goodness, and Faithfulness, wherewith His Divine Providence hath irradiated an Indian Wilderness. (1.25)

This passage suggests that Mather's political views have guided his explorations of a transplanted Puritanism.[11] In "flying from the depravations of Europe," Protestant reformers encountered shifting structures in both civil and personal authority. England in the 1630s seemed a society on the brink of religious reaction and political autocracy. John Winthrop urged his immigrants "to seek out a place of Cohabitation and Consorteship under a due forme of Government both civill and ecclesiasticall" largely because he and the Puritan leadership with him found the government in England deficient (*Winthrop Papers* 2:293). Larzer Ziff in *Puritanism in America* has argued that "dominant Puritan culture had in the 1630s defined itself through defining deviancy from [England]" (70). Darrett Rutman feels that New England's fractured separation from England produced a climate where "disparity of doctrine and even practice was the rule and not the exception" (112). Rutman sees American Puritanism as a chance confluence of cultural and religious forces and heterogeneity, not unanimity.

After the suspension of the first charter, the New England colonies suffered a fairly rapid erosion in their apprehension of what Mather meant by the "conscience of Truth." Truth, difficult to determine in 1640, was even more elusive in 1690. Many persons reconsidered the origins of cherished assumptions about New England's authority and legitimacy.

Mather's opening passage in *Magnalia* is a characteristic hybridization of traditions that sought to capture the importance of the past in order to better understand present confusing circumstances. Mather invokes biblical authority, and (later) he appeals to historical precedents in order to situate his role as a historian.[12] In "writing the wonders" of New England, Mather sought to reconstruct the culture of the colony so that young settlements might have a bright "candle" of a chronicle to hold against England's "well-lit" histories. "A field thus being prepared," Mather writes, *Magnalia* becomes a work that combines "truth" and exhortation in the best Puritan hortatory tradition. Mather's history, different in execution from the histories that preceded it, nevertheless was anchored in sixty years of Puritan historiography. William Bradford wrote his *History of Plimouth Plantation* (1642) with a singular regard for "the simple truth in all things." Edward Johnson wrote, under the pressure of parliamentary debates in England over church governance, *The Wonder-Working Providence of Sion's Saviour in New England* (1650), a history dedicated to the building of pure churches shielded by strong civil powers. Nathaniel Morton published "a word of Advice to the Rising-Generation" in his jeremiad *New Englands Memoriall* (1669). William Hubbard published a lackluster *General History of New England* (1682), which Increase Mather and many of his fellow ministers considered a failed attempt to heed Urian Oakes's call, in *New England Pleaded With*, for a Puritan historian who would be the Lord's "Remembrancers; or Recorders."

Mather's preoccupation with "considerable matters" provides an index to his own particular understanding of his role as "remembrancer." The narrative that Mather anticipates in the "General Introduction" hinges on his use of a specialized realism for depicting the political challenges facing Puritanism at the close of the seventeenth century. Mather's key distinguishing mark as a Puritan historian emerges in the last paragraph of his introductory statement:

> Let my readers expect all that I have promised them, in this *Bill of Fare*; and it may be they will find themselves entertained with yet many other passages, above and beyond their expectation, deserving likewise a room in History: in all which, there will be nothing but the Author's too mean way of preparing so great entertainments, to reproach the Invitation. (1.25)

This passage betrays an astute recognition that narrated history is more the product of "the Author's too mean way of preparing so great entertainments" than it is the "assisted" ventriloquization of God's utterances. It argues that readers see his text as sometimes organized around centers different from those familiar to the anachronistic (after 1691) Puritanism that he inherited. Mather was cognizant that what was happening in Boston was part of a more comprehensive imperialistic design that was unfolding in many places simultaneously. His political activities and writing benefit from this "bifocal" knowledge. Richard Johnson describes the changing imperial design as a movement based on commercial and strategic considerations. These interests produced a high degree of English political intervention and promoted the extension of royal control into the Caribbean and American colonies:

> This movement assumed new form and intensity amidst the dramatic political changes attempted on both sides of the Atlantic during the last years of Charles II's rule. . . . the crown sought to reduce and consolidate all bastions of local particularism: by 1686, as the Dominion of New England took shape, legal action had been ordered against every extant colonial charter. (29)

Significantly, Mather sometimes organizes his historical material around a keen awareness of this political context. His perception is so keen that large portions of *Pietas in Patriam* seem organized around little else besides political rhetoric. Most critics have been absolutely correct in saying that most of *Magnalia,* in both intention and execution, appears to follow the "singular prerogatives" implied in purely sacred histories. That is the pretext of the first paragraph in the "General Introduction." But there are moments of political brilliance that challenge the notion that politics is only a marginal, peculiar, and anomalous feature of the text. Mather captures significant moments, placed at rather strategic junctures, where he draws attention to his blending of the exegetical "historia" of his sacred material with the "fabula" of political activity. Mather's "mean preparations" steadily produce new levels of correlation between sacred history and political activity, and he shifts and refigures the narrative possibilities of both. Mather's *Magnalia,* at such moments, addresses the constitutive conventions that govern both Puritan ideology and colonial identity. By his support of *Declaration,* Mather ironically "measures his abilities in appearances; while he acknowledges to himself having 'greatly miscarried in Secret,' he celebrates the spotlessness of his reputation in public" (Richards 171). Similarly, *Magnalia* attempts to record Mather's abilities as a political critic even though his admitted interests created deviations in his concern for Puritanism's importance. Mather's politically refigured concerns are further organized around the "several prerogatives" expressed in his own culture—concentrated and diffuse personalities, economic and political competition. By bridging Puritan historiography and politics, Mather hoped to embed radical possibilities within the thematic and rhetorical conceits of *Magnalia.* Mather's textual labors, often marked by elaborate metaphor or textual denseness, were accessible to other readers who could realize Mather's text in readings that were different from his own. The "openness" that political engagement brought to *Magnalia* is analogous to Jauss's belief that literature has the power to change readers' social as well as literary expectations (40–41).

The relative distance between Mather's opening paragraph and his last (in the first section of the "General Introduction") is itself a reliable index to this "political" angle of vision. The first paragraph, which relies on abstract words like *truth, wisdom, goodness,* and *faith,* is linked to a notion of divine providence. Mather's opening is calculated as a classical invocation of sacred history. According to authorities like Sir Walter Raleigh in his *History of the World* (1614), sacred history "setteth down expressly the true and first causes of all that happened." Cotton Mather easily accepted the notion that *Magnalia* would be seen by many readers as a demonstration that sacred history had particular ramifications for the "exceptional" facts of New England experience. Mather wrote, "But of all History it must be confessed, that the palm is to be given unto Church History; wherein the dignity, the suavity, and the utility of the subject is transcendent" (1.28). The opening paragraph, taken alone, suggests that Mather fully intended his readers to connect his text with other prominent examples of sacred history like Thomas Fuller's *Church-History of Britain* (1655) or John Vicars's *Magnalia Dei Anglicana* (1646).

Sacred history is what Timothy Woodbridge, minister of Hartford, had in mind when he wrote in his prefatory attestation, "The dead ones here, so much alive are made, / . . . Hark! how they check the madness of this age, / The growth of pride, fierce lust, and worldly rage" (1.21). The Puritan clergy in New England viewed the Bible as the prime historical narrative that formed the foundation of subsequent histories through binding precedents.

The biblical exegesis of the first- and second-generation Puritans had a medieval basis. Medieval exegetes considered the historical or "literal" reading of events in Scripture to be one principle among four that were brought to bear on textual interpretation. Readings that capitalized on "historia" were counterbalanced by the moral implications of tropology, the hidden spiritual readings made possible through allegory, and the eschatological insights of anagogy. Protestant reformers, following Martin Luther's dictum that "the historical meaning was the real and true one" of the four and John Calvin's assertion that historical meaning corrected extravagant allegories, considered historical readings of Scripture to be the primary exegetical tool of the ministry.

Mather's opening paragraph claims that his work draws on the energy of first- and second-generation exegetes, and, by doing so, he establishes the characteristic representational conventions of these earlier ministers. John Cotton had argued that reading Scripture as a historical drama frequently exposed a meaningful duplicity. It became the task of Puritan exegetes of the first and second generation—ministers like John Cotton, Thomas Hooker, Thomas Shepard, John Winthrop, and others who drafted the Cambridge Platform of 1648—to work out ways for best appropriating the biblical precedents in any given scriptural text to the understanding of contemporary events. The Puritan hortatory that emerged from biblical exegesis relied on interpretation by means of exemplary readings, typological interpretation, and proportional exegesis.

Exemplary readings of Scripture looked for narrative events within the Bible that, because they presented a persuasive precedent, permitted or required a course of present action. John Cotton declared that such scriptural examples were patterns for imitation. Mather recognized this tradition in his work: "the Son of God hath redeemed and purified unto himself . . . a peculiar people . . . [who conform] themselves unto the Truths and Rules of his Holy Word" (1.28).

Typological interpretation depended on types, which Samuel Mather in *The Figures or Types of the Old Testament* (1683) called "some outward or sensible thing ordained of God under the Old Testament, to represent and hold forth something of Christ in the New" (52). Most Puritan ministers (John Cotton being a notable exception) viewed types as predictive of future spiritual realities. Types, by their innate character, pointed beyond themselves, and visible types were said to be abolished when they found fulfillment in Christian antitypes. Examples, in contrast, bore meaning on their surfaces and endured in Scripture as perpetual models for Christian behavior. By the time Cotton Mather came to write *Magnalia*, he was using a greatly expanded notion of Puritan typology.

Proportional exegesis served an important function for ministerial practice because it addressed those religious situations whose variety and unpredictable nature were not adequately explained by examples and types. Proportional exegesis depended on a system of synecdoche, a figure where a part represents a whole, and metonymy, a figure where an attribute of a thing stands for the thing itself. Proportional readings of sacred history often centered on arguments that applied general rules such as those embodied in the Puritan conception of civil law to cases that entered the "gray" area of the Mosaic code.

Mather's intense self-scrutiny, aided by the pressures of political behavior, fed his desire to depict a New England that was in the process of undertaking a sophisticated and earnest attempt to check New England's control over the colony. The places where Mather marks his text with his political concerns describe an evolving cultural experience. The baroque and Mass-like rhetorical style of the book in part stems from Mather's attempts to portray a politicized reality within an exploratory narrative. Lukács's definition of realism (which I offered in the Introduction) mentioned that a writer's concerns "enacted contortions" within the stated intentions of his or her work. Political life and "realistic" writing are sometimes purposefully messy affairs.

Puritan historians writing before Mather's *Magnalia* depicted New England history as an unceasing record of providential interventions. William Bradford found it easier to illuminate what (to him) were "simple truths." As David Scobey has suggested, "almost invariably orthodoxy looks to its history for the 'Rule' by which it guides action and erases ambiguity. Either it locates this 'Rule' in a scriptural text or it turns history itself into a kind of scripture, endowing the past with interpretative authority" (30). What Mather did, was to suggest that perhaps these rules did not exist in any meaningful way until they were manufactured or organized according to some logic that was directly connected to urgent political necessities. Further, these rules, which justified the exercise of authority, were often highly subjective interpretations of complicated events. After all, the entire conceit of New England as a Dominion with federated economic and government interests was an "invention" born from English commercial and economic needs. To an extent, the basic character of authority in the period between charters depended on who created and defended the most satisfying "fiction." Mather's "realistic" treatment of cultural rules become translated into narrative passages that seem to anticipate and then modify readers' expectations. Mather's contingent political realism is quite different from Bradford's simplistic complaisance with biblical authority. Mather, as Breitwieser in *American Puritanism and the Defense of Mourning* has suggested for Mary Rowlandson, was relatively unconcerned with the adequate representation of Puritanism per se. If Bradford was concerned with adequate representation (as he had suggested in his description of life in New England as being organized around the bass note of the pilgrimage), then Mather was interested in the original charter's suspension and the problems and opportunities that political action initiated. The loss of chartered identity triggered wide-ranging disruptions in Puritanism's representational conventions.

For Bradford, New England's declension was a gradual crumbling of a static ideology. Things happened so quickly in New England that social pressures erupted along "fault lines" where Puritanism's moral authority seemed to falter. For Mather, however, the problem was not strictly an issue of declension. Instead, it was Puritanism's inability to dominate those impossible aspects of politics that had divided New England culture between moderate and popular factions. The ministerial class was socially linked to the moderate faction; but, ideologically and politically, ministers were sympathetic to the views of their congregations. Mather's position, like that of many other Puritan ministers, depended on how effectively he mobilized resources and built coalitions in a new political climate where compromise and accommodation were fast becoming the norm. If Puritan ministers had to seize on anomalous circumstances to reinforce an anxious connection to their congregations, then it seemed natural that their public would begin to see Puritanism in a multiple and alternative light. Although *Magnalia* does not legislate directly that reappraisal, it nevertheless entertains Mather's expectation that his audiences can profit from his political self-definition as a writer.

In retrospect, Mather's attempts to utilize the same resources that were available to some of his contemporaries were quite feeble. As Russell Osgood has noted, Mather's exceedingly strong defense of the charter of 1691 eventually caused his political alienation. Significantly, as his high-profile role diminished his influence, a member of his congregation, John Clark, formed highly effective coalitions with Elisha Cooke (both Sr. and Jr.) and rose to the top of the popular party hierarchy. At the time Mather wrote *Magnalia* (when the popular party was in an emergent stage), he saw his participatory politics and writing as an important means for managing his own position within a rapidly changing society.

Mather's attempt to manage both political activity and writing hearkens back to Lukács's definition of realism. Mather's realism was attuned to Puritanism's need to find a hermeneutic cure for chaotic social conditions after the Boston rebellion. His arguments in favor of the charter negotiated by his father brought many of these political insights to a personally satisfying closure, but some of the episodes recorded in *Magnalia* are designed to leave his actions open to review.

Cotton Mather's political filtering of history isolates moments where his stated intentions as an author and the message he sends to his readers are quite divergent. Engaged in the political context and hampered by the inherent limitations of language, Mather made certain assumptions about his own identity and the identity of his culture that became structural in the text of *Magnalia*. It is important to note, however, that while both Cotton and Increase were self-consciously making investments in new personalities after the suspension of the charter, both men were easily seen by their contemporaries as contradictory exemplars. If the revolution in New England was grounded on the principle that power should belong to people and not to individual persons, then Cotton's and Increase's attempts to consolidate political power were in some measure attempts to bring into the light of day that which was impossible to embody. Cotton Mather's need to mediate or disguise this contradiction was expressed through his involvement in revolutionary politics and the emerging print culture. To ameliorate a generally unfavorable image of himself, Cotton Mather sought to shift the arena of political power from the context of town meetings and market-street conversations, where he was inhibited by his reputation, to the new realm of a public constituted in writing and print.[13]

Because his account is "faithful" to the realities he has encountered, Mather tells his readers in the last paragraph of the "General Introduction" to expect that some portions of his account will overcome the heuristic capacities of his audience. Above and beyond anything with which his readers may be familiar, Mather aims to show his readers observations "which likewise deserve a room in history" (1.25).

The "General Introduction," aside from setting forth his subject and suggesting his place within a prior tradition, is a sign that Mather's political engagements have narrowed what he claims as his own significance. "But whether New-England may *live* any where else or no, it must *live* in our History!" (1.27), Mather says optimistically. But later, emphasizing that his politics have qualified his embrace of abstractions, he concedes,

> I commit the fault of a egotistical discussion . . . to excuse whatever other fault of inaccuracy or inadvertency may be discovered in an History, which hath been a sort of rhapsody made up (like the paper whereon 'tis written!) with many little rags, torn from an imployment multifarious enough to overwhelm one of my small capacities. (1.34)

The "General Introduction" establishes a point of intersection between the political anxiety of the Mather who collaborated on *Declaration* and the Mather of *Magnalia*, who is a cross-generational exemplar of American Puritanism.

The two documents, considered together, give us important glimpses of a public political figure and a private writer whose sincerity in matters of politics translates some of this experience to reading audiences. Mather connects the confusing drama of public culture, with its specific and local details, with Puritan hortatory. Mather's readers are offered a glimpse into literary processes where the restraints an author places on his narrative actually point the way to several new possibilities embedded in the rhetoric of the text.

Clearly, Mather's introduction is concerned with putting forward not just one "self" but at least two: (1) a man whose politics have made him self-aware of Puritanism's paradoxical situation after the "legal" basis of New England society has disappeared; and (2) a man whose practice of authorship appears less autonomous because of that knowledge. Although Mather pretends to control the apprehension of reality, the texts he creates can insist on the recognition that what seemed a conscious effort was actually only a contingent and fleeting illusion. The significance of *Declaration* and the "General Introduction" for better understanding the political Mather is this: these texts prepare his readers for a fundamental apprehension of isolated moments that complicate the simple assumption that a writer relates a "truthful" historical account of events. This calculated narrative effect displaces readers' expectations. Such moments are placed in the text for the purpose of setting up resonances between what one reads in books and what one experiences as a citizen.

Mather claims in both texts that he is merely an "arranger" whose primary role has been to sort through events that testify to a variety of motives, actions, and consequences. He is, at best, only partially in control of his actions both as a writer and as a politician. And, Mather goes on to suggest, there is something fundamentally important about being a circumstantial figure if one wants to be an authoritative politician or writer. Because the "General Introduction" signals his readers to be attentive to tense moments in his text, Mather is also signaling his readers to be attentive to moments that were shaped by politics.

At its root, Mather's observation that Saint Jerome said, *"Non bene fit, quod occupato Animo fit* [No one can bestow his *whole* attention upon several things at the same time]"* (1.33), is really a candid admission that his political experience has warned him to shelter himself. "Methinks I might perswade my self, that it [*Magnalia*] will find another sort of entertainment from those good men who have a better spirit in them" (1.36), he writes, anticipating that his history might find readers because of an opacity between writer and subject. By limiting his claims to authority about New England's "truths," Mather suggested a personal identity that corresponded to the regional limitations imposed by the 1691 charter. Mather said, "As I live in a country where such recompences [of enormous wealth and fame] never were in fashion; it hath no preferments for me, and I shall count that

I am well rewarded in it, if I can escape without being heavily reproached, censured and condemned, for what I have done" (1.37).

The resolutely dialectical relationship posed between Mather's involvement in politics and his authorial practice brings Mather's readers to the point where each activity can be considered through the lens of the other. In this way, Mather's accounts violate a certain principle of innocence. They are overdetermined.

Mather tried to make his readers sense that ambiguous circumstances permit extensions of civil authority. His involvement in politics, marking his commitment to "American" principles, enhanced his authoritative image for those New Englanders who wrote attestations to the significance of his book. Like Roger Williams, Mather made a distinction in his writing between the authoritative, to which respect is willingly granted, and the authoritarian, which at best is merely obeyed. Mather presented his *Magnalia* as an authoritative text. By contrast, many of the Andros proclamations and orders had passed themselves off as authoritarian.

Portions of *Magnalia* form an emblem of New England's potential for self-determination. "The discoveries which I may happen to make of my apprehensions, that *Scripture*, and *reason*, and *antiquity* is for it [the history] . . . is not far from a glorious resurrection" (1.36). The specific textual passages Mather uses to make such points are limited in number and may not entirely displace the "dignity, suavity, and utility" of New England's "transcendent" origins. Nevertheless, they do encourage readers to consider critically that events between 1684 and 1691 have been, politically at least, a labor of overcoming New England's original (theocratic) limitations.

Mather wanted to locate his *Magnalia* within a broader cultural context that linked his project to other texts that attempted to locate New England's significance. Politics diverted (even if only momentarily) his readers' attention to the fact that what had passed for stability under the first charter was only an illusion based on rhetorical strategies. Because *Magnalia* recapitulates a cultural moment through successive acts of rereading New England's context, it illuminates how politics can erode cultural coherence. The modern philosopher Michel Foucault claims that politically motivated writing like Mather's plays a fundamental role in managing cultural discourse: "the statement circulates, is used, disappears, allows, or prevents the realization of desire, serves or resists various interests, participates in challenge and struggle, and becomes a theme of appropriation and rivalry" (*Archaeology* 105). Mather's self-fashioning in writing and politics unveiled to his readers a need to grasp more fully the "constructedness" of both. An occasional diversion of his readers' attention to colonial realpolitik was Mather's best means for countering the criticisms he saw arrayed against his text.

Anticipating an event not yet accomplished (the ouster of Sir Edmund Andros), *Declaration* also presaged the erasure of the author(ity) by conceal-ing Mather's true identity and allegiances. After the rebellion, when conse-quences would be felt by all the signers, Mather could invoke his authorship (or lack thereof) to rule out perverse readings of his complicity. The knowl-edge that public personalities could be exercised almost at will to a variety of purposes under the concealment of writing allowed Mather to anticipate one of the great themes of his *Magnalia*—that writing that turned upon the personality of its author was likely to confuse persons about "original" mo-tives. In the rhetorical disclaimer of *Declaration*, Mather found an authorial stance that sanctioned his supreme inventiveness while his writing simulta-neously deflected public accountability.

Paradoxically, *Declaration* served equally the purposes of both the mod-erates (who desired only to direct the course of social movements they had been powerless to prevent) and the theocrats, like Cotton Mather, who wel-comed the advent of rebellion as the successful result of their Puritan propa-ganda. On the very day of rebellion, Cotton Mather was to have been taken into custody for preaching sedition.[14] Mather's moderate stance on the brink of a radical event allowed him to share in the success of resistance against Andros. Should history's judgment claim that he was responsible for a great crime (as it did when he held a similarly ambiguous stance at Salem in 1692), the same moderate stance gave him an alibi. A participant but not a signa-tory, Mather could say with confidence that he had not been present when the incriminating documents were signed. An unsigned work maintains a writer's freedom though the work itself is somehow "wounded" by the ab-sence of agency. Mather capitalized on this notion in the "General Introduc-tion," where he delays revealing his true identity. Mather reiterates the "silk-worms motto: The more closely she toils, the more closely she hides" (1.34).

In the "General Introduction" the "author" is more the product of the legal and institutional systems that circumscribe, determine, and articulate the realm of discourses in New England culture. The role(s) of the author that Mather taps into maintains a plasticity. In *Magnalia*, through a series of precise and complex narrative procedures similar to the efforts of Christian exegetes who seek to establish the value of a text by determining the holiness of its author, Mather uses identity as both a sign of vanity and an illusion. In

De viris illustribus (A.D. 393), Saint Jerome explains that homonymy alone is not sufficient to identify legitimately authors of more than one work: different individuals could have had the same name, or one man could have illegitimately borrowed another's patronymic. Mather draws on Jerome as he attempts to complicate authorship in the "Introduction": "I would have tried whether I could not have Anagrammatized my name into some concealment" (1.34). The concept of author in Mather's text does not refer simply to an actual individual (Mather's claim that "the greatest part of histories are but so many *panegyricks* composed by *interested hands*"); instead, it refers to a variety of postures.

In the "Introduction," Mather gives us several: the "Gentleman" Renaissance historiographer, the pious son of Puritan luminaries, the "soldier" of international reformation, and the cosmopolitan cultural critic. Each of these roles afforded Mather not one but many options for narrating his story. The several narrative positions within his text allow Mather to choose how he "inhabits" his own narration. They also allow him to remove himself from the work by ventriloquizing the words and acts of others. Mather's "representative" status is thus always somewhat illusory and hard to grasp. His style of narration makes it so.

Readers who find it easy to credit an author as exemplifying the traits of his subject are made to question this conceit. Mather's rhetorical strategies ask his readers to balance the contemplative aspects of his subject with the added understanding that political writing tries to manipulate as well as inform. Mather's text not only changes the habits of many of his "Puritan" readers but inaugurates distinctions between collective versus solitary modes of reading. *Magnalia* educates readers at a time of crisis to pause and consider the degree to which New England culture sanctions a dangerous reification of political and historical reading.

In his "General Introduction," Mather insists that there are real disjunctions between the intentionality of an author and the registered effects that his writing has for others. At times, Mather is overt about his purposes; but, as we have seen, that confidence is often a shield against circumstances that are highly contested and openly tenuous. Mather's narrative roles provide his history with a great deal of authority that appears to be released from his direct control. A political narrative design allowed Mather to liberate William Phips from the criticism that he was ignorant, brutal, violent, and covetous. Mather did not find Phips culpable of the climate in which he was forced to govern. Mather drives that point home to readers by showing how the reductive phrase "he served his country" depreciated other elusive values that Phips exemplified. Political efficiency, Mather suggests, is a function of refiguring human identity into simplified forms that the public desires. Similarly, Mather suggests that he is not to be made responsible for the accounts he has provided. "Readers should exercise leniency towards historians, and bear it in mind that they cannot be infallible in every thing," he writes, with the knowledge that he has constructed his narrative voices to resist isolating any one for excessive criticism (1.29). A notion of "escape clauses" was important to him because it seemed best to convey the political necessity of his time.

Mather makes any historical belief seem dangerous. Like Pierre Bayle's *Dictionnaire historique et critique* (1697), Mather's *Magnalia* exposes elements of deception, credulity, and error that constitute our sole knowledge of the past. What we had assumed passed for factual truth, Mather informs us, was in fact nothing more than a process that always extended beyond the range of the individual scholar. Mather's continual erosion of the stability of the past is a persistent feature of his history.[15]

The admission that mistakes may be made in *Magnalia* accomplishes two aims: it licenses the sort of history where dramatic confrontations that never actually occurred may be arranged because they express relevant and genuine points of view, and it associates his church history with an immutable ambivalence that is a hallmark of culturally useful art. We are right to suspect that behind all Mather's apologies is a more carefully calculated stance. Mather saw that no one, outside the limits of myth, could be Adamic; the human world was one of continuous existence, and the sinful choices of the past created powerful limitations on the freedoms of the present.

The Mather who will depreciate all of his own best work as vaguely erroneous and will repeatedly lament that he was inadequate to his appointed task is also interested in insinuating his personality into the mandarin networks of culture in decidedly daring ways. Mather's rhetorical contrivances are meant to be obvious in their elaborateness. They have an almost reflexive tendency to combine writerly values with the statecraft of *Declaration*:

> Every writer forms mistaken judgments of his own productions. I observe that learned men have been so terrified by the reproaches of pedantry, which little smatterers at reading and learning have, by their quoting humours, brought upon themselves, that, for to avoid all approaches towards that which those feeble creatures have gone to imitate, the best way of

writing has been most injuriously deserted. . . . As for such unaccuracies as the critical may discover, in the course of a long work, I appeal to the courteous for a favourable construction of them; and certainly they will be favourably judged of, when there is considered the variety of my other imployments; which have kept me in continual hurries. (1.31–32)

Mather's own spiritual and political anxieties were contained and consoled by the tenets and practices he used while writing *Magnalia*. His elaborate portrayal of himself and his project illustrates that Mather thought his function as an author could reveal the manner in which cultural discourse is sometimes articulated. He knew that *Magnalia* would identify him within New England society and so establish the specific modes of history available for others.

The Boston Town House and *Pietas in Patriam*: Political Personality

If Mather's hand in writing *Declaration* seemed to suggest an ambiguous cultural framework for future actions, then his appearance at the Boston Town House was an even more elaborate contrivance designed to signal his pre-eminence on the stage of postrebellion politics. When approximately one thousand armed militiamen had seized Captain John George of the H.M.S. *Rose* along with several key leaders of the Andros administration, others went to the Town House where they read the prepared *Declaration*: five of the magistrates of 1686 (including the former governor, deputy governor, and secretary); five Dominion councilors: William Stoughton, Adam Winthrop, Samuel Shrimpton, Thomas Brown, and Bartholomew Gedney; four merchants of Boston; and five Puritan ministers including Cotton Mather. A short time later, Andros, captured from his hiding place at the fort, was brought by the militia to the Town House, where those assembled placed him under arrest. Palmer attested in the postscript to his "Impartial Account" that at this moment the revolt seemed to be coordinated by the ministers present.[16]

Cotton Mather's appearance at the Town House seemed an anointed moment far different from the anxious years of delay he had endured waiting to assume a respected place alongside his father in the pulpit of the North Church. During a period of four years, 1680 to 1684, Increase had resisted repeated votes of his church members to make his son a co-pastor. Increase's reluctance has never been fully explained, though many critics point out that Cotton posed an intellectual threat and in many important ways was different from his father. Among other things, Increase felt that his son's piety was exaggerated, that he was flamboyant and exhibitionistic, and that he was profoundly extroverted. These traits presented a contrast to Increase's severe, ascetic, ideologically simpler approach to life.

The extent of Increase and Cotton's loving competition for authority came to the surface in July 1682 when Increase thanked his congregation for choosing Cotton as a colleague: "You . . . have so many ways obliged me, that I cannot think my Son, or anything that is mine, too good or too deare for you. . . . And I am really sensible to your affection manifested to myself in the great love and respect you have shown to one . . . so nearly related to me" (*Practical Truths*, Preface). After Increase delivered this speech, he delayed Cotton's ordination for three years. In the personal sphere, the two Mathers were already making investments in personality that would determine their involvement in the political and historical affairs of 1689. Between them, a public image was being tested that would later inform Cotton's development of a historical persona in *Magnalia*.

The departure of Increase Mather for England on April 7, 1688, made clear to many in New England that Increase would prevail in his efforts for the colony on the English stage. Increase's Anglo-centrism left his son with the duty to act purposefully for interests in Massachusetts. Cotton Mather's actions at the Town House, a spontaneous coronation of sorts, appeared to vindicate the youthful aspirations of a third-generation Puritan who had labored under an oppressive "anxiety of influence" bequeathed him from his forebears. For the third generation, fragmentation, declension, and partial recoveries were the established order of things. Cotton Mather, on his appearance at the helm of a civil uprising, saw himself as investing a new order aided by the resuscitated forms of his father's generation.

Palmer's sense of the rebellion as peculiarly "Puritan" made plain that the behavior at the Town House engendered a symbolic subjectivity that was constituted in and through Puritan rituals. Arranging the potency of Puritanism past at the Town House, the leaders of the rebellion succeeded in reclaiming a moral high ground from a colonial enterprise that was symbolically bankrupt of anything except administrative efficiency. The authority of the sublimated Puritanism of his fathers was transferred to Cotton Mather's surrogate position as "leader" of the colony. Cotton Mather's easy adoption of a highly representative position within Massachusetts society would, in later years, fuel his own declension as figures like John Clark claimed the political success that Cotton thought was reserved for his own line.

However, at the time of the rebellion, the willingness to "stand in" for a changing Puritan ideology paid dividends because it allowed Cotton Mather to construct the first in a series of "personally sufficient" identities. As he did in the literary "General Introduction," Mather deployed several personally sufficient public identities that carried forward his public agenda. Kenneth Silverman has pointed to these identities in his biography: Andros's former underlings and supporters privately referred to Mather as the "young Pope"; Randolph complained that "Young Mr. Mather" and "others of the gang" continued to promote antimonarchial principles and opposed "all commands from their Majesties which will not serve their interests"; and Samuel Myles charged Mather with fomenting acts of desecration against King's Chapel (74). At the Town House on April 16, 1689, Cotton Mather's public identity was fully social, discursive, and historical. It was shaped by complex cultural and familial inheritances that constrained and released options that were not purely imaginary but instead were (according to John Palmer) "faithful" responses to particular events. Accordingly, Mather constitutes the identity of William Phips in *Magnalia* out of the same cultural and familial contexts. Phips is "conjured" out of the opportunities of the Glorious Revolution:

> IF such a renowned chymist as Quercetanus, with a whole tribe of "labourers in the fire," since that learned man, find it no easie thing to make the common part of mankind believe that they can take a *plant* in its more vigorous consistence, and after a due *maceration, fermentation* and *separation*, extract the *salt* of that plant, which, as it were, in a *chaos*, invisibly reserves the *form* of the whole, with its vital principle; and, that keeping the *salt* in a *glass* hermetically sealed, they can, by applying a *soft fire* to the glass, make the *vegetable* rise by little and little out of its *ashes*, to surprize the spectators . . . by the like method from the *essential salts of humane dust*, a philosopher may, without any criminal *necromancy*, call up the *shape* of any *dead* ancestor . . . carrying in it some resemblance of these curiosities, which is performed, when we do in a *book*, as in a *glass*, reserve the history of our departed friends. (1.165)

This passage, which has drawn the attention of many critics, is important because it situates Mather's design for creating a politically representative narrative that considers the relationship of leadership to the public. Mather's and Phips's identities are linked by the unstable formulations presented in this passage. Phips, the charismatic governor, emerges from the "chaos" of frontier life because Mather effectively invents an image of a worldly and decisive man of action. Mather, whose principal job has been to apply the "soft fire" of his political experience to a further understanding of the New England enterprise, connects his success to his ability to invoke out of manuscript sources "surprises" for his spectators.

The "representative nature" of politics and of writing feeds off a self-styled necromancy in order to equate public and private values. The opening to "The Life of Phips" is the most dramatic moment in *Magnalia*. There, Mather employs an analogy (occult sciences/pneumatic philosophy) that outdistances Puritan notions of exemplaristic personality. The code words that Mather employs show the rhetorical complexities that are required to invest public political leaders with "necromantic" significances. As Parker Johnson has said, "An author who begins an important piece of writing with a sentence of over 250 words in eleven clauses embedded at several levels of subordination is no doubt trying to tell us something. . . . metaphors always seem to reverberate; the plot implicit in [this] metaphor can extend to every level of experience" (237, 245). The authoritative and the subversive in this opening passage are connected and dependent on one another. David Watters has shown that "in comparing his method to that of the necromancer, Mather at least anticipates the questions about witchcraft and magic that plagued the Phips administration. But he also reveals the degree to which witchcraft troubles him in its resemblance to other acts of the imagination, such as the writing of romances and biographies" ("Spectral Identity" 224). Mather's method for introducing "The Life of Phips" rhetorically expands to reveal the shadow of the designing consciousness and the shadows of other selves. The astonishing realism supplied by Mather's politics lies in his suggestion that beneath the constitutive elements of political authority there may be real vacancies. Under the smoke and mirrors may be insubstantial ideas and many masks of personality.

Mather considered his partnership with his father and his leadership in the rebellion as opportune moments that could suggest to an unsophisticated public a coherent moral or political creed.[17] The investiture of a son alongside the father in the pulpit itself replicates similar events recorded in the Bible. The true significance of Mather's "personal" experience lay in the opportunities made available for fashioning an effective identity. At the

Town House and in the first sentence of "The Life of Phips" Mather (with some labor) bridged a momentary "fold" in the fabric of cultural knowledge. In *Pietas in Patriam*, he fashioned an identity for a governor (Phips) whose decision to stop the witch trials was the only thing he did that the home government in Whitehall approved. In Boston, at the Town House, Cotton fashioned another identity, one that was capable of faithfully manipulating his familial and intellectual myth of origins.

"The Life of Phips" registers several political insights of Mather's. All relate directly to the issue of representative personality. Phips provided the example of a man whose leadership and authority tend to condense the half-spoken desires of the populace. Mather writes,

> Sir William Phips applied himself to consider what was the most signifi-cant thing that could be done by him for that poor people in their present circumstances. . . . when King James offered, as he did, unto Phips an opportunity to ask what he pleased of him, Sir William generously prayed for nothing but *this*, "That New-England might have its lost priviledges restored." (1.175)

Mather drew Phips in such heroic proportions because he hoped to conceal some of the more glaring deficiencies in his record.

Mather knew that in politics it was important to inflate the public image of the leadership. The larger the perceived image, the more easily the appa-ratus of government is distanced from the direct consequences of policy decisions:

> Sir William Phips, who might in a *calm* of the commonwealth have admin-istered all things with as general an acceptance as any that have gone be-fore him, had the disadvantage of being set at *helm* in a time as full of *storm* as ever that province had seen; and the people having their spirits put into a *tumult* by the discomposing and distempering variety of disas-ters . . . it was natural for them, as 'tis for all men *then*, to be *complaining*; and you may be sure, the *rulers* must in such cases be always complained of, and the chief complaints must be heaped upon those that are *com-manders in chief*. (1.224)

Some of Phips's policies were far from popular, and, at times, actions he took as governor were seen in England as prime examples of New England's basic inefficiency for managing its own affairs. Nevertheless, Mather felt that if he could paint Phips on a large canvas, his image would work to camouflage varieties of political action that were unambiguously contrary to English expectations.

During his tenure, Phips was said to have thrashed Jahleel Brenton with his cane and fists; to have scuffled with the captain of the frigate *Nonesuch*, after which he imprisoned the man among "witches, villains, negroes and murderers" for nine months; to have engaged in illicit trade; and to have sponsored a law exempting Massachusetts from the requirements of the Navigation Acts.[18] Despite these incidents, Mather invests Phips with an illusion of popularity that appears to excuse these acts (or he claims that they were the work of lesser aides): "I have not all this while said *he was faultless.* . . . if the anguish of his publick fatigues threw Sir William into any faults of passion, they were but *faults* of *passion* soon recalled: and *spots* being soonest seen in *ermin*, there was usually the *most* made of them that could be, by those that were least *free* themselves" (1.227).

The image of Phips that Mather creates is celebrated because it affords New Englanders the opportunity to "forget" just how tenuous their position was under his leadership. Mather claims that it was a failure of popular support that plagued the Phips administration. According to Mather, New England missed the value of Phips's "native" grandeur, which worked to conceal some of the nasty business of the colony itself. After all, New England had routinely subverted royal enforcement of the Acts of Trade by enacting obstructive laws and manipulating local juries. Phips was the perfect icon for distracting English eyes from questionable practices within New England:

> I must with a like freedom say, that great was the fault of New-England no more to value a person whose *opportunities* to serve all their interests, though very eminent, yet were not so eminent as his *inclinations*. If this whole continent carry in its very name of AMERICA an unaccountable *ingratitude* unto that brave man who first lead any numbers of Europeans thither . . . I must believe that the ingratitude of many . . . for such *benefits* as that country of New-England enjoyed from a governour of their own . . . was that which hastned the removal of such a benefactor from them. (1.228)

In his biography of Phips, Mather capitalized on the notion that the effigy of a political leader establishes a personal link between that leader and the populace. Phips is altogether one of the plain folk: "upon frequent occasions of uneasiness in his government, he would chuse thus to express himself: 'Gentlemen, were it not that I am to do service for the publick, I should be much easier in returning unto my broad-ax again!' " (1.221). Phips provided not only a referendum for political action but a climate that organized for the people a set of choices.

As Mather himself anticipated, his portrait of Phips hearkened to something deep and irrational that was co-extensive with the politics in which Phips engaged. Phips was a "type" manufactured not from the Bible but from the social setting of revolutionary New England. He was at once the product, the example, and the bait of popular political beliefs. Phips's life becomes equivalent to the originality of the civil experiments being practiced in Massachusetts:

> So *obscure* was the *original* of that memorable person, whose actions I am going to relate, that I must, in a way of writing like that of Plutarch, prepare my reader for the intended relation, my first searching the archives of antiquity for a parallel. . . . And in America, the first that meets me is Francisco Pizzaro, who, though a *spurious offspring* . . . so thrived his adventures there. . . . if anything hindered his Excellency Sir WILLIAM PHIPS from affording of a *parallel*, it was not the want either of design, or of courage, or of conduct in himself, but it was the fate of a *premature mortality.* For my reader now being satisfied, that a person's being obscure in his original, is not always a just prejudice to an expectation of considerable matters from him, I shall now inform him . . . he was, as the Italians express it, "a son to his own labours!" (1.166–67)

Mather here equates the life of Phips with the name of Pizarro. Pizarro invited the reigning Inca Atahualpa to a banquet, had him imprisoned, and commenced a wholesale butchery of his subjects. Afterward, he forced Atahualpa to disclose his treasures and then perfidiously put him to death.

Pizarro's power, a function of the terror he inspired, and Phips's oversight of the Salem witchcraft delusion are intended to dovetail. Mather's allegorical suggestion of conquering personalities is calculated to raise anxious questions about authority and reputation in a revolutionary society.[19] Reading in the sense that Mather intends here does not consist of stopping the chains of systems at work—colonial power, esteemed public images, high-handed tactics, and opinions. Nor does it establish a singular truth, a legality of the text. To see Phips as a passive reflection of popular opinion is misguided and leads the reader into errors. Instead, Mather suggests that his "design" of Phips co-implicates the writer and his reading audience. In effect, these passages trigger what semioticians call "suture,"[20] which relates the degree of credulity, involvement, and critical distance of the reader to the concrete experience of the words on the page. The importance of Mather's dramatic passages and offbeat associations lies in their power to create a textual space for the negotiation of meaning that relates the reading subject with the chain of discourse.[21] Breitwieser reaches essentially the same conclusion, saying,

> Mather writes extensive biographies of Winthrop, Jr., and Phips precisely *because* they are clear cases of the disjunction between Puritan holiness and worldly accomplishment. . . . Mather's belief that an inimical and hostile alterity doubled and dogged his filiopious attempts to return selflessly to the same; in the biographies of Winthrop, Jr., and Phips, however, the alterity that eludes and evades hagiographic patterning is . . . chosen, developed, presented, and even celebrated by Cotton Mather; and these two biographies . . . allow us to speculate that Mather's *antinomies of the other* are evidence of the filiopious self in the act of circumscribing and disavowing those parts of the whole, rich character that are potentially discordant. (*Cotton Mather and Benjamin Franklin* 144–45)

What Mather accomplishes in his biographies closely parallels John Cotton's use of figural realism to explicate historical knowledge. Unlike John Cotton, however, Mather wanted his readers to learn how to read public personalities on more than one level. If Puritanism generally described a politics where the common man was asked to "trust the teller" because he lacked the tools to explain the tale, then Mather's biographies, by incorporating a great many conflicting codes, overcome his readers' dependence on the author. Mather's account of Phips, disjunctive when compared to the "public record," enables readers to perceive different configurations of personality in *Magnalia*.

What Mather has added to Cotton's tradition is a sense of the political urgency that attaches to illusions of leadership. Each of Mather's subjects is simultaneously figural and historical.[22] In the acutely self-conscious uses of imagery, Cotton Mather's technique continually calls attention to itself. The pictures he develops do not create a stable image. Instead, his exegesis indirectly conveys the inadequacy underlying all forms of representation.[23]

In his "Life of Phips" Mather asks his readers to read the familiar and the known. Mather's *Pietas in Patriam* offers to the public their own like-ness—clarified, exalted, and superbly elevated into a type. The populace could be expressed and heroicized through such a man, but not without the perception of the unsettling inauthenticity that always accompanies the handshakes of the political leadership.

We can question whether Mather was being fully truthful when he writes, "I do not know that I have been, by any personal obligations or circum-stances, charmed into any partiality for the memory of this worthy man," but if we grant Mather a sophisticated understanding of political necessity, it becomes easier to see how he expected his readers to respond to his prose (1.227). Political necessity dictated that the popular will be expressed defin-itively in the personality of the governor, but Mather (the self-critical author) would ask his readers to look beneath the slogan "He loved his country" and reflect. Responsible political participation requires that individual au-tonomy be allowed to persist even though individual actions were continu-ally betrayed by political action that was, in many cases, hidden from view. Mather allowed his readers to penetrate his account of Phips so that they might become aware of the need to construct their own hermeneutic. Math-er's invitation may be indirect, but it is nevertheless there—marked—in the contorted language and dramatic plot.

"The Life of Phips" purportedly appears in *Magnalia* as an example of a political figure whose life contains "formal parallels in the conversion expe-rience." But in his *Diary* Mather admits that "the life of Phips was intended, in part, to confound 'base Tories' opposed to Phips who based their oppo-sition to Phips on his errors in judgment" (qtd. in Watters, "Spectral Iden-tity" 226, 229). *Pietas in Patriam* attempts to render personality as the prod-uct of a collective exchange. Mather's negotiations within the "controlled chaos" of political personalities depend on his personally sufficient judg-ments about his relationship to the governor. He passes his estimate of the governor as a qualified "truth" available for public inspection. Cotton Math-er's authority consistently portrays him as an impartial historian. Mather viewed the fashioning of human identity as an important conduit for con-flicting and divergent cultural values.[24]

Mather possessed an acute self-consciousness about the fashioning of per-sonality; he viewed the process as a manipulable, artful process. For Mather, *Pietas in Patriam* is neither a lie about his admiration for the governor nor a confession that he desires a dictatorial authority: it is an inflection of his political understanding. The chapter materializes out of the alchemist's jar.

His interest in politics and the specifics of Phips's life "naturally" combine the concept of Christian resurrection and illicit alchemy. William Phips is the signifier who animated the signified—New England's historical past encouraged the arrogation of many (sometimes unfamiliar and unexpected) attributes of nationhood.

Underneath Mather's praise of Phips lurks his inventiveness. In constructing perpetually self-reflexive biographies of Puritan leaders (perhaps drawn from the conventions of Tudor biography and Lives of the Saints), Mather implied the possibility of other unfulfilled identities that could be opened and examined as cultural conditions permitted.[25]

One of the most elaborate passages addressing new circumstances is Mather's account of the three hundred thousand pounds of Spanish treasure that Phips recovered from Haiti in 1687. Mather uses this embroidered account to stand in for the larger and considerably more difficult political negotiations that Phips undertook when he handled the fight against Sir Edmund Andros in 1689, the expedition against Port Royal in 1690, and the government of Massachusetts from 1692 to 1694:

> So *proper* was his behaviour, that the best noble men in the kingdom now admitted him into their conversation; but yet he was opposed by powerful enemies, that clogged his affairs with such demurrages, and such *disappointments*, as would have wholly discouraged his designs, if his patience had not been *invincible*. . . . Thus his indefatigable *patience*, with proportionable *diligence*, at length overcame the difficulties that had been thrown in his way. . . . he set sail for the *fishing-ground*, which had been so well *baited* half an hundred years before: and as he had already discovered his *capacity for business* in many considerable actions, he now added unto those discoveries, by not only *providing* all, but also by *inventing* many of the instruments necessary to the prosecution of his intended *fishery*. . . . in a little while they had, without the loss of any man's life, brought up *thirty-two tuns* of silver. . . . Thus did there once again come into the light of the sun, a treasure which had been half an hundred years *groaning under the waters*. . . . But there was one extraordinary distress which Captain Phips now found himself plunged into: for his men were come out with him upon seamen's wages, at so much *per* month; and when they saw such vast litters of silver . . . they knew not how to bear it, that they should not *share* all among themselves. . . . In this terrible distress . . . he then used all the obliging arts imaginable to make his men true unto him. . . . they declared

themselves *content*. . . . [he] did acquit himself with such an exemplary honesty, that partly by his fulfilling his assurances to the seamen, and partly by his exact and punctual care to have his employers defrauded of nothing that might conscientiously belong unto them, he had less than *sixteen thousand pounds* left unto himself. . . . Accordingly the King, in consideration of the service done by him, in bringing such a treasure into the nation, conferred upon him the honour of knighthood; and if we now reckon him *a knight of the golden fleece*, the stile might pretend unto some circumstances that would justifie it. Or call him, if you please, "the knight of honesty"; for it was *honesty* with *industry* that raised him; and he became a mighty river, without the running in of muddy water to make him so. (1.171–74)

Mather's text treats his readers to another disruptive and anamorphic paradox so that the man who recovers a pile of lost treasure (Phips is recovering *stolen* goods) becomes the icon of honesty. Mather's rhetorical depiction validates an argument made by David Watters that the supposed Puritan hostility to sensory meditation between earthly and divine attributes was not explicitly forbidden in political considerations. In his adventurous account here, Mather has seemingly negated a Puritan instruction not to let sensory experiences become interesting in themselves. If a "traditional" Puritanism distrusted images because they easily subsided into falsity, then Mather's biographies turn themselves into "self-consuming artifacts" because the thrill of their experience is limited by the fact that they have ceased to influence the very cultural networks they represent.

The significant units of Mather's biography of Phips are exaggerated for the needs of a popular audience. They have a high potential for overcoming the entrophy of an outmoded antiquarianism because the vitality of Mather's images mediates the "low" concerns of the citizenry with the "high" divinity of his subject. The importance of Mather's "Life of Phips" is not the efficiency with which it projects a long-standing intellectual order on the present; instead, it is significant because the experiential immediacy of politics dictates a glorious representation of a troubled attempt at self-governance.

Mather's momentary hesitation, in the passage cited above, between the knight of the golden fleece[26] and Phips, whose political machinations in New England were anything but motivated by benign interest, invites the reader to connect both stories. Placing them in conversation, Mather sincerely probes Phips's role and his relationship to the prosperity of the region.

In "The Life of Phips," which gives its support to Phips's administration of the government established by the 1691 charter, Mather exercises his populist doctrines. As he does in *Wonders of the Invisible World* (1692), whose composition Perry Miller vividly re-enacts in *Errand into the Wilderness* as a fevered cover-up, Mather clarifies much less than he screens. The assemblage of redundant fragments and the repeated stalls in *Wonders of the Invisible World* make everything seem the prologue to a prologue, "creating an effect of endless jerky beginnings. . . . A simultaneous saying and unsaying, the book resembles a gigantic stammer. . . . Mather's defense . . . seems in context half-hearted and forced, for Mather hedged it around with hints of coercion, warning winks at the reader, tipoffs to his discomfort" (Silverman 115–16). As Murdock notes in "Cotton Mather," "Increase must have found it difficult to admire or even to accept his son's clumsy and confused pages, but paternal affection conquered whatever distaste he felt, and in the postscript to *Cases of Conscience* (1692) he stoutly declared that he had read and approved *Wonders* before it was printed" (12). Similarly, Mather's opacity in portraying Phips is meant to encourage a second look at the readerly and writerly values that are being expressed.

"The Life of Phips" and *Wonders* resonate strongly in the deeply unsettled attitude toward Salem that Mather records in *Magnalia*:

> In fine, the last courts that sate upon this *thorny business*, finding that it was impossible to penetrate into the whole meaning of the things that had happened, and that so many *unsearchable cheats* were interwoven into the *conclusion* of a mysterious business, which perhaps had not crept thereinto at the *beginning* of it, they *cleared* the accused . . . if we consider, that we have seen the whole English nation alarumed with a *plot* [Gunpowder plot of November 5, 1605], and both Houses of Parliament, upon good grounds, voting their sense of it, and many persons most justly *hanged, drawn,* and *quartered,* for their share in it: when yet there are enough who to this day will pretend that they cannot comprehend how much of it is to be accounted *credible.* However, having related these wonderful passages, whereof, if the *veracity* of the relator in any one point be contested, there are whole *clouds of witnesses* to vindicate it, I will take my leave of the matter with an wholesome caution of Lactantius, which it may be, some other parts of the world besides New-England may have occasion to think upon: it is one of the chief arts of evil spirits, to make things which have no reality seem real to those who witness them. (1.212–13)

Having thus *publicized* his view on the matter, Mather then attempts to bring his inventiveness into line. His extensive use of Phips's legacy is gratuitous, the result of an overzealous "revaluation" that was organic and necessary to his own project of insinuating his historicity into present circumstances. Mather saw Phips as a historical locus—a place where he was willing to allow readers to pass out of the world of the obstructive present in order to better apprehend their own roles as citizens under a new regime. Mather made errors, but he was joined by many others.

Social energy flows through Phips, but it is the people who must sanction or question the quality of colonial leadership under the 1691 charter. *Pietas in Patriam* attempts to facilitate the direction of this social energy through literature.[27] Self-reflexive interrogations of the social networks that contain and condition the formation of Phips's and Mather's personalities are examples of those moments anticipated in the "General Introduction," where "the author's too mean way of preparing great entertainments" forms an "invitation" for readers' participation. "Mather expected his readers to accept some 'magic' in biography," writes David Watters, "for the lives of the great should be a sort of looking-glass, in which I may see how to adjust my own life" ("Spectral Identity" 224). Fictional possibilities illustrate complex needs for both writing and political planning. Mather's work bends a mastery of political facts to the reader's imaginative inquiries.

Arrest, Persecution, and Political Aliases

In January 1689, a warrant was sent out for Mather's arrest. It was sworn by Edward Randolph, who declared Mather to be "the abettor, if not the author of a scandalous libel" (*Andros Tracts* 1:212). Randolph's contrived charge implied that Mather had edited the anonymous pamphlet published by his father Increase, *A Brief Discourse Concerning the Unlawfulness of Common Prayer Worship* (1686). Randolph had earlier used Increase Mather's correspondence with Abraham Kick, a correspondent in Amsterdam, to prove treason, when in fact the letter said to prove this claim was shown to be a forgery. Wait Winthrop, a longtime friend of the Mathers, quashed the order of arrest. However, a few days before his birthday in February 1689, Cotton was again brought under the scrutiny of the Andros administration for alleged violations of the Act of Uniformity.

The threat of Mather's prosecution lingered for over two months until news arrived in Boston of William of Orange's invasion of England. Abundant rumors circulated earlier in the year about the Glorious Revolution in England, but confirmation came on April 14, when John Winslow returned from the West Indies with a copy of a document proclaiming William king. On April 18 Cotton was to have been arrested, but Boston took arms against the Dominion government.

If some of Mather's roles in the events between charters seem almost heroic, it helps to humanize the situation when we recall the almost constant threats of arrest and persecution he regularly encountered. The two criminal proceedings launched against Mather reiterated the dangers to personal liberties expressed in the *Declaration*:

> All men have with admiration seen what methods have been taken that they might not be treated according to their crimes. Without a verdict, yea, without a jury sometimes have people been fined most unrighteously; and some not of the meanest quality have been kept in long and close imprisonment without the least information appearing against them, or an *Habeas Corpus* allowed unto them. (*Andros Tracts* 1:14–15)

Cotton Mather's political innovations (like almost all colonial initiatives since settlement) were totally devoid of genuine, enforceable authority. As Phillip Haffenden explains, "the astute politicians of Massachusetts had maintained a form of independence until 1684 by careful observation of the conflicts, tensions, and divisions of English political life" (2).

News of Monmouth's Rebellion sent chilling messages to Puritan leaders and their supporters about the penalties that could be faced for political miscalculations. Increase's arrest on December 24, 1687, which was engineered to prevent his departure for England, and the seizure of Cotton, planned for April 18, 1689, gave notice that Massachusetts was a potentially dangerous environment. The charges leveled against the Mathers showed that substantiated facts were unnecessary for instituting criminal proceedings. To Cotton Mather, it was clear that authority and power were intimately associated with contingent and dangerous forces. Furthermore, the means used to quell public dissent could be accidental and irrational in practice. The oppressive presence of force, finitude in self-government, and the innumerability of threatening appearances were cited as evidence that Mather's New England was a collective chaos. As Palmer noted, "Persons do not understand Euclid or Aristotle; for the knowledge of the law, cannot be attained without great industry. . . . What a miserable condition are [New Englanders] in now, that instead of not knowing the law, there is no law for them to know?" (*Andros Tracts* 1:44–45).

Mather's provision of additional or intermediary options in telling his history enabled him to retain a greater artistic flexibility, both in his cognitive appraisal of situations and in his capacity to develop alternative courses of action. In psychological terms, however, this position caused Cotton Mather a great many problems. *Magnalia* partially fulfilled Mather's need for safety and security, esteem, self-actualization, and an interpretive frame for understanding his own danger. One tradition he had at his disposal was the example of the Puritan minister. In his practice of the ministry, Cotton Mather frequently departed from the authority invested in the ministry by lowering himself into the matrices of cultural negotiation that his congregation daily confronted. The proscription of relying for proofs and texts on anything save Scripture was easily abandoned in the legal and constitutional perils he himself faced.

Mather allowed that human authors and past Christian practices could help illuminate present circumstances. He used those examples to arrange his source materials. Mather's competence in balancing and managing a flexible interpretive scheme produced confusion among his peers, but it also served to heighten his innovative status. Mather's encounters with legal authority inculcated a flexibility in reasoning similar to Roger Williams's. Legal precepts are created out of uncertainty in human affairs, and Mather's direct engagement with colonial politics heightened his plurisignifying rhetoric.

The "worldliness" of Mather's hermeneutic was sometimes extended so far as to include dramatic examples of practices and persons whose very existence seemed to undercut Puritanism's vaunted authority. Mather's interest in counterfeit ministers marks one place in *Magnalia* where political aliases and the ministerial role he held hearken back to a conservatism that was associated with the "disciplined" Puritanism of his father:

One cannot easily ascribe unto a truer cause, than a *Satanick energy*, the strange *biass* upon the minds of a multitude, forceably and furiously sometimes carrying them into follies, from whence the plainest reason in the world will not reclaim them. What but such an energy could be upon the minds of many people in Boston, after the arrival of one that went by the name of Samuel May. . . . The wonderful success of Mahomet upon a world, where Christianity was to another degree lost than it yet is in Boston, was no longer a wonder unto us, when we saw the success of May. . . . It was all over pure *enchantment!* (2.544)

Mather's political experiences had taught him that aliases were a natural consequence of public involvement. Most effective political action is accomplished by aliases. The various roles that a political figure deploys exact a mounting emotional cost for the freedom they provide.

Mather, in the chapter devoted to counterfeits plaguing New England churches, suggests that his alternative political roles sometimes return as uninvited guests. They frame his anxiety, compromises, and partial control over events. Cotton Mather answers to this reality in *Wonders of the Invisible World*, where he uses spectral identity to link his project of "countermining the whole Plot of the Devil against New-England . . . as far as one of my Darkness can comprehend such a work of Darkness" to the understanding that "a man may come to walk about invisible . . . applying the Plastic Spirit of the World unto some unlawful purposes" (211, 246). In many ways, the rhetorical personality that Mather uses to narrate *Magnalia* is irradiated by his discussion of oppositional figures like Anne Hutchinson and Roger Williams. Contingent and marginal figures are Mather's "dark doubles" who haunt his text. The constant intrusion of controversy into Mather's chapter *Ecclesiarum Prælia* (*The Battles of the Churches*) celebrates his enacted self's range of encounters.

Mather used the image of the counterfeit to evoke the desolation of those who are forced to adopt roles and attitudes that exceed the interior life. The false minister was a warning to an evolving revolutionary society to never underestimate the power of forces that are outside society's power to contain. As Jeffrey Richards comments, "Mather shifts radically from nonconformist tradition by making faith not only a dialogic combat but also a spectacle; he celebrates a self large enough to be a nation. . . . Mather appropriates the Antinomian prerogative . . . and converts it to a social, and not merely an individual, imperative" (172). The root of revolutionary politics is the admission that the departure from a singular point of origin produces a plurality of secondary effects. As Mather said in *Wonders*, "It has been a most usual thing for the Bewitched persons, at the same time that the Spectres representing the witches Troubled them, to be visited with Apparitions of Ghosts, pretending to have been Murdered by the witches then represented" (237). According to Mather, when a Puritan minister is supplanted from his sacred duty by a dancing instructor, a barber, or a tanner, the political spectacle has degenerated into outrageousness. Mather's political compromises, which occasionally put him into an impostor's role, heightened his sense of contingency.

As a political actor, Mather sometimes had difficulties acknowledging the depth of his commitments. After the failure of Phips's expedition into Quebec in 1690, the political atmosphere of Boston was particularly tense. The failure of the expedition contributed to public dissatisfaction with Bradstreet's interim government. Cotton Mather fueled the unrest. He was accused of being the author of a populist newspaper, *Publick Occurrences*, which was unlicensed, contained dubious reports of events, and criticized the government (Kenneth Silverman 75–76). People believed Mather was behind it. He issued a proclamation denying "he had published the scandalous thing." In the same effort at denial, however, he said he considered the newspaper "noble, useful, and laudable." And he reported to his uncle John Cotton that "the publisher had not one line of it from me, only as accidentally meeting him in the highway, on his request, I showed him how to contract and express the report of the expedition" (*Selected Letters* 27–28). Mather's involvement with the paper shows his familiarity with aliases. On the one hand, there is the "official" Mather whose loyalty to the Bradstreet government prevents him from openly criticizing its policies. This Mather issues the ardent proclamation that he has nothing to do with the underground press. On the other hand, there is the "unofficial" Mather whose complicity with the publishers of the *Publick Occurrences* attempts to explain Phips's actions against the French as having failed because of poor government in Boston. This Mather is an "alias" operating surreptitiously within revolutionary politics. Mather's political entanglements found him in several of these tenuous positions. Certain episodes in *Magnalia* are colored by that tension.

The "Introduction" to *Magnalia*'s seventh book points to this uneasiness:

> I disdain to make the apology once made by the Roman historian, *Nemo Historicus non aliquid mentitus, et habiturus sum mendaciorum comites, quos Historiæ et eloquentiæ miramur authores.* [There is no historian who has not told some falsehoods, and I shall have as my companions in mendacity those whom all admire as models of historic truth and eloquence.] (2.583)

In the "General Introduction," Mather supplied his audiences with the observation that "Histories are but so many panegyricks composed by interested hands, which elevate iniquity to the heavens, like Paterculus, and like Machiavel" (1.29). Further along in the same passage, Mather's deep-seated anxiety erupts as a half-composed confession: "Me, me, adsum qui scripsi; in me convertite ferrum [I wrote it! — I! — vent all your spite on me!]. I hope 'tis a right work that I have done. . . . It will not be so much a suprise unto me, if I should live to see our Church-History vexed with *Anie mad-versions* of calumnious writers" (1.34). Mather's wordplay "Anie-mad-versions" speaks volumes about the construction of historical authority he has undertaken in *Magnalia.* The phrase connotes "animadversions," those critical comments that usually imply censure, and "any mad versions," suggesting heretical separatist doctrines that were also intended to reach an English audience.

The doubleness and imagined deception that determine the tone of this chapter stem from Mather's fear that his political roles engendered unexpected subversive repercussions. Mather often uses the example of heretical beliefs to unveil the private, subversive forces that he set out to contain in the book's design.[28] The complexity of "face value" representations is a "realistic" insight of Mather's. Under a system where social rank no longer guaranteed a fixed political position, Mather occasionally had to assume compromising positions in order to accomplish laudatory goals. Because counterfeit ministers reopen substantive questions about the author's connection to his time and place, a careful reader rightfully asks, how do I judge the narrator of the "authorized" history of New England? Mather says,

> Men are too insensible of the horrid *villainy* and *blasphemy* in the crimes of those fellows, who set up for *teachers* to the people of God, when God knows they are wicked *vagrants* and *varlets*, designing to abuse the honest people, if they imagine it a *severe* thing to stigmatize them in view of all the affronted churches. The faults of the *penitent*, indeed, should be *concealed*; but these pretended preachers of repentance are not known to *practice* the *repentance* which they *preach*. . . . Our laws not providing such a punishment for them, they that would be faithful to the churches, will do well . . . to set them up in an *history*, instead of a *pillory*, with a *writing* as it were in capitals, to signifie, THESE WERE IMPOSTORS THAT WOULD HAVE BEEN ESTEEMED MINISTERS. (2.540)

Mather is careful to project onto the community as a whole the contingencies he knows so well, thus suggesting that the populist desire for autonomy has exposed a "wolf in sheep's clothing" who barks at the English government in Whitehall.

Many of the anxieties about inside/outside, authority/deception, and truth/untruth that Mather encountered in his political life he projected into his chapter on counterfeit ministers. As his role in the Salem imbroglio became more and more disruptive of the civil order, we can surmise that Mather sometimes felt like the minister Lyford, who "at his first coming did caress the good people at Plymouth with such extream show of affection and humility, that the people were mightily taken with him; nevertheless, within a little while he used most malignant endeavours to make *factions* among them, and confound all their *civil* and *sacred* order" (2.540). Mirroring a deep split and ambivalence in Mather's own life, his account of false ministers is a study in miniature of the relationship between dominant and subversive ideologies in seventeenth-century New England.

In cases like Samuel May's, two genres of ideology—the overtly political and the subverting self-interest—are mutually constitutive. Mather's attention to impostors "novelizes" his own role as a historian. By suggesting an enlightened worldliness that often exceeds his readers' expectations, Mather creates cultural logics that seize on the irrational grayness, perversity, and peculiarity that counterfeit ministers impose on a sacred community. Mather's specific case studies are potent reminders that the bizarre in history exists within everyday reality. Such anxious moments momentarily isolate alternative versions of events that alter the meaning of "official" histories.

The cultural identity of the minister is shaped by the doubled reality of illicit and proper behavior. As Mather concludes,

> Who would have believed it, that in a town so illuminated as Boston, there should be any people of such a principle, *that if the greatest villain in the world should arrive a total stranger among us, and for his true name give us perhaps only the first syllable of his name, and of a barber turn a preacher, the pastors here must immediately set him up in the publick pulpits, or else the people unjustly load them with all the calumnious indignities that can be thought of?* (2.547)

Mather's discussion of counterfeit ministers enabled him to suggest rhetorically that "historians" were capable of shuttling among several positions in their efforts to capture political events. Furthermore, the political spectacle forces the responsible historian to consider not just the primary event in which he is interested but also the concealments his method produces. Important aspects of Mather's subject may be compromised by his bias.

Certain passages in *Magnalia* do not attempt to reconcile these forces, nor do they try to organize them into a coherent sensible pattern. Ambiguity functions as a public space that allows a shifting series of superficially incompatible impulses to coexist inside the narrative. Although the importance of narrative style as a self-conscious strategy for dealing with conflict cannot be overemphasized, Mather in fact did not rely only on narrative conventions. Mather's political knowledge must be understood as partly independent of the social system in which it operated. Indeed, the governmentality[29] that Mather promulgated capitalized on transactional realities that existed at the mutable interface of political power. Mather knew that print culture and the narrative structures it allowed alone would not satisfy the American desire to inhibit England's colonial rule. *Magnalia*, located as it is on this frontier of political power, constituted in print a problematic space where experimental innovation (both in narrative and in government ideology) was thought to be actively shaping the development of a unique political technology. Mather exploited "knowledge" broadly defined. He held a shared sense of a European influence on the construction of North American ways of knowing. Consequently, his history, convoluted and introspective, seeks to invoke the sense of transformation that had begun long before John Winthrop but had entered the American context along with that first generation of Puritan settlers. Further, Mather's conceits in *Magnalia* deliberately signal that his knowledge-based power was much more flexible than what the social structure of New England accommodated. The book's success rests, for his own and future readers, on its ability to preserve frequent areas of common ground (though sometimes *congested* and *contested*) between groups apparently sharply divided. Politics is oftentimes reduced to anxious moments of composition. In one anxious moment of composition, Mather describes the spectacle of the revolution he has lived through:

I have sometimes, not without amazement, thought of the representation which a celebrated *magician* made unto Catherine de Medicis, the French Queen, whose impious curiosity lead her to desire of him a *magical exhibition* of all the Kings that had hitherto reigned in France, and yet were to reign. The shapes of all the Kings, even unto the husband of that Queen, successively showed themselves, in the *enchanted circle*, in which that conjurer had made his invocations, and they took as many *turns* as there had been years in their government. The Kings that were to come, did then in like manner . . . namely, Francis II., Charles IX., Henry III., Henry IV., which being done, then the two cardinals Richlieu and Mazarine, in red hats, became visible in the spectacle: but after those cardinals, there entred wolves, bears, tygers and lions, to consummate the entertainment. If the people of New-England had not imagined that a number of as *rapacious animals* were at last come into their government, I suppose they would not have made such a *revolution* as they did, on April 18, 1689. (1.139)

By distancing himself from "those who made such a revolution as they did," he draws attention to the distinction between the enacted and enacting selves that we have encountered elsewhere in *Magnalia*. The little scene that Mather "conjures" is symbolic of the transformational process at stake here. The rulers of New England, like those of France, were veritable wolves in sheep's clothing. The passage cited above is a spectacle of political danger not unlike Hawthorne's depictions of portentous political masques.

The conjunction between the magical dance and the political heritage of France is not an accidental situation. Mather raises the point in order to say something about the political situation in New England. Moderate politicians attempted to use the threat of external French aggression to smooth the internal dissension within the colony. Mather uses a different pose than either Machiavelli (a major figure who shapes the historical logic within *Magnalia*) or Bradford. Either of these men might confidently see the situation described above as a clarification of human political behavior. Cotton Mather's rhetorical "truth" was of a different order. It was capable of cancelling, but not making plain, human politics. In many instances *Magnalia* imitates classical examples of republics (Greece, Rome, Florence) and describes with a definable bias certain aspects of New England. But Mather's work illuminates politics not with faith in human perfection but rather with his literary imagination.

It becomes Mather's right, once he has confused his relationship to his own text, to survey the world he has constructed, to deliberate on the worthiness of representations that would make plain what New England was in danger of losing and what the meaning of that loss might become. The incursions and pollutions that Mather records in his chapter on false ministers contribute to the climate for New England's well-developed repressive apparatus of rumors, accusations, and legal proceedings (those strategies that were deployed in reaction as a corrective to realignments made possible under the second charter). The everyday reality of Massachusetts between the charters made the subversive seem omnipresent. The relation between orthodoxy and subversion, at the time of *Magnalia*'s composition, was both perfectly stable and dangerously volatile.

The politically adept person, a man like Cotton Mather, conveys a sense of authority and power. He has that status precisely because power's quintessential mark is the ability to impose one's fictions upon the world. Like the magician's act paraded before Catherine de Medici, the more outrageous the fiction, the more impressive is the manifestation of power.

Political Fables and the Political Negotiation of Meanings

In June 1691, armed with a parallel text of the old and proposed charters, Increase Mather, William Blathwayt, and the other Lords of Trade met and negotiated a framework of government for the Dominion of New England. Their efforts combined precedents from the old charter with patterns of political authority that the Lords of Trade had employed in Virginia and the West Indies. Despite a final round of direct appeals to William III, Increase Mather eventually supported a charter that preserved for an enlarged Bay Province a greater number of liberties than in any other jurisdiction in America. But the new charter decisively eliminated the supremacy of Congregational churches in political and cultural affairs.

The charter attempted to centralize England's imperial control, but it also effectively legitimated factional conflict among interest groups in New England. The charter guaranteed that open disagreement would be tolerated in a government characterized by political pluralism. Executive power was concentrated in the governor general's office. The earlier paradigm of the governor as the symbolic head of an ideologically consistent populace was replaced by a consummate political manager who needed to use power in a variety of ways to control a faction-ridden political body. The emergence of the governor's office diminished the authority that assistants had formerly held over political affairs.

The "external" apparatus brought to bear on Massachusetts politics is also the core of Mather's "government" of representation in *Magnalia*. Prior to 1686, when the General Court was in session, assistants were the upper house in the legislature and shared executive and legislative authority with the deputies. During the remaining five to six months of the year, the assistants operated Massachusetts's government, regulating town and county affairs, registering land deeds and probate records, controlling the admission of voters, and constituting the court of appeals for the colony. These diversified powers had enabled the assistants to engage in a great deal of social management, but under the new charter they were to remain the upper house and execute the powers of advice and consent. Consequently, they found themselves to be increasingly an advisory body mediating conflicts between the governor and representatives, the two major power centers in the new scheme.

Every May, the representatives were able to nominate twenty-eight councilors representing various territories within the province and present them to the governor for confirmation. Councilors chosen under this system ceased to be conservative defenders of Puritanism and became instead political moderates acceptable to both imperial and popular interests.

To secure public acceptance of the new legislative scheme, Increase Mather provided in the second charter for an assembly that would (1) elect all civil officers who performed nonjudicial duties; (2) control the assessment, collection, and disbursement of public money in the province; and (3) organize courts in Massachusetts. This final provision created a voting prerogative based purely on property qualifications. Increase Mather's original intention to preserve a degree of religious orthodoxy as a standard for political participation ultimately resulted in the most liberal set of voting laws in America.

Finally, Mather's negotiated charter provided for a guarantee of religious freedom for all Protestants. This final provision, excluding Puritans from the mechanisms of civil government, enabled dissenting groups to pursue their interests with some degree of protection from the executive branch of government.

When the charter was proclaimed in New England on October 7, 1691, it seemed an almost total reversal of providential history. Freedoms were to be unambiguously legislated by civil authorities. The very real need for a workable government had produced a document that reflected patterns of shifting priorities. Cotton Mather's political role, like that given to assistants under the new charter, was to mediate between his father and a generally disagreeable popular faction.

There was no hoped-for "outside" to the new charter that would renew the original Puritan mission of John Winthrop. The charter established elaborate structures, instituted a necessity for diligent negotiation, and renewed the ever-present competition over ambiguous areas of political involvement. The keys to success in the world invented by this new charter were principally efficiency and social currency—prized attributes for translating ideology into government practice.

The accommodationist tendencies that Cotton Mather embraced after 1691 flowed from his conviction that political insights and blindness were co-implicated in the processes of statecraft. He drafted a series of political allegories that thinly concealed his desire for public acceptance of the terms his father had negotiated. It was his view that New England could capitalize on the vitality of its illusions. Especially useful were those experiments in self-government forged out of the uncertain period between charters. The scattered experience of the past five years had shown Mather that wealth, power, and prestige could be manufactured according to political necessity. The need to consolidate the effects of the Boston rebellion influenced Mather to write his political fables. Spectacles of excess could effectively inform the writing of fiction, and, in turn, the fiction could be used to forge a connection to the commonweal.

The political fables were schematic. The complex experience of the region was made to communicate by means of public symbols drawn from myth and the fantastic. The ease with which the fables incorporated a wide range of formerly contentious issues paralleled the 1691 charter's attempt to safeguard some of the liberties the colonists had worked to achieve. Both documents seemed to overcome the initial contingency of their artificial relationship to the people and ideas they framed.

For Mather, a culturally constructed world became a meaningful world that could be bartered in the marketplace of colonial politics. The charter was not an end unto itself but rather a means for establishing a cultural standard. What had at times during the governorships of Andros and Phips been unintelligible was now intelligible and self-consistent even though fables were only an approximate analysis of actual opinion.

Mather wrote four fables in defense of the 1691 charter: *The New Settlement of the Birds in New England, The Elephant's Case a Little Stated, Mercury's Negotiation*, and *Story of the Dogs and the Wolves*. They were intended to counter harsh criticisms. Some in New England (Elisha Cooke, for example) believed that Increase had sacrificed too many of the old rights expressed under the original charter. The fables were circulated in manuscript in 1692. Fables had a long tradition in England. John Dryden's *Fables An-*

cient and Modern (1700) were important pieces of cultural criticism that, through short stories with a moral lesson, were often fantastic associations of the marvelous and mythical. Mather's fables used the common generic conventions of animals or mythic gods to represent key political players in New England. New Englanders were represented as birds and sheep; Increase Mather was an eagle and Mercury; Sir William Phips was the king's-fisher and the elephant; the foes of New England (governors and "moderates") were represented as harpies, bruins, or foxes.

The New Settlement of the Birds in New England allegorizes the events from the original charter's suspension in 1684 to Increase's decision to make the mission to Whitehall. "When they had lost their charters, those poetical birds called harpies became really existent, and visited these flocks, not so much that they might build nests of their own, as plunder and pull down the nests of others," Mather wrote (*Selections* 363). He was referring to New England's final entrapment in English colonial policy. Prior to 1684, New England had been successful in contending for rights without fully acknowledging the responsibilities owed to the mother country.

Mather continues, describing his father's travel to "Jupiter's court" where he attempted to better decipher James's equivocal intentions in restoring Catholicism or the imperial dominion (or both). His father, as agent of a powerful colony, assumed he could accept or reject the royal proposals as he deemed appropriate. Increase Mather contended vigorously with the government of William III and was able to win the acceptance of a provisional government under Phips's leadership. "He offered that the king's-fisher should have commission to be their governor until they had settled what good orders among them pleased" and "the birds might everlastingly be confirmed in their titles [to land]" (*Selections* 364).

The Elephant's Case a Little Stated recapitulates the contentious experiences of Phips's provisional government: "The elephant was as good as he was great. . . . But [they] said they feared he was but a shoeing-horn; in a year or two either Isgrim the wolf, or Bruin the bear, would succeed him" (*Selections* 365). Mather uses the fable to suggest that, after James's abdication and William's accession, the danger to New England was no longer with the ways English governors interfered with the region's autonomy but instead was with the threat of French encroachment. "My desire is," says the king's-fisher, "that Jupiter may have the satisfaction of seeing you saved from the dangers of perishing either by division among yourselves, or by invasion from abroad" (*Selections* 366).

Mercury's Negotiation concentrates on Increase Mather's efforts to win the 1691 charter from King William. To those in favor of the charter, the new instrument provided complementary measures designed to supplement the natural regulations that were thought necessary for rulers. Increase Mather stressed how the new charter secured liberty and property, and he also pointed to the ability of Puritans to worship as they had before (though other religions had to be granted liberty of conscience). The governor could no longer make laws or impose taxes without the consent of a representative assembly. Increase stressed his unique achievement in obtaining "peculiar Charter privileges which no other English plantation in the world has" (*The Revolution in New England Justified*). Despite Increase's lobbying efforts, opposition to the charter was widespread. The royal governor, lieutenant governor, and secretary were given large powers, including a veto over acts of the General Court. "When Mercury returned to the sheep, he found them strangely metamorphosed from what they were before. . . . such things as the sheep would have given three quarters of the fleece on their backs to have purchased . . . they were now scarce willing to accept" (*Selections* 367). Cotton Mather portrays himself as Orpheus who must play a tune to placate the sheep. He defends the new charter by telling people that Increase financed his own mission to England, won favors for Harvard, preserved trading privileges, bought time during which Massachusetts could recover all its lost liberties through legal channels when conditions permitted, was not authorized by the people themselves to refuse the king's conditions, and was not the proper judge to balance Christian and English allegiances. As Cotton Mather says in the conclusion to the fable, the sheep were "a little better satisfied; but Mercury was not much concerned. . . . he wished the sheep would have a care of all the snakes in the grass, who did mischief by insinuating . . . discord" (*Selections* 370).

Story of the Dogs and the Wolves is a brief warning to the colony that its discontent is playing into the hands of French enemies. New Englanders had become fragmented, "the dogs were not only divided into three or four several bodies which had little disposition to help one another, but they were also very quarrelsome among themselves" (*Selections* 371). The result, Mather suggested, was that the revolutionary heritage might end in a deflationary moment: "said he, monsieurs, let's have at them: we shall easily play the wolf upon them that have played the dog upon one another" (*Selections* 371).

Mather's use of allegory accomplished the merger of contemporary social circumstances with myth that he had intended. In writing these fables, Mather knew that his best hope for short- and long-term success depended on his equating the great questions of New England's political life with his own biography. He tried to capture the power of politics by using recently enacted public dramas to direct these allegories. In so doing to the fullest extent that his temperament and historical consciousness allowed, he betrayed himself as an ambitious historical fictionalist reaching out for community. He wanted to connect with a community that enjoyed the past glory of Puritanism, and he wanted to maintain contacts with the popular leadership.

Because Mather opened this "new" role for himself as a Puritan historian, he was able to apotheosize the first and second generations. At the same time, he was interjecting ironic notes, suggesting that the first- and second-generation leadership had precipitated New England's present confinement under the 1691 charter. Both Cotton and his father had been radically subverted as narrators of New England's meaning. Each chose to "look elsewhere for the rewards of [their] charitable undertakings" (*Selections* 370).

Mather's extravagant focus on the "paranoid" public attitudes against his father suggested a need to match these complex responses with public fictions that could overcome the resistance his father's work had generated. Cotton Mather's ironic fictions (like his fables and the charter), which initially seemed inadequate to calm public dissent, would ultimately become the fictions that purchased New England's cultural stability. The desire of the Mathers to identify themselves by reference to a wider community formed Cotton Mather's specific ambition to demonstrate to English audiences the worthiness of the New England enterprise that they had helped to manage. *Magnalia*, by demonstrating in literature how the skill and fortitude of the politician could be employed to consolidate privileges and superior virtues, played a significant part in Mather's translation of his past perils into a promising legacy.

In *Magnalia*, Mather's personal accommodation of the charter echoes in his description of the colony's public debt. Mather's theory of cultural capital compares the value of the Massachusetts enterprise to the "value" of his own narrative. The issue of the public debt has both a personal and a communitarian dimension. The colony's ambivalent appreciation of its self-worth is the context that frames Mather's discussion of New England's public debt:

Every one will easily conclude none of the least consequences to have been the *extream debts* which that country was now plunged into; there being *forty thousand* pounds, more or less, now to be paid, and not a penny in the treasury to pay it withal. In this extremity they presently found out an *expedient*, which may serve as an *example* for any people in other parts of the world, whose distresses may call for a sudden supply of money to carry them through any important expedition. The general assembly first passed an act for the levying of such a sum of money as was wanted, within such a term of time as was judged convenient; and this *act* was a *fund*, on which the *credit* of such a sum should be rendered *passable* among the people. Hereupon there was appointed an able and faithful committee of gentle-men, who printed from copper-plates, a just number of *bills*, and flour-ished, indented, and contrived them in such a manner, as to make it im-possible to counterfeit any of them, without a speedy discovery of the counterfeit: besides which, they were all signed by the hands of three be-longing to that committee. These bills being of several sums . . . did con-fess the Massachusetts-colony to be endebted unto the person in whose hands they were. . . . The publick debts to the *sailors* and *soldiers*, now upon the point of *mutiny*, were in these bills paid immediately: but that further *credit* might be given thereunto, it was ordered that they should be accepted by the treasurer . . . in all publick payments, at five per cent. more than the value expressed in them. . . . The people knowing that the tax-act would, in the space of two years at least, fetch into the treasury as much as all the bills of credit . . . wherein it was their advantage to pay their taxes, rather than in any other specie; and so the sailors and soldiers put off their bills, instead of money, to those with whom they had any dealings, and they circulated through all the hands in the colony pretty comfortably. Had the government been so settled, that there had been any doubt of any obstruction, or diversion to be given to the prosecution of the tax-act, by a total change of their affairs, then depending at White-Hall, 'tis very certain, that the bills of credit had been better than so much ready silver; yea, the invention had been of more use to the New-England-ers, than if all their copper mines had been opened, or the mountains of Peru had been removed into these parts of America. The Massachusetts bills of credit had been like the bank bills of Venice, where though there were not, perhaps, a ducat of money in the bank, yet the bills were es-teemed more than twenty per cent. better than money. . . . But many people being afraid that the government would in half a year be so overturned as to convert their bills of credit altogether into *waste paper*, the *credit* of them was thereby very much impaired; and they who first received them could make them yield little more than fourteen or sixteen shillings in the pound; from whence there arose those idle suspicions in the heads of many more ignorant and unthinking folks concerning the use thereof, which, to the incredible detriment of the province, are not wholly laid aside to unto this day. (1.190–91)

Mather sensed that part of New England's difficulties with England stemmed from an unclear understanding of how the economic and spiritual pursuits of the colony were linked with English imperialism.

The suspension of the original charter showed the basis of the partnership between Old and New England to be a manipulative one. Mather adeptly perceived that the hindrances caused by a division of purpose between mother country and colony would license new opportunities for himself. Communication between Old and New England had been extremely limited. But, as the writing of *Magnalia* itself shows, that period, for Mather at least, was to end when his father brought the colony a new blueprint for the partnership. Mather's role as a politician seemed better defined by the 1691 charter than did his role as author. The discussion of the debt shows a Mather determined to maintain the illusion in his work that he was intermediate between the concerns of the dominant culture and what he took to be its inventive core. The description of New England's public debt draws on its typically colonial nature: contingent, historical, and fabricated. Mather uses that representation to argue metaphorically for his own acts as a writer—he can "mint" his own artistic currency in ways that will transform the reality he describes.

The Massachusetts bills of credit were, in effect, managed currencies. When the instability of exchange rates grew too profound, Governor Phips interceded by buying the depreciated bills in order to restore public confidence in a fluctuating currency. Those "ignorant and unthinking folks" continued to view money as a standard of value and a medium of exchange. Money was not a simple concept that expressed a fixed value; its worth was regulated through a process of negotiation and agreement. Mather's consideration of monetary worth is not a slight shading of economic terms but rather a complete renegotiating of ways to determine cultural value. The piecemeal efforts to impose a consolidated political façade always seemed (in Mather's experience) to be localized improvisations to a more general problem. Ultimately a "loose and scattered" condition continued to prevail despite the earnest attempts of others to manage public policy.

The discussion of the debt is an example of cultural purchase. It reflects the extent to which secular and civil matters intersect with larger allegorical processes of reading and writing. Mather's understanding of money here is one that could not have been formed without an active interest in politics. When Mather asserts that currency is a manufactured standard that has less to do with "innate" value than with "apparent" value, he is putting forward representations of the world based on "material emanation and exchange." Each of the passages I have looked at in *Magnalia* bears these textual traces of Mather's revolutionary politics. Stephen Greenblatt writes:

> If the textual traces in which we take interest and pleasure are not sources of numinous authority, if they are signs of contingent social practices . . . we can ask how collective beliefs and experiences were shaped, moved from one medium to another, concentrated in manageable aesthetic form, offered for consumption. We can examine how the boundaries were marked between cultural practices understood to be art forms and other, contiguous forms of expression. We can attempt to determine how these specially demarcated zones were invested with the power to confer pleasure or excite interest or generate anxiety. (*Shakespearean Negotiations* 5)

Magnalia, because it is centered on the emergent aspects of New England that were a particularized combination of historical circumstances, becomes a great working-out of the boundary between politics and the practices of the historical writer. Notice that Mather, in the passage on the public debt, characterizes the committee as being "indentured." He means that in executing the agreement in as many counterparts as there were parties, the enterprise became a communal undertaking where the relative significance of any singular person was subsumed by the interests of the whole. This notion of "indentured" activity helps Mather to connect his fictional approximations of political influence with his public statements that his history is meant to memorialize public experience. Mather's account of money, not of what it actually purchases but of owning the potential of capital, is a remarkable foreshadowing of the theory behind the gold standard the United States adopted in 1834. Mather hoped his books would be used to accomplish the cultural tasks of repaying debts, setting a standard for (historical) value, and

creating a demand for more writing in a similar vein. Those are many of the
same functions that money performs for national economies.

Although Mather deals with some of the same cultural concerns as his
predecessors, his understanding of the negotiational dynamics involved between writing and politics signals his distance from someone like John Winthrop. The details that Mather uses to construct notions of saintly divines
and the associations he draws between events form an ironic ventriloquism
to the intended authority of his own narrative. Mather is not always the
symbolic figure controlling his own discourse. At key moments he is nothing
more than a manager of discursive strands that depend on a reader's response.

Mather's description of the debt embarrasses the simplicity of a "new
myth" that saw the return to the dictates of the old charter as a providential
resurrection of the old leadership in the midst of its final eclipse. Mather's
continual evocation of the first generation ultimately makes the point that
the present political world is redundantly overspecified. It has a contingent
and even, in a sense, a facetious life of its own.

We have seen in this chapter how Mather's politics frequently shaped
some of the rhetorical strategies he deployed in *Magnalia*. The ability he
showed for recording political commentary into an authoritative text on the
Puritan experience in New England did not form a coherent "system" for
telling that story. What it did do was record his political inflections in such
a way as to cluster his public life and commitments around key interests that
he had as a historical writer: which "genre" conventions to uphold and modify when narrating a politically aware narrative; how to depict the "constructedness" of representative personalities; how to cope with the reality of
aliases in writing and political life; and how to translate political knowledge
into cultural forms that can be useful to those who want to shape the opinions of others. Each of these writerly concerns is borne in markers, or textual
traces, that Mather used to narrate the identity of the colony for an eager
reading public in England. In constructing a narrative in this way, Mather
was both characteristically traditional and iconoclastic. The historians of the
third generation like Edward Johnson and Cotton Mather occupied a unique
literary moment in which personal covenantal involvement transformed the
traditional forms of history.[30] The acceptance of the notion of corporate self-
hood gave the historian's role a striking resemblance to that of the auto-
biographer. Spiritual autobiographies written during the crisis years of the

1690s present new, self-centered protagonists. Thus, by the beginning of the eighteenth century, the genre had become above all else a way to separate the private soul from a frightening world[31]—except, in Mather's case, the insidious aspects of that frightening world were constantly viewed as part and parcel of private identity.

The initial euphoria of the rebellion in Boston held forth the promise of popular rule, rapid economic growth, the redistribution of social importance, cultural regeneration, and the specter of regional greatness. It was these considerations, certainly dimly perceived at the moment the *Declaration* was read from the balcony of the Town House, that fed Cotton Mather's sense that he was near the center of a valuable undertaking.

In reading and remembering the sequence of events leading to the charter's suspension, Mather knew that the restoration of civil stability was impossible under the Dominion. The clouded lines of authority, the empty notions that the "city on a hill" held relevance for a rapidly modernizing international state, were part and parcel of the regional consciousness. The fractured reality that Mather anticipated became the context that Puritanism would have to engage if it were to enter contemporaneity and restore itself. As the days and weeks after the initial uprising made clear, the agenda undergirding the revolution became increasingly attenuated.

The near-millennial hopes of a political deliverance for Massachusetts—once vested in men like Increase Mather and Simon Bradstreet—were becoming more diffuse. This trend increased until late in 1691, when the new charter was implemented. Phips's charismatic leadership, which Mather celebrated in *Magnalia*, was systematically dissolved as the expedition into Canada tarnished New England's reputation for even limited self-government. The forward motion of the colony that Mather discerned in the early post-revolutionary phase was replaced by a complex, uneven, and many-directioned movement. The atmosphere in Boston at the end of 1691 indicated that the rebellion had created less a sense of progress than a feeling of agitated stagnation. No doubt, it was Cotton's frustration with this situation that fueled an intense period of preoccupation with eschatology. Beginning with *Things to be Look'd for* (1691), Mather published more than forty sermons on the millennium and the events leading up to the cataclysm. Mather's eschatological view underwent considerable revision throughout his life, but as he aged, he openly disagreed with his father Increase—and with many of their mutual friends—on such issues as the National Conversion of the Jews, the Conflagration, and the New Jerusalem of the New Heavens and the New Earth. Mather's unpublished manuscript essay "Problema Theolo-gicum" (1703), *Triparadisus* (begun in 1712 and finished in 1726), and "Biblia Americana," his compendium to the Bible, left unfinished at his death in 1728, are important works written after *Magnalia* that reflect theologically his impatience with the social order after the new charter. As these writings attest, Mather's architecture for a pietist ecumenism, his endeavor to unite all creeds in one Church Universal through his "Maxims of Piety," and his desire for a more progressive government, were steady and pronounced after the Glorious Revolution.

What Mather initially viewed as a rapid, broadly coordinated social, eco-nomic, and political advance was, in 1691, a continuation of the major issues facing the colony in the immediate prerevolutionary period: New England was engaged in a collective activity aimed at defining, creating, and solidify-ing a viable cultural identity that retained the ideological distinctiveness that had characterized its founding. That activity was now seriously circum-scribed by the larger imperial designs of England.

The political markers of the text become important for other writers look-ing for authoritative sources to work from in their attempt to reconcile an-tiquarianism with political issues in Jacksonian America. Mather's markers of a political experiment that produced disappointing outcomes become ac-cents of the struggles confronting writers investigating the consequences of participatory democracy. The republication of *Magnalia* is the focus of the next chapter.

Part Two

Reading *Magnalia Christi Americana* in the Nineteenth Century

Chapter Two

Participatory Democracy and Robbins's 1820 Edition of *Magnalia Christi Americana*

This chapter begins by considering Thomas Robbins's republication of *Magnalia* in 1820 and then suggests that the text helped to define a broader cultural moment of national self-definition in the writing of Hawthorne, Stowe, and Stoddard. The 1820 edition constituted one of the most significant publishing events of the American Renaissance when considered from the standpoint of the history of the book in New England. Perry Miller and Kenneth Murdock have called *Magnalia* the most sustained jeremiad produced in seventeenth-century New England. Readers have always considered Mather's history to be more than the sum of its individual chapters, but never more so than in 1820. Exhibiting all the characteristic traits of the jeremiad—cryptic renderings of the Puritan divines; the failings of a people attended by social, spiritual, and political disaster; inevitable punishments; and identity politics riddled by a haunting sense of mission and destiny—the American edition was the crucial publication for the production of a new and highly self-conscious literature. Despite the profound differences between Mather's original audience and his potential audience in the first half of the nineteenth century, Thomas Robbins played a pivotal role in the formation of a literary tradition by making available a uniquely "American" text.

Many who read Mather's text understood it as a celebration of the literary competencies of newly empowered readers and as a substantial, expensive, and encyclopedic book embodying New England's Puritan legacy. Possession of *Magnalia* indicated certain social (and perhaps scholarly) inclinations of the reader. As Robbins himself said in the Preface in 1852, "The demand for the work is now increasing. The History of New England cannot be written without this authority" (Mather, *Magnalia* vi). After the edition became available, the macro-observations of Mather's time—neatly summarized in Mather's original map, which Robbins insisted be included in the American edition—were ardently translated and dispersed among a democratic readership.

Thomas Robbins was born in Norfolk, Connecticut, on August 11, 1777. Like Cotton Mather, he was a third-generation minister who stood at a rather distant point within a long-standing ministerial dynasty. Robbins's father, the Reverend Ammi Ruhamah Robbins, was the minister at Norfolk for fifty-two

Rev. Thomas Robbins (1777–1856) (1801), oil portrait by Reuben Moulthrop. (The Connecticut Historical Society, Hartford; photograph by Arthur Kiely)

years; his grandfather, the Reverend Philemon Robbins, was minister at Branford for thirty-nine years. In 1811, while he was the pastor at East Windsor, Connecticut, Thomas started in earnest to expand a library that he had started to assemble in 1793. In his diary he recorded that

> After much deliberation, and endeavors to seek divine direction, I have concluded to attempt to lay a foundation of a permanent Library. I have now about THREE HUNDRED VOLUMES, which I conclude to number. . . . I hope to be enabled to add the value of *One Hundred Dollars* a year, at least as long as I live. . . . The object of my Library is, first to assist the Divinity Student in the investigation of the Holy Scriptures, . . . secondly, to assist the Lover of History in his researches.

At the end of 1841 Robbins had thirty-three hundred volumes along with thousands of pamphlets, proclamations, newspapers, almanacs, and manuscripts. His acute interest in political utterances led him to collect election sermons feverishly. Interestingly, the peak of his search for election sermons coincided with the year he republished *Magnalia*: 1820. By 1823, Robbins could say with obvious satisfaction, "Of one hundred and nine [election sermons] printed in this State [Connecticut], I now have one hundred and eight" (931).

In 1820, Thomas Robbins reissued Mather's text through a small publisher of antiquarian curiosities, Silus Andrus. When he decided to reissue *Magnalia*, Robbins wrote that he "had long been sensible of the great demand for the work, both by literary men and all others who wish to be acquainted with the early history of our country" (Mather, *Magnalia*, Preface). Robbins's expectation for sales was small, but the edition sold steadily and a second edition was called for in 1853. Robbins's edition was essential for a New England readership trying to "image" itself during a period when the cultural legacy of the seventeenth century seemed hopelessly obsolete. As a textual artifact, *Magnalia* "arranges" aspects of seventeenth-century culture. The text communicates by squarely implicating Cotton Mather within the cultural forces that guided the production of a marketable text. Robbins was eager to make possible a correct text that was capable of becoming widely known.

Secondarily, in advertisements and reviews of the book, Robbins's volume is used to "image" the varieties of taste and responsibility expected of a democratic readership. This reciprocity of author and reader is rooted in the strategies of early American publishers, who attempted to invent a native literature with the ability to exploit for readers both old, familiar roles and new, potentially profitable ones. Robbins's efforts amply illustrate Cathy Davidson's point that beneath every text lies "an overt and covert cultural agenda, an ideological subtext, [which] is encoded in the writing, publishing, reprinting, binding, titling, retitling, pictorializing, advertising, distributing, marketing, selling, buying, reading, interpreting, and, finally, the institutionalizing (within literary criticism and historiography) of any text" (7). Indeed, at the time of the American Revolution, James Rivington, the notorious New York Tory publisher, recognized the political implications of *Magnalia*. He considered a new edition in 1773 but never launched the project.[1] Rivington, it may be surmised, saw a reflection of himself in Mather's text. As Tebbel tells us, Rivington practiced a form of journalism similar to Mather's writing for the *Boston Gazette*: "Rivington wielded a clever, vitriolic pen—it attacked the patriot cause with diabolical ingenuity and savage wit. [He] did not hesitate to print the most scurrilous forgeries . . . and [he] printed gossip freely" (88).

Robbins knew that Rivington's failure to tap *Magnalia* presented him with the great "theme" of his time: the extension of "democracy" and its effects on American desires. On the one hand, New Englanders were receptive to the re-establishment of true community; on the other, democratic readers were continually becoming cognizant of competitive individualism. Robbins wrote in the Preface to the first American edition:

> *Magnalia* is a standard work with American Historians, and must ever continue to be such, especially, respecting the affairs of New-England. To this portion of our country, always distinguished for emigrations, a great part of the population of New York, the most important state in the American confederacy, and of all the western states north of Ohio, will always trace their origin. . . . The great object of the first Planters of New-England was to form a CHRISTIAN COMMONWEALTH—a design without parallel in ancient or modern times. The judicious reader would expect to discover, in the annals of such a people, characters and events not to be found in the history of other communities. (Mather, *Magnalia* v)

Robbins surmised that readers were drawn not to the church history aspects of the work but rather to its fascinating grasp of political and historical realities. There is some evidence that he used *Magnalia* as a personal guide for

better understanding the erosion of his own Federalist position by Democratic political successes. Robbins read Mather's book steadily from 1800
until his death. In his diaries, he wrote "read *Magnalia*" in 1801, 1811, 1812,
and 1813. Robbins observed in 1817 that "the effects of democracy are astonishing. . . . Democracy appears to have obtained a perfect triumph. . . . I
hope and pray that we may not long be given up to the rage of the wicked.
I consider it the success of inequity against righteousness" (*Diary* 699, 716).
Robbins's political views expressed in his diary show him clinging to republican virtues antithetical to the excesses of Jacksonian politics. Robbins's
keen interest in nostalgic histories was expressed in acquisitiveness. As the
owner of the finest ministerial library in Connecticut, Robbins knew that
Mather's text was an important means for reading the shifting political context that he dramatically experienced in East Windsor.

The fascination of the book for many came from the manner in which it
spoke to the enormous growth of the nation. The period beginning around
1820 has been commonly viewed as a *locus classicus* in American literary
history. As applied by critics like Douglas, Matthiessen, Pease, and Tompkins, the term *American Renaissance* designates a moment in America's history when "original" works laid claim to an "authentic" cultural achievement. Mather's *Magnalia* was an important touchstone for this revival of
culture, and it may represent the key to understanding the rise of democratic
readership before the Civil War. The Puritans, according to Robbins's Preface, had completed their Christian work: "And now we may say, by the favor
of HEAVEN—THE WORK IS DONE." For readers of Robbins's generation, it
was important to draw connections between Mather's time and their own
remarkable experiences as a young nation. "The world looks with amazement on a great Country, united in one territory, more extensive than Rome,
a great population in rapid increase, all looking for Salvation."[2] After the
election of Andrew Jackson in 1828, intellectuals interested in theology, history, and literature were debating about secular and democratic consciousness.

During this period of nascent nationalism, democratic pressures generated unrelieved anxiety. Riotous urban mobs, persistent lawlessness, corruption in business and politics, all seemed so closely intertwined that a standard for building an authentic tradition was needed to counter a confused
present. "The work now presented to the American public," Robbins wrote
in his Preface, "contains the history of . . . New England, for about eighty
years, in the most authentic form." Sacvan Bercovitch has noted that "the

generation that bought up Robbins's 1820 edition discovered in Mather a prophet of their own ideals" (*Puritan Origins* 87). In the mid-1820s, anxiety was emerging in public dialogue, and by the 1850s political and economic anxiety in New England had become metaphorical, as Hawthorne demonstrated in his descriptions of blighted Salem in *The House of the Seven Gables* and "The Custom House." According to William Gilmore,

> the increasingly avid reading engaged in by so many families was proving to be a subtle curse. . . . By the mid 1830s it had become demoralizing [in New England] to read about expansion and success elsewhere. . . . Such heightened awareness elicited complicated intellectual and emotional responses. More detailed knowledge of geography, politics and government, economics, and social relations, and of their interconnections was doubly ironic because knowledge of the real world was accompanied by a noteworthy exploration of speculative, dream, and fantasy realms. (13–15)

Over the period considered by this study, reading enriched the awareness of ambiguities inherent in New England's description of itself as a place with a special mission, and it planted the seeds of alienation necessary for the creation of the allegorical symbolism that began to enshroud the popular images of Puritan personalities.

Theologians, a major audience interested in *Magnalia*, used Mather to mediate a dispute between orthodox and Arminian varieties of Calvinism. The argument over Mather's reputation, Lawrence Buell informs us, "is a legacy of the Unitarian controversy. The Unitarians latched onto Mather as a scapegoat through whom to assail all that they disliked in the Puritan tradition: superstitiousness, officiousness, self-righteousness, hypocrisy—and modern anti-Matherite scholars have followed their lead" (*New England Literary Culture* 218). The fracturing of Protestant orthodoxy, which progressed at a blistering pace in the early nineteenth century, had two core disputants: Arminian Unitarians and orthodox Calvinists.

Orthodox Calvinists were increasingly alarmed by what they considered to be the dangerous narrowing of the distinction between Calvinism and Arminianism. That movement was evident in the preaching of Nathaniel Taylor and Lyman Beecher.[3] Liberal theologians, who believed that creeds, doctrines, ecclesiastical polity, and Scripture—as products of historical eras—were not literally binding on contemporary worshipers, suggested the superiority of reason and enlightened knowledge. Conservatives espoused a spirit of reformation Calvinism in which the literal dictates of Scripture continued to control present practices. This theological dispute spilled over into the larger issues of the facts, meaning, and authority of the New England past.

Two dominant paradigms for viewing New England's history emerged. In one view, history was an evolution from defective original principles toward greater enlightenment. According to the other view, the early founders of New England exemplified a piety that needed to be maintained free from present corruptions. As Buell admits, the debate seldom had this degree of definition: "In practice the debate became more subtle than this, because the Orthodox were ready to admit that the Puritans had sometimes been limited by the prejudices of their age, while the liberals, in their statements about the founders, departed markedly from filiopietism only when reprobating doctrinal narrowness" (*New England Literary Culture* 217). In 1820, the year in which the Reverend Thomas Robbins prepared a new American edition of *Magnalia*, an extreme, militant orthodoxy seemed to be on the rise in New England theology. Consequently, the liberal response to the renewed image of Mather as a champion of pro-Puritan sentiment intensified the debate over Mather's importance to the nineteenth century.[4]

For a historian like George Bancroft, Mather offered a way out of a historical situation that had existed in the country from about 1800 to 1830. Bancroft wanted to say that New England's influence could be harnessed into the larger national project of Manifest Destiny. During the first thirty years of the nineteenth century, there was a weak national sense of identity. After Jackson's election, it was supplanted by Bancroft's calls for a nationalist political agenda. To Bancroft, Mather's mistakes in the witch trials made Mather seem like an aberration that induced people to reject the Puritan legacy and to look to civil and less theocratic forms of government. In Bancroft's view, Mather epitomized all of the limitations of the "New England Way," and his downfall enabled truly democratic reform to begin. In his *History of the United States*, Bancroft wrote that Mather "was ever ready to dupe himself" and was "an example of how far selfishness, under the form of vanity and ambition, can blind the highest faculties, stupefy the judgement, and dupe consciousness itself" (2.266). But as Nathaniel Hawthorne, a writer who benefited from Bancroft's network of political patronage, knew, Mather was important for historians trying to align themselves along a sliding scale of democratic value. Hawthorne shared Bancroft's liberal democratic sympathies; but, knowing the source materials of Puritan history as well as he did, he could not subscribe to Bancroft's caricature of Cotton Mather's significance.

As Robbins predicted, "the history of New England could not be written" without Mather's authority. Bancroft—like fellow historians Francis Parkman, Richard Hildreth, and William Prescott—looked to Mather's example to write histories of the early republic that, in Bancroft's words, "explain how the change in the condition of our land has been accomplished . . . to follow the steps by which a favoring Providence, calling our institutions into being, has conducted the country to its present happiness and glory" (qtd. in Smith 1033).

The 1820 Robbins edition of *Magnalia* was a palimpsest in the sense that it continually reconstituted Puritan history for authors who shared different opinions of Puritanism's relevance to Jacksonian democracy. In the course of subsequent revisions, it became "saturated" with history. Robbins drew a parallel between his culture's need for answers and Mather's pressing urgency to manage a Puritanism faced with structural change. As Peter Gay puts it in *A Loss of Mastery*, "everyone owned [Mather's] history, everyone read it, everyone, consciously or not, absorbed its views and employed its categories" (87). Robbins wrote in his Preface, "The situation and character of the author afforded him the most favorable opportunities to obtain the documents necessary for his undertaking." In an admission that Mather's political sophistication merits close attention from nineteenth-century readers, Robbins continues, "no historian would pursue a similar design with greater industry and zeal."

In 1832, Robbins was installed as associate minister in Mattapoisett, Massachusetts (in the town of Rochester). Later, in the text of Stoddard's *The Morgesons*, he would be transformed into Dr. Snell, a character who at first glance appeared to be a typical liberally educated "moderate" Calvinist displaced by more sectarian, evangelical, seminary-trained successors.[5] It was there that he made the acquaintance of the young woman who would become Elizabeth Stoddard, who liberally borrowed from his collections.

Robbins quickly became one of New England's largest customers for bookcases. With each new bookcase came his public appeals for more manuscripts from "known" collectors, and former governors were asked to donate portraits to the growing collection that was to become the Connecticut Historical Society. In 1844, Robbins retired from the ministry to become the Historical Society's librarian. His retirement from Mattapoisett was not entirely voluntary.

Robbins had become the target of criticism within his parish. He himself did not record the exact nature of his disputes with his church. But several recorded instances appear to implicate him in a scandal involving the construction of a new meetinghouse. At one point in 1843, Robbins seems to have misunderstood or miscalculated the strength of his opposition in Mattapoisett. In a memorandum for a precinct meeting, he says, "I sent them a paper relinquishing claims for salary for the current year on account of their embarrassment in business and the erection of the meetinghouse" (qtd. in Harlow 8). The next year finds Robbins rather anxious to have alternatives. His sister Sarah Battel wrote to him: "Frank made some enquiries about the institution [Historical Society] & was informed they were getting along slowly for want of funds. . . . in the meantime you must leave your present situation the first opening that looks favorably. We are all unwilling you should be exactly in the neighborhood of Hartford for it looks like dancing attendance and we well know how uneasy you would be to have no constant employment" (qtd. in Harlow 8–9).

The same entrepreneurial spirit that motivated his publication of *Magnalia* served Robbins well as the librarian of the Connecticut Historical Society. From 1846 until 1854, he continued to preach, he attended historical and clerical meetings, and he cultivated a group of donors who gave generously to the Society. His suggestive entanglements in the decidedly postcolonial Mattapoisett and his negotiations for a dignified position as Connecticut's most prominent antiquarian indicate that he was a careful student of Mather.

As we saw in the previous chapter, Mather marked his text with his understanding of politics and writing. Sometimes, he suggested, his writing practices stem from ideological commitments. Hawthorne, Stoddard, and Stowe all used Mather's "General Introduction" to *Magnalia* as the mainspring for narratives that explored, renewed, and changed some of the generic conventions of historical romance. Their literary experimentation contributed to the resuscitation of a genre that, by the time they undertook their books, had become tired and afflicted with associations of genteel amateurism. In subsequent chapters, I consider these works individually in the order in which they were written. Each of these writers attempted to explore carefully Mather's text for the lessons about the past that it offered. Even though Robbins may have felt that *Magnalia* would lend itself to the notion of a "usable past," the various adaptations of the text tended to undermine any such notion, despite the fact that a "usable past" seemed to be a natural corollary to Jacksonian democracy. The problem, then, was anticipated by Mather from the outset: the search for consensus ultimately devolves into spectacle. I look to these nineteenth-century works for examples of political commitment that makes possible the rehearsal of *Magnalia* in new and different contexts. The term *rehearsal*, borrowed from Steven Mullaney, conveys the desire of these writers to use Mather's material for cultural performances of stunning variety and energy. A rehearsal brings with it experimental possibilities and outcomes; in contrast, *influence* is often used by critics to provide apparently objective standards for construing the mind of the author. When considering Mather's insights into Puritanism, it is important to consider "the attention towards [how] strange ways and customs reveal an ambivalent and even paradoxical rhythm; in such [rehearsals], the maintenance and production of the strange takes on its most dramatic form, as a process of cultural production synonymous with cultural performance" (Mullaney 68). In their recapitulations of *Magnalia*, each writer brings forward Mather's conceit of "preparing entertainments" that were deserving of a "room in [the] History" of New England. Hawthorne makes Mather the subject of a children's story. Stowe brings Mather's political intrigues before the gaze of an audience whom she understands will not read narratives uncritically or assume that fictional characters actually exist. Stoddard "ventriloquizes" Mather's anxieties about the relation between his ambition and tradition.

Hawthorne's, Stowe's, and Stoddard's uses of *Magnalia* best reflect the convergence of literary vocation with antiquarian impulses. Hawthorne struggled throughout many of his romances to invest his antiquarianism with a great deal of cultural resonance. Hawthorne's *Grandfather's Chair* was not just an attempt to bring historical considerations to center stage but a calculated effort to exploit a large market for children's fiction. In 1834, Hawthorne submitted a large manuscript to Samuel Goodrich, who had published individual stories from the *Provincial Tales* in the annual *The Token*. At this early stage of Hawthorne's career, Roy Harvey Pearce informs us, "his fortunes as a writer—if he was to survive financially—were still dependent on opportunities offered him by Goodrich, or someone like him" (288). Hawthorne was aware that he was writing historical material of great sophistication and was interested in "marketing" his texts to a wide popular audience. In 1836, he edited six issues of Goodrich's *American Magazine of Useful and Entertaining Knowledge*. When he had finished *Grandfather's Chair*, he remarked, "by occupying *Grandfather's Chair*, I really believe I have grown old prematurely" (qtd. in Pearce 290). Nevertheless, *Grandfather's Chair* engendered a favorable review by Evert Duyckinck in the January 1841 *Arcturus* and netted him a project (in collaboration with Henry Wadsworth Longfellow) to produce a school book. Horace Mann saw opportunities for *Grandfather's Chair* in a planned book for the Massachusetts Board of Education. In a letter to Longfellow (June 19, 1837), Hawthorne claimed the book would "revolutionize juvenile literature" (Longfellow I.265–66). Likewise, Stowe and Stoddard were using *Magnalia* to explore niches in a crowded and popular market for regional historical fiction. In 1842, Stowe published her "Mayflower Sketches" in *Harpers*, and she regularly contributed historical sketches to the *Atlantic Monthly* and the *Christian Union* before she published *Uncle Tom's Cabin*. Stoddard wrote for the *Alta* newspaper in California. According to Lawrence Buell, she took the world as her subject in the *Alta*, but "her literary imagination is rooted in the kind of small, ancient, ingrown New England seaport town in which she grew up" (Stoddard 15).

Hawthorne contrived fictional strategies that could be used to establish resonances among scattered artifacts of culture. Scattered, removed, and flawed artifacts had an uncanny power for determining value in a democratic culture. Consequently, he was sensitive to Mather's value-laden exchanges recorded in political narrative and their echoes in *Magnalia*. Stoddard's narrative strategies capitalize on Mather's notion of political aliases whose alien stance to matters of sacred concern tell us much about a culture's definition of identity. Stowe drew heavily on the notion of representative personalities that Mather used in *Pietas in Patriam* to explore tyrannical properties behind charismatic leadership.

Hawthorne merged his concerns with the work being done by two other contemporaries: Charles Willson Peale and George Bancroft. Peale, an artist and museum owner deeply committed to public education, created in Philadelphia a democratic forum that was principled and economically oriented. Bancroft held a romantic notion of a usable past, which he attempted to recover in his *History of the United States* because it formed the prologue to a story of America's manifest destiny. George Bancroft, for whom Hawthorne contributed to the *Democratic Review*, was an icon of the shifting alliances and inventiveness that defined democratic politics. Hawthorne's affiliation with Bancroft allied him with a historian who thought America was a place of "even justice" where "invention is quickened by the freedom of competition; and labor rewarded with sure and unexampled returns" (qtd. in Smith 1032). If Hawthorne's role as a writer of historical romance dimmed some of Bancroft's optimism, Bancroft nevertheless shared Hawthorne's engagement with the vernacular materials of the past. Amid that clutter, Hawthorne found democratic security from the antiquarianism of Salem's William Bentley and others of the "worm-eaten aristocracy" that his work challenged. Hawthorne's appreciation of Mather illustrated that questions of cultural value are ultimately decided in forums outside the control of the artist, despite self-conscious measures to equate the identity of the collector with the artifacts he presents.

Stowe saw in Aaron Burr a panoply of problems affecting Jacksonian democracy. She was aware, as all were at the time, that Martin Van Buren, the "Little Magician" behind the Jackson organization, was Burr's heir in his command of political tactics and organization.[6] Stowe perceived in the operation of American politics the unsettling power with which people embraced Van Buren's contrivances. Political life seemed seductively stage-managed, and persons with an ill-defined set of core beliefs eagerly embraced a power structure that was becoming increasingly centralized. Stowe was able to distill into the figure of Aaron Burr these scattered concerns about the "authenticity" of American life and art and its continual perversion.

As a counterpoint to what she saw as dangerous European manners, masculine ambition, and political greed, she created the character of Mary Scudder, whose feminine intuition, New World religious piety, and Republican sincerity triumph over the corruptions of Burr. Stowe's strategy for depicting Mary Scudder is related to Mather's explorations of exemplaristic personality in *Magnalia*. Stowe found in Mather's text (marked with clues for interpreting the evolution of the nation) the basis of a complex narrative that demanded political responsibility and an enhanced role for women in public affairs.

Stoddard, like many others restrained by the reigning patriarchy, saw the opportunity to engage the public through novels that tapped the public's interest in spiritual mediums. News that Kate and Margaret Fox of Hydesville, New York, were witnesses to spirit rappings drew the attention of literati like James Fenimore Cooper, George Bancroft, William Cullen Bryant, and Horace Greeley, who attended private seances at the home of a Rochester minister in 1850. The fascination that the "Rochester knockings" held for the elites stemmed from the idea that women could serve as mediators for "unbroken communication" with the past. Spiritualist writers like Cora

Wilburn had written in "the persuasive accents of inspired woman's tongue," and Stoddard considered that writing a historical novel that drew off the suggestiveness and contingency afforded a woman addressing the public might be a successful strategy for engaging democratic politics.

An engaging, self-determined woman, Stoddard viewed with suspicion prescriptive cultural knowledge that held the home to be the locus of religiosity and domesticity. She ironically undercuts domestic spheres by her depiction of Cassandra Morgeson. In her literary practice, Stoddard referred to herself as using the "planchette"—a device employed to facilitate spiritual communication among untrained persons within the home—for writing *The Morgesons* (see page 204). The planchette generates the anxious, focused gathering that Stoddard wanted her readers to experience. It was Stoddard's suggestion, drawn from Mather's powerful accounts of effective work performed by enacted aliases, that *The Morgesons* would direct her readers to examine the construction and maintenance of Jacksonian political structures.

In the chapters that follow, *Magnalia* functions as a masterplot of nationalist, politically inflected stories of New England's experience between the charters. Because of the transitory nature of that period, Mather's accounts frame interrelated (and sometimes conflicting) tales of New England's origins and experience of danger. With the intervention of Robbins's edition, the "plot" of New England history that Mather provided shapes in the works of Hawthorne, Stoddard, and Stowe allegorical passages that require readers to consider the fusion of the emblems and political rhetoric of Puritanism with their own participation in democracy. Allegory is important for considering readers' interpretation of Puritanism because each of the writers discussed here "disguises" the hermeneutic potential of Puritanism within popularized discourse. Hawthorne's, Stowe's, and Stoddard's stories about *Magnalia* are narratives of disguise: allegory is not merely a way of writing but also a way of reading. These writers suspend the reader somewhere between credulity and incredulity so that, as Roger Chartier suggests, "belief in what is read is accompanied by a laugh that gives it the lie; the reader's acceptance is solicited, but a certain distance shows literature for what it is. . . . This delicate balance permits multiple readings that fluctuate. . . . Thus the reader could simultaneously know and forget that fiction was fiction" (*Cultural Uses* 335–36). In each case the juxtaposition of democratic concerns with a sophisticated and playful antiquarianism was intended to create this degree of anxiety among readers.

The experience of reading in antebellum America allowed readers and writers to be co-present in what the sociologist Erving Goffman calls a "focused gathering." In moments of reading, readers and writers cooperate with each other.[7] In the focused gathering generated by historical narratives, Hawthorne, Stowe, Stoddard, and their readers sustained a joint focus of attention on the democratic problems and opportunities presented by Mather's *Magnalia*. Acts of reading historical romances were presented in order to encourage several ways in which readers might cooperate to sustain the occasion.

These writers were deeply interested in ways in which their readers might move from the state of being unengaged politically to being engaged through the experience of literature. As Janice Radway has argued in her reading of popular fiction, "Although romances are technically novels because each purports to tell a 'new' story of unfamiliar characters and as-yet uncompleted events, in fact, they all *retell* a single tale whose final outcome their readers already know" (198). By translating some of the political concerns made available in Robbins's authoritative edition of *Magnalia*, Hawthorne, Stowe, and Stoddard enacted narrative strategies that encouraged readers to see democracy as a "spectacular invention" formed by utterances and gestures that were arranged and exchanged beforehand. Hence the exchanges and responses to these works examined the series of conscious decisions that individuals had to undertake as responsible citizens participating in antebellum democracy.

Because the period from 1820 to 1859 was one of unrelenting social change, the theory of accents put forward by Voloshinov is important for considering Mather's translation into the nineteenth century. The textual traces of Mather's political and historical contingency that we looked at in *Magnalia*—narration that implied multiple vantage points in the "General Introduction," representative personality "conjured" from inventive circumstances, enacted aliases that operate from within narrative, and fictional constructs that standardize a cultural meaning—were not limited to Mather's Puritan context. And they are not univocal in the possibilities they create for expression. In fact, they formed a viable system of signs in a culture where political activity generated a renewed interest in how the past could be used to cope with the present. The utility of Mather's markers of political involvement for nineteenth-century writers comes not only from their rhetorical character (their use of metaphor and other figurative devices) but from the different political accents they summarize. Voloshinov describes it this way: "the very same thing that makes the ideological sign vital and mutable is also that which makes it a refracting and distorting medium. . . . This inner dialectic quality of the sign comes out fully in the open only in times of social crises or revolutionary changes" (23).

Hawthorne, Stowe, and Stoddard use political accents to describe the "democratic terrain" that unfolds in their novels. These accents can sometimes be detected in the way the writer understands her or his material. Harriet Beecher Stowe is concerned with politics from the moment of production. She places Aaron Burr into her text to show dangerous tendencies competing with Puritan sensibilities. At other times, these political accents are an active presence in the reception of a work.[8] Stoddard shows in her complex narrative that historical understanding depends deeply on modes of transmission and reception. She draws on popular notions of mediums in order to make her readers question the specific conveyances (the persons and mechanisms) of authority in Jacksonian society. In some cases the political accents of these writers originate in the codes of dominant genteel culture. In other instances they derive from residual and emergent alternative or oppositional culture. Hawthorne's, for instance, emerge from genteel culture—the theories of museology displayed in Peale's museum in Philadelphia. Stoddard's, in contrast, draw from the emergent feminist ideology of spiritual mediumship as it was practiced by Lizzie Doten, the Fox sisters, Cora Wilburn, and others.

Both sets of accents, the dominant and oppositional, are fought over in Jacksonian culture at large. They are taught, learned, excluded, appropriated, reinterpreted, subverted, and co-opted many times over in cultural processes. These more conscious and intentional places in historical fiction, where the ideological battles over the meaning of these accents is exposed, represent highly significant points where the scope and direction of the American Renaissance can be better explained.

Clearly Hawthorne's wonder-cabinets and archives, Stowe's desire for communion with her audience, and Stoddard's extrasensory narration were all textual devices used to link the writers' works with the sensibilities of their readers. History, *Magnalia* told this nineteenth-century audience, requires explicit repeated signs, numerous discontinuities, and approximations. Each of the three writers and many of their readers were bent on heightening the uneasiness that a democratic readership encounters when history is received as an act of reading replete with brief coherent textual unities (chapters, titles and headings, summaries, and images) describing their social experience. Roger Chartier's notion of "popular reading," explained in *The Cultural Uses of Print*, can help to explain the various markers contained in Hawthorne's, Stowe's, and Stoddard's works:

> This popular reading requires explicit and repeated signs, numerous titles and headings, frequent summaries and images. It is only at ease with brief, complete sequences, seems to require only minimal coherence, and proceeds by the association of textual unities (chapters, fragments, paragraphs), which are themselves disconnected. Discontinuous, approximate, hesitant: this way of reading guides editorial strategies in giving form to the printed objects offered to the largest numbers, and guides the work of adaptation. . . . This other manner of reading also defines a specific relationship to print culture, a specific mode of comprehension that creates a cultural frontier based on the varying uses made by different classes of readers of the same texts rather than on the unequal distribution of texts in society. (30)

On the one hand, *Magnalia* was a cultural event that mediated the discourse of specialists (ministers, historical scholars, antiquarians). On the other, it delivered a fund of narrative possibilities that could be readily adapted to the interests of children and the needs of women—two different kinds of readers who were expanding the market for historical literature, two different kinds of print consumers. *Magnalia* was a significant contribution to specialized knowledge; moreover, Hawthorne's, Stowe's, and Stoddard's use of Mather's version of the Puritan past was also grounded in market opportunities. Each of their specialized interests merged with the professional's entrepreneurial concern with changing market dynamics.

Magnalia created an unusual space that distributed the public and the private, the specialized and the common, the anecdotal and the epic. It is probably better to see *Magnalia* as an advance in technological opportunity rather than as a simple literary moment. Like other technological advances with which we are familiar—the telephone, the computer network, the notion of virtual reality—*Magnalia* organized a fundamentally new space that supported a great variety of *interactive* responses that both empowered users with new abilities and intimidated because those interactions were not easily managed.[9] Those things that, for the sake of discussion, we tend to view as binary oppositions were in fact fully supported in the contractual space made available by the text. *Magnalia* is both *work* and *text*—so much so that what we are dealing with, in the final analysis, is a form of "virtual reality" whereby the reader is free to become the writer and vice versa. From the perspective of the *work*, the tradition that Mather established was both a common domain and a private preserve. From the perspective of the *text*, *Magnalia* was repeatedly "broken" into lexias, coded sequences, and narrative anecdotes, so that out of the various "borrowings" readerly "classical" works were marketed, ready to be undone by the writerly acts of reading.[10] The net effect, then, was the creation of radically participatory relations in which individual selection and control became a matter of manipulating the various *technologies* (accents, markers, allegorical readings, symbolic structures, ideological constructs) that became available to Hawthorne, Stowe, and Stoddard through the Robbins edition. The mutual implication of literature and politics (or perhaps the appearance of mutual implication) is mediated exclusively by the "virtual" connections that form in the marketplace. Consequently, the open architecture of *Magnalia* and the various attempts to link historical projects with its "authority" culminated in the distribution of its contents to more diverse and emergent audiences and multiplied the frequency with which such knowledge was wasted, dispersed, or lost.

Chapter Three

Hawthorne's Rehearsals of Puritanism and Peale's Museum

+

Resonance and Wonder in Cultural History

In the clutter of historical anecdotes contained in *Magnalia*, Hawthorne discovered a persuasive metaphor—the wonder-cabinet—for historical fiction. To explain Hawthorne's rehearsal of *Magnalia*, one needs to look at Charles Willson Peale's museum in Philadelphia. Peale's museum displayed artifacts in a way that was designed to educate as well as stimulate visitors. Hawthorne was captivated by the concept of the natural history museum, and he wrote "The Virtuoso's Collection," in part, as a response to the museum's potential for literature. *Grandfather's Chair* is the text that best represents Hawthorne's attempts to balance what Stephen Greenblatt calls "resonance" and "wonder" in historical romance. Cast as a tale for children, it has a narrative complexity that brings forward for the benefit of readers the notion that an author's identity coincides with the "arrangements" of his art.

Hawthorne struggled throughout many of his romances to imbue his antiquarian impulses with cultural resonance. Hawthorne merged his literary concerns with the work being done by two other contemporaries: Charles Willson Peale and George Bancroft. Peale's museum defined the entrepreneurial necessity for balancing the need for income with principled activity, thus history was freely negotiable. Bancroft had a fixation on the notion of a usable past. In his *History of the United States* he attempted to recover the usable past because it formed the prologue to a story of America's manifest destiny. Bancroft was the man responsible for creating and maintaining the "gloomy-stern-righteous-democratic" myth for which he held Cotton Mather to be the prime example.[1]

Peale's museum, which was supported exclusively through paid admissions, needed to stage evening entertainments that presented to the viewing public a variety of "wonders" designed to educate while amusing. After a brief period of management as a joint-stock company after Peale's retirement, Moses Kimball and P. T. Barnum acquired the building and the collections in 1850. They brought a highly commercialized and bizarre dimension to the institution. Blurring the boundaries between museums and carnival shows, Peale's museum was a prominent example of the exchanges between the real and the contrived in antebellum America. For Hawthorne, the voyeurism of the American public and the vast commercial success of Barnum made a powerful statement about the value of the material objects of the past. Mather's wonder-cabinet of Puritanism greatly assisted Hawthorne's rummaging through America's attics and archives.[2]

George Bancroft, for whom Hawthorne contributed to the *Democratic Review*, exemplified the opportunities newly available to historians eager to associate their careers with political concerns. Hawthorne's interest in Bancroft was an admission of the potential for history in the nineteenth century. Hawthorne realized, through his work on the *Democratic Review*, that the art of government was not expressed in transcendental rules. Instead, the work of historians like Bancroft was beginning to equate the specific reality of the Jacksonian period with a presumed rationality.

Bancroft had been elected to the Massachusetts state legislature by the Workingman's party in 1830 but had declined to serve. Later he ignored the pleas of Springfield's Jacksonian paper to run for Congress, and he published an essay discouraging talented young men from entering politics at all.[3] But Bancroft played politics from two sides. He also wrote an unfriendly piece about the second Bank of the United States—an article that pleased Van Buren. Like his fellow Democrat Benjamin Hallett, Bancroft seemed to be a man who manipulated politics to personal advantage. According to Schlesinger, "Bancroft's whole life had been a series of minor revolts against the 'natural aristocracy,' " who developed a "precarious balance of loyalties, [which produced] a vacillation which was by no means evidence of insincerity" (161).

The romance writer in Hawthorne recognized quite clearly that the art of government, in the writings of historians like William Bentley, Bancroft, and Francis Parkman, was spreading and developing subtly in an age of expan-

The Long Room, Interior of Front Room in Peale's Museum (1822), watercolor by Charles Willson Peale. (Founders Society Purchase, Director's Discretionary Fund, The Detroit Institute of the Arts)

sion, free from the political and economic tensions that afflicted the seventeenth century. If Hawthorne seemed exceptionally interested in the vernacular artifacts of the past, it was because the matrix of Puritan government (which had rested on the presumption of a convenanted social contract) was now imbued with a new inventiveness. The mutual pledge of ruler and subjects (modeled on the notion of the family), which had been the basis of Mather's analysis in *Magnalia*, yielded in the nineteenth century to a recognition that new networks of relations between persons, territory, and wealth were determining the course of American politics.

Hawthorne was aware that the celebration of historical resonance cost him as an artist. Sidney George Fisher had decried Bancroft's politicized history: it "was poor stuff, filled with unnecessary details, without just thought, facetious in sentiment, weak, tawdry and diffuse in style. . . . He spins it out because he sells it by the volume" (qtd. in Smith 1033). Similarly, Hawthorne faced charges of crass opportunism and involvement in patronage politics. Curiously, these disparagements were implied by Elizabeth Stoddard, whose career was deeply affected by her inability (for reasons of genre and gender) to enter the "school of Hawthorne." Such criticisms were the natural consequences of Hawthorne's wish to engage the marketplace as Mather had been forced to do. In other words, the increasing objectification of Jacksonian democracy, which Hawthorne exaggerated in his fiction, turned the discussion of government away from Mather's concern with the open-ended and experimental question of how to govern New England and toward an apprehension of the techniques that were being used to govern. Increasingly, democratic spaces such as the museum and novel were constituted as hybrid forms that coupled the public ability of politics with private authority.

The logic of displaying artifacts enshrined in Charles Willson Peale's museum plays a determining role in Hawthorne's rehearsals of New England history in his historical fiction. Christopher Looby has said that "the decisive conjunction in Peale's life of republican political sympathies, dissatisfaction with trade, and predilection for the labor of artistic representation is characteristic of his complicated personality and his ambitious creative program" (363). So too Hawthorne invites us, as does the figure in Peale's self-portrait (see page 112), to enter the contextual space of the museum of New England history: we witness the artist's rehearsals of culture even as the artist encourages our own untutored groping among the scattered relics contained there.

The term *rehearsal* applies here because Hawthorne's use of early New England history reflects concern for the authentic portrayal of the past. This concern is evident in the introductory notes to *Mosses from an Old Manse*, as well as in "The Custom House," *Grandfather's Chair*, "Old News," and "The Virtuoso's Collection." Like Peale's museum and Mather's *Magnalia*, Hawthorne's historical concerns are fragments arranged in a wonder-cabinet. The objects that Hawthorne places in his fiction participate in an artistic process that negotiates his readers' perceptions of wonder and resonance. The images and themes that Hawthorne brings to his fiction from the past are calculated to reveal the ambivalent and even paradoxical rhythms that they produced for his culture (and, by extension, produce for our own). The maintenance and production of strange things from New England's Puritan past take on their most dramatic form in the works discussed here. The usefulness of these materials, besides their obvious qualities as art, comes from our recognition that Hawthorne has explained a process of cultural production that is synonymous with cultural performance.

Neal Doubleday, in his study of Hawthorne's historical materials, stresses that Hawthorne's use of American materials gave Hawthorne a convention suited to "American needs and possibilities" (31). Michael Bell, writing in *Hawthorne and the Historical Romance of New England*, reminds us that Hawthorne brought to his histories of the Puritan past many attitudes, prejudices, and problems that he had in common with his less famous and more conventional contemporaries. Bell concludes that Hawthorne's use of Puritan images was well suited to the cause of literary nationalism and the secular typology of American romantic history. More recently, George Dekker, in *The American Historical Romance*, has suggested that Hawthorne's work is laden with historical ironies and that the historical imperatives of the Puritans endowed Hawthorne's works with special capacities that showed that history was the product of unintended consequences. Michael Colacurcio brings this form of analysis to a higher level of intensity when he claims in *The Province of Piety* that "Hawthorne had a nearly flawless sense of the way some text always comes between the observer and the origins he would observe, making the historian's own tale twice-told at its very most original. . . . Hawthorne indeed possessed the critical mind of a modern intellectual historian" (1). The *text* that came to influence Hawthorne's reading of the specifically Puritan past was Cotton Mather's *Magnalia Christi Americana*.

My own views on Hawthorne have affinities with the treatment offered by Dekker and Colacurcio, but unlike them, I am interested in the ways Hawthorne's historicism and the type of antiquarianism exhibited in Charles Willson Peale's museology combine to form what Erving Goffman calls a "focused gathering" surrounding Hawthorne's reading of Mather. Scholars working on a variety of subjects—Lawrence Levine, David Hall, Janice Radway, Michael Denning, Richard Brodhead, and Jane Tompkins—all make reference to the way different reading situations can modify, sometimes decisively, the cultural work done by a given text.[4] My suggestion, in the following reading of Hawthorne's use of Mather, is to show how Mather and Hawthorne, working as fundamentally ironic historians, inscribed traces of Puritanism's legacy within a cultural poetics organized around object-choices and object-investments.

Such a cultural poetics gave Hawthorne the ability to manipulate what Tompkins refers to as the "fine power of a culture"—that is, power that does not merely fill the brains of an enlightened readership but fills them so they are alike in fine detail.[5] Along with Hall, Denning, Brodhead, and several critics of mass culture, the cultural work performed by Hawthorne and Mather engaged the grainy spaces and even the "dream life" of private and secret spaces of the text's audience.

Hawthorne's wry manipulations of museums and literature express the sense that a symbolic exchange often takes place not just *within* the account of a cultural process—say, Peale's "shaping" of his visitors' symbol systems—but with the *writing* of cultural studies and history itself. That is, Peale, Mather, and Hawthorne invariably employ certain tropes, metaphors, constructions of cultural levels (like an epochalist or essentialist orientation of an artifact's significance), and symbols of urgency to a given *contemporary* situation, to "design" the past, to make it more readable.[6] This underlying theme, of Hawthorne as a Jacksonian explorer of the divide between freedom and order, organizes this chapter.

A common thread links these pieces of Hawthorne's literary output with the cultural work performed by Peale's museum and Mather's *Magnalia*. All three works are metaphorically related to the concept of the *wunderkammer* (wonder-cabinet), and that relationship is calculated to induce a viewing audience to recognize wonder in the culture around them. The rehearsals of culture accomplished by these "texts" are capable of unlimited replication. Reliance on "wounded" artifacts is central to Hawthorne's conception of democracy. For Hawthorne, the exercise of political power operates outside a domain that is "natural" and necessary. In Peale's museum, political persuasiveness is demonstrated in the artificial relationships of authority and subordination of arranged items. Thus, government is constituted already in existing social economic relations and the display of governmentality is mirrored in the egoistic interests of the artist and collector. The object lesson of Peale's museum is that the regulatory framework of government (which at first glance seems to emerge from a "natural" order) is in fact conjured out of a forced continuity between society's relations and the emblems of history. It is in the name of democratic society and its economic processes that Hawthorne and Peale constantly arrange and rearrange the forms of the past; through their invention the mechanisms of "self-government" within the state are both criticized and demanded. Ultimately, democratic society is not divinely sanctioned, nor is it articulated in the rhetorical apparatus of text. Instead, it is a transactional reality that equates the individual with the political technology of history. Because the primary sources of historical insight are implicated in the technological machinery of politics, the historical claims of Puritanism prove to be a particularly fertile ground for experimental innovation. Further, at the level of individual interests, needs, and opportunities, the subscription to liberal democracy expressed through such technologies makes persons absolutely governable. In other words, the consumer's demand for spectacle ensures the government of those same individuals because the identity of the viewer is determined by the degree of attachment or displacement from the scene viewed.

The cultural work of Mather, Hawthorne, and Peale was designed to show that resonance (the feeling that the artist and his culture are mutually constitutive) ought to predominate over the sense of wonder. One aim of their work was to show that a writer's grasp of the past is an act of self-fashioning. The artist's relationship to the work he has performed simultaneously evokes and dissipates a dream of possession, order, and significance. If Mather's, Hawthorne's, and Peale's projects for determining culture have been successful, it is because through the rehearsal (and performance) of these works the viewer (or reader) comes to recognize the contingency within the individual work, a contingency shaped not only by what the performance allows us to see but also by what remains unseen.[7] It is as if the works of Mather, Hawthorne, and Peale contain shelves and cases filled with unseen wonders that constitute the prestigious property of the collector.

Peale's Museum

Gary Kulik explains Peale's museum by referring to Charles Willson Peale's self-portrait, which shows the artist

The Artist in His Museum (1822), oil on canvas by Charles Willson Peale. (The Pennsylvania Academy of the Fine Arts, Philadelphia. Gift of Mrs. Sarah Harrison. The Joseph Harrison, Jr., Collection)

lifting a theatrical crimson curtain to reveal the Long Room of the Philadelphia Museum, a museum he first conceived of in 1786. On the two visible walls stood cases of stuffed birds, stacked four high, surmounted by a double row of portraits of Revolutionary heroes and statesmen. Half-hidden behind the curtain stood the principal object of the museum, the skeleton of a large mastodon exhumed in 1801. In the foreground was the first object placed in the museum, an Allegheny River paddlefish, along with a stuffed turkey from the Long Expedition, a taxidermy kit, a painter's palette, and several large mastodon bones. In the far background, reduced in scale in comparison to the dominating figure of the artist, Peale painted his audience: a contemplative man musing over birds, a father instructing his child, and a proper woman with her arms raised in astonishment as her eyes met the mastodon. Peale had captured the order, diversity, and pedagogical intent of America's first serious museum. (3)

Charles Willson Peale dedicated himself to the idea of a museum of natural history, its purpose "to bring into one view a world in miniature" for an audience that would receive both enlightenment and pleasure (Kulik 4–5). Perhaps most of all, Peale's museum was a "temple" in the sense that Francis Taylor meant when he described the museum as "the encompassing catch basin for all those disparate elements of hereditary culture which are not yet woven into the general educational fabric of society" (8). Peale's museum was intended not as a gallery for the display of masterpieces but rather as a visual reference for American cultural history. For Looby, Peale's museum was "an unfamiliar perspective on the era of Revolution, Constitution, and new nation," and was a collection of "amusingly unbalanced activities [which] have in common the principle of copying" (365). For Peale, history is delineated not by the study of individual masterpieces but from the study of collections in all their variable worth—from the "lowbrow" pandering of human exploitation to the "highbrow" appreciation of organ music delicately infusing a world of natural unity presided over by great statesmen. The larger the collection—in this case indexing everything from masturbation to patents and printing—the more intense the incongruity and variety seem and the more opportunities a museum like Peale's has for shaping the popular imagination.[8] Serving a cross section of the public, Peale's museum gave people the chance to question the omniscience of the expert even as it worked in a multitude of ways to enhance the social status and identity of its founder.[9]

On July 13, 1787, a New Englander, the Reverend Manasseh Cutler, visited the museum and recorded his impressions in his diary:

I observed, through a glass at my right hand, a gentleman close to me, standing with a pencil in one hand, and a small sheet of ivory in the other, and his eyes directed to the opposite side of the room, as though he was taking some object on his ivory sheet. Dr. Clarkson did not see this man until he stepped into the room, but instantly turned about and came back to say, "Mr. Peale is very busy, taking a picture of something with his pencil. We will step back into the other room and wait until he is at leisure." We returned through the entry, but as we entered the room we came from, we met Mr. Peale coming to us. The Doctor started back in astonishment, and cried out, "Mr. Peale, how is it possible you should get out of the other room to meet us here?" Mr. Peale smiled. "I have not been in the other room," says he, "for some time." . . . When we returned, we found the man standing as before. My astonishment was now equal to Dr. Clarkson; for, although I knew what I saw, yet I beheld two men, so perfectly alike that I could not discern the minutest difference. . . . This was a piece of waxwork which Mr. Peale had finished, in which he had just taken himself. So admirable a performance must have done great honor to his genius if it had been any other person, but I think it is much more extraordinary that he should be able to so perfectly take himself. . . . By this particular method, our particular friends and ancestors might be preserved in perfect likeness to the latest generation. (259 ff.)

This entry frames succinctly the ability of the museum to "fabricate" a version of culture for consumption by an audience. Cutler's comments make plain that the cultural functions of the museum also serve to elevate the stature of the collector.

The self-fashioning of America is co-extensive with the self-fashioning of the collector's identity. Peale's museum frames four points about Hawthorne's appropriation of Mather's historiography:

1. The museum concept supplies a representational logic for both writers' depictions of New England's fragmentary significance.
2. The arrangement of fragments is deeply connected with the writer's creation of an interpretive space that is used to mask and unmask narration. In this way, historical specificity is continually conditioned by authorial ambivalence.
3. Some of the objects that the museologist-historian displays are calculated to arrest the viewer's attention, evoking exalted attention to a display of uniqueness.
4. The entire enterprise, be it a wonder-cabinet of history or a prosaic

recollection of tales intended for children, is meant to serve as a model of democratic freedoms.[10]

Gary Kulik isolates the source of Peale's genius in Peale's recognition of an American democratic culture in which scholarship and entertainment were compatible ideas. Museums played a significant role in shaping public values because they revealed a basic and secure order underneath the apparent chaos of daily commerce (6).[11] To see Hawthorne's historical fiction and Peale's museum as parallel "texts" is important because the sensibility of culture's worth is conveyed as the sum of its various parts. In the plenitude of this diversity lay the secure foundations of democratic potential. The medium for telling history, then, must be intentionally antithetical to singular ways of formulating experience. As a mode for apprehending the past, the museum concept and the combination of museology and literary practice turn Puritanism's apparent isolation into a potent device for negotiating present circumstances.

The Inducement to Wonder

In the sketch titled "The Virtuoso's Collection," Hawthorne had Peale's museum in mind when he wrote: "I stepped into a new museum . . . directly in front of the portal was the bronze statue of youth with winged feet. He was represented in the act of flitting away from the earth, yet wore such a look of earnest invitation that it impressed me like a summons to enter the hall" (476). Once the author is induced to enter Hawthorne's museum, his appreciation of wonder increases with each room he passes through: a choice collection of stuffed animals, a multitude of stuffed birds, a random collection of curiosities including Franklin's cap of asbestos, an ancient library, entomological collections, and sculptures of classical origins.

The museum described in "The Virtuoso's Collection" is a cabinet of curiosities, a *kunst* or *wunderkammer*: a space originating in the late Renaissance and characterized primarily by its encyclopedic appetite for the marvelous or strange.[12] Hawthorne's fascination with strange things comes from the fact that places like the virtuoso's collection withhold simple categorization. The randomness of objects and their apparent disconnectedness make the museum a space that neither specifies nor defines but rather sets objects aside and grants them the freedom to remain as they are. The wonder-cabinet maintains its artifacts as "extraneous" objects, placing them outside the bounds of cultural hierarchies or definitions.

In the museum of "The Virtuoso's Collection," the system determining the organization of objects on display is curiously complex: it is an admixture of epochalist and essentialist traditions for preserving the past. Steven Mullaney describes such spaces as places where "things are on holiday, randomly juxtaposed and displaced from any proper context; the room they inhabit acts as a liberty or sanctuary for ambiguous things, a kind of halfway house for transitional objects, some new but not yet fully assimilated, others old and headed for cultural oblivion, but not yet forgotten or cast off" ("Strange Things" 67). As Peale's portrait suggests, the display of strange things gives the artist an opportunity to fashion an order where none seemed apparent and a space to define himself in relation to the objects he has collected.

For literary men like Hawthorne and Mather, such wonder-cabinets supplied a representational logic for their depictions of New England's significance. There are, to be sure, restrictions to be placed on seeing one's region as a collection of scattered artifacts, but the cultural accumulations that both men collected exist because Hawthorne and Mather desired to invoke our attention as readers, auditors, and spectators for the rehearsals of the past that they concocted. That curiosity, which begins with an invitation provided by the artist, draws our attention to the cultural dynamics of an age that was ostensibly devoted to the cultivation of wonder for the past but in sometimes paradoxical ways pointed in other directions. As we still see in the cases of Mather and Hawthorne, the resonance (between the old and new, the residual and emergent, and otherwise strange renderings of culture inherent in their historical works) creates the space whereby each writer works to mask and unmask his activity.[13]

In many of Hawthorne's historical fictions the concepts of resonance and wonder form the core of his literary approach to the past, but that core logic is marked extensively by a recognizable ambivalence.[14] The term *resonance*, as employed here, means the power displayed in objects that causes them to reach out beyond their formal boundaries to the larger world, the capacity of objects to evoke in their viewers the complex, dynamic, cultural forces from which they have emerged. An object's resonance has a metaphorical connotation and a synecdochic aspect, for a viewer understands that the object is a significant marker for several discourses. The concept of wonder, another of Hawthorne's favorite tropes, describes the power of objects to stop a viewer in his or her tracks, the ability of objects to suggest an arresting sense of uniqueness, and to evoke an exalted attention.

Several of Hawthorne's most important texts that "arrange" the materials of the past express in fiction the commingling of the epochalist and essentialist traditions of the seventeenth century. Epochalist and essentialist distinctions reflect millennialism's impact on explanations of the Puritan mission in America. An essentialist historian tended to view the experience in America as the final episode in a millennialist drama about to be suddenly concluded. The epochalist, by contrast, tended to view the American experience as merely one more transitional and intermediate stage toward a deferred conclusion. Mather, in *Magnalia*, was deeply undecided about his relationship to these two traditions. At times (in Books Six and Seven) he adopts an essentialist posture; at other times (in Books One, Two, and Three, for instance) he seems assured that the final analysis of New England's mission is yet to come. The tone that these traditions bring to *Magnalia* is quite important because what later critics have called American exceptionalism, New England legacy-ism, a consensus model of the Puritan imagination, and so on, all derive from the essentialist tradition, which singled out and isolated those aspects of the culture that tended to set New England apart from other places. These historical representations, especially in the decisive *Grandfather's Chair*, enjoy a great range of sophistication; but, more important, Hawthorne's own attitudes and methods are consistently more ironic in these tales for children than in his more "serious" novels. A crucial moment in the midst of Hawthorne's plural literary renditions of New England culture may well have been his discovery of the contradictions and ambiguities concerning epochalism and essentialism that inhered in Mather's work.[15]

Of course, many other scholars have recognized Hawthorne's penchant for contingency. Millicent Bell, in *Hawthorne's View of the Artist*, writes of Hawthorne's antagonism toward the romantic-idealist exaltation of the ego. For Bell, Hawthorne's impulse for contingency stemmed from a deep distrust of the effects of the free play of economic and social forces. Post-Jacksonian America—as it is portrayed in "The Custom House," for instance—was demonstrating that the democratic scheme was capable of producing all-encompassing personalities and a faceless, bewildered, and un-individualized industrial population.[16] Consequently, Hawthorne looked with stern suspicion on "occult perspicacity," which claimed to give the artist the power to pierce external reality. Hawthorne thus manipulates the romantic machinery he had available to him only to expose its hidden weaknesses. In

Bell's opinion, Hawthorne's most important judgments are anti-romantic, and his art is rooted in distinctions between the real and the ideal (5–7).

Hawthorne's appreciation of the inspector at the Salem Custom House rests on the fact that he "certainly was one of the most wonderful specimens" likely to be discovered in a lifetime's search. Hawthorne "used to watch and study this patriarchal personage with, I think, livelier curiosity than any other form of humanity" ("The Custom House" 16, 18). Hawthorne's inducement to see this man as an object of great interest depends on his rare attributes: "He was, in truth, a rare phenomenon; so perfect in one point of view; so shallow, so delusive, so impalpable, such an absolute nonentity, in every other." Hawthorne continues, describing the inspector as an admixture deprived of normal human constitution, as if this man were merely instinct somehow coaxed from the corporeal body and displayed in some hall of natural history. "My conclusion was that he had no soul, no heart, no mind; nothing, as I have already said, but instincts; and yet, withal, so cunningly had the few materials of his character been put together, that there was no painful perception of deficiency, but, on my part, an entire contentment with what I found in him" (18). As Hyatt Waggoner notes in *The Presence of Hawthorne*, Hawthorne's portrayal was in many important respects "modern."

Hawthorne signals to his audience that his curiosity about constructed aspects of personality springs from interests shared with the museum collector. From excavated bones, Peale constructed his "mastodon," adding when appropriate the flourishes that he felt placed the creature in a revealing light.[17] Not all of the creature is bathed in light, to be sure, for the brand of history visible here aspires to the condition of historical deconstruction. Hawthorne's literary mode is never typological in the American Puritan sense; its epistemology is always suggestive of duplicitous meaning. Hawthorne wrote not of what he believed in but of unsought-for truth hidden in the most common objects.

Hawthorne uses the portrayal of the Custom House inspector (and other fictional characters—for instance, in "The Old Apple Dealer") to drive home the point that the inspector is a living remnant of a dusty past, much like Peale's reconstructed mastodon. The possibility of restoration, here caught in the image of a Custom House inspector, is one of several inducements for Hawthorne's appreciation of resonance. "It might be difficult— and it was so—to conceive how he should exist hereafter, so earthy and sensuous did he seem" (18). Like the curator, working with his wires and instincts, the problem for the writer in Hawthorne comes in his need to make a sketch of a civil servant "materialize."[18] And, as Waggoner suggests, that materialization has much to do with Hawthorne's convictions about man's nothingness and difficulties and the dangers and opportunities that knowledge holds for the artist. Hawthorne feared a consensus view of history; he preferred to conceal his knowledge in irreducible layers of mystery.

Hawthorne's deep appreciation that he has somehow been "mothballed," stored away in the confines of the Custom House, suggests to him that the past holds meaningful clues:

> I cared not, at this period, for books; they were apart from me. Nature,— except it were human nature,—the nature that is developed in earth and sky, was, in one sense, hidden from me; and all the imaginative delight, wherewith it had been spiritualized, passed away out of my mind. A gift, a faculty, if it had not departed, was suspended and inanimate within me. There would have been something sad, unutterably dreary, in all this, had I not been conscious that it lay at my own option to recall whatever was valuable in the past. ("The Custom House" 26)

This is the sense of estrangement that flows naturally from our direct apprehension of the mysterious or disordered when it touches our lives directly. A good museum induces us to feel somehow shut out from the objects that surround us. For Hawthorne in "The Old Manse," that sensibility is an important motivation to discover a sense of resonance in art. When it can be grasped and felt, "as when I used to pick up Indian arrow-heads in the field near the Old Manse," Hawthorne says, it joins with the promise of restorative labor to produce a form of pleasure. The prodding of these influences forces Hawthorne to an enlightened rehearsal of the figure of Surveyor Pue and his historical context:

> I chanced to lay my hand on a small package, carefully done up in a piece of ancient yellow parchment. This envelope had the air of an official record of some period long past. . . . There was something about it that quickened an instinctive curiosity, and made me undo the faded red tape, that tied up the package, with the sense that a treasure would here be brought to light. . . . I found it to be a commission . . . of one Jonathan Pue. . . . I remembered to have read (probably in Felt's Annals) a notice of the decease of Mr. Surveyor Pue, about fourscore years ago; and like-

wise, in a newspaper of recent times, an account of the digging up of his remains in the little grave-yard of St. Peter's Church, during the renewal of that edifice. Nothing, if I rightly call to mind, was left of my respected predecessor, save an imperfect skeleton, and some fragments of apparel, and a wig of majestic frizzle; which, unlike the head that it once adorned, was in very satisfactory preservation. But, on examining the papers . . . I found more traces of Mr. Pue's mental part, and the internal operations of his head, than the frizzled wig had contained of the venerable skull itself. ("The Custom House" 29–30)

It is important to quote such accounts at length (this is only a fragment of an involved discussion connecting Pue with his official duties) in order to convey the amazing elaborateness of Hawthorne's susceptibility to resonant objects, the staggering range he is able to draw from so limited a contact with Pue's manuscript, the sheer energy that an intimate contact with history animates, and the attention to detail that marks Hawthorne as a collector of merit. A passage like this shows quite clearly how adept Hawthorne was at "imaging" a museum as a high-quality organization. His use of elements is a major part of the physical communication in the graveyard, and the accumulation of detail has a profound effect on the interpretation of displayed objects.[19]

Such a passage reminds us of Folsom's claim in *Man's Accidents and God's Purposes* that Hawthorne was fascinated by the accidental. Hawthorne's deep respect for Pue is a function of the surveyor's close proximity to an ambiguous symbol, the embroidered "A," that neatly frames a series of ethical and moral concepts. The fact that the "A" exemplifies alternative moral and ethical reasoning heightens Hawthorne's own historicism because it works as an anti-exemplum. The "A" confuses the origins of Hawthorne's insights as much as it reveals them.

Hawthorne's antiquarian interest was in fact two separate, competing ideologies. David Watters has discovered, in Hawthorne's antiquarian impulse, a desire to advance the epochalist tradition of historiography. Watters traces the epochalist tradition through William Bentley and the founders of the Essex Historical Society, on whose estimate of Salem's material legacy Hawthorne relied. That tradition, embodied in the Mary English chair, "recalled for Bentley, and later for Hawthorne, the conflicts of the witch trials" (Watters, "Hawthorne Possessed" 31). Bentley's acquisition and conservation of the Mary English chair embodied a political pretension that "hearkened back to republican values he saw embodied in the simple, old-fashioned furnishings of ancient Salem households. A member of the educated elite, his nostalgia was expressed in acquisitiveness" (32–33). Bentley's position reflected notions of New England's significance similar to those that Mather anticipated in Boston after the rebellion. At that time, the aesthetic appreciation of New England culture was profoundly implicated in the general sweep of providential history.

The simple republican virtue, because it made the past a static object of contemplation, was socially de-provincializing but, given the realities of nineteenth-century Massachusetts, psychologically forced. Hawthorne's fascination with the past was tinted by a "democratic resentment," which he expressed in reference to the portraits in the Essex Historical Society: "Nothing gives a stronger idea of old worm-eaten aristocracy—of a family being crazy with age, and of its being time that it was extinct—than these black, dusty, faded antique-dressed portraits" (qtd. in Watters 32). A neat division between Bentley and Hawthorne must be qualified: Hawthorne knew more than a little of "historic portraits." It was easy for Hawthorne to criticize Bentley, for they were wrestling with many of the same issues of the proper context in which to display the fragments recovered from their historical investigations.

Estrangement, pleasure, and the antiquarian impulse are combined in the great invitation to resonance that Pue's materials offered to Hawthorne. The real importance of Jonathan Pue, however, is the fact that he is Hawthorne's invented double, and the work performed by each depends on Mather's suggestion in *Magnalia* to invent a personality to record events that cannot be experienced firsthand:

The ancient Surveyor—being little molested, I suppose, at that early day, with business pertaining to his office—seems to have devoted some of his many leisure hours to researches as a local antiquarian, and other inquisitions of a similar nature. These supplied material for petty activity to a mind that would otherwise have been eaten up with rust. A portion of his facts, by the by, did me good service in the preparation of the article entitled "MAIN STREET." . . . The remainder may perhaps be applied to purposes equally valuable, hereafter; or not impossibly may be worked up . . . into a regular history of Salem, should my veneration for the natal soil ever impel me to so pious a task. Meanwhile, they shall be at the command of any gentleman, inclined, and competent, to take the unprofitable labor off my hands. As a final disposition, I contemplate depositing them with the Essex Historical Society. ("The Custom House" 30–31)

As Hawthorne makes clear, the prospect of historical recovery feeds the artistic impulse. His impulse on opening Pue's document is not merely to learn how to judge the world it describes but rather to learn how it opens avenues for Hawthorne's own participation in the world as an actor among the rest. In "The Custom House," the presence of clutter, the fact that there are many potential sources of historical resonance, allows Hawthorne to unfold an entire theory of romance. The cluttered attic and the deserted parlor are necessary spaces for Hawthorne's practice of literature:

> There is the little domestic scenery of the well-known apartment; the chairs, with each its separate individuality; the centre-table, sustaining a work-basket, a volume or two, and an extinguished lamp; the sofa; the book-case; the picture on the wall;—all of these details, so completely seen, are so spiritualized by the unusual light, that they seem to lose their actual substance, and become things of intellect. . . . Thus, therefore, the floor of our familiar room has become a neutral territory, somewhere between the real world and fairy-land, where the Actual and Imaginary may meet, and each imbue itself with the nature of the other. (35–36)

The appearance of a wonderful aspect to otherwise common and familiar objects opens a valuable and rich interpretive space. If an artist can succeed in attaching wonder to everyday domestic furniture, it offers him a "neutral-ground" where he can work to restore a powerful awareness of the openness of interpretation.

Again, a significant number of Hawthorne critics have seized on this aspect. Nina Baym sees this "space" as especially reflective of Hawthorne's singular literary sensibility, which defined a way of writing that could embody the imagination and justify it to a skeptical, practically minded audience (*The Shape of Hawthorne's Career*). Darrel Abel, in *The Moral Picturesque*, argues that Hawthorne's elaborate descriptiveness is an important mode for figuring the archetypal experiences concerning the paradoxical relation of the real and the ideal. Abel does not see such instances as historically significant; rather he sees open interpretive spaces as entrances to Hawthorne's psychologizing approach to experience.

Before discussing the importance of openness as a primary inducement for the artist's craft, let us look at Hawthorne's "The Old Manse," in which the inducement to excite wonder in his readers flows from a desire to be like a tour guide inviting his guests to reconsider along with him the importance of place: "Perhaps the reader—whom I cannot help considering as my guest in the old Manse, and entitled to all courtesy in the way of sight-showing—perhaps he will choose to take a nearer view of the memorable spot" (6). Like the figure of Peale drawing back the curtain to his Long Room, Hawthorne easily assumes the responsibilities of a guide. His inducement to recreate the past is linked to his enlistment of others. The guidance of an expert is sometimes necessary because the most obvious places are not always the most significant. In Hawthorne's work, the strong emphasis on participation may have represented as well Hawthorne's response to democratic education.

In the stance put forward in his introductions, "The Custom House" and "The Old Manse," Hawthorne was not content to reserve interpretation for the work of the scholar alone; instead, he expressed a public sense of generosity as he sought to disseminate his understanding as widely as possible.[20] In the following passage from "The Old Manse," Hawthorne takes great pains to attribute the techniques of archaeological exploration to others, largely because he himself benefited from Henry David Thoreau's example. The importance of cultural artifacts becomes in some sense a civic responsibility, passed from individual to individual:

Many strangers come, in the summer-time, to view the battle-ground. For my own part, I have never found my imagination much excited by this, or any other scene of historic celebrity. . . . There is a wilder interest in the tract of land—perhaps a hundred yards in breadth—which extends between the battle-field and the northern face of our old Manse. . . . Here, in some unknown age . . . stood an Indian village. . . . The site is identified by the spear and arrow-heads, the chisels, and other implements of war, labor, and the chase, which the plough turns up from the soil. You see a splinter of stone, half hidden beneath a sod; it looks like nothing worthy of note; but, if you have faith enough to pick it up—behold a relic! Thoreau, who has a strange faculty of finding what the Indians have left behind them, first set me on the search; and I afterwards enriched myself with some very perfect specimens, so rudely wrought that it seemed almost as if chance had fashioned them. Their great charm consists in this rudeness, and in the individuality of each article, so different from the productions of civilized machinery, which shapes everything on one pattern. (10–11)

There is always, it seems, an "authentic reality" buried or neglected in the objects that Hawthorne recovers, and his antiquarianism frequently bears the message contained in these fragments to a world becoming increasingly inauthentic and modern. Authenticity is the effect of certain kinds of residuum that lend themselves easily to allegory. Resonance, however, does not describe these codes but rather is the focused gathering that organizes them and reaches out to a larger context of narrative possibility. In *A Week on the Concord and Merrimack*, for example, the arrowheads Thoreau encounters on his journey are "authentic," but they resonate for him in the sense that they give him a point of identification whereby his own journey, however significant, will never connect with the past. Passages like this one reflect Hawthorne's spiritual anxieties that a culture without direct access to the wonders of the past is in danger of losing the value of tradition altogether.[21]

Hawthorne repeatedly sees his labors as contributing to the formation of a cultural context that can adequately support national ideals. In "The Old Manse," toiling in his garden becomes a metaphor for his choice to make cultural work an object for living: "I felt that, by my agency, something worth living for had been done. A new substance was borne into the world. They [crook-necked winter squashes] were real and tangible existences, which the mind could seize hold of and rejoice in" (15). The fact that Hawthorne viewed his antiquarian interests as a preserve of democracy is somewhat illustrated by his positioning himself in the attic of the Old Manse. There, he sorts through the accumulated artifacts of a two-centuries-old house; his rifling through the attic of the house becomes continuous with his interest in creating the archive for his nineteenth-century readers:

> The old books would have been worth nothing at an auction. In this venerable garret, however, they possessed an interest quite apart from their literary value, as heirlooms, many of which had been transmitted down through a series of consecrated hands, from the days of the mighty Puritan divines. Autographs of famous names were to be seen, in faded ink, on some of the fly-leaves; and there were marginal observations, or interpolated pages closely covered with manuscript, in illegible short-hand, perhaps concealing matter of profound truth and wisdom. . . . The rain pattered upon the roof, and the sky gloomed through the dusty garret-

windows; while I burrowed among these venerable books, in search of any living thought, which should burn like a coal of fire, or glow like an inextinguishable gem, beneath the dead trumpery that had long hidden it. . . . In fine, of this whole dusty heap of literature, I tossed aside all the sacred part, and felt myself none the less a Christian for eschewing it. . . . Nothing, strange to say, retained any sap, except what had been written for the passing day and year, without the remotest pretension or idea of permanence. There were a few old newspapers, and still older almanacs, which reproduced, to my mental eye, the epochs when they had issued from the press, with a distinctness that was altogether unaccountable. It was as if I had found bits of magic looking-glass among the books, with the images of a vanished century in them. (18–20)

But as soon as that connection is forged, Hawthorne would have us ironically consider that such musty items may be of extremely limited use in his present age. Here is a plausible and basic justification for wonder-cabinets and the pursuit of history: to be the arbitrator of democratic freedoms. Hawthorne believed in the nineteenth-century maxim that the library and the museum were the two halves of the public memory, and in his self-conception of himself as an author he established himself as a prime figure managing them both for the benefit of his readers. But within that attempt, Hawthorne is careful to maintain the position that the "power" fixed in these institutions is highly variable.

As Mather suggested, when the colonial mission waned, it required augmentation even to the point where invention made the process of an artifact's meaning appear co-extensive with the meaning of the person who described it. In its spirit and outlook, Hawthorne's project is very similar to Mather's interest, expressed in *Magnalia*, in establishing from available sources a cultural archive for all generations. The laudable aims of the novelist turned historian are to study man not as a singular intellect presiding over his destiny but as the product of those creative expressions that have survived him and to recognize those elements that have contributed to the general welfare of humankind by virtue of their careful arrangement by a collector.

Now it should be stressed that Hawthorne's interest in becoming a manipulator of the cultural archive was paralleled by his interest in being made a part of the cultural apparatus to which an emergent middle class aspired. The attention Hawthorne focuses on items whose charms "consist in their rudeness and individuality of each article" anticipates the consumer fetishism of the late nineteenth century. The so-called Colonial Revival and the Arts and Crafts movements sought an American aesthetic to replace European-inspired and technologically sophisticated styles. Hawthorne's evincing a concern for traditional American materials, then, neatly frames his need for both a democratic form for expressing history and a tentative essentialist position with respect to culture: one that draws from local traditions in a psychologically immediate but socially isolating way.

That point emerges from the following passage, in which Hawthorne makes plain that the New England influence as it operates for him no longer is burdened by the weight of theological formalism; instead, his narrative of the past is calculated to draw a wide popular audience. Hawthorne makes this point in "The Old Manse":

> I turned my eyes towards the tattered picture . . . and asked of the austere divine, wherefore it was that he and his brethren, after the most painful rummaging and groping into their minds, had been able to produce nothing half so real, as these newspaper scribblers and almanac-makers had thrown off, in the effervescence of a moment. The portrait responded not; so I sought an answer for myself. It is the Age itself that writes newspapers and almanacs, which, therefore have a distinct purpose and meaning, at the time, and a kind of intelligible truth for all times; whereas, most other works—being written by men who, in the very act, set themselves apart from their age—are likely to possess little significance when new, and none at all, when old. (20–21)

So it is that two writers, Hawthorne and Mather, perhaps ironically, establish themselves as writers concerned with the immediate cultural moment, preserving their significance for their own and future generations. Both would agree that, in principle, artifacts of the past are potentially democratic. They are so abundant that they can be utilized to replace romantic preconceptions with scientifically derived knowledge, as Peale thought. The irony, without which we miss a great deal, is that such uses are far from inevitable. Often the historian treats only genealogically relevant things, as Hawthorne did when he looked at two chairs that had a significant family connection.

The usual historical treatment of artifacts, the dark side to Peale's museum, is that objects are seen not as descriptive of their times and places but rather as mere disjointed items wrenched out of their vital historical contexts. The task that a visitor to the museum must complete is an accurate historical "reading"; a visitor must recognize in the museum the principles that reinforce the notion that the museum is a setting that consecrates the objects placed within it.

The parallel between Peale's museum and *Magnalia* is this: both semiotically offer a proposed contract to those who would understand the culture inscribed within. The mechanisms by which we are to accomplish our readings of culture within museums depend on a relationship among three things: (1) the museum as an abstract entity expressed by the organization of space; (2) the objects on display; and (3) the visitor who receives these messages and either interprets them or simply accepts them as they are. In its use of these mechanisms, the museum places visitors in a situation where a particular reading depends both on the skill of the observer and the techniques of display. Thus, in these operations, the status of each factor involved is capable of manipulation: the museum, the objects on display, and the visitor who is a cognitive subject. One needs to be energetic and have a reference to personal values in order to read and judge for oneself.

Both Mather's writing of *Magnalia* and Peale's creation of a museum depend on competence and self-assurance. The ability to make oneself into a subject and the quality of writing that acts upon readers precisely through an ethos of cultural conservation become the roots of literary genius in both Mather and Hawthorne.

The wonder-cabinets of Hawthorne—his historical tales—and Mather's history are at least as much about possession as they are about display.[22] The wonder derived from them originates with the sense of resonance on which these works capitalize; they are bound up not with the evocation of an absent culture but with the acuity with which a great man manipulates rare and precious things. And the things they transform into wonder are not necessarily beautiful; the marvelous in Hawthorne, Mather, or Peale is bound up with the excessive, the surprising, the literally outlandish, and the prodigious. The marvelous could be the manifestation of the artistic skill possessed by human makers, as Peale's portraits of statesmen were, or Mather's biography of Phips. But it could just as easily be uncannily small or large bones, stuffed animals, or Indian arrowheads. And, most important, in the logic of the wonder-cabinet, it was not necessary that the objects that attracted visitors' most rapt attention be those specifically set out for prominent display:

Genius, indeed, melts many ages into one, and thus effects something permanent, yet still with a similarity of office to that of the more ephemeral writer. A work of genius is but the newspaper of a century, or perchance of a hundred centuries.

Lightly as I have spoken of these old books, there yet lingers with me a superstitious reverence for literature of all kinds. A bound volume has a charm in my eyes, similar to what scraps of manuscript possess, for the good Mussulman. He imagines, that those wind-wafted records are perhaps hallowed by some sacred verse; and I, that every new book, or antique one, may contain the "Open Sesame"—the spell to disclose treasures, hidden in some unsuspected cave of Truth. ("The Old Manse" 21)

Our reading of "The Custom House" and "The Old Manse" has moved back and forth between the postulate that Hawthorne's interest in the past defines an artistic vocation and an opportunity to take part in the cultural technologies of one's age.

If we see Hawthorne's writing as constituting a wonder-cabinet filled with surprising variety, then the objects he describes may not only arouse wonder but also communicate a sense of astonishment as a report of marvels seen. Mather's *Magnalia*, with its extensive coverage of wonders not always seen by the writer himself, has much in common with textual collections of wonders from medieval times. Friar Jordanus's *Marvels of the East* and Marco Polo's *Book of Marvels*, when viewed in the light of Hawthorne's claim that "the ancient Surveyor, in his garb of a hundred years gone by, and wearing his immortal wig,—which was buried with him, but did not perish in the grave,—had met me in the deserted chamber of the Custom House" ("The Custom House" 33), indicate that the marvelous can be theorized as a principally textual phenomenon.[23]

Hawthorne's wondrous apprehension for the past and its artifacts is synonymous with the recovery of the past. In both "The Custom House" and "The Old Manse," we have seen that the writer's aim has been to recover as far as possible the historical circumstances of an object's original production and consumption. Hawthorne's method is to analyze the relationship between these original circumstances and his own. Hawthorne declared that in his rendering of Pue's documents "I must not be understood as affirming, that, in the dressing up of the tale, and imagining the motives and modes of passion that influenced the characters who figure in it, I have invariably confined myself within the limits of the old Surveyor's half a dozen sheets of foolscap" ("The Custom House" 33). Hawthorne's defense for his fiction rests on his claim that he is not trying to reduce to isolation the individual masterpiece given to him by Pue; rather he wants to restore the tangibility, the openness, the permeability of the boundaries that enabled this object to come into his possession in the first place. The purpose of the prose "frames" that Hawthorne uses to enclose his works suggests that openness, the finished quality of art, is never taken for granted. In "The Custom House" and "The Old Manse" Hawthorne places his artifacts precariously to help his readers imaginatively re-create the work. Peale's museum and Hawthorne's two prefatory introductions function, partly by design and partly in spite of themselves, as monuments to the fragility of the culture preserved within them.

Analogical and Causal Links to Puritanism

"The Old Manse," "The Custom House," *Grandfather's Chair*, and "Old News" are all tales in which Hawthorne uses material artifacts to evoke an analogical or causal link to Puritanism. In "The Old Manse" the author's house constitutes the link to the seventeenth century. "Certainly it had little in common with those ordinary abodes which stand so imminent upon the road that every passer-by can thrust his head, as it were, into the domestic circle," Hawthorne says of this parsonage in Concord (3).

> In its near retirement, and accessible seclusion, it was the very spot for the residence of a clergyman; — a man not estranged from human life, yet enveloped, in the midst of it, with a veil woven of intermingled gloom and brightness. . . . I took shame to myself for having been so long been a writer of idle stories, and ventured to hope that wisdom would descend upon me with the falling leaves of the avenue; and that I should light upon an intellectual treasure in the old Manse, well worth those hoards of long-hidden gold, which people seek for in moss-grown houses. Profound treatises of morality; — a layman's unprofessional, and therefore unprejudiced views of religion; — histories, (such as Bancroft might have written, had he taken up his abode here, as he once purposed,) bright with picture, gleam-

ing over a depth of philosophic thought; — these were the works that might fitly have flowed from such a retirement. . . . It was here that Emerson wrote "Nature." . . . When I first saw the room, its walls were blackened with the smoke of unnumbered years, and made still blacker by the grim prints of Puritan ministers that hung around. These worthies looked strangely like bad angels, or, at least, like men who had wrestled so continually and so sternly with the devil, that somewhat of his sooty fierceness had been imparted to their own visages. (4–5)

At a moment like this, Hawthorne reminds us that this house is a balancing point between his present concerns and those of the past.

Such reflections may help us to understand how Hawthorne, who felt the competitive rivalry of Ralph Waldo Emerson's transcendental personality, could occupy the same dwelling and construct from its varied influences a literature different from the literature of the inhabitants who had lived there before him. As von Abele argues, Hawthorne held a pseudo-Platonic conception of the nature and function of art. In his symbolic techniques employed in the passage quoted above, he defined his position as a "serious" artist in a democratic society whose work might appear to appeal only to elites. Hawthorne's tenure in the Old Manse came after the death of Ezra Ripley, the minister who he had conjectured had "penned nearly three thousand sermons." Ripley's death on September 21, 1841, was a foreshadowing of great changes in Concord. His old meetinghouse was undergoing extensive alterations, even to the point of being shifted around to face in the opposite direction, a fact some of his parishioners deemed theologically significant. Hawthorne's comments, in their repetitive sounding of the themes of renovation and renewal, draw their resonant force from his association with Ripley's house and heighten a perception of his "status anxiety." Ralph Waldo Emerson, quick to grasp Ripley's passing as the symbolic closing of an era, dwelt on Ripley's character:

He has identified himself with forms at least of the old church of the New England Puritans, his nature was eminently loyal, not in the least adventurous or democratical and his whole being leaned backward on the departed, so that he seemed one of the rear guard of this great camp and army which have filled the world with fame and with him passes out of sight almost the last banner and guidon of a mighty epoch. Great, grim, earnest men, I belong by natural affinity to other thoughts and schools

than yours, but my affection hovers respectfully about your retiring foot-
prints, your unpainted churches, strict platforms, and sad offices; the iron-
gray deacons and the wearisome prayer rich with the diction of ages. Now
in his old age when all the antique Hebraism and customs are going to
pieces, it is fit he too should depart, most fit that in the fall of laws a loyal
man should die. (qtd. in Ellen Tucker Emerson 90)

Hawthorne's natural affinities leaned more toward Ripley and less toward
Emerson. In fact, with Ripley's passing and Hawthorne's subsequent residence in the house emblemizing prior tradition demonstrated his tacit ac-
knowledgment that his art needed a Puritan source.

The Old Manse, a structure subject to continual rearrangement by its
occupants, has, in every era, served as a place where literary culture has
repeatedly been rehearsed. Hawthorne wrote, "Houses of any antiquity in
New England are so invariably possessed with spirits that the matter seems
hardly worth alluding to. Our ghost used to heave deep sighs in a particular
corner of the parlor, and sometimes rustled paper, as if he were turning over
a sermon in the long upper entry. . . . Not improbably he wished me to edit
and publish a selection from a chest full of manuscript discourses that stood
in the garret" (17). As Ripley's haunting of the Old Manse suggests, Hawthorne's connection to the house affirms the vital imaginative force of Puritanism.[24]

In "The Custom House" it is Hawthorne's genealogical connection to the
town of Salem that energizes his memory of Puritan times:

This old town of Salem—my native place, though I have dwelt much away
from it, both in boyhood and maturer years—possesses, or did possess, a
hold on my affections, the force of which I have never realized during my
seasons of actual residence here. . . . The sentiment is probably assignable
to the deep and aged roots which my family has struck into the soil. It is
now nearly two centuries and a quarter since the original Briton [1625],
the earliest emigrant of my name, made his appearance. . . . And here his
descendants have been born and died, and have mingled their earthy substance with the soil; until no small portion of it must necessarily be akin
to the mortal frame wherewith, for a little while, I walk the streets. (8–9)

After reading "The Custom House," it is fairly easy to understand why Hawthorne praised Stoddard's *The Morgesons* "as genuine and lifelike as anything that pen and ink can do" (N. Hawthorne to EDS, January 26, 1863, Berg Collection). Stoddard's novel vividly recalled his own early years in Salem and his confronting the traces of a declining Puritan tradition. Stoddard's toying with the notion of a haunted place is neatly echoed in Hawthorne's own appraisal of an image of Puritanism that crosses generations:

> The figure of that first ancestor, invested by family tradition with a dim and dusky grandeur, was present to my boyish imagination, as far back as I can remember. It still haunts me, and induces a sort of home-feeling with the past, which I scarcely claim in reference to the present phase of the town. I seem to have a stronger claim to a residence here on account of this grave, bearded, sable-cloaked, and steeple-crowned progenitor,—who came so early, with his Bible and his sword, and trod the unworn street with such a stately port, and made so large a figure. . . . He was a soldier, legislator, judge; he was a ruler in the Church; he had all the Puritanic traits, both good and evil. He was likewise a bitter persecutor; as witness the Quakers, who have remembered him in their histories, and relate an incident of his hard severity towards a woman of their sect, which will last longer, it is to be feared, than any record of his better deeds. ("The Custom House" 9)

In "The Custom House," Hawthorne's own spiritual anxieties were contained and consoled by the notion that he had somehow become re-Puritanized by his employment in Salem. His interest in local history and the depravity of his ancestors have made him a careful explorer of his Puritan origins:

> I know not whether these ancestors of mine bethought themselves to repent, and ask pardon of Heaven for their cruelties. . . . At all events, I, the present writer, as their representative, hereby take shame upon myself for their sakes, and pray that any curse incurred by them—as I have heard, and as the dreary and unprosperous condition of the race, for many a long year back, would argue to exist—may be now and henceforth removed. (9–10)

Admiration for his ancestors and a desire to atone for their misdeeds do not permit Hawthorne to efface the disturbing estrangement that his connection to the past creates. Ultimately, what Hawthorne characterizes as his relationship to his ancestors is the recognition that his ancestors see in him an ironic choice of vocation:

> Doubtless, however, either of these stern and black-browed Puritans would have thought it quite a sufficient retribution for his sins, that, after so long a lapse of years, the old trunk of the family tree . . . should have borne, as its topmost bough, an idler like myself. No aim, that I have ever cherished, would they recognize as laudable; no success of mine—if my life, beyond its domestic scope, had ever been brightened by success— would they deem otherwise than worthless, if not positively disgraceful. "What is he?" murmurs one gray shadow of my forefathers to the other. "A writer of story-books! What kind of a business in life,—what mode of glorifying God, or being serviceable to mankind in his day and generation,—may that be? Why, the degenerate fellow might as well have been a fiddler!" Such are the compliments bandied between my great-grandsires and myself, across the gulf of time! And yet, let them scorn me as they will, strong traits of their nature have intertwined themselves with mine. ("The Custom House" 10)

For our purposes of describing Hawthorne's historical intentions, no tale is more important than *Grandfather's Chair*. Hawthorne's engagement with the cultural poetics of *Magnalia* in *Grandfather's Chair* characterized his entire career.[25] In the early years of his vocation, *Magnalia* represented a link to the "neutral territory" of literary historicism, but in later years Mather's text became a highly specific articulation of literary democracy. Hawthorne's exploration of the utility of Mather's text was like the narrative designs he experimented with in *The Story-Teller*: "Frames perhaps more valuable than the pictures themselves . . . embossed with groups of characteristic figures of our native land" ("Passages from a Relinquished Work" 408–09). *Magnalia* framed Hawthorne's interest in the historical arrangements that appear in *Grandfather's Chair* and that fully flowered in his later historical romances. Michael Colacurcio completely misreads *Grandfather's Chair* in *The Province of Piety* when he says that it recapitulates New England history in childlike good faith with the "reticence of a symbol." David Watters is closer to approximating the significance of *Grandfather's Chair* when he describes it as a transformation of an "old Puritan relic" whose purpose is to "create oral traditions livelier than 'official' history. . . . epitomizing Hawthorne's historical method—the chair is polysemic, reinterpreted and refurbished by each owner in her or his time, yet each owner's experience is part of an historical tradition" (Watters, "Hawthorne Possessed" 36–37).

In fact, *Grandfather's Chair* claims historical authenticity precisely because the narrative operates through the agency of the chair; the chair is, so to speak, the actor that acts upon the story, disrupting the present and functioning as the artifact that animates history. And through this use of the chair as the actant in the narrative, as a "wounded artifact," the local Puritan past is edified because the authoritarian vantages on Puritanism, represented by Bancroft, become destabilized. It gives us the key, the education necessary to understand the contours of the essentialist tradition: what is quaint in a Vermont village betokens economic privations, and what appears handcrafted according to "traditional" practices is more often than not the commodities offered to a middle-class public so that conservation work can continue in spite of its seeming uselessness.

In all of the Hawthorne canon, *Grandfather's Chair* makes the most elaborate use of a type associated with Puritanism to connect events in figurative strategy. In this work, Hawthorne turns key moments in Massachusetts history, recast from a variety of historical sources, into exempla of persecution, intolerance, suffering, and violence that puzzle his juvenile auditors. To fully understand Hawthorne, we must take very seriously the perception that a material artifact drawn from a Puritan context carries with it the basis for historical narrative. Grandfather's chair is not, in other words, simply a rhetorical device or an unconventional allegorical mode; it is a central and enduring response to the ways history can be rehearsed. Hawthorne makes this claim in his "Preface":

> Setting aside Grandfather and his auditors, and excepting the adventures of the chair, which form the machinery of the work, nothing in the ensuing pages can be termed fictitious. The author, it is true, has sometimes assumed the license of filling up the outline of history with details, for which he has none but imaginative authority, but which, he hopes, do not violate nor give a false coloring to the truth. . . . The author's great doubt is, whether he has succeeded. . . . To make a lively and entertaining narrative for children, with such unmalleable material as is presented by the somber, stern, and rigid characteristics of the Puritans and their descendants, is quite as difficult an attempt, as to manufacture delicate playthings out

of the granite rocks on which New England is founded. (*Grandfather's Chair* 6)

Hawthorne is careful to connect grandfather's chair with its Puritan source. "It came across the Atlantic with Lady Arbella, who allowed ministers to sit in it on shipboard. This male-female, elite-plebeian pattern of identification is repeated for the next two hundred years, as the chair passes from radical men and women such as Roger Williams, Anne Hutchinson, Mary Dyer, and Sam Adams, to aristocrats, magistrates, and ministers such as John Winthrop, John Hull, Cotton Mather, and Governor Hutchinson" (Watters, "Hawthorne Possessed" 38). In a very real sense, the chair's involvement with Puritan culture closely replicates the substance of Mather's *Magnalia*. As a focus for the narrative, the chair becomes the site where images that Mather suggested in his book come to life before the children's eyes. Sir William Phips, before rising to the governorship, repaired the arm himself, and the tale that ensues brings forward Mather's idealized image of Phips, the original self-made man (*Grandfather's Chair* 56). Like Charles Willson Peale's *Perspective Views with Changeable Effects*, Hawthorne's chair animates the early years of the Puritan settlement, covering in a brief space what Mather had described in prolix detail.[26]

> First, the gentle and lovely lady Arbella would have been seen in the old chair, . . . then Roger Williams, in his cloak and band, . . . then the figure of Anne Hutchinson, with the like gesture as when she presided at the assemblages of women; then the dark, intellectual face of Vane. . . . Next would have appeared the successive governors, Winthrop, Dudley, Bellingham, and Endicott, who sat in the chair, while it was a Chair of State. Then its ample seat would have been pressed by the comfortable, rotund corporation of the honest mint-master. Then the half-frenzied shape of Mary Dyer, the persecuted Quaker woman. . . . Then the holy apostolic form of Eliot would have sanctified it. Then would have arisen, like the shade of departed Puritanism, the venerable dignity of the white-bearded Governor Bradstreet. Lastly, on the gorgeous crimson cushion of Grandfather's chair, would have shone the purple and golden magnificence of Sir William Phips. (*Grandfather's Chair* 66)

The grandfather's chair is most obviously a bravura display of Hawthorne's ability to hang historical pageantry on a museum piece, elsewhere manifested in his rendering of the artifacts in "The Virtuoso's Collection." Grandfather without the chair is a man of very small and very secondary imagination—at best an amanuensis; but when he narrates through the chair, he is a first-rate historian. A chair may make a parlor a pleasant place to grow up. But it is analysis, which leads away from a concern with the object itself and toward the ideas that were the cause of the chair's existence, that grandfather supplies to his youthful auditors. Strictly speaking, the ideas in the mind of a maker can never be enumerated, but the scholar can venture close to comprehension of the mind's activities and of the maker's intent through deep play with components, sources, and models of process. Hawthorne's fondness for the meaningful detail that links his writing to a suggestion of Puritanism is more often than not expressed through a fully fleshed portrait of "the thing itself."

In his writing, Hawthorne's remembrance is renewed by rehearsals of an object's place in the cultural atmosphere from which it emerged. The rhythm that emerges from these texts is one of exhibition, followed by exclusion or effacement. Exhibition, seen in Hawthorne's bringing to light the lost manuscript of Surveyor Pue and his ushering of guests through the rooms of the Old Manse, is the unveiling of a sacrificial offering—the placing of an object in public view for a time preliminary to its removal from view after a full and indulgent display. The removal comes after Hawthorne adapts the object in question, thus forming his own narrative in response to the original source. In "The Custom House" Pue's documentation, so patiently brought to the surface, and his tattered relic, the scarlet "A," are removed from the narrative that follows but are retained in the author's possession.

The rhythm of exhibition followed by exclusion or effacement—a process of observation and review—does not merely precede the subsequent revision in prose but is intimately related to it. This is the personality that is attributed to most of Hawthorne's narrators. The prop of the unreliable narrator is a frequent touchstone of Hawthorne's technique. The recursiveness of Hawthorne's narrators preserves intentional ambiguities through fortifying Yvor Winters's notion of a "formula of alternative possibilities" and exploiting what Matthiessen termed a "device of multiple choice." For Hawthorne, this rhythm is the primary trope for explaining the course of New England's evolutionary change in "Old News":

In short, newer manners and customs had almost entirely superseded those of the Puritans, even in their own city of refuge.

It was natural that, with the lapse of time and increase of wealth and population, the peculiarities of the early settlers should have waxed fainter and fainter through the generations of descendants. . . . It tended to assimilate the colonial manners to those of the mother-country. (143)

The collection of artifacts bearing a Puritan significance for Hawthorne is a rehearsal of popular culture with a self-consuming end in mind. As Michael Bell suggests, Hawthorne's antiquarianism is aimed at revealing the supposed contradictions between the advocacy of liberty and the denial of it. The true nature of democracy's potential for the masses produced the central tensions of Hawthorne's historical romances, and a close examination of source materials is directed at resolving that tension (13). We have only to recall the passages in Mather's church history that revealed his deep frustration with licentious behavior in the streets of Boston, to recollect that popular culture in the Puritan era was of decisive importance. Recalling some of the editions of the *Boston News-letters* that Cotton Mather contributed to and the editions of the *Boston Gazette*, Hawthorne assures his readers in "Old News":

There is no evidence that the moral standard was higher then than now. . . . There seem to have been quite as many frauds and robberies. . . . there were murders . . . and bloody quarrels, over liquor. . . . Some of our fathers, also, appear to have been yoked to unfaithful wives—if we may trust the frequent notices of elopements from bed and board. . . . in short, as often as our imagination lives in the past, we find it a ruder and rougher age than our own. (135)

Characteristic, then, in Hawthorne's fictional method is the display of an object rescued from antiquity followed by the displacement of the object into a drama of resonance. The association of a house with a genealogical connection to the witch trials in Salem becomes, in its fully rehearsed form, *The House of the Seven Gables*. The packet of documents and the scarlet letter become, in their fully rehearsed form, *The Scarlet Letter*.

What we have been concerned with here is Hawthorne's role as a collector in the introductory passages to longer, more extensive works treating themes of Puritan history. The examples cited from "The Custom House" and "The Old Manse" in particular represent a practice session for Hawthorne, the collector of Puritan curiosities, to arrange resonant items from his wonder-cabinets prior to a more extended public display. As we will see in the following three sections, Hawthorne's use of the items he selects gives him ample opportunity to tap their resonance in a forum where alternatives can be staged, unfamiliar roles tried out, and the range of his power to convince or persuade explored with relative freedom. The adaptation of fragments of Puritan history is a performance common to both *Magnalia* and Peale's museum, but it is one in which the customary demands of decorum and the expectation of a final perfected form are compromised for the sake of the author's experimental historical negotiations.

Estrangement in the Wonder-Cabinet

If variety and possibility are a part of the wonder-cabinet's appeal for collectors, estrangement is also an important part of the total effect. Hawthorne's collection is presented as a blending of old and new forms.

> "That," answered the Virtuoso, "is the original fire which Prometheus stole from Heaven. Look steadfastly into it, and you will discern another curiosity."
>
> I gazed into that fire,—which, symbolically, was the origin of all that was bright and glorious in the soul of man,—and in the midst of it, behold! a little reptile, sporting with evident enjoyment of the fervid heat. It was a salamander.
>
> "What a sacrilege!" cried I, with inexpressible disgust. ("The Virtuoso's Collection" 488)

Hawthorne's visitor expresses a confusion born from the oddity of the place. Is the original light a wondrous object to behold or an infernal representation in which a respected image finds itself appropriated by pagan craft?

The wonder-cabinet's ability to fascinate as well as alienate its viewer has its place in Hawthorne's rehearsals as well. As critics, perhaps we would do well to see "The Custom House" and novels such as *The Scarlet Letter, The House of the Seven Gables*, and *The Blithedale Romance* as the traps of historical ingenuity.[27] Hawthorne's employment at the Custom House betokens an estrangement of the author:

> Literature, its exertions and objects, were now of little moment in my regard. I cared not, at this period, for books; they were apart from me. . . .

It might be true, indeed, that this was a life which could not, with impunity, be lived too long; else, it might make me permanently other than I had been, without transforming me into any shape which it would be worth my while to take. ("The Custom House" 25–26)

The Ripley property in Concord, seen from Thoreau's old rowboat, the *Lily-pad*, by Hawthorne's friend Ellery Channing, has the power to confuse the senses through its fusion of memory and desire, history and the present:

Of all this scene, the slumbering river has a dream-picture in its bosom. Which, after all, was the most real—the picture, or the original?—the objects palpable to our grosser senses, or their apotheosis in the stream beneath? Surely, the disembodied images stand in closer relation to the soul. But, both the original and the reflection had here an ideal charm; and, had it been a thought more wild, I could have fancied that this river had strayed forth out of the rich scenery of my companion's inner world;—only the vegetation along its banks should then have had an Oriental character. ("The Old Manse" 22)

Hawthorne's response in this passage reflects a profound transformation of the experience of being in Concord—the experience of wonder. For a man of his tastes, that wonder held a great many problems for his art because the ideal, though still registering the celebrity of its collector and a sense of market value, has at the heart of its mystery the sense that it is unique, authentic, and reflective of a tremendous visual power. Ideally displayed, nature benefits from a heightened charisma. The Concord River rewards the intensity of a viewer's gaze, and it seems to manifest the genius of its maker, "a straying forth from the rich scenery of his companion's inner world" (22).

Hawthorne's ambivalent attitude toward anything transcendental is due to the fact that the democratic freedoms of the wonder-cabinet, the ability to select and define resonance according to one's own preferences, are inverted in the transcendentalists' view.[28] Where all effort is directed to the demonstration of wonder expressed in perfected forms, the fantasy of possession that the wonder-cabinet maintains is no longer central to art; the object in its essence seems not to be a possession but rather is the possessor of what is most valuable and enduring.[29] Hawthorne preferred stuffy closets filled with ephemera that others might consider trash to supreme temples devoted to the display of wonderful articles. "In this world, we are the things of a moment," he writes in "Old News," "and are made to pursue momentary things, with here and there a thought that stretches mistily towards eternity, and perhaps may endure as long. All philosophy, that would abstract mankind from the present, is no more than words" (133). A close connection to the materials of the past has the ability to strike a note of estrangement in viewers.

Grandfather's young auditor Laurence, after being told the story of John Eliot and his Indian Bible, expresses an estrangement caused by the relic that seems, as many of the children's responses to the tales do, to far exceed his age:

> "My heart is not satisfied to think," observed Laurence, "that Mr. Eliot's labors have done no good, except to a few Indians of his own time. Doubtless, he would not have regretted his toil, if it were the means of saving but a single soul. But it is a grievous thing to me, that he should have toiled so hard to translate the Bible, and now the language and the people are gone! The Indian Bible itself is almost the only relic of both." (*Grandfather's Chair* 49)

In Laurence's comments, we can almost discern the note of uncertainty that Hawthorne himself may have felt, because so much of his fictional enterprise was bound up with resurrecting the obscure from the darkness of history.

In Hawthorne, relics like the Indian Bible are calculated to problematize the author's relationship to his culture. We are correct, in Hawthorne's view, to see this Bible as a prime example of a writer attempting to recirculate the resonance of an alternate tradition within his own. We know this to be true because Eliot's Bible becomes the vehicle through which the colonial presence in New England is rehearsed in this tale: "[Eliot] was visited by learned men. . . . They, like himself, had been bred in the studious cloisters of a university, and were supposed to possess all the erudition which mankind has hoarded. . . . Mr. Eliot would put into their hands some of the pages, which he had been writing; and behold! the gray-headed men stammered over the long, strange words" (46). Conversely, it would be wrong, by the same reasoning, to see the Indian Bible as an object of wonder, for that status closes the openness of the artifact, removes its precarious qualities, and nullifies its usefulness as a tool for researching the historical circumstances of its original production and consumption. Hawthorne himself summarized the importance of the distinction between resonance and wonder in a passage from "The Virtuoso's Collection":

> But the deep simplicity of these great works was not to be comprehended by a mind excited and disturbed as mine was by the various objects that had recently been presented to it. I therefore turned away, with merely a passing glance, resolving, on some future occasion, to brood over each individual statue and picture, until my inmost spirit should feel their excellence. In this department, again, I noticed the tendency to whimsical combinations and ludicrous analogies, which seemed to influence many of the arrangements of the Museum. (493)

This response to a finished work of art is one that Hawthorne wishes for his readers. In his invocations of the past, the intention is almost always to bring the significance of another time or place into conversation with present circumstances. The probability that there will be missed cues, or a slippage in the meaning that the author intended to convey, is of little consequence; the significance of a museum like Peale's, broadly conceived, is its special power to promote further inspired rehearsals rather than isolating a privileged few.

Resonance is a trait commonly found among the clutter of wonder-cabinets. There, meaning is more often than not a celebration of the vernacular. Exceptional, yes, but the collections are directed toward displaying for a time the possibility of otherness, a performance that demands that objects gain their value through possession by a collector seized by a momentary attraction. Estrangement is an invitation for a writer like Hawthorne to undertake an exercise in cultural mnemonics, an effort to displace or re-create cultural memory. Estrangement is but one feature of an artifact that tugs at the collector's imagination; it is one incentive for the museum curator to consider an artifact's display.

Wounded Artifacts

Many of the items that resonate with Puritan culture are overdetermined and gain their stature through their association with a collector's intelligence and the accumulation of historical detail. For instance, the newspapers that form the basis for the trilogy of tales that is "Old News" had an indescribable picturesqueness, not to be found in the later ones. Whether it be something in the literary execution, or the ancient print or paper, and the idea that those same musty pages have been handled by people—once alive and bustling amid the scenes there recorded . . . so it is, that in those elder volumes, we seem to find the life of a past age preserved between the leaves, like a dry specimen of foliage. It is so difficult to discover what touches are really picturesque, that we doubt whether our attempts have produced any similar effect. (160)

"The Custom House" has two material aspects that become overdetermined by Hawthorne's involvement: the town and the scarlet "A." About the town, Hawthorne writes:

The spell survives, and just as powerfully as if the natal spot were an earthly paradise. So has it been in my case. I felt it almost as a destiny to make Salem my home; so that the mould of features and cast of characters which had all along been familiar here—ever, as one representative of the race lay down in his grave, another assuming, as it were, his sentry-march along the Main-Street—might still in my little day be seen and recognized in the old town. (11)

As though providing explanatory material in a collection guide for a museum display that reads "Fabric 'A' embroidered by Anne Hutchinson," Hawthorne tells his readers:

It was the capital letter A. By an accurate measurement, each limb proved to be precisely three inches and a quarter in length. It had been intended, there could be no doubt, as an ornamental article of dress; but how it was to be worn, or what rank, honor, and dignity, in by-past times, were signified by it, was a riddle which (so evanescent are the fashions of the world in these particulars) I saw little hope of solving. . . . Certainly, there was some deep meaning in it, most worthy of interpretation, and which, as it were, streamed forth from the mystic symbol, subtly communicating itself to my sensibilities, but evading the analysis of my mind. (31)

In Concord, the white pond-lily gains favor in the author's eye because it embodies both beauty and a close relationship with the antithetical. "It is a marvel . . . springing, as it does, from the black mud . . . where lurk the slimy eel, and speckled frog, and the mud turtle, whom continual washing cannot cleanse. . . . Thus we see, too, in the world, that some persons assimilate only what is ugly and evil from the same moral circumstances which supply good and beautiful results" ("The Old Manse" 7).

Perhaps the best example of all of a "wounded artifact" in both a literal and a figurative sense is Grandfather's chair: "it was very large and heavy, and had a back . . . curiously carved in open-work, so as to represent flowers and foliage, and other devices, which the children had often gazed at, but could never understand what they meant. On the very tiptop of the chair . . . was the likeness of a lion's head" (*Grandfather's Chair* 10). Supplementing the purely visual appeal of the chair is the fact that it had an enormous allegorical significance. This significance accounts for the chair's being a "wounded artifact." It has been the seat of all the early governors of Massachusetts (456); it is inherited by Simon Bradstreet, "the sole representative of that departed brotherhood" of Puritan settlers (483); and it is the principal site where Mather's *Magnalia* routinely resurfaces (494). "Grandfather, for aught I know," says Hawthorne, "might have gone on to speak of Maryland and Virginia; for the good old gentleman really seemed to suppose, that the whole surface of the United States was not too broad a foundation to place the four legs of his chair upon" (30). Its superadded meaning draws special consideration from the company of children who consider the chair to be as interesting as "conscious being":

> Even Charley, lawless as he was, seemed to feel that this venerable chair must not be clambered upon nor overturned. . . . Clara treated it with still greater reverence, often taking occasion to smooth its cushion, and to brush the dust from the carved flowers and grotesque figures of its oaken back and arms. Laurence would sometimes sit a whole hour . . . and, by the spell of his imagination, summoning up its ancient occupants to appear in it again. (31)

These, and many other references that Hawthorne makes to Puritanism, are overdetermined because the tableau of culture they are understood to represent is polymorphous; they stand for more than what a single object or a group of objects should be able to contain.

Hawthorne's interest in these curiosities was expressed in "The Virtuoso's Collection," which reflected contemporary newspapers' interest in presenting impossible curiosities. The hairy ears of Midas reported in Hawthorne's notebooks later became the mysterious ears of Donatello in *The Marble Faun*. Members of his family and some of his friends contributed ideas for his scheme. His wife Sophia Peabody contributed "Some Egyptian darkness in a blacking jug." Hawthorne suggests that present-day culture is made over by its contact with these things. The present is made strange but capable of imagination in those places where a simple chair can be made part and parcel of many pivotal events in a region's history. The true significance of places like the Salem Custom House, peopled with its odd, shiftless fellows, and the Old Manse, with its cracked windows gazing out over the site of the shot heard around the world, is that they are cultural expressions that depend on periodic resuscitation among an audience unmindful of original conditions.

Instead of dimly lit raw materials vaguely associated with another time, these places (and their curious contents) are "points at which one cultural practice intersects with another, borrowing its forms and intensities or attempting to ward off unwelcome appropriations" (Greenblatt, "Resonance and Wonder" 79). In the sense that several differing modes of representing a culture's identity are at work, both Mather and Hawthorne capitalize on their abilities to make a simple item profuse with meaning supplied by their artistic labors. To take but one example, both men attempt to sketch a portrait of William Phips. Mather's portrait, which he hung in the "gallery" in the chapter of *Magnalia* entitled *Ecclesiarum Clypei* (Shields of the Churches), mixes the first generation's reverence toward conversion and enlightened leadership and his own epoch's experience of commercial expansion and imperial progress. Hawthorne, too, makes his image of Phips a combination of history and (auto)biography—but with the superadded influence of a romantic sensibility that comes from his contextual arrangement of these three traditions:

> Few of the personages of past times . . . seldom stand up in our imaginations like men. The knowledge communicated by the historian and biographer is analogous to that which we acquire of a country by the map,— minute, perhaps, and accurate, and available for all necessary purposes, but cold and naked, and wholly destitute of the mimetic charm produced by landscape painting. These defects are partly remediable, and even without an absolute violation of literal truth. . . . A license must be assumed in brightening the materials which time has rusted, and in tracing out the half-obliterated inscriptions. . . . Fancy must throw her reviving light on the faded incidents that indicate character. ("Portrait of Phips" 227)

The biographical miniature of Phips (which Mather put forward in eighty pages) and Hawthorne's own brief sketch of Phips (composed as it is out of fragments residing in his wonder-cabinet of Puritan sources) amply illustrate that wounded artifacts are compelling to viewers not only because they are evidence of historical change but because they are monuments of subsequent human involvement. A wounded artifact forms a direct link to the openness that was the original condition of an object's creation.

In a sense the narratives that Hawthorne and Mather create exist to replace the contexts that are subtly effaced by the appropriation of historical opinion into their work. According to Greenblatt,

> The most familiar way to recreate the openness of aesthetic artifacts without simply renewing their vulnerability is through the skillful deployment of explanatory texts in the catalogue, on the walls of the exhibit. . . . The texts so deployed introduce and in effect stand in for the context that has been effaced in the process of moving the object into the museum. ("Resonance and Wonder" 81)

If it is fair to call some of Hawthorne's historical fictions and Mather's *Magnalia* wonder-cabinets designed to encourage rehearsals of cultural significance (as I think we can, for both examine and display anointed objects of specific local interest through a continually shifting arrangement), then we have reached a new understanding of how a church history composed of scattered fragments drove the imaginative productions of Hawthorne and the writers to follow.

The chairs, papers, and clothing that Hawthorne examines at the Old Manse in Concord are not simply decorative but are a compelling representation. They are the material basis of a rehearsal that impinges on the text's overall designs, enabling readers to better see the circulation of social energies that such rehearsals put into motion. Hawthorne's representational practice informs the portrait of the inspector whom Hawthorne calls "the Custom-House in himself . . . the main-spring that kept its variously revolving wheels in motion. . . . by an inevitable necessity, as a magnet attracts steel-filings, so did our man of business draw to himself the difficulties which everybody met with. . . . I had met with a person thoroughly adapted to the situation which he held" ("The Custom House" 24–25). The assorted material artifacts that set Hawthorne as the "Surveyor walking the quarter-deck" unsettle those forces that seemed to hold Hawthorne's confidence as an author loose. The infirm Weighers and Gaugers seem to say through their glances, "The little power you might once have possessed over the tribe of unrealities is gone! You have bartered it for a pittance of the public gold" (34). At last, it is among the objects in the Custom House that Hawthorne renews his desire to bring *The Scarlet Letter* before the public:

> No longer seeking nor caring that my name should be blazoned abroad on title-pages, I smiled to think that it had now another kind of vogue. The Custom-House marker imprinted it, with a stencil and black paint, on pepper-bags, and baskets of anatto, and cigar-boxes, and bales of all kinds of dutiable merchandise. . . . Borne on such a queer vehicle of fame, a knowledge of my existence, so far as a name conveys it, was carried where it had never been before, and I hope, will never go again. ("The Custom House" 27)

What is haunting about Hawthorne's project, which intermingles resonance with wonder, is the self-reflexiveness it demands and, with this self-reflexiveness, self-estrangement. That is the essence of Hawthorne's self-explanation as an artist willing to barter principle for financial rewards. His surveyor's stamp becomes an ironic reminder of his aspirations at literary fame; it is a wounded artifact in that it carries so much of the author's personality in such a simple form. But as a suggestion of literary ambition, the stamp fits perfectly with Hawthorne's sense that an author should strive to make readers aware of the constant risks involved when a writer becomes identified with his subject. Because Hawthorne's signature does not claim to perfectly merge the identity of great art with the genius of its creator the connection is seen to be almost accidental, or at least dictated by external forces. Finally, Hawthorne's signatures attached to flour barrels and to his fiction are indicative of his anxieties about the marketplace. Both signatures destabilize and maintain his art in relation to the material conditions of its production.

Hawthorne's chair circulates the elements of "remarkable events" in Massachusetts history by focusing the arrangement of parts into a temporary and shifting context.[30]

> The chair is made to pass from one to another of those personages, of whom he thought it most desirable for the young reader to have vivid and familiar ideas. . . . On its sturdy oaken legs, it trudges diligently from one scene to another, and seems always to thrust itself in the way, with most

benign complacency, whenever a historical personage happens to be looking around for a seat. (*Grandfather's Chair* 5)

The chair's versatility stems not only from its focusing powers but from the
fact that it helps Hawthorne to arrange the print sources that have aided him
in his project. Significantly, both Hawthorne and Mather recognize that textual contextualism is limited unless it also has some connection to a material
basis.

Like Peale's raising of the curtain in his self-portrait, Mather was careful
to let some of his subjects speak in their own words; and Hawthorne, at the
end of *The Scarlet Letter*, leaves his readers with Hester's tombstone, which
in some way parallels and intersects with his own formal work of art. Summarizing the lasting value of the wonder-cabinet, Steven Mullaney writes,
"What comes to reside in a wonder-cabinet are, in the most reified sense of
the phrase, strange things: tokens of alien cultures, reduced to the status of
sheer objects, stripped of cultural and human contexts in a way that makes
them eminently capable of surviving the period that thus produced them"
("Strange Things" 68). Granted that so many objects are preserved in the
print of Hawthorne's work, his function as a contextual historian rests with
his ability to develop and improve the hermeneutic potential of the wonder-
cabinet. The wonder-cabinet is so useful because it helps Hawthorne rehearse the significance of the past in a way he could not do unaided. "The
life of the Custom-House lies like a dream behind me," he says at the conclusion to his prefatory notes. "Soon, likewise, my old native town will loom
upon me through the haze of memory, a mist brooding over and around it;
as if it were no portion of the real earth, but an overgrown village in cloud-
land. . . . Henceforth, it ceases to be a reality of my life. I am a citizen of
somewhere else" ("The Custom House" 44). Representation is always a form
of repetition, but Hawthorne's tenure in Salem conspired to achieve a paradoxical end: not the affirmation that he is a man wedded to a single place,
but the erasure or negation of any single place for totally describing his
identity. Hawthorne's involvement with Salem, he is careful to note, is not
to represent it but to perform it for the sake of another audience.

The ritual of accepting employment in the Custom House is important
insofar as it re-establishes a connection to Puritan sources; it is organized
around the elimination of its own pretext. The Other—that is, his recovery
of place—is celebrated as the narrative flows back completely into the seventeenth century, where the fascination he felt in the garret is renewed in a

larger dramatic space. The significance of so many objects stuffed into the narratives of Hawthorne and Mather is the preservation of a rich source of ambivalent things that could be mined for exhibition and display.

Mather, Hawthorne, and Unexpected Survivals

Both *Magnalia* and Hawthorne's tales depend on things that unexpectedly survived within their works.[31] Mather's great accomplishment—seen, for example, in his *Life of John Winthrop*—was his ability to convert the scant historical record of a given time and place into the kind of historical portrait that has made *Magnalia* a source book for the study of colonial New England.

This conversion is made possible in the first place by taking one man's limited public accomplishments—Winthrop's plain style of dress and conversation, his aversion to drinking toasts, his easy intercourse with inferiors, and a number of his most important speeches—and transforming them through the author's imaginative comparison of the man to a wide range of exemplary figures drawn from classical sources and the Reformation. As a chronicle history, *Magnalia* links the lives of many of Mather's cherished figures with published and unpublished documents in an effort to depict Winthrop within the framework of an ongoing historical enterprise.

We see similar signs of this process in Hawthorne's description of the General Collector, a man whose unexpected survival through the battles at Fort Ticonderoga gives Hawthorne the material he needs to resurrect his portrait. As Hawthorne describes this labor, "To observe and define his character, however, under such disadvantages, was as difficult a task as to trace out and build up anew, in imagination, an old fortress, like Ticonderoga, from a view of its gray and broken ruins. Here and there, perchance, the walls may remain almost complete; but elsewhere may be only a shapeless mound, cumbrous with its very strength, and overgrown" ("The Custom House" 21).

We know that Mather brought the significance of his own family line and a sense of his personal reputation to *Magnalia*'s presentation of a comprehensive historical design within his church history. "I feel the Lord Jesus Christ most sensibly carrying on, the Interests of His Kingdom, in my soul, continually," wrote Cotton Mather, and so directing "me to become a Remembrancer unto the Lord, for no less than whole Peoples, Nations, and

Kingdoms." The self that Mather vaunted he thought to be the fulfillment of the suprapersonal destiny that Ezekiel had promised. In becoming representative of what a person of his stature could do by arranging carefully the aspects of the past that he had acquired, Mather sought to be the bridge between himself and the world that was slipping away.

In his description of Mather, Hawthorne takes great pains to draw parallels to the vision he gave to readers of himself as an avid scavenger among cluttered spaces. In *Grandfather's Chair*, Mather is made over into an enacted self for Hawthorne, a wax figure like the one in Peale's exhibition room:

> On entering the room you would probably behold it crowded, and piled, and heaped with books. There were huge, ponderous folios and quartos, and little duodecimos, in English, Latin, Greek, Hebrew, Chaldaic, and all other languages, that either originated at the confusion of Babel, or have since come into use.
>
> All these books, no doubt, were tossed about in confusion, thus forming a visible emblem of the manner in which their contents were crowded into Cotton Mather's brain. And in the middle of the room stood a table, on which, besides printed volumes, were strewn manuscript sermons, historical tracts, and political pamphlets, all written in such a queer, blind, crabbed, fantastical hand, that a writing-master would have gone raving mad at the sight of them. . . . In this chair, from one year's end to another, sat that prodigious book-worm, Cotton Mather, sometimes devouring a great book, and sometimes scribbling one as big. In Grandfather's younger days, there used to be a wax figure of him in one of the Boston museums, representing a solemn, darked-visaged person, in a minister's black gown, and with a black-letter volume before him. (93–94)

The relationship, formed in the special connection between the writer and his sources, is what Hawthorne aspires to in "The Custom House" when he writes, "as if the printed book, thrown at large on the wide world, were certain to find out the divided segment of the writer's own nature, and complete his circle of existence by bringing him into communion with it" (3–4).

But, as Hawthorne knew, in "The Minister's Black Veil" both his own work and the admired work of Mather operated in such a way as to shield the innermost personality of the writer behind the very profundity of culture that they strove mightily to place in their books.

But as thoughts are frozen and utterance benumbed, unless the speaker stands in some true relation to his audience, it may be pardonable to imagine that a friend, a kind and apprehensive, though not the closest friend, is listening to our talk; and then, a native reserve being thawed by this genial consciousness, we may prate of the circumstances that lie around us, and even of ourself, but still keep the inmost Me behind its veil. (18)

The fact that Mather showed how a historian could manipulate a history based not only on the consideration of a lost or destroyed sensibility but through its unexpected survival attracted Hawthorne to the idea that a historian could form a work that intimated the presence of a larger community of voices and skills.

A passage in Hawthorne's "Custom House" makes clear the potential of contextual history:

It will be seen likewise, that this Custom-House sketch has a certain propriety, of a kind always recognized in literature, as explaining how a large portion of the following pages came into my possession, and as offering proofs of the authenticity of a narrative therein contained. This, in fact,— a desire to put myself in the true position as editor, or very little more, of the most prolix among the tales that make up my volume,—this, and no other is my true reason for assuming a personal relation with the public. In accomplishing the main purpose, it has appeared allowable, by a few extra touches, to give a faint representation of a mode of life not heretofore described, together with some of the characters that move in it, among whom the author happened to make one. (4)

That the historian himself could join with his sources as part of the entire project was also a source of great pleasure. *Magnalia* made the pursuit of history a search driven by a fantasy of possession. History, seen as a resonant exhibition like *Magnalia*, pulls its viewers away from the celebration of isolated things and directs attention toward a series of implied, half-visible relationships and questions. Hawthorne's visitor to the virtuoso's collection feels the allure of possession but is surprised, as many are, that an illusion like the one conveyed in Peale's self-portrait is at work.[32]

I observed a curtain that descended from the ceiling to the floor in voluminous folds, of a depth, richness, and magnificence which I had never seen equalled. It was not to be doubted that this splendid, though dark and solemn veil, concealed a portion of the Museum even richer in wonders than that through which I had already passed. But, on my attempting to grasp the edge of the curtain and draw it aside, it proved to be an illusive picture. ("The Virtuoso's Collection" 492)

Hawthorne tells us that another of these half-visible relationships was the fact that Grandfather's chair held private chats with a select few of its owners, including Phips and Mather. " 'And have you often held a private chat with your friends?' asked Grandfather. 'Not often,' answered the chair. 'I once talked with Sir William Phips, and communicated my ideas about the witchcraft delusion. Cotton Mather had several conversations with me, and derived great benefit from my historical reminiscences' " (207). Though Mather chose, by his arrangement of individual biographies, to suggest a line of narrative development leading to a conclusion—namely, that the story of New England was in an intermediate position between fulfillment and greater fulfillment of the original "errand into the wilderness"—that conclusion is not the only one possible.[33] Part of *Magnalia*'s great appeal is that by its very variety and strangeness, it is by itself capable of importing a great deal of studied ambiguity into any discussion of Puritanism. Like Grandfather's chair, Mather's history has a generational appeal that moves forward in history in spite of its enormous weight. In fact, the representative nature of the work depends as much on properties associated with the collector and arranger as it does with the sources themselves.[34] The Grandfather who describes Mather to his grandson is well aware of this forward progression: "*Magnalia* is a strange, pedantic history, in which true events and real personages move before the reader, with the dreamy aspect which they wore in Cotton Mather's singular mind. . . . as he was the author of more books than there are days in the year, we may conclude that he wrote a great deal, while sitting in this chair" (92). A history that bears traces of an author's manipulations amplifies the reader's confusion between events and the objects implicated in the actions that describe the event itself. That is the implication of Peale's pulling back the curtain to reveal the inner contents of his museum.

The notion that a man can be so completely subsumed in the rhythms of cultural rehearsal is paramount to the authenticity we sense in Peale's museum, in *Magnalia*, and in novels like *The Scarlet Letter*. But the openness displayed in each of these can easily make us lose sight of the fact that the people responsible for these rehearsals might be pursuing other aims—financial enrichment, public displays of egotism, and creative marketing in a competitive marketplace. This possibility became increasingly important for Hawthorne's work because he was aware that Jacksonian democracy consistently used the inheritable past as a "currency" for waging intracultural debates on liberty, individualism, and manifest destiny. Further, Jacksonian democracy was a culture feeding on consolidation, and Hawthorne, in his pioneering exploration of different arrangements of history's materials, sought to reterritorialize New England's historical situation. Consequently, this fiction combining the antiquarianism of museums with political sensibilities educates Hawthorne's readers. Hawthorne's *Grandfather's Chair* makes plain that literature is both an artificially framed world with an organized structure governing its interpretation and a part of a larger structure determined by economic, institutional, and ideological forces that govern its composition, its publication, its circulation, its reading, and the end—canonization or obscurity—to which it is read.[35] A consequence that emerged from Jacksonian democracy was the fact that someone like Peale could manufacture a self and make that self appear to be engaged in purposeful work. The Reverend Cutler's mistaken identification of the wax figure for the flesh and blood Peale is a classic recognition of a strange but powerful suggestion about wonder-cabinets and their collectors. If the likeness of the collector can be so convincing among the items in his collection, people can assume that his identity is co-extensive with its context when, in fact, the artist's true interests may lie elsewhere altogether. Peale's wax figure, in a slightly different guise, is a logical consequence of the openness we have already established as a precondition of cabinets of curiosity.

Hawthorne's Foregrounding of Resonance

Both Mather and Hawthorne labored hard to present a public face that would conceal their personal commitment to aspects of life that they knew ran at cross-purposes to the expectations of readers who thought their work somehow symbolic. The importance of being a writer whose work evokes in readers a continual sense of resonance (as opposed to wonder) is a lesson that Hawthorne learned from *Magnalia*. Mather, who erected an image of himself as the redeemer of the intentions of the first settlers' vision, was in fact aware that their vision was based on an order that could not survive in America. Although to many, Mather was simply the distinguished, filiopietistic son of Increase Mather, he actually engaged in activities that involved multiple self-fashionings, and many of those selves worked conspicuously against the designs of his father's beliefs. Mather's interest in reaping the excitement of physico-theology in the witchcraft delusion, his need to be an insider in the political order initiated by the new charter, and his paradoxical interest in the Royal Society at a time when he was one of the foremost adherents of chiliasm in New England, all indicate that Mather's identity as a third-generation "divine" was being pushed to the very edge of what had been previously expected of a Puritan minister. To be of one's own time and yet capable of entering fully another, prior culture was Cotton Mather's legacy, embodied in the 1820 edition of *Magnalia*.

A position like Mather's—multiple, dispersed in the interests and materials of his culture offered Hawthorne the greatest artistic license to practice his own rehearsals of New England. It is appropriate to think of Hawthorne, Stowe, and Stoddard in terms of cultural separations—personal motives from politics, the past from the present, authority from identity. Each of their works to one degree or another reconciles this crisis in legitimization as Mather did: by positing an anthropological fallacy at the center of all representations of historical destiny. Emerson's "humble-bee" is a mere token of the virtuoso's collection (554).

Recall D. H. Lawrence's observation about Hawthorne: "You must look through the surface of American art, and see the inner diabolism of the symbolic meaning. Otherwise it is all mere childishness. That blue-eyed darling Nathaniel knew disagreeable things in his inner soul. He was careful to send them out in disguise" (93). Lawrence's point is that Hawthorne knew that the American preoccupation with anthropological fallacies made transcendentalism blind to social reality. Transcendentalism's highly wrought symbolism is an art of high ideals removed from social reality, and that is why it was so easily valorized by this century's modernists.

If Grandfather's chair generates any historical significance, it does so because it echoes many of the resonant discourses that have touched it, not because it is an object of unmitigated wonder. Grandfather says:

> any other old chair, if it possessed memory, and a hand to write its recollections, could record stranger stories than any that I have told you. From

generation to generation, a chair sits familiarly in the midst of human interests, and is witness to the most secret and confidential intercourse, that mortal man can hold with his fellow. . . . The imagination can hardly grasp so wide a subject, as is embraced in the experience of a family chair. (65)

Hawthorne could not subscribe to a "visionary compact" as Donald Pease has suggested he did along with Whitman and Emerson. His view of the writer in connection to history was deeply at odds with the transcendentalists' views, primarily because their notion that the self is rendered in a truthful relation to its surroundings was meant to evoke wonder, to celebrate man's image at the expense of contingency. Hawthorne knew (and Mather would have guessed) that Emerson's all-seeing eye implied that the human self was capable of standing in a privileged relation to the culture that supports it.

If Hawthorne were to create a distinctively New England voice, involving "psychological" characteristics, popular mythologies, and his choice to be under the influence of Puritanism, had to be conceived according to his role as a writer somewhat at odds with the prevailing tenets of Romanticism. The fact that he conceived of himself as fundamentally different from the other literary men of Concord is a point that Hawthorne made at the conclusion of "The Old Manse." There he said, "The treasure of intellectual gold, which I hoped to find in our secluded dwelling, had never come to light. No profound treatise of ethics—no philosophic history—no novel, even, that could stand, unsupported, on its edges. . . . such trifles, I truly feel, afford no solid basis for a literary reputation" (34). Hawthorne's rehearsals of culture, in referring back to openness and historical contingency, depend on echoed truths buried in the past. There is seldom an idealized symbol in Hawthorne's work. The scarlet "A" is a prime example. Whatever significance it has is the product of the many discourses—feminine, sexual, historical, moral, aesthetic, Puritan, occult—behind it.

The example of Colonial Williamsburg also has some bearing here. That community, founded to be a "living museum" depicting colonial Virginia life, is not really a single town but two towns. One Williamsburg is the one offered for easy consumption by day-tripping visitors interested in handcrafted antiques of great value. The antiquarian, the connoisseur, the tourist, and the wealthy are drawn to the sense of wonder in a place that uses the materials and techniques of the past to produce objects of great beauty that are synonymous with the labor and skill of its artisans.

The other Williamsburg is the town that appeals to cultural historians, preservationists, and students. This town is marked by decaying structures, archaeological digs, and construction materials hidden by "weather-beater" paint. Long ago, a decision was made to try to supplant the notion of wonder created by Williamsburg with a sense of the resonance of the place. Consequently, Williamsburg's mission, in its fullest articulation, has been to act as a vital example of a wonder-cabinet of early Virginia history in which the mindless details and implements of kitchens, fields, taverns, blacksmith shops, and government centers are fully displayed and rehearsed for the public according to the normal cycles of the days of the year. Although people are no doubt astonished by the beauty of the Wren building on the campus of William and Mary, or awed by the governor's house in the center of the village, Williamsburg works because it is dedicated to the idea that portraying the "authentic" rhythms of rehearsed life in another time is the best way to bring the resonance of the past to audiences of the present. Of course, Williamsburg is the very essence of well-studied intention, but the same general approach for understanding the importance of Puritanism— the evocation of resonance through accumulated detail—lies at the heart of Hawthorne's contextual history.

Chapter Four

"Wreathing the Pearls upon the Straight Thread of Puritan Life"

✛

Penelopean Rehearsals of New England History in *The Minister's Wooing*

This chapter considers the rehearsal of Mather's *Magnalia* in Harriet Beecher Stowe's novel *The Minister's Wooing*. Mather was concerned with the representation of political personality in *Pietas in Patriam*. Stowe is also concerned with exemplaristic personality, and she creates two characters, Aaron Burr and Mary Scudder, to dramatize the operation of fictional identities that organize her own (and her readers') sense of historical contingency. Stowe connects her novel with Mather's "Life of Phips" in order to show how New England's political ambition (rooted in notions of regional exceptionalism) works to isolate further and disable effective political activity. Mather's "Life of Phips" became "multiaccentual" as New England's political machinery faltered in the sectional politics of the 1850s.

Stowe's novel animates the presence of New Politics (which demoted sectional points of view in favor of a "national" policy) after Zachary Taylor's election in 1848. In the first section of this chapter I describe Stowe's fictional method as being a "Penelopean" effort in which her female protagonist moves repeatedly across the boundaries defining political power. The second section examines the sheltering of politics within domestic fictions. And in the third I suggest that Stowe inverts the generic conventions of romance in order to suggest to her readers that New England's political aspirations have conspired to frustrate the course of sectional politics before the Civil War.

In *The Minister's Wooing*, Stowe frames New England politics in a highly complex way. She examines politics from three interrelated and dependent vantage points: the 1690s, the 1790s, and the 1850s. Stowe examines New England's political legacy from the 1690s as a competition among Calvinist ideologies. She depicts Cotton Mather as exemplifying a counter-tradition to her own Connecticut Valley experience of Edwardseanism. Stowe uses Mather to accomplish a technical criticism of "disinterested benevolence" by humanizing an evangelical Congregationalist doctrine through a recovery of Mather's contingent portrayal of the state of religion in *Magnalia*. Stowe saw opportunity in Mather largely because the decline of Puritanism became pronounced in the early national period. The uncertainty over Calvinism's core ideology in the early nineteenth century provided Stowe with an ideal literary setting in which to modernize Calvinist belief: Newport in the early national period.[1] Her revaluation of the past was necessitated by a residual Unitarian and orthodox Calvinist culture. Her interest in New England's legacy-ism was motivated in part by biographical circumstance and by market opportunities for specifically New England fiction. During a time when many in New England realized that their futures depended on the settlement of the West, Stowe took an inward turn by choosing to re-examine a New England in danger of becoming anachronistic. George Bancroft (and Unitarian liberals like Hawthorne) had defined Calvinism as the germ of the spirit of liberty. Stowe and other less liberal critics charged that Calvinism's "distinguishing doctrines" referred to social realities unaccounted-for by liberal formulations of Calvinism. Stowe felt that her literature must address a greater nominalism within Calvinism in order to be true to spiritual and social realities that were obscured by attempts to reduce Calvinist ideology to moral universals or specious concepts (Buell, *New England Literary Culture* 273).

In the context of the 1790s—the early national period—Stowe saw in Aaron Burr a panoply of problems affecting the Jacksonian democracy of the 1830s and 1840s. The correlation between Martin Van Buren, the "Little Magician," and Aaron Burr is indicative of the manner in which Stowe views government. For Stowe the imperative of democratic leadership is to merge the government of souls and lives, families and children, and the state and its leaders with the issue of how to become the best possible governor.[2] Van Buren was aided in his efforts on behalf of Jackson by a group known as the Richmond Junto: Thomas Richie, editor of the *Richmond Enquirer*; Duff Green of the *United States Telegraph*; Amos Kendall, editor of the *Argus of Western America*, a Jacksonian paper in Kentucky; and Vice President John

C. Calhoun. Van Buren worked extensively to develop local political organizations in all the states, and he sought to form a national chain of pro-Jackson newspapers. In his advice to Jackson, Van Buren urged vagueness, and his recommendations produced satisfactory results, for Jackson pledged to pursue careful tariffs and purge the corruption of John Quincy Adams's administration and defined himself as a supporter of states' rights. Van Buren and his aides were very successful in their creation of an extensive political machine. Jackson committees were created on community and county levels. They were joined to a state "central committee," which coordinated their activities and raised money. Van Buren staged numerous political events at which "Hurra Boys" presided over parades, barbecues, and rallies.

In the era of New Politics, Stowe savagely attacked the duplicitous character of politicians like Burr, Van Buren, and Zachary Taylor. These men, so lacking in their capacity as leaders, demanded that government be defined in a manner that differentiates between traditional (and primarily male) abilities and the power of politics to coordinate social activity. To this end Mary Scudder and the domestic tactics that Stowe employed in *The Minister's Wooing* are meant to demonstrate that the sovereignty of government resides in the things it manages. If readers accept this inversion, the multiform tactics of the marital relationship are much more effective than obedience to legislative law. Later in her life, Harriet would see her brother Henry Ward Beecher drawn into the political jungle of the Republican party. In columns written in the *Independent*, Henry would discover that behind the seemingly simple façade of northern and southern political rhetoric lay deeply deterministic notions of the manifold ways in which an industrialized society abused the lives of its citizens. In Van Buren and Burr, Stowe encountered directly the early stirrings of Jackson's hold over the people.

Writing about a European trip that Stowe made shortly after the publication of *Uncle Tom's Cabin* in 1850, Milton Rugoff claims, "although [Stowe] was still conservative in her moral judgements, an innate romanticism persuaded her to let down her guard. . . . she was seduced by Europe's art, so she was intoxicated by the sensuous rituals—the incense, organ music, stained glass—of the great Catholic cathedrals" (334–35). That experience of a local realism threatened by romantic corruption forms a major subtheme in *The Minister's Wooing*. The subversion of local tradition by specious ideology also frames her political insights into the nature of democracy in the nineteenth century. Burr was an ideal character on which to hang these scattered considerations, for he bridged the Calvinist past (he was Jonathan Edwards's grandson) and was a harbinger of the new politics of the 1850s (a political model for Martin Van Buren).

Aaron Burr represented the corruption of New England's sturdy ideals. As an artist, Stowe recognized that romances aided a more general corrosive program being enacted in party politics. In Paris, the painters John Vanderlyn and Washington Allston received the patronage of Aaron Burr. He sent them to Gilbert Stuart as pupils and personally underwrote a trip for them to France. Their experience of failure despite financial patronage was allegorically significant to Stowe. Page Smith informs us that "After years of study in Paris and Rome, Vanderlyn returned to the United States to waste a substantial talent painting second-rate versions of a third-rate school of painting" (922). Allston painted the unfinished *Belshazzar's Feast*, which was intended as a "national specimen of American art" but instead was seen by Americans as "a metaphor of the uncertain state of the visual arts in the republic" (Smith 923).

Stowe was able to provide her feminine audience with convincing examples of authentic domestic government because the basis of democratic life was not the objective ensemble of "subjects" and "territories." Instead, legitimate power was constituted within the relationships that exist between the governing and the governed. Again, because these relationships were seen to be "sincere" and best managed by women, the nexus of political activity was seen as consummately feminine. Readers, no doubt confused by the triple layering of historical periods and concerns, were made to understand Stowe's conceits by means of the ingenious character of Mary Scudder. Mary Scudder reflects, under the guise of simplistic purity, a personality recognizable as the popular antebellum stereotype of the "female saint," and she is also "an exemplum of humanization within the Edwardsean tradition" (Buell, *New England Literary Culture* 275). In creating the character of Scudder and framing larger cultural questions about how American identity expressed itself in historical romance, Stowe capitalized on Mather's *Magnalia*. In that text, she saw clues for insinuating an author's literary commentary within larger debates about regional and national identity. The physical surroundings of Newport and the exemplaristic types that Stowe carefully depicts never act as a neutral filter or frame. Instead, they always point to the cultural encoding of Puritanism, which, as Mather suggested, is tenuously linked to the political circumstances of authorship.

At a crucial point in *The Minister's Wooing*, Stowe pauses to tell her readers, "There is no word in the English language more unceremoniously and indefinitely kicked and cuffed about, by what are sensible people, than the word *romance*" (598). Stowe's concern with romance is important because it signals that her novel, a superficially domestic romance treating social customs and moral conditions in post-Revolutionary Newport, is really a double enterprise.

In the scant criticism available on *The Minister's Wooing*, the novel is consistently read as a text intimately concerned with Edwardsean Calvinism. Lawrence Buell finds the novel useful in "tracing the legacy of Edwardseanism, which used to be known as *the* 'New England theology' " ("Calvinism Romanticized" 119). Christopher Wilson sees the novel's central protagonist—a "reincarnated" Puritan, Mary Scudder—as a pious maiden whose "intuitive, feminine influence counterbalances, and ultimately outperforms, the stoical and all-too-logical doctrine of post-Edwardsean Calvinism" ("Tempests and Teapots" 554). Both of these critics identify the basic hybrid nature of Stowe's text: *The Minister's Wooing* is "about" a representative figure of Puritanism and "about" a peculiarly New England tradition. Buell and Wilson see the experience of Mary Scudder as fully emblematic of a mode of religious piety struggling to maintain authority in a secularized world.

Viewing *The Minister's Wooing* as a sophisticated act of historical criticism better explains Stowe's continuing interest in Puritanism. Within the novel, Puritanism is depicted as a philosophy whose exigent unfolding leads inexorably to a conclusion, fully anticipated in advance by readers. Stowe's romanticism demands that the historical legacy of New England be told in a succession of feminine anecdotes. However, *The Minister's Wooing* is far from being an absolute, unavoidable, and self-realizing phenomenon (as might be said of Hawthorne's portrayal of Puritan themes). Stowe repackages *Magnalia* as so many *historemes*—the smallest units of historiographic fact—that the heroines experience in peculiar and eventful moments. Because Stowe correctly assumed that Puritanism was the "already" realized end of New England history, the determining force of that tradition momentarily unfolds into an otherwise formulaic romance. Further, it is in the momentary recollections of its own historicity that Stowe's narrative, with its twin plot structures, comes to merge with its inevitable conclusion. The spirit of Puritan authority is registered in the domestic anecdote.

Stowe's suspicion of the nineteenth-century belief that all history had to be rewritten in forms that testified to a retrospective and evolutionary sense of progress guided her forays into Mather's historicism. Stowe found it advantageous to animate her political and social concerns within the apparent boredom of ordinary life. Her romantic antiquarianism was not harmless or trivial, however, for she endeavored to write fiction that seemed to flow naturally out of democratic ideals of domesticity. Many critics have addressed Stowe's sophisticated manipulations of domestic ideology.[3] In this chapter, I am less interested in covering this familiar territory than in tracing Stowe's spectacle of a domestic fiction that "sheltered" a political sensibility originally recorded in Mather's *Magnalia*.

In practice, Stowe's fictional "criticism" of the particular "past" of Newport society during the early republic has two aspects. First, it is a glimpse into the author's potential to become a "feminine authority" in a world where few existed. Second, Stowe's criticism tries to contain a complex, legendary fiction about New England's origins within a narrative frame that points out its own constructedness.

The Minister's Wooing animates many of the religious and political concerns in antebellum New England. Set in the slave-trading community of Newport at the close of the eighteenth century, Stowe's historical romance centers on the experiences of the moral exemplar Mary Scudder. Mary is a pious "little Puritan" who stands at the center of a community of Congregationalists that is growing ever smaller under the guidance of a post-Edwardsean minister, Dr. Hopkins. Throughout the book, Mary's intuitive feminine and republican cast of mind is balanced against Dr. Hopkins's stoic and logical theology.

Mary's faith is tested by the suspected drowning of her beloved cousin James Marvyn and by her betrothal to Hopkins, whom she loves more out of maternal duty than passionate interest. In the end, Mary's feminine faith outperforms the logically correct theology of Hopkins. With him, as with many other important characters in the book, Mary manages to establish a new order of belief where a previous doctrine had failed.

Mary's intuitive negotiations of personal matters, though central to the plot of the book, are only a segment within the larger historical tableau that Stowe arranges in the narrative. *The Minister's Wooing* is a novel populated by freed slaves, an avaricious businessman, a visiting French aristocrat and his wife, and a fictive (but potent) Aaron Burr. The locus of Burr's importance for Stowe, of course, is the fact that he is a renegade grandson of Jonathan Edwards. "Harriet paints Burr as a hypnotically fascinating mixture," says Rugoff. "Having abandoned the religion of his grandfather Jonathan Edwards, he seemed to illustrate the dangers of both religious over-indoctrination and complete rejection. . . . As we have since learned, Aaron Burr was indeed sexually a satyr" (*The Beechers* 347).

Doubtlessly, Stowe divided herself (and her sympathies) unequally among these various characters. Dorothy Berkson, who has considered Stowe's millennial politics in light of her feminist opinions, writes, "[She] was in a unique position to understand the pervasive influence religion had on political and social institutions" ("Millennial Politics" 246). However, most critics, including Berkson, have faulted Stowe for seeing through the particularities of her own time in favor of a theocracy that Parrington called "enveloped in a haze of romance" (*Main Currents* 2:371).[4] Predictably, most of these accusations derive from her portrayal of Jonathan Edwards's role in New England intellectual history in *Oldtown Folks*. Stowe's rejection of Edwardsean Calvinism in that book has been seen as an act of rebellion against her father's influence and authority over her and a possible explanation for her embrace of Anglicanism.

Charles Foster's original claims about Stowe's "influence" derived from Puritan documents fail to account for her close reading of Mather's *Magnalia*. If we view the rejection of Edwards's position by the light of that book—which is to say a somewhat *strange* light—Stowe's rejection of a doctrine rooted in experience was only a shrewd and knowledgeable reading of Mather's claim for a fundamental contingency within Puritanism itself.[5] If we examine more closely the processes of historical negotiations registered in the novel, I am persuaded that we will find not only a complicated and rich narrative work that surpasses the limiting accounts of Stowe as a novelist concerned with a simple dialectic of themes (the competition of head versus heart) but also the portrayal of a liberalized theology.

Stowe capitalized on the various (re)presentations of history made available by the publication of the 1820 Robbins edition of *Magnalia*. She used Mather to negotiate a cultural space for the practice of her authorship and to promote a compelling and counterfactual reading of New England's position within an evolving national culture. *Magnalia* was a very important text for Stowe. Forrest Wilson claims that "along with the *Arabian Nights*, Mather's *Magnalia* was Stowe's favorite childhood book, for these wonderful stories of witches, of Indian raids, and of awful punishments that had overtaken sinners, were about America and were, moreover true" (53). In her autobiographical notes, Stowe wrote about the Hartford edition of 1820: "There was one of my father's books that proved a mine of wealth to me. It was a happy hour when he brought home and set up in his bookcase Cotton

Mather's *Magnalia* in a new edition of two volumes. What wonderful stories those! . . . Stories that made me feel the very ground I trod on to be consecrated by some special dealing of God's providence" (qtd. in E. Wilson 117).[6]

Stowe, like Mather before her, frames reading events in order to make the point that her characters (and all of us) decisively modify the cultural work done by a text. Stowe's aim is to free up the present generation of readers (and writers) for meaningful political and moral action of its own by placing the past in a critical or realistic perspective. At the heart of Stowe's historical enterprise is the underlying question, Why do we subscribe to fantasies that cannot nourish or sustain an individual's political autonomy? Stowe's answer to that question, in part, is power: power's quintessential sign is the ability to impose one's fictions upon the world. The more outrageous the fiction, the more impressive is the display of power. Stowe's specifically political intent in *The Minister's Wooing* to address the New Politics in American culture.

When Zachary Taylor was asked in 1848 if he would consider being a presidential candidate, he declared the idea "too visionary to require a serious answer." Taylor wrote that "the thought had never entered my head nor is it likely to enter the head of any sane person" (qtd. in Smith). Taylor, a man who was assumed to be a Whig in the Mexican War but who had never voted in any election, was typical of the New Politics engendered by sectional interests. Taylor was a wealthy Kentucky plantation owner (one of only eighteen hundred who owned more than a hundred slaves), and he publicly hinted that he was opposed to the extension of slavery to the western territories. His only real claim to the office of president, besides his obscure political views, was the record of his victories in the Mexican War, which he had opposed. In the familiar pageantry of presidential elections, the contest between Lewis Cass and Taylor was marked by the burning of Whig headquarters in New Orleans and the arrest of a drunken prostitute in Philadelphia who gave her name as Rough and Ready.

Only when we pass from the apparent confidence, flexibility, and authenticity of Stowe's historical romance to the deeply contentious and anxious social realm in the troubled decade prior to the Civil War do we see lived experience as a threatening, absurd proposition. To many, the election of Zachary Taylor seemed to suggest that American politics was a dangerous balance of rickety alliances. Taylor's "authority" came from his attempt to be all things to all people, and he positioned himself as being above narrow party politics. Nevertheless, the election results showed that Taylor's success had as much to do with Van Buren's hatred of Lewis Cass, which split the Democratic party, as it did with Taylor's strength as an executive leader. The chaos inherent in the New Politics frames Stowe's occasional realism in *The Minister's Wooing*. A satirical verse from the Taylor campaign bears affinities to Stowe's recognition that her culture was moving away from romantic illusions:

Extra Cass—
Pray, tell me, Rough and Ready,
How did it come to pass
That you were made a President,
And I was made an ass?

Rough and Ready—
Sir, you would play the demagogue,
And practice mystifying,
Until enveloped in a fog,
All human eyes defying;
In such a guise, no friend could C you;
And so, poor *ass*, they tho't they'd flee you. (qtd. in Smith 1062)

This verse, betraying a cynical and insubstantial democracy, neatly framed a political situation in which sectional antagonisms emerged in congressional resolutions that Thomas Benton of Missouri called "false in their facts, incendiary in their temper, disunion in their object, nullification in their essence, high treason in their remedy, usurpation in their character" (qtd. in Smith 1064). Taylor's incoherent origins as a president were substantially overcome when his work on the Wilmot Proviso and the Fugitive Slave Law showed him to be quite judicious in the execution of government. His premature death served only to foster the illusion that "the exciting topics of a sectional character" were in the saddle and threatened to trample the democratic process.

Stowe's novel responds to the New Politics through its rhetorical allusions to the readers' world. The agreement she forms, with the aid of Mather, is to shuttle back and forth between the characters of Mary and Aaron Burr so that when Mary enters the social stage of politics, her moral importance is heightened, and when she is forced to "retreat" into the kitchen, that move does not diminish her moral authority. Mather's anticipation that weakness becomes strength in a shifting setting where the moral landscape is frequently out of synch with political reality is a favorite aspect of Stowe's reading of *Magnalia*. Mary Scudder and Aaron Burr establish a set of correspondences between the disparate social and spiritual, public and private, and theological and political realms. The democratic concern of Stowe's authorship is an act of making history that shapes the rhetorical reality of the novel according to a political design. Stowe's novel manufactures historical meaning in the same manner that Mather's "Life of Phips" made William Phips an icon of New England's historical significance: it convinces people through the vigor of its representation of the virtues exemplaristic personality. Mary Scudder prevails in the novel because she has laid claim to the self-fashioning power that Zachary Taylor expressed in presidential politics. As sentimental fiction, Mary's politics are rendered as being contingent and circumscribed by her domesticity. Stowe attempts to convert the patriarchy of Mather's *Pietas in Patriam* into a matriarchal knowledge whose power to conceal purposeful political activity can be salvific to New England's political diminishment in sectional politics.

Stowe's direct concern with political representation resides in three linked aspects of the novel: the "Penelopean" activities of the novel's protagonist Mary Scudder and Stowe's narrative voice; the framing of democracy within domesticated fictions; and the counterfactual representation of New England as a moral icon for national history.

Mary Scudder is Stowe's means for fully animating the religious and political spirit of seventeenth-century Puritanism recorded in *Magnalia*. As a representative figure, Mary Scudder is committed to establishing and elaborating a system of exemplaristic representation.[7] Mary is a late-blooming Puritan in a veritable hothouse of competing and hypocritical interests. Her activities in Newport as a counselor are a means of exerting control over the dispersive and centrifugal energies of republican New England. Her own stature is powerful *because* it challenges the moral standing of the community at large.

The way in which Stowe makes Mary Scudder into an exemplary figure accords well with the thematic coherence of Puritanism. Experience is subordinated to idea in Mary's life, as she constructs the minutiae of life as instances of archetypes. Stowe informs us, "New England presents probably the only example of a successful commonwealth founded on a theory" (609). In the best tradition of Puritanism, Mary's ascent becomes a conference of significance on the novelty of New England life, and her life serves to fortify the authority of Protestant discourse.

Mary's rehearsal of Puritanism, which subordinates lived experience for some abstract exceptionalism, is just one aspect of Mary's personality. The other aspect is her ability to reveal a critical image of New England history. Mary is positioned within the novel so that three different historical periods—from the 1690s to the early eighteenth century of Jonathan Edwards, the post-Revolutionary period, and Stowe's own mid-nineteenth century—intersect in her daily activities. In this arrangement of the past, Mary condenses New England's identity. Consequently, Mary is a highly mobile heroine whose easy access to various strata of society enables her to perform subtle manipulations in the lives of others.

Stowe, in her complex use of narrative strategies, shows us that Mary frequently uncovers a distracting patina of particularity, unfamiliarity, and anomaly in the people and places she encounters. But as a character, she translates Stowe's highly refined interest in history into a feminized evangelicalism that urges readers to examine the minute details of Newport culture for evidence of an overall plan that could be used to explain the social pattern of their lives.

Stowe draws on the representational reserve of all her characters. She is careful in the novel to assert the pre-eminent role that fashioned identities play in creating the moral topography of Newport's colonial venture. Using Mary Scudder as a focal point for competing discourses about femininity, theology, and philosophical understanding, Stowe asks Mary Scudder to serve as a norm of identity for all "good" persons. Stowe uses Mary Scudder as a hermeneutic device for deciphering what James Fenimore Cooper called "names" and "things" in government. Cooper argued in *The American Democrat* (1838) that there was a "necessity of distinguishing between names and things in governments, as well as in other matters. The institutions of no country are rigidly respected in practice, owing to the cupidity and passions of men" (80). Because her role is forged in a direct experience of history, Mary uneasily bridges the perceived surface of the novel's romantic plot and its darker, more chaotic, subtexts.

Mary makes possible a collective scrutiny of Newport life. Her work operates on behalf of the community, staving off and regulating the excesses of Newport's immoral economy. She lifts the dissonances of actual historicity toward a certitude of readily recognizable abstractions that clarify (even as they coerce and legitimate) the social order of the 1790s. Following in the

Puritan tradition of Mather, Stowe pursues social power not through direct and explicit means but through the deployment of a core ideology composed of particular and hybrid local forms. And, as in *Magnalia*, the illusion of coherent representation is frequently undone by countervailing narrative strategies.

The emphasis of *The Minister's Wooing* is Stowe's development of a radical form of literary realism. Through passages that are technically brilliant and wickedly ironic, Stowe inserts moments of realism into the conventions of formulaic romance for the express purpose of disrupting and modifying her narrative's presumed meanings. Her novel unfolds according to a principle of partial concealment. The moments of intense realism in her story are realistic not because they are faithful reportage but because they form an account that *breaks through* or *outdistances* Stowe's (and her culture's) dominant means of representation.

The Minister's Wooing becomes, through its insistence on integrating historical understandings, a continuation of Mather's political specificity. Like *Magnalia*, Stowe's novel does not exist as a fully composed and tranquil recollection properly judged by its formal accomplishments. Rather, the novel gives form to furtive identifications, recognitions, and appreciations of Stowe's political insights. These epiphanic moments play constantly across the structured field of her text.

Stowe's seriousness in defining realism in conjunction with romance betrays her deep wish for a definition of realism that can be most useful for treating her politics. Her experiments in literary form are not immune from disparaging criticism. At one point in the novel Stowe says, "we foresee grave heads beginning to shake over our history, and doubts rising in reverend and discrete minds whether this is going to prove anything but a love story, after all" (601). At another juncture, Stowe senses impatience among her readers:

> Will our little Mary really fall in love with the Doctor [Hopkins]? — The question reaches us in anxious tones from all the circle of our readers; and what especially shocks us is, that grave doctors of divinity, and serious, stocking-knitting matrons seem to be the class who are particularly against the success of our excellent orthodox hero, and bent on reminding us of the claims of that unregenerate James, whom we have sent to sea on purpose that our heroine may recover herself of that foolish partiality for him that all the Christian world seems bent on perpetuating. (636)

As Christopher Wilson notes in "Tempests and Teapots," these passages "suggest the double-edged quality of Stowe's appeal to 'love-story' strategies." Wilson is content to see such instances in light of "orthodox religious objections" to Stowe's fiction. In any case, Stowe's intrusions into the reader's activity suggest the seductive and controlling nature of political narrative.

Stowe's theory of realism finds its clearest expression in the brief chapter titled "Which Treats of Romance." This chapter, coming as it does soon after James's departure at sea (thus setting the inexorable romantic machinery fully into motion), begins with the premise that "romance" has become an impoverished term in the popular discourse of Jacksonian culture. For the average reader, Stowe writes, all but the "dead grind" of making money is thrown "into one waste 'catch-all' and labelled *romance*" (598). In the Jacksonian period, when men have been reduced by economic circumstances to puerile calculations, the potential of the romance to stir the imagination is only a faint echo of poetry and courtship rituals: Mrs. T, the opera-going socialite, has only dim memories that "there was a man so noble, so true, so good" that to live with him in poverty was "a something nobler, better, purer, more satisfying, than French laces, opera-boxes, and even Madame Roget's best gowns" (599). Because Americans were weakened by a lust for foreign social rituals and tied to a petty capitalism, Stowe felt that translating the grace of a forgotten Puritan sensibility had become impossibly difficult by 1859.

What Americans needed, Stowe suggested, was a glimpse of the poetry of everyday life. Americans needed a stirring moment when the significant details of local experience could significantly outdistance any expectations forged in the pedantic operations of business and domesticity. It takes a person of "very common, self-interested aims and worldly nature" who is "busy with the *realities* of life" to re-ignite forgotten pleasures. As soon as Stowe has made this suggestion, she places it back into her larger concern for preserving the authority of Christianity: "Let us look up in fear and reverence and say, 'GOD is the great maker of romance. HE from whose hand came man and woman,—HE, who strung the great harp of Existence with all its wild and wonderful and manifold chords, and attuned them to one another,—HE is the great Poet of life'" (600). Here, Stowe's ideology of romance turns on the shuttling movement we have been describing in Mary's character. In a major key, Stowe asserts a totalizing presence of divinity. Stowe's humility before an authoritative abstraction, similar to the Puritan's own self-understanding, becomes a sign of the author's own attainment of grace. Puritan humility in the face of a complex natural and divine order thus becomes an emblem of the enlightened democratic individual. But, in a minor key, that self-abasement tends to show, in a stridently individualistic society, that there is a "history" trying to emerge from behind the romance.

Further, that "history" has a great deal to say about the limitations a romantic ideology places on human authority. The author is only "a second-hand recorder" (601). Stowe subscribes to the illusion that novelists who make romance sometimes merely delude the people who read romances. Her knowledge, transmitted to a largely unprepared audience, is the crux of Stowe's interest in raising the attentiveness of her readers. Using her theory of romance, Stowe attempts to bridge a gulf in her readership. As author, she is concerned with countering among democratic readers an ignorance that undermines fundamental civic virtues. The problem with Newport, Stowe suggests, does not lie in the fact that Hopkins and Brown represent the twin corruptions of theology and business. Rather, it lies in the fact that they are so easily convinced of their self-importance. Stowe's theory of romance penetrates and reconstructs naive estimates of character that Cooper pointed to in *The American Democrat*:

> Large democracies . . . are unable to scrutinize and understand character with the severity and intelligence that are of so much importance in all representative governments, and consequently the people are peculiarly exposed to become the dupes of demagogues and political schemers, most of the crimes in democracies arising from the faults and designs of men of this character, rather than the propensities of the people, who, having little temptation to do wrong, are seldom guilty of crimes except through ignorance. (128)

An informed readership ultimately serves the nation because it critically judges the versions of events that seem to most satisfy our deepest beliefs and longings. Stowe's political acuity is not validated through her fiction's connection to actual conditions in Newport (though her fiction is remarkably accurate in these details), nor is the novel principally concerned with the overhaul of inherited religious doctrines; instead, her textual strategies produce "reality effects" that attempt to disguise or arrest the intrinsic disbelief of her readers.

Restating then, Stowe's novel draws on a tradition of manufacturing exemplaristic personalities that serve the purpose of animating an ideological position. Mary Scudder's biography is a spiritualistic account of heroism similar to Mather's biographies of Winthrop, Phips, or Eliot. The lives of these Puritan divines suggested the overall boundaries of an ideology that could be crafted in accordance with the logic of an author's individual experience. The accounts of their lives aim at ordering the reader's perceptions of subjective democracy. Drawing on a set of *options* suggested by Mather's *Magnalia*, Stowe proceeds to narrate the story of James and Mary's conversion and love in such a way that the political ramifications of a corrupt democracy (illuminated by Puritanism) occasionally surface in moments that invite the reader's participation.

Stowe's episodes, because of their startling opacity, outdistance both the culture they refer to and the culture in which they are placed. In other words, Stowe's realistic moments complicate our original notions of exemplary figures as pure and transparent mediums of the ideology they express. At the same time, Stowe's work questions the visions and expectations of the culture engaging her work.

Stowe decides to deploy the comparatively ingenious insights of *Magnalia* by sequestering it in a darkened antechamber removed from direct light of day. In *The Minister's Wooing*, a proper discussion of Mather's role begins not at the beginning but in the seclusion of Katy Scudder's garret. There, Stowe informs us, "Garrets are delicious places . . . for people of thoughtful, imaginative temperament" (676). Stowe knew that readers would inevitably compare her room full of artifacts suggesting "quaint, cast-off, suggestive antiquity" — "worm-eaten chests," "rickety chairs," "boxes and casks full of odd comminglings" — to the historical realities of Newport, which she had taken great pains to bring into her narrative.

Stowe places *Magnalia* within her novel because it is one of those works "which you wish your Charley or your Susie to be sure and read." It is packed away in some obscure corner where inquisitive minds always go. And, in the midst of all the complicated plot twistings, which recall the moral theology of Jonathan Edwards and Mary Scudder's ascendant femininity, *Magnalia* resides like the "delicious pages of some romance which careful aunts had packed away at the bottom of all things." *Magnalia* situates itself within the novel's political and explicitly cultural concerns. Unwieldy though it is, *Magnalia* is "a trunk of stimulating rubbish . . . if the book be at all readable . . . and by any possible chance can make its way into a young mind, you may be sure that it will not only be read, but be remembered to the longest day they have to live" (676). If Mather's historiography is fundamentally ironic, then it appropriately resides in quarters alongside "a grand easy chair of stamped leather, minus two of its hinder legs, which had genealogical associations through the Wilcoxes with the Vernons" (recalling perhaps Hawthorne's *Grandfather's Chair*), and an "old tarnished frame, of a woman whose tragic end strange stories were whispered." Whether or not the book in the garret is actually the Robbins edition, this passage, when read in conjunction with the statement in her diary that *Magnalia* and the *Arabian Nights* were her own favorite childhood books, indicates that she sees Mather as "necessary" reading.

Where *Magnalia* enters *The Minister's Wooing*, it immediately frames the historical and political issues of Stowe's own times as a relationship between the surface and depths of Puritan ideology. To be sure, Jonathan Edwards and his theology dominate the novel's "surface." Edwardsean theology informs the plot and logically organizes choices made by the protagonists. The Edwardsean strain, which has been eagerly followed by the handful of critics who have discussed *The Minister's Wooing*, is quite pronounced. Hopkins is a "type" of Edwardsean Calvinist doctrine. There is not always an external occasion quite so explicit and notorious as Jonathan Edwards's renegade grandson appearing to woo the idealized, beautiful figure of a young Puritan lady in contact with "true virtue." Burr triggers the reader's realization that political forces are being played out according to an unpredictable script that Mather himself employed. Stowe implies that we should not always be looking to the Edwardsean theme for explanations. Rather, we should be attuned to a Mather whose political beliefs are so well known to Stowe that they must be considered "internal."

Stowe's use of a historically contingent literary realism transcribes some of the astonishing realities of Jacksonian democracy. The novel turns on moments that are discursively harmful to the novel's "romantic" texture. James, for instance, is raised to heroic stature, and Hopkins and Burr suffer a demotion. Stowe's manipulation of realism does not form an extradiscursive, extratextual, or extrahistorical authority; instead, it remains fully implicated in the specific coherences that Stowe sought to achieve. Nonetheless, her success sometimes becomes a contrary intention that she is powerless to control.

Believing that democracy frequently succeeded in advancing its causes through falsified or distorted frames of reality, Stowe shows ruthlessly that human destinies inevitably exceed a character's capacity to control matters.

Sharing a fundamental position that Mather held in *Magnalia*, Stowe suggests that human connections to history are fraught with reminders of human limitations and ironic episodes. Within our consciously held worldviews are immutable discrepancies between our intentions and actual performance. Stowe's partial concealments are wickedly mirrored in the thematic aspects of her work.

Within Stowe's interest in advancing an evangelical feminism is the realistic image of a woman knowledgeable about the secular and impure traffic of business and politics. In *The Minister's Wooing*, the definition of feminine individuality is developed dialectically by the interplay of Mary (prim, Puritan, Christ-like) and Virginie de Frontignac (adulteress, Catholic, corrupt). Karen Haltunnen assures us that "if Harriet Beecher Stowe shared with Henry Ward Beecher a sense of the diabolical powers of the fallen woman, she moved beyond him in seeing the positive potential of that demonic energy" ("Gothic Imagination" 122). This theme of a Puritan "realism" is challenged by a Catholic "romanticism." Poised as she is between her pious mother and the fallen Virginie, Mary has to steer a delicate course. Her intense need to filter romantic preoccupations through politics is mirrored in popular tales of young Protestant girls deceived and led astray in a world of hopelessly complicated and cryptic choices. Mary shows that a woman's exemplaristic status depends on a collateral exchange between ideas and experience.

A palpable subtext of Puritanism contains and shapes Mary Scudder's own "Penelopean" work in the novel. Anticipating Stoddard's later characterization of her historically minded protagonist Cassandra Morgeson, Stowe connects Mary to the obscure power that Mather tried to manage in his own world: "The face wears weird and tremulous lights and shadows; it asks us mysterious questions, and troubles us with the suggestions of our relations to some dim unknown. . . . A vague shuddering of mystery gave intensity to her reverie. It seemed as if those mirror-depths were another world" (774). Stowe's interest in democratic illusions requires that we see through the many beguiling surfaces into the depths Mary has seen. For instance, during the "theological tea" Stowe tells us, "You must not understand that this was what Mrs. Brown *supposed* herself to be thinking about; oh no! by no means! All the little, mean work of our nature is generally done in a small dark closet just a little back of the subject we are talking about, on a subject we suppose ourselves of course to be thinking;—of course we *are* thinking it; how else could we talk about it?" (555). How else indeed, unless we know that Mather has shown a receptive generation a decidedly ingenious way for recording the historical concerns of New England as a direct function of political authorship.[8] Stowe's and Mather's notions for animating history depend on the spirit (and the place) in which they ask their questions. As the narrator of *The Minister's Wooing* puts it, "New England presents . . . a distinct experiment in the problem of society. . . . Nobody, therefore, . . . was in the least surprised when there dropped into their daily life these sparkling bits of ore [that] . . . served to raise the hackneyed present out of the level of mere commonplace" (609–10). This observation captures the historical intent of both *Magnalia* and *The Minister's Wooing*. Each book is devoted to telling stories of cultural origins grounded on sound Congregational theory, which, by virtue of its contact with a chaotic, disruptive political environment, devolves into "sparkling bits of ore" that infrequently illuminate some fragmented but significant design.

"Some Special Dealing": Mary Scudder as Political Exemplar

Stowe crafted a novel combining a region's unique moral heritage with a corrective to a harsh theology. Mary Scudder is the figure who is made to carry the standards of the region. Stowe invests her with collective importance just as Mather made Winthrop live for all the Puritan divines. As Buell has pointed out, Mary's importance in the novel, for all its spiritual content, is primarily as a historical construct: "*The Minister's Wooing* is finally not a spiritual autobiography but historical fiction. Even its fantasy elements are responses to history as well as expressions of the author's psychic needs" ("Calvinism Romanticized" 122). In order to create a vessel capable of carrying the weight of the Puritan past into the late eighteenth century, Stowe was forced to create a character out of exceedingly complex materials.

In the *Odyssey*, Telemachus's mother frequently enters the narration in order to disrupt it. Penelope, who practices an artistry based on the "loom and the distaff," resists the pressure of her household to choose a new husband by performing the tedious task of unweaving at night the funeral pall for her father-in-law, Laertes, that she has woven during the day. Remaining in her bedroom, where all the men expect to find her, Penelope uses her work as a secret passage away from the expectations placed on her by the men around her. In the tedious interior of her room, she resists the entreaties of her suitors, even though they are fully aware that she is delaying for her own advantage. The moral exemplar, Penelope, helps frame the type of art that Stowe creates in *The Minister's Wooing*. Peggy Kamuf defines Penelopean art in these terms: "It ravels—which is to say it both untangles, makes something plain or clear, and entangles, or confuses, something. An alternative definition of the transitive verb 'to ravel' is 'to unravel.' . . . Penelopean work blurs the line between historical prerogatives and fictional pretensions, always deferring the promised end of its labor, unravelling clear historical patterns at its fictional border" (154–55).

In Mary Scudder Stowe creates an icon of a faithful, pious, chaste Puritan girl who shuttles between the figures of power in Newport. Mary's movement between the interior and exteriors of Newport's elite society, her intercession between the violence and poetry of Burr and Virginie, and her role in the working and simultaneous unworking of history in her contacts with the Reverend Hopkins frame the issue of a woman occupying a designated sphere while (at the same time) she negotiates the importance of the cultural discourse around her. Virginie, sitting at the spinning wheel, initiates a dialogue with Mary:

> "Do you know Burr told me that princesses used to spin? He read me a beautiful story from the 'Odyssey,' about how Penelope cheated her lovers with her spinning, while she was waiting for her husband to come home;— he was gone to sea, Mary,—her true love,—you understand." She turned on Mary a wicked glance, so full of intelligence that the snowdrop grew red as the inside of a sea-shell. (711–12)

Stowe, a Penelopean novelist-historian, describes within the text places where her story indicates its own undoing. She composes *The Minister's Wooing*, with all its complexities of invention, by ravelling the twin threads of fiction and history.

Mary's Penelopean work is Stowe's enacted self—it is her way of addressing the "infection in the sentence" raised by her source. The self-interruption, which echoes Mather, becomes symptomatic of the author's anxious temperament. Using Gilbert and Gubar's term "anxiety of authorship," we may say that the interrupted narrative in *The Minister's Wooing* reflects "an anxiety built from complex and often only barely conscious fears that authority which seems to the female artist to be by definition is inappropriate to her sex" (*Madwoman in the Attic* 51). Consequently, as Stowe reconstructs the historical example of Mather's *Magnalia*, she frequently breaks through the surface of her own text (thereby amply illustrating its "constructedness") in order to demonstrate that perceptions of human reality are concerted— and disconcerted—by systems of meaning through which gender is construed.[9] According to Robyn Warhol, Stowe relies on engaging narrative when her readers' sympathy is most crucial to her rhetorical purpose. Stowe's interruptions help to extend the referentiality of her fiction. The involvement of the author thus becomes an instance of metalepsis; the author's entrance into the narrative avoids reminding readers of the fictionality of Mary's identity. Fused as a heterdiegetic "I," Stowe and Mary equally work history from within and without the text ("Towards a Theory of the Engaging Narrator" 814–15).

Stowe's political allegory relies on abyssal self-representation: Mary Scudder attempts to inhabit two different and mutually exclusive spheres of understanding simultaneously. Consistent with her purpose of bringing Edwards into the mid-nineteenth century, Stowe is intent on diminishing his "authority" in the literary sense. Consequently, Stowe tips off her readers by saying that the story can tell itself only if she gets out of the way. Her narrative self-effacement is a logical outgrowth of her ongoing project to insinuate her activities as a writer into the political discourses she frames in the text. Mary, in her attempt to inherit the Puritan past fully and yet to engage in social negotiations, is made to occupy two different and mutually exclusive traditions at once. She is primarily a shuttling figure who mediates and enables historical understanding by weaving the fictional bases of New England (past and present) with the apprehension of a new order.

The complexity of Mary's character is sounded early in the novel: "There was something in Mary, however, which divided her as by an appreciable line from ordinary girls her age. From her father she had inherited a deep and thoughtful nature, predisposed to moral and religious exaltation" (539). Mary is made to mirror both the authentic and the illusory. In Mary, the importance of the New England past assumes a sort of theatricality in which the false, base, and threatening aspects of New England culture are commingled with the equally illusory and counterfactual presence of moral and cultural stability. The combined forces of Protestantism and democracy enabled American women to be more independent and morally self-controlling than women living in more structured or aristocratic societies.

Consequently, Mary is better able to read Burr for what he is, a sexual satyr, than is Virginie, who is preoccupied with his masculinity. Mary typifies one version of the "moral exemplar" in American fiction "who enacted Margaret Fuller's clarion pronouncement: 'Women of my country . . . if you have power, it is a moral power.' The power of the moral exemplar grew in proportion to the decline of reliable male authority figures" (David S. Reynolds, *Beneath the American Renaissance* 343). And it is this quality that marks her as a Penelopean figure. It is at the novel's end that the full significance of the Penelopean parallel is realized. Penelope endured the twenty-year absence of her husband, Odysseus. Throughout that period, she was forced to withstand noble suitors (like Mary's Burr and the Reverend Hopkins) who remained only to waste her revenues and force her remarriage without considering her own passions. Mary's bridging status is the very locus for the negotiation of individual choices in a democratic atmosphere in which conspiracies against the individual, both major and minor, were routine. Mary becomes an embattled vessel because she is constantly made to be the vehicle through which parallel forces are made to come to terms.

Mary's continual blending of Puritan simplicity and Catholic profaneness is representative of her agility. In this passage, Mary, a vision of purity, stands in opposition to the corruptions of Stowe's readers:

> a petite figure in a full stuff petticoat and white short gown, she stands reaching up one hand and cooing to something among the apple blossoms . . . and we, that have seen pictures, think, as we look on her girlish face, with its lines of statuesque beauty, on the tremulous half-infantine expression of her lovely mouth, and the general air of simplicity and purity, of some old pictures of the girlhood of the Virgin. But Mrs. Scudder was thinking of no such Popish matter, I can assure you,—not she! I don't think you could have done her a greater indignity than to mention her daughter in any such connection. (538)

Stowe proceeds to place Mary in the context of the sacred and the profane, prefiguring the mechanisms through which New England virtues will be seen to prevail over the imperfections of the rest of the nation.

There is always, Stowe seems to alert us, a "real" self buried or neglected behind Mary's prim exterior. And Mary's hidden self is subject to insidious temptations that she negotiates as much by luck as by foresight. One notable effect of Mary's circumstantiality is to heighten our awareness that Mary presides over a world that is "a thing of Man's creation, a dark and dreary fraud . . . a veil whose folds will hide deep remorse, sins and shame." Stowe evinces corruptions to her readers by suggesting that politics operates in dream lives and in secret spaces just beyond the author's direct control:

> We fancy such a one lying in a rustling silk negligee, and, amid a gentle generality of rings, ribbons, puffs, laces, beaux, and dinner discussion, reading our humble sketch; — and what favor shall our heroine find in her eyes? For though her mother was a world of energy and "faculty," in herself considered, and had bestowed on this one little lone chick all the vigor and all the care and all the training which would have sufficed for a family of sixteen. . . . She could not waltz or polka or speak bad French, or sing Italian songs; but, . . . she could both read and write fluently in the mother-tongue. She could spin both on the little and great wheel. . . . She had worked several samplers of rare merit, that they hung framed in different rooms of the house, exhibiting every variety and style of possible letter in the best marking-stitch. . . . Her knowledge seemed unerring and intuitive; and whether she washed or ironed, or molded biscuit or conserved plums, her gentle beauty seemed to turn to poetry all the prose of life. (538–39)

This playful juxtaposition of Mary and Stowe as a moral heroine against a hypothetical reader who encounters tainted American values is so easily acknowledged and ignored that its fundamental importance to the novel is overlooked. Passages such as this one make the argument that literature has a fine power over readers. Historical romances connect a writer's public agenda with the grainy spaces of an audience's private life. Mary's shuttling between Stowe's politics and an audience's responses urgently engages both parties in the effort to "design" the past.

Mary's abyssal constitution demands from readers a constant and incisive self-awareness. When Mary's pure individualism is tested for the first time by her sudden immersion into the swirling social forces present at Wilcox's party, we are reminded that Mary is abyssally represented:

> Her dress, which, under Miss Prissy's forming hand, had been made to assume that appearance of style and fashion which more particularly characterized the mode of those times, formed a singular, though not unpleasing contrast to the sort of dewy freshness of air and mien which was characteristic of her style of beauty. It seemed to represent a being who was in

the world, yet not of it. . . . The feeling of being in a circle to which she
did not belong, where her presence was in a manner an accident, and
where she felt none of the responsibilities which come from being a com-
ponent part of a society, gave to her a quiet, disengaged air. (654)

Of course, it is at this crucial point that Stowe unleashes her comic recognition that she is restructuring history by fictitious means. At this very moment, Mary is introduced to Aaron Burr, and her detached complacency is
shattered as she is brought squarely to the center of one of the century's
great historical events. Mary, that pious representative of a Puritan order
described by Mather, is suddenly handed the opportunity to involve herself
in the conspiratorial milieu of antebellum America.

As Burr's influence begins to reverberate through the novel, it registers at
once in two dimensions of femininity: the pure and vulnerable and the
tainted but questing. Burr stands as the nagging problem of conspiracy in
early American history—one simply cannot find out who is causing what,
with whatever degree of intention. Balancing precariously the forces that
define the divide between Scudder and Burr, Stowe relates that Mary

> felt within herself the stirring of dim aspiration, the uprising of a new
> power of self-devotion and self-sacrifice, a trance of hero-worship, a cloud
> of high ideal images,—the lighting up, in short, of all that God has laid,
> ready to be enkindled, in a woman's nature, when the time comes to sanc-
> tify her as the pure priestess of a domestic temple. But alas! it was kindled
> by one who did it only for an experiment, because he felt an artistic plea-
> sure in the beautiful heat and light, and cared not, though it burned a soul
> away. (666)

From this portrait of an Eve about to be tempted by the vanity hidden in
the garden (which perhaps reveals some latent anxieties of Stowe's own efforts to romanticize history), Stowe turns the attention of her readers to the
sketch of a woman who has "fallen" and now aspires to reclaim the qualities
Mary commands. Stowe's narrator says:

> Look in with us one moment, now that the party is over, and the busy hum
> of voices and blaze of lights has died down to midnight silence and dark-
> ness; we make you clairvoyant. . . . opposite, resting with one elbow on
> the toilette table, her long black hair hanging down over her night dress

... sits Virginie, looking fixedly into the dreamy depths of the mirror. ...
She struggles feebly and confusedly with her fate, still clinging to the name
of duty, and baptizing as friendship this strange new feeling which makes
her tremble. ... It is one of the saddest truths of this sad mystery of life,
that woman is, often, never so much an angel as just the moment before
she falls into an unsounded depth of perdition. And what shall we say of
the man who leads her on as an experiment. ... Of old, it was thought
that one who administered poison in the sacramental bread and wine had
touched the very height of his impious sacrilege; but this crime is white,
by the side of his who poisons God's eternal sacrament of love and de-
stroys a woman's soul through her noblest and purest affections. (666)

In passages such as these, Stowe's allegory of a democratic microcosm is
geared toward re-educating her audience to the unique stance she is formulating about authority—about who has it and how it works. Far from imply-
ing imperfections in Mary's ability to comprehend the contents of the text,
Stowe nevertheless uses overjustifications in the same way Mather did: to
overcome the reader's potentially limited ability to read the complexity of
historical processes. This mandarin complexity echoes again and again in
The Minister's Wooing.

Mary's power stems from her remarkable ability to interact with the potent forces of economic and political corruption arrayed inside her home
and community. As she balances and negotiates, she alternately reveals herself to be either the icon of a virtuous wife, whose constancy buttresses her
image as a moral exemplar, or the manipulator behind fictions that conceal
the extent of her control over the organs of power.[10]

Penelopean activity is the basis for the representational logic of *The Minister's Wooing,* but a distinction has to be made between Mary's functioning
as a shuttling figure and Stowe's role as author-historian. Mary's activities
are made to speak for the community at large. Mary is Stowe's "enacted"
self whose discourse is made to arrogate the right to speak for all the "other"
discourses present in nineteenth-century culture. Stowe's activity, in contrast, is metatextual and designed to problematize the author's apparent control over her subject matter. Stowe constantly signals her readers to notice
that she stands dramatically apart from the fiction she has created.[11] This
separation from her work is an attempt to carve out a sanctuary where her
intellectual project (which is quite antinomian in that it grants women exceptional powers for deciding spiritual issues) can be defended. Stowe's legiti-

mization for revising the history her readers experience is justified (like Mather's) by her provisional location outside the narrative. One might think of Stowe as a puppeteer pulling the strings that animate her characters while she remains fully shielded by a curtain. Only the occasional intrusion of strings gives readers a clue that some calculating presence is manipulating the show.

The deflection of identity that Stowe achieves through Mary paradoxically gives her greater latitude to experiment with narrative strategies. By refusing to adopt a universal, panoptic stance, Stowe shields her counterfactual versions of New England society. It is acceptable for her protagonist Mary Scudder to remain fully confident that her intuitive negotiations are valid and supportive of a humane order, but it is quite a different case for the novelist to become wedded to the "truths" of her fiction. The essence of Stowe's Penelopeanism is not the half of the myth that remains exclusively faithful to one's prior commitments. Instead, Stowe's emphasis is on the coy wooing of suitors to accept and be convinced of the sincerity of her fictional pattern, even though her readers sense the inherent falsity of her designs.

In practical terms Stowe's method, which depends on her audience recognizing that her characters exist neither as real people nor as metaphorical types, allows her to insist on allegorical readings that equate the type of experience rendered in the text with the masterplot of democratic culture. Stowe deploys a host of familiar "hooks" that are meant to snare her readers into a fuller understanding of their roles as consumers in politics and culture. But, in her attempts to assert that opinion is the moving power behind America's fatal attraction to foreign influences, Stowe uses her audience's narcissism to argue against the consumption satisfaction that Aaron Burr and Virginie de Frontignac (and also, perhaps, James and Mary's ironic embrace of comfortable reclusiveness at the novel's end) ultimately come to represent.

The Domestic Framing of Democratic Culture

Stowe recognized that women in the early nineteenth century operated under a "pink and white tyranny." Ann Douglas tells us that the rituals of sentimental literature, such as those appearing in *The Minister's Wooing*, were directed at "the active middle class Protestant women whose supposedly limited intelligences" caused them to be flattered by liberal piety:

"These women did not hold offices or own businesses. They had little formal status in their culture. . . . Increasingly exempt from the responsibilities of domestic industry, they were in a state of sociological transition. . . . the drive of the nineteenth century [was] to gain power through the exploitation of their feminine identity as their society defined it" (6–7). Men, as husbands and providers, acted on behalf of the family in the wider world of public and economic activity. Women, as wives and mothers, held primary responsibility for the household. Protestant mothers were charged with the maintenance of a nurturing (and overwhelmingly Christian) atmosphere and the routine functioning of the domestic economy. As Mary Kelley notes, popular literature played a particularly important role by constructing alternatives to the cultural hegemony that separated the spheres of men and women:

> The literary domestics inadvertently revealed to the public much of the woman's act in private. . . . Theirs was a prose of heroines with only a sprinkling of heroes. . . . Their public prose reflected the concerns, even obsessions of their privately recorded thoughts, just as their letters, diaries, and journals documented what was for them the bewildering, anxious reign of private women as public, popular writers. (9)

Domestic sensibility fortifies Stowe's cultural poetics in *The Minister's Wooing*. Mather's original probing of public and private selves was useful for Stowe's later affirmation that private experience could illuminate experience, not only at the level of large historical events (such as the correction of slavery) but all the way down to a level of individual specificity (such as the recovery of a childhood text from a small garret in a woman's home).

The primary bond in nineteenth-century family life joined the interests of mothers and their children. It was assumed that when the connection with the home was severed, the children would rise or fall in the uncertain society outside the home on the basis of what they had acquired during childhood. As children left the home, they were confronted by a world of choices that every year was becoming more sophisticated and complex. Stowe's novel draws on a popular image of nineteenth-century femininity beset by disorienting social dangers. Virginie's seduction by Aaron Burr is a glimpse at the vision of a lone woman facing the ultimate female jeopardy. The most complicated portion of the social message for women in novels like Stowe's sets the social obligations for women in tension with one another. Lawrence Buell, summarizing data for 276 New England authors, notes some of the feminine "themes" that Stowe insinuated into her characterizations of Mary and Virginie:

> the woman writer working from the basic situation of housewife or depen-
> dent daughter [was motivated] by some sense of family financial emer-
> gency. . . . The overall professional picture for women writers [was] more
> polarized for women than men. . . . it exhibits a contrast between writers
> who were able to dabble or immerse themselves in writing because they
> were financially secure [and those] who were thrust completely into the
> marketplace. (*New England Literary Culture* 381–82)

Mary Scudder, in her work at executing a feminist cultural poetics, reflects these more generalized social pressures on women. Her culturalism is an *intrinsically* progressive work because it produces its end in the course of her relationships. Her culturalism does not begin with a preordained end to which the facts of her life conform.

By the 1840s, family life was commonly considered to be the appropriate pattern for the larger democratic culture of the nation (Wiebe 266–67). Stowe's novel both reflects and complicates this conception of family life. The Scudder household is limited by its contact with a Congregationalism leaning toward consociationism, yet the peculiar dynamic that it contains helps to elaborate a fictional construct that conceals some of the cultural energies the home circulates.

The Minister's Wooing is an extended literary examination of the feminine role in maintaining a pattern of culture that was, in fact, being unworked from within. As Lisa MacFarlane writes, "Although presuming to stabilize the relations between men and women, the doctrine of separate spheres was itself unstable. . . . the doctrine . . . simultaneously endows woman with a worldly power yet requests that she refrain from using it; it mobilizes her yet curtails her motion" (282). Mary celebrates her ability to function effectively outside the home by elaborate (and direct) confrontations with male author-ity. Her melodramatic challenge of Burr by the seaside is only one instance among several where Mary appears to have a political effectiveness that pre-vents her immobilization within the home.

The revolution in choices that typified the antebellum culture of New England broke with the eighteenth-century notion of the family as a hierar-chical set of superior and inferior relations. Children, upon leaving the home, were no longer perpetual dependents but were emerging adults at a point of departure from which there was no return. American society after 1820 depicted life's tests along parallel lines. The fact that individuals and groups competed against themselves rather than against one another constituted the basis of democratic freedoms. Parallelism minimized the frictions of competition and maximized the possibility of new opportunities and fresh starts. In *The Minister's Wooing* this parallel lifestyle illustrates that the Scudders are better citizens than Simeon Brown. Neither family cancels the other through direct competition; instead, each is accommodated within one community. A child's leaving home meant that a new parallel track was being established. Each child was then encouraged to internalize a set of absolute principles to carry on life's impersonal journey.

The freedoms and dangers inherent in the new democratic society had numerous psychological implications. Mrs. Scudder is continually haunted by the thought that she may not have translated the absolutes of her husband properly to Mary; the Marvyns have been remiss in curtailing the wanderlust of their son James. The image of the youth's irreversible departure held great sway in the psychological and social implications of antebellum culture, although in some areas of society this norm did not apply. Stowe recasts this theme of parental responsibility versus the determination of the child by developing a complex relationship between Mary Scudder and her mother Katy.

If Katy represents a neo-Puritanical form of motherhood, Mary is the child who confronts directly the multitude of corrupting dangers in antebellum society. Mary therefore becomes a significant example of a personality distilled from the networks of culture that Stowe enacts. Stowe and Mary both felt themselves to be supremely constructed selves. Each, in her own sphere, claims to be a primary negotiator of the Puritan past, and each tries to erect a plausible foundation for a moral culture.

Stowe makes Mary into a "Penelopean figure"[12] whose involvement with the diversity of Newport culture allows her to express a rhetoric of evocation in which objects, texts, and images all contribute to the materialization of the past. Mary's role, at least as viewed by early-nineteenth-century readers, was to illustrate that New England was on the brink of civil war and found itself emptied of history. Mary, in contrast to her society, was already attempting to remake history on her own terms. Essential to that task was the critical redeployment of the cultural power in Mather's *Magnalia*. That project, as we have seen, was exceptionally anamorphic in the sense that Stowe's interpretations contained clues betraying the fictions underneath historical observation. Mary's intuitive responses to crises that surface are both true to the spirit of past and radical extensions beyond them. Further, her revisions of the past carry a self-conscious significance because they have been forged through a direct and threatening contact with subversive powers. For example, Mary's prime convert is Virginie de Frontignac—a woman whose romantic aura has contributed a great deal to Mary's own sense of right and wrong; yet Virginie is an admitted adulteress, the motive force behind political conspiracies against the republic, and a Catholic trained in the convent. Virginie is the personification of Roman Catholic corruption mirroring an "idolatrous" threat to democracy.

Many of Stowe's readers would have recognized that Virginie's presence in New England was dangerous. To paraphrase André Malraux, a heritage is not transmitted; it must be conquered. Stowe's creation of a female figure who is adept at shuttling between the moral and immoral, between abstract dogmatism and unbridled romantic impulses, and between the refinement of a republican gentility and a democratic acceptance of blacks, Jews, and Europeans is intended not only for purposes of enactment but for representing the spirit of Stowe's historical knowledge.

The Minister's Wooing traces a shifting outlook on Protestantism.[13] Stowe rejects a strict delineation of human activity into two separate spheres. She places her historical romance into a new political matrix that valued at least limited degrees of autonomy and individualism. Since the time of the American Revolution, the period roughly conveyed in *The Minister's Wooing*, the asymmetry of sexual relations had entered public discourse as writers like Stowe tried to define a place for women in postrevolutionary society.

As America enlarged the scope and ideological power of republicanism, it was also busily trying to accommodate meaningful roles for women. For Stowe, her placement in the mid-nineteenth century made earlier literary efforts seem rather limited. In *The Minister's Wooing* she attempts to recast the era as a meaningful juncture in the history of American culture that ought not to have passed by unnoticed. As New England's political impotency increased during the 1850s, Stowe's recording of values in the woman's sphere (which validated women's moral influence on their husbands and lovers) became a self-questioning theme in her novel.

Stowe's general stance in *The Minister's Wooing* reflects the ideology of republican womanhood; the understanding was that women played world-historical roles that served large social and political purposes. Further, the complexity and efficiency of women's activity in the cultural realm brought the woman's sphere into close proximity with the world men were thought to inhabit. In Stowe's case, at least in *The Minister's Wooing*, the language of domesticity is used to erect a façade of conservative political choice. Mary Scudder is not yet a feminist; but, according to Linda Kerber, "[her] world maintained itself by the spinning gyroscope of successive decision and choice" (21). Political rules in Stowe's era existed in a world from which familiar boundaries had been erased. The complex negotiations of freedom in the free territories in the West were mirrored everywhere in the 1850s. New social relationships needed continual redefinition, and the new spheres of competition made most Americans characteristically anxious.

Stowe's historicism is quite direct in its problematizing of the several domestic fictions that "contained" historical romances written by women. The Scudder home, which appears initially as an icon of American domestic orthodoxy, claimed that for every interior space there was an object appropriate to it. The Scudder house celebrated the fact that New England homes were well ordered and self-sufficient.

For every question posed within the domestic enclosure there was presumed to be an answer. The home defined a space where the identities of nineteenth-century Americans were forged and their social and political interactions were organized. The domestic enclave was supposed to provide a firm base for the actions of men, women, and children. The values fostered there were intended to support loyalties that applied inside its walls and without. "The most important characteristic of this new domestic space was its ability to integrate personal and national goals. It fostered uniform communities, molded socially homogeneous human beings, and produced a set of predictable habits among contemporary Americans," writes Kathryn Sklar. "To do this and at the same time to defend the virtues of self-reliance, freedom of choice, and independence of mind required considerable ingenuity" (12). This was a culture that raised the past to an apex of social ritual. On the Fourth of July, in the newly regularized Thanksgiving holiday, and on all sorts of national and local election days, the American citizen reverentially recalled the past before thinking to project ahead. The domestic fiction of the home helps to conceal and enable the essentially democratic character of Mary Scudder's Penelopean activities.

Stowe, like many other women writers of the period, occupied a relatively safe position, for her literary role appeared to be an extension of her domestic roles. Mary Kelley writes:

As popular writers, as public figures, economic providers, and creators of culture, the literary domestics in a very real sense left the "shade" for the "sunny places of life." . . . But they were torn between a desire "for something out of their condition" and a conflicting and contradictory desire for "a right appreciation" of their condition. . . . Beset by a lingering conviction that private domestic women were the humblest performing the "lowest office," they nevertheless sought dignity through dutiful performance in the private domestic sphere. Reluctant and fearful to claim more, they condemned any woman for doing less. (10–11)

It is little wonder, then, that in *The Minister's Wooing* the figures of Candace, Cerinthy Ann, and Prissy are made heroic and central although they remain firmly enmeshed in the networks of the domestic economy. Prissy, in particular, bears the stamp of anxiety felt by Stowe herself.

It is ironically fitting that Miss Prissy broods over the realm of the material, of clothes, despite all of Stowe's pointed remarks about the deceptive materialism of a democratic society. Christopher Wilson suggests that "Miss Prissy signifies the unresolved status in Stowe's epistemology of art and artifice, of self-abnegation and selfishness, of woman's role as artist (influence) or artifact (ornament)" ("Tempests and Teapots" 577). And, if we are to believe Ann Douglas, the interaction between Mary and Hopkins, with all its barely concealed contempt of a male authority over the home, may be seen as "part of Stowe's long-standing attempt to supplant her father and obtain his ministerial authority" (247).[14] It is easy to underrepresent the degree to which Stowe was involved in the public sphere. Her involvements there helped to determine many of the authorial attitudes and contingencies regarding the political nature of domestic enclosure expressed in *The Minister's Wooing*.

Stowe's novel dramatizes how the homely fictions of domestic enclosure enhance the practice of storytelling and the practice of force: by providing material support for ingenious narrative designs, by offering strategies for controlling a culture's discourse, and by modifying in important ways the determination of a woman's place within that culture. The work becomes implicated in her readers' predicaments, and, as in all anamorphic situations, her readers cannot fail to read themselves even as they read the pages before them. This is no ordinary Puritanic or republican virtue but rather an assertion that typic heroism lay behind Stowe's present. Antitypic glory stretched ahead; but in between, in the difficult wounded present of Newport in the eighteenth century, urgent self-examination and anxiety alone sufficed for the moral historian:

> Our scene opens in the great, old-fashioned kitchen, which on ordinary occasions is the family dining and sitting-room of the Scudder family. I know fastidious moderns think that the working-room wherein are carried on the culinary operations of a large family must necessarily be an untidy and comfortless sitting-place. . . . The kitchen of a New England matron was her throne-room, her pride; it was the habit of her life to produce the greatest possible results there with the slightest possible discomposure. . . . The floor,—perhaps, Sir, you remember your grandmother's floor, of snowy boards sanded with the whitest sand; you remember the ancient fireplace stretching quite across one end,—a vast cavern, in each corner of which a cozy seat might be found. . . . across the room ran a dresser, on which was displayed a great store of shining pewter dishes and plates that always shone with the same mysterious brightness; and by the side of the fire, a commodious wooden "settee," or settle, offered repose to people too little accustomed to luxury to ask for a cushion. . . . Oh, that kitchen of the olden times, the old, clean, roomy New England kitchen!—who that has breakfasted, dined, and supped in one has not cheery visions of its thrift, its warmth, its coolness? The noon-mark on its floor was a dial that told of some of the happiest days; thereby did we right-up the short-comings of the solemn old clock that tick-tacked in the corner, and whose ticks seemed mysterious prophecies of unknown good yet to arise out of the hours of life. How dreamy the winter twilight came in there,—when as yet the candles were not lighted,—when the crickets chirped around the dark stone hearth, and shifting tongues of flame flickered and cast dancing shadows and elfish lights on the walls, while grandmother nodded over her knitting work, and puss purred, and old Rover lay dreamily opening now one eye and then the other on the family group! With all our ceiled houses, let us not forget our grandmother's kitchens! (536–37)

Stowe's elaboration of the kitchen is not a mere concentration on the material aspects of a woman's place in a well-ordered world, but rather it is an elaborated discourse on the allegorical type of historical meaning that Stowe unfolds in the novel. The influence of time, the romanticized images of dancing figures and "mysterious prophecies," the "righting-up" of shortcomings in the instrumentality of time—these things are invoked and contained within the ritual space of the kitchen. The things in Stowe's kitchen evoke the multivocality of such signs for her readers. Such a private space, publicly offered for her readers to view and encounter, points to a way for understanding a culture's political and social unconscious as it becomes overdetermined in that culture's self-consciousness.

The garret-boudoir of the Scudder household is another space that becomes the apotheosis of New England's cultural importance:

> Was there not there a grand easy-chair of stamped leather, minus two of its hinder legs, which had genealogical associations through the Wilcoxes with the Vernons and through the Vernons quite across the water with Old England? and was there not a dusky picture, in an old tarnished frame of a woman whose tragic end strange stories were whispered, — one of the sufferers in the time when witches were unceremoniously helped out of the world, instead of being, as now-a-days, helped to make their fortune in it by table-turning? . . . The next spread was spun and woven by Mrs. Katy's beloved Aunt Eunice, — a mythical personage, of whom Mary gathered vague accounts that she was disappointed in love, and that this very article was part of a bridal outfit, prepared in vain, against the return of one from sea, who never came back, — and she heard of how she sat wearily and patiently at her work. . . . mated to it was one of the blankets which had served Mrs. Scudder's uncle in his bivouac at Valley Forge. (677–78)

The Scudder house is a domestic archive of New England history that prefigures and enables the activities of the present.

Describing the Scudder home is Stowe's strategy for controlling the historical discourse in the novel. In the descriptions, Stowe practices rules of exclusion.[15] She also defines her place as an author within the house of fiction—that is, the framing of the fictional house also frames Stowe's authorship. Therefore, the Scudder house informs the social appropriation of her work, for her readers' view of social reality is shaped both by the text and by the domestic world it describes. In her primary negotiation with a Puritan community, she continues to respect a contemporary New England society that reflects the pernicious, calculating mind of the entrepreneur. Stowe's restorative quest has its jeremiadic purpose. In the Puritan community she portrays, there are treasured secret mementos: hope chests revealing Indian lace, Oriental designs, Madonnas from far-off lands. The ornamentation of Puritanism in all its various forms bespeaks Stowe's abiding interest for romance. Her presentism, however, sees Newport in a different light; the "dead grind" of making money has been thrown into "one waste catch all and labelled romance" (598). As Christopher Wilson notes, Stowe's characters are presented either as highly romantic figures (when aligned with Puritanism's influence) or as figures somehow diminished by their contact with purely present concerns.

Within this "house of fiction" it is Mary who shuttles easily between the work of history and the unworking of fiction. If *Magnalia* was a text that presented its readers with the metaphor of the historical banquet on a jeweled table, then Stowe's refiguring of the past ushers us into the special places where the banquet was prepared. Supplanting the sermons of illustrious ministers, the platforms of synods, and the systematization of belief, Stowe's evocation of the grandmother's kitchen (a nice parallel to another material artifact—Hawthorne's grandfather's easy chair, which is also used as a platform for the reissue of past stories) pulses with allegorical possibilities for her readers. Stowe's history is a materialist one, and Mather's was a history based on intellectual documentary. Stowe's version of the New England past is rendered in folk terminology. Consequently, when it invokes the ordered chaos of the Puritan legacy, it often comes without dramatic anecdote. Though the well-sanded kitchen floor might seem less portentous than Mather's description of a minister delivering a stirring sermon on the likeness between thunder and moral states (even as his own house is burned by lightning in a terrific storm), the historical hearts of both Stowe and Mather are powerfully similar.

Formally, the cultural grammar of Stowe's kitchen and Mather's Florentine table are alike. At the surface are complications that can be stripped away to reveal a common pattern of historical invention. Romance was a versatile and legitimating ideal for both writers. Their accounts of New England ranged freely into literary allusiveness; speculations not only ornamented the contours of their pages but subtly refashioned the interpretations contained within.

Mather and Stowe capitalized on an elaborate "fiction" put forward for the purpose of securing some sense of self within the history they describe so brilliantly. Taken at a deeper political meaning—since that is what Stowe expects her readers to do by presenting the kitchen as some sort of evidence that New Englanders, despite their divergences, can at least be united in the realm of their grandmothers' kitchens—the domestic environment contains and provides the basis for the historical explanations that follow. As Henry

Glassie has so perceptively remarked, "In folk art, the deep geometry of reason forces itself upward to the sensate surface, preventing characterological discourses, inhibiting the elaboration of incident, confining ornamentation, and manifesting itself in repetitive patterning" (84).

In *The Minister's Wooing* the homely fiction of domestic enclosure disguises a more worldly feminine role. Though men like Mather and Edwards make the abstract theological systems that appeal so much to the intellect, women must deal with the emotional reality that resides within them:

> These hard old New England divines were the poets of metaphysical philosophy, who built systems in an artistic fervor, and felt self-exile from beneath them as they rose into the higher regions of thought. But where theorists and philosophers tread with sublime assurance, woman often follows with bleeding footsteps;—women are always turning from the abstract to the individual, and feeling where the philosopher only thinks. (541–42)

Joan Hedrick sees Stowe as replacing the abstractions of Hopkins's *System* with networked relationships: "The terrifying individualistic vision of Edwards" is replaced by "a communal vision in which women are spinners and weavers of the social fabric. . . . In this women's world the 'high' and the 'low' are replaced by a complex set of peer relationships" (321). The historical determination of woman's place is itself conditioned by a fiction.[16] The empowerment of women that springs from a domestic basis is many times used for liberating purposes rather than limiting ones. At the quilting party, for instance,

> serious matrons commented on the cake, and told each other high and particular secrets in the culinary art, which they drew from remote family-archives. One might have learned in that instructive assembly how best to keep moths out of blankets,—how to make fritters of Indian corn indistinguishable from oysters,—how to bring up babies by hand,—how to mend a cracked teapot,—how to take grease from a brocade,—how to reconcile absolute decrees with free will,—how to make five yards of cloth answer the needs of six,—and how to put down the Democratic party. (803)

The image of a culture so intricately elaborated through painstaking feminine political inquiry seems completely subsumed in the "romance" of real life. However, the quilting party dramatizes the pernicious effect of a culture that is constituted by beguiling forms of authority. The fluidity, informality, and experiential basis of women's culture hearkens back to the era of the 1840s, when the parallel tracks in antebellum society appeared relatively undisturbed. By merging a vision of feminine evangelizing with a nostalgic (and counterfactual) rendering of the true state of American society in 1859, Stowe demonstrated a great deal of complicity with the culture she wished to change.

New England as Political Icon

The Minister's Wooing frames a crisis in parallelism in American culture prior to the Civil War. Before 1820, America's web of institutions was neutral: it neither affirmed nor denied the existence of a unified nation. There was a widespread belief that America was a land of egalitarian opportunity in which respectable Americans constituted a commonality that did not impinge on their manners of living. After 1820, sectionalism accelerated rapidly. A simplified array of institutions in the South eased the assimilation of these strands into a sectional network.

Institutional complexity in the North tended to hinder the development of sectionalism. Many northern churches and reformers in the early nineteenth century espoused an optimistic nationalism that largely ignored the fact that slavery and business enterprises often interchanged or combined the same methods for state, regional, or national commerce. National stability before the war hinged on the maintenance of parallelism.

In the 1840s, America's institutional networks mobilized the values of the culture into a national standard for inclusion and exclusion. As enormous changes began to mobilize the nation's politics, sharp lines divided the virtuous from the corrupt, progress from decay, and respectability from the cheap. The pattern of democracy in antebellum culture demanded that acceptability be the norm for participation in the free choices the nation had to offer. Where one stood in relation to this line of authenticity became the preoccupation of many in post-Jacksonian America. We know that Stowe was exposed to human brutality in Cincinnati but that she sided with New England respectability in the main. A town plagued by street riots, Cincinnati was a gateway to the West, one of the more significant outposts in America where the parallelism of America was sorely tested. Early-nineteenth-century society had dispersed responsibilities among national, state, and local elites, blurred the division of rights among its ranks of citizens, and shaded the boundary between a republican people and a society's residue. Harriet's sympathies were with a republican age and not a democratic one. Milton Rugoff notes that Stowe's failed project to convert the West for Calvinism was an admission that she would opt for a theology quite different from the version she found in Ohio, which was interlinked with all areas of the new democracy. "Thus even as the discovery of gold in California was setting off the greatest westward movement in American history . . . the Beechers were drifting back to the East. . . . they retreated, almost instinctively, to the scene of ancestral triumphs" (247). As *The Minister's Wooing* shows, the historiographical emphasis of a nostalgic New England of the 1790s—its social structures and the textures of New England life, rituals, and folkways—became her *donnée*. Lacking gradations in a flattened society, respectable Americans in 1850 drew a line—in or out—and "concentrated on preserving their one significant distinction" (Wiebe 322). The drawing of this line seems to have been a strong impetus behind Stowe's writing of *The Minister's Wooing*.[17] Lawrence Buell comments, "*The Minister's Wooing* is the start of a fictional retreat from confrontation of contemporary issues . . . back to the past of her childhood and her parents' lives. As she does, she increasingly suspends her critical judgment and gives way to nostalgia, although she continues to use the convention of the disengaged narrator and the escape-from-orthodoxy plot" (*New England Literary Culture* 279). The interrelations among these scattered "tiers" become the frames we use to direct attention to the more central issue of Stowe's political and historical veracity.

"Never was there a community where the roots of common life shot down so deeply, and were so intensely grappled around things sublime and eternal," claims Stowe as she traces an outline of New England as a moral and intellectual beacon to the rest of the nation. Her desire to renew an image of regional significance mirrors Mather's:

> In a community thus unworldly must have arisen a mode of thought, energetic, original, and sublime. The leaders of thought and feeling were the ministry, and we boldly assert that the spectacle of the early ministry of New England was one to which the world gives no parallel. Living an intense, earnest, practical life, mostly tilling the earth with their own hands, they yet carried on the most startling and original religious investi-

gations with a simplicity that might have been deemed audacious, were it not so reverential. All old issues relating to government, religion, ritual, and forms of church organization having for them passed away, they went straight to the heart of things, and boldly confronted the problem of universal being. (727)

Stowe's plotting of history owes much to the dominant figurative modes that Mather used to describe the relative importance of New England's position at a time when the earlier "simplicity" of the original founders was being modified to meet new challenges. "New England was one vast sea, surging from depths to heights with thought and discussion on the most insoluble of mysteries," Stowe claims, "and no man or woman accepted any theory or speculation simply as theory or speculation; all was profoundly real and vital, a foundation on which actual life was based with intensest earnestness" (728). Stowe's "reinvention" of the past represents a stage in the development of a parent strain of Puritan culture. Stowe anatomizes the Puritan past.

The argument between the two poles of Puritanism itself, Mather and Edwards, sheds light on the arguments of many who quietly, perhaps unconsciously, expanded the limits of natural ability and those who anxiously or intentionally determined to hew the hard line of a more consistent Calvinism. As Stowe reminds us, this debate reached its climax with Edwards's *Nature of True Virtue*, where his analysis of Puritanism is less doctrinally technical, more psychological, and potentially more literary than one Mather suggested.

But, as Charles Foster shows in *The Rungless Ladder* (even if he does not openly admit it), Stowe uses Mather and Edwards to effect a doubled reading of everything usable in New England's origins. Cotton Mather's position is championed by Stowe because he read his culture exceedingly well—his urging of inoculation for smallpox seemed to confirm his position as a physician for his time. Edwards, in contrast, failed to see his culture with competent accuracy—his death from an unsuccessful inoculation allegorically proves his false reading of the times (26). When there is a choice between deploying the cultural logic of Edwards or of Mather, Mather many times prevails.[18]

Stowe makes Mary into a stable moral center that is defined by the diametric opposition of contending moral perversions that Mather and Edwards both occasionally authored. The differential intimacy Stowe shows in relation to Puritan community accords well with the terms of the Arminian/ Unitarian debates raging in the early nineteenth century. The orthodox view saw the Puritans as Mather did: as the best models of piety and conduct for the 1800s. The Arminian appreciation of the Puritans depended on their being a transitional stage along a continuum of evolution into a modern society.

Stowe, of course, seizes on the terms of orthodox and Arminian distinctions (which were really no more than ill-defined antagonisms at the time she was writing *The Minister's Wooing*) to depict a post-Edwardsean sensibility in keeping with her Litchfield exposure to evangelical Protestantism. Occasionally Stowe falls back into a pre-Edwardsean sensibility that is acutely ironic in its deconstruction of the nineteenth century's confident belief in progress. The tenuous balancing of Edwards and Mather became central to her futile definition of New England politics in 1859.

Mather's portrayal of Phips had isolated him on the political fringe. Similarly, Stowe's ironic retreat into the nostalgia of James and Mary redeemed by reformed Calvinism reflects New England's isolation in the nativist concerns of the American (Know Nothing) party. Stowe underscores the importance of regionalism as an effective fiction that works to homogenize the disparate discourses that together come to make up our idea of the nation. But in practice, regionalism fell prey to the worst forms of narcissism. Similar to the fictional containment provided by domesticity, which we examined in the previous section, regional allegory itself is complicit in a legitimizing ideology. We, as readers implicated in the process of receiving Stowe's message, are led to the realization that the problems engendered by a regional discourse—problems of insufficient political leadership typified by Franklin Pierce, the erosion of moral stability uncovered by James Bierney, and the inability to preserve a native ideal through the exercise of exclusion and discrimination represented in Henry Gardner—could not be resolved by a genre that refused to be implicated in these same problems.

To isolate just one example, Stowe's chapter "Last Words" ushers her readers into the grand foyer of the chambers where she has been spinning her Penelopean narrative. Her readers, anxious to gain a prize, follow along complaisantly even as the schemes Stowe has employed unfold slowly. *The Minister's Wooing* does not image the things it indicates; it calls to mind images of the things it indicates. Consequently, Mary, "the fair poetic maiden, the seeress, the saint, has passed into that appointed shrine for woman, more holy than a cloister, more saintly and pure than church or altar,—*A Christian home.*"[19] James Marvyn "was one of the most energetic and fearless supporters of the Doctor in his life-long warfare against an inhumanity which was entrenched in the mercantile interests of the day, and which at last fell before the force of conscience and moral appeal" (870). Hopkins "was always a welcome inmate in the house of James and Mary. . . . he married at last a woman of fair countenance. . . . his theological system was published . . . nor did his words cease to work in New England till the evils he opposed were finally done away" (871). Burr, "chased from society, pointed at everywhere by the finger of hatred, so accursed in common esteem that even the publican who lodged him for a night refused to accept his money when he knew his name," is taken in by a kindly woman near the end of his life: "The New Testament was always under his pillow. . . . Patient, gentle, and grateful, he was, as to all his inner history, entirely silent and impenetrable" (872–73). Madame de Frontignac, in a personal letter, writes Mary the coda to all the trials and tribulations in the novel:

> But Marie, how unjust is the world! how unjust both in praise and blame! Poor Burr was the petted child of society; yesterday she doted on him, flattered him, smiled on his faults, and let him do what he would without reproof; today she flouts and scorns and scoffs him, and refuses to see the least good in him. I know that man, Mary, and I know, that sinful as he may be before Infinite Purity, he is not so much more so than all the other men of his time. Have I not been in America? I know Jefferson; I knew poor Hamilton,—peace be with the dead! Neither of them had a life that could bear the sort of trial to which Burr is subjected. When every secret fault, failing, and sin is dragged out, and held up without mercy, what man can stand? (875)

At the novel's conclusion, where meaning is shifted under the weight of Stowe's retroactive voice, Stowe succeeds in endowing the past events that the novel has reviewed—the collapse of strict Calvinism, the morally bankrupt practices of the slave trade, the political schemes and subversion of the American political system in the Burr-Hamilton episode, the presentation of an authenticated American way of acting that effectively displaces a stale European precedent—with the allegorical similarities between historical reality and the structure of her fictions.[20] Many of Stowe's examples recall her intense focus on the exceptional details of New England, which are combined to produce a supremely "edited" version of each character's public and private interactions.[21]

In *The Minister's Wooing*, a whole "Pequod" of secular politics masquerades as Puritanized history. It forms a nearly irresistible source book of matters for the New England mythographer. Each of the political allegories in the novel, like Mather's own constellations in *Magnalia*, requires some sort of vindication by an age that seemed categorically more liberal but was in fact only relatively more secular and more idolatrous of the illusion of progress. Stowe's presentism merges the anxiety of the New England American (Know-Nothing) party with the conventionalized forms of romance. Lawrence Buell claims, "Stowe expresses no Hawthornian reservations about her fictional subject as dreamlike, cut off from present-day actualities . . . not withstanding that technological and social change and intellectual liberalization were in the process of making obsolete [that fictional reality]" (*New England Literary Culture* 268). In part, Stowe's conclusion refers back to Know-Nothingism's demonstration of disillusionment with existing party alignments. New England nativism, in its attempt to curtail the extension of slavery, was also dependent on a theory of the region's exceptionalism. Richard H. Dana wrote that nativism was a great setback which "[has] arisen to divide the Counsels of the North and weaken our influence on the Slave Question, at a time when a united front from the North is so necessary" (qtd. in Smith 1097). Stowe's ending, which too neatly puts to rest the contentiousness and difficult political circumstances between Mary and Burr, is calculated to re-engage her readers' sense of the utility of New England's past legacy. In Stowe's novel Newport becomes an unstable metaphor of the national culture. It speaks allegorically for both the strengths and the weaknesses that she perceives in New England's character. If Hopkins is made the unstable container of Edwardsean Calvinism, then Newport as a community becomes the unstable container for national history as Stowe perceived it in 1858.

In the last analysis, because Stowe has taught her readers to "see through" this process of construction, sentimental fiction becomes a mode for deconstructing the mechanisms of the beguiling authority it projects so well. That education has important ramifications for cultural ideology and the potential of democratic society outside the domain of purely literary practice. Stowe did not think that she could rehearse the New England past as one long, unbroken train of *magnalia*. Error, infirmity, and crime were abundant in Newport. They exist there to dot the landscape of the historical imagination.

The village of Newport was a place where the logic and sentiment of New England encountered a reality that was fast becoming unmanageable. A good deal of evidence in *The Minister's Wooing* suggests that Stowe regarded America's various theories of its own exceptionalism as theologically misguided and politically dangerous. Newport is both a comic miniaturization of national concerns and a potent example of a community deceived by powerful illusions about the morality and security of its course of behavior. Stowe's town, and its fictional inhabitants, are not unlike this ideal portrait of New England at midcentury given by Theodore Parker:

> The welfare of a nation consists in these three things; namely: first, possession of material comfort, things of use and beauty; second, enjoyment of all the natural rights of body and spirit; and, third, the development of the natural faculties of body and spirit in their harmonious order, securing the possession of freedom, intelligence, morality, philanthropy, and piety. It ought to be the aim of a nation to obtain these three things in the highest possible degree. (*Collected Works* 271)

The playful interplay of the local and the national—so easily glossed over and missed in Stowe's descriptions of Newport—deserves special emphasis. Stowe breaks her text's congruency with the world it tries to represent. By undermining the fantasy that Mary's negotiations create, Stowe brings forth the provenance of the text, nudging her readers to question the received rules of narrative and genre and to reconsider the limits of representation itself. If the text remains congruent with the world in her readers' eyes, then the novel risks becoming accommodationist in its nostalgic appreciation of the past.

The conclusion of *The Minister's Wooing* carries with it a significant ironic clarification of Stowe's attitudes toward formalistic endings and of her status as a historian. Stowe's ending recognizes that she was highly self-conscious about her own deep divisions of political feeling. She embodied her own ambivalent attitudes in a series of literary gestures that had explicit designs on the credulity of her readers.

Stowe's attempt to preserve choices and parallel definitions in fiction was a response to the gradual closing of options in national politics. As George Templeton Strong wrote, Know-Nothingism was an "awful vague, mysterious, and new element" in the political sphere, and "If the Know-Nothings were only political, not politico-religious, I'd join them" (qtd. in Smith 1097).

For Stowe, the marginalization of New England's importance for negotiating national policy became an ideal vehicle for fictional accounts of Puritanism's recovery into the nineteenth century.

If *The Minister's Wooing* had a compelling effect on the reading public because it aimed at the improvement of the people, then it merited popularity according to the degree it brought readers close to the illicit and the dangerous. As James Wallace notes, "[Stowe] was quite aware of what the reading public expected to find in a new novel, and strove according to her own temperament to satisfy the prevailing taste" (183). *The Minister's Wooing* is an extended negotiation between Stowe and the reading public and consequently scores its successes and generates its anxiety in that audience according to the reception it receives. As a reader of historical fictions, Stowe seemed to say with this novel that everyone might yet become his or her own historical critic. She wanted her readers to become more genuinely and deeply involved about New England's past than an official historian could afford to be.

Chapter Five

Historical Negotiation as "Planchette"

✛

Elizabeth Stoddard's *The Morgesons*

> I suppose it was the environment that caused me to write these nov-
> els; but the mystery of it is, that when I left my native village I did
> not dream that imagination would lead me there again, for the simple
> annals of our village and domestic ways did not interest me; neither
> was I in the least studious. . . . Of literature and the literary life, I and
> my tribe knew nothing; we had not discovered "sermons in stones."
> Where then was the panorama of my stories and novels stored, that
> was unrolled in my new sphere? . . . One day when my husband was
> sitting at the receipt of customs, for he had obtained a modest ap-
> pointment, I sat by a little desk, where my portfolio lay open. A pen
> was near, which I took up, and it began to write, wildly like "Plan-
> chette" upon her board. . . . As my stories and novels were never in
> touch with my actual life, they seem now as if they were written by a
> ghost of their time. It is to strangers from strange places that I owe
> the most sympathetic recognition.
>
> —Elizabeth Stoddard, 1901 preface to *The Morgesons* (259–61)

This chapter looks at Elizabeth Stoddard's framing of *Magnalia* in *The Morgesons*. Stoddard demonstrated a knowledge that Mather's text ad-
dressed the "primitive" desire of some in the nineteenth century to locate power and authority in diffuse and often unexpected places. An aspiring but commercially unsuccessful writer, Stoddard was quite attuned to living in the "shadows" of writers like Mather and Hawthorne.[1] This chapter considers her ingenious attempt to create a spiritualistic narrative that draws on

Mather's political aliases. For both writers, political efficiency depended on the ability to create viable alternative selves who could engage in activities that were sometimes censurable. Important spiritualistic enthusiasms framed Stoddard's model for democratic culture. Stoddard employs the suggestiveness of witchcraft and oppositional culture in the narration of her novel. Her indirectness and recognition of contingency were valid literary and political responses to a patriarchal order that subverted female ambitions by denying women roles outside the domestic sphere.

Like many aspiring women, Stoddard saw the opportunity to engage the public through novels that tapped the public's interest in spiritual mediums. The fascination of many readers for spiritualists and their special modes of communication provided Stoddard with a perfect opportunity for testing the ability of democracy to connect with a removed past. The "national allegories" that seemed validated in the many recorded psychophysiological events were usefully applied by Stoddard in crafting a literature in which *nation* is either unavoidably difficult to define or simply a reminder of a vanished state. George Templeton Strong mentions in his diary the publication of a book consisting of transcribed communications from George Washington, Andrew Jackson, Thomas Jefferson, and Margaret Fuller, "most of them using very questionable grammar." Stoddard, a writer who desired to rewrite the genre conventions of historical romances like Hawthorne's *House of the Seven Gables*, knew that mediumship was closely identified with femininity. As Susan Harris suggests, Cassandra Morgeson creates a "new set of values for women's novels and a new kind of narratee to receive them" (153). The new social movements that sprang up around figures like Cora Wilburn held profound consequences for individuals enmeshed in populist and authoritarian politics. Hawthorne himself, we are led to believe, recoiled from the specter of modernity and repression involved in spiritual communication.

Spiritualists used the language of electricity, also expressed in mesmerism and phrenology, to describe the relative positions of men and women in spirit communication. Circles at seances were best composed of equal numbers of persons in whom respectively the positive (male) and negative (female) elements predominate. Stoddard's apprehension of spiritual electricity was meant to ensure that the space where a Puritan past and a democratic present met was multitudinous and highly charged with danger. Stoddard used this notion to allegorize political power structures in antebellum New England culture. The conceit of the "planchette" became the critical framework for a novel that viewed the advancing of a particular conception of government (and a specific literary genre to depict it)—the nation—as inherently unstable and potentially fatal. Cassandra taps the power of spiritualism's logic of representation to tell the story of her feminine development under repressive Puritan influences. Within the story of a young girl's development from "undisciplined immaturity" to adulthood "lies an exploration into the nature of female sexuality and the process of self-creation that has not hitherto been undertaken by any female American writer" (Harris 152). She is "alien" to that culture and, like Mather's political aliases, her story involves her strange and hackneyed relationship to Ben Somers, who acts as her amanuensis. As Ann Braude notes, because the planchette was designed for widespread home use, the device was metaphorically democratic and tended to blur the distinction between "game playing" and "serious" communication. Planchettes imported from France were available in spiritualist bookstores during the 1850s. In the 1860s they were being mass-produced domestically.[2]

> The introduction of the planchette facilitated the mediumship of untrained family members within the home. A heart-shaped piece of wood mounted on three casters, the planchette was believed to respond to magnetic forces passing through the bodies of those who placed their fingers on it, thus communicating messages from spirits. It could be used either with a copy of the alphabet, on which it would point to letters to spell out communications, or with a pencil inserted into a hole on its back, so that a spirit could use the planchette to write. (24)

In 1857, it was public knowledge that the Fox sisters struggled with alcoholism, secret marriages, and poverty. In *The Morgesons* Stoddard afflicts Ben Somers with many of these problems. Stoddard's politics, drawing off the emergent and oppositional culture of feminism, suggests that figures like Anne Hutchinson and other antinomian personalities chart important strategies for women's freedom of expression.

In form as well as subject matter, *The Morgesons* focuses on the political exchanges possible between a New England familiar to Mather and Stoddard's own literary vocation. In the 1901 preface to her three novels Stoddard provided an important key to understanding the technique and artistic sensibilities that she employed in appropriating the Puritan past for literary romance. The citation quoted as an epigraph to this chapter—referring to the pervasive effect of the "environment," her portrayal of her clan as a

Advertisement for "The Boston Planchette" (1860?).
(American Antiquarian Society, Worcester, Massachusetts)

"tribal" authority incapable of deciphering "sermons in stones," and its description of Stoddard's writing as a spiritualistic exercise—recapitulates many of the major themes and suggests a core logic for representing the Puritan past in *The Morgesons*.

Stoddard's connection to her historical subject—the intuitive gesture of self-definition of a young New England girl in a post-Puritan society—helped her to envisage herself as somehow exterior to the places and things she describes with exceptional force. As she said in her preface, "it is to strangers and strange places that I owe the most sympathetic recognition." Because she assumes an "alien" stance to the subject of her novel, Stoddard's characters inhabit and sustain a premodern concept of culture. Her creation of an authorial stance, by its appropriation of the significance of witchcraft and spiritualism, helps her to accommodate her work as a historical critic with other, competitive antiquarian strategies. Stoddard's novel resists appropriation by readers who looked to the Puritan past as a justification for Jacksonian politics. The conflicting programs of Puritan determinism and democratic tyranny are rendered in the novel as intractable problems that defined American politics at midcentury: social inequality, ideological hypocrisy, totalitarian responses to racial heterogeneity, and urban oppression of rural life. In frequent and sustained references to Puritanism, Stoddard vividly illustrated the fact that all efforts at the legitimization and identification of the state must end in failure.

The idea that Puritanism could, as an immortal, disembodied, and continuous reality, animate the operations of the modern state was abandoned by Stoddard in favor of a depiction of nationalist dialogue as exiled and irrational. Nowhere is this more evident than in the voice of the anxious first-person narrator, whose grasp of her own story as "living" speech is constantly betrayed as written or missing text. The cyclical idea that an author's (or politician's) illocutionary force could constantly be betrayed or obliterated exactly conveyed Stoddard's deep sense of alienation both from the world she inhabited and from the literary communities (peopled by the likes of Hawthorne and Stowe) that had claimed Puritan history as their own special province. The impossibility of merging her personality with her writing allowed Stoddard to indict a broader political establishment by claiming that language is complicit in the representation of authoritarianism. The prolific increase in historical fiction during the American Renaissance was to Stoddard evidence of her era's total removal from historical understanding. Because her characters are so invisible and impossibly atypical, Stoddard's argument that her readers were forever "hidden from history" gives the novel an incredible postmodern force.

The Morgesons tells the story of Cassandra Morgeson. Cassandra's tale is a rare female *bildungsroman*, tracing the maturation of a girl into womanhood in the New England provincial town of Surrey. During her developmental years, Cass negotiates two extended and entangled romances; the second involvement leads to her marriage. Like most first novels, *The Morgesons* has a decidedly autobiographical slant. The activity in the novel centers on Cassandra's childhood home in Surrey, based on Mattapoisett, Stoddard's hometown. At the novel's beginning, Cassandra is ten years old. Her relatives think that she is "possessed" because she is actively inquisitive and contentious with her elders. Locke Morgeson, her father, runs a shipping enterprise; Stoddard describes him as "the richest man in Surrey," the person responsible for "turning Surrey from a herring-weir into a whaling port." Cassandra's mother is a gentle, pious woman whose disapproval of her daughter's ill regard for traditional religious beliefs controls their relationship. Veronica, Cassandra's younger sister, is a consumptive figure who shares many of Cassandra's mysterious dispositions but is generally more reclusive and passive than is Cass.

The early chapters of the book show Cassandra to be a girl not easily tamed; she is expelled from the local school for taunting her teacher, and she upsets the decorum of one of her mother's tea parties. At fifteen, Cassandra attends school in nearby Barmouth (Fairhaven). In Barmouth she stays with her grandfather Warren and her mother's sister Aunt Mercy. The Warren house is an old-fashioned Puritan enclave. Barmouth is a center of traditional Puritanism, and her schoolteacher, Miss Black, runs her classes with a stern orthodoxy. Cassandra's liberality is victimized by the spite of her classmates, and when she suffers an injury, she returns to the more familiar surroundings of Surrey. A previously unknown cousin, Charles Morgeson, visits the family in Surrey and proposes that Cassandra continue her education at Roseville Academy. When she is eighteen, her parents agree to the proposition, and Cass goes to live with Charles and his wife Alice.

Roseville greatly enhances Cassandra's intellectual and social circle, and her experiences there awaken her intense private passions. As she makes progress both in the Academy and around town, a passionate bond grows between Charles and Cass. Having little regard for his wife, Charles puts increasing pressure on Cassandra to consent to his romantic designs. As part of her initial resistance, Cassandra befriends two schoolmates, Helen Perkins and Ben Somers. Ben is remotely related to the Morgesons and hails from the decaying seaport town of Belem (Salem). Ben, who is just as "possessed" as Cass, tries to disrupt the relationship between Cassandra and Charles but cannot break the bonds of affection that isolate him on the periphery of Cassandra's feelings. Because of Cassandra's remoteness, Ben visits Surrey and cultivates a love for Cass's sister, Veronica. In Roseville, Cassandra rejects a marriage proposal from one of Alice's cousins and admits to herself that she wants to risk an affair with Charles. She goes out riding with Charles, a man who loves to break wild horses, and the two have an accident. Charles is killed, and Cassandra's face is permanently scarred. Cass confesses to Alice that she did indeed love Charles but never had the opportunity to consummate their love. At the midpoint of the novel, Cassandra returns once more to Surrey.

During a period of emotional recovery, Cassandra travels with her father on business and becomes a spectator of Surrey's religious revival. Then Ben Somers reappears. He invites Cassandra to his family home in Belem so that she might help clear the way for his marriage to Veronica. Surrey is small, predictable, and provincial. Roseville is more liberal, thoroughly Unitarian, and much like Concord in the mid-nineteenth century. Belem is a cosmopolitan nexus of capitalism, high society, and cultural significance in steep decline. The Somerses live at the frayed edges of Belem. Ben and his family have a proclivity for alcohol but nevertheless possess a great deal of wealth in the form of a trust that will be shared by all the Somers children when they reach maturity. The birth of another Somers, however, threatens to postpone the inheritance for two decades, and the delay compels Ben to seek financial security through marriage. The visiting Cassandra is regarded as a fortune-hunter by Mrs. Somers, and the two have an embarrassing midnight encounter in the parlor. Cassandra fares better with Ben and Adelaide Somers and their profligate brother Desmond. High-spirited, drunk, and arrogant, Desmond becomes attracted to Cassandra, and though Ben tries to avert another ill-conceived romance in Cass's life, Cassandra falls in love with Desmond. When Desmond's sordid past becomes known to Cass, she leaves Belem with Desmond's hollow promise to reform his manners and with Ben's dire prediction that ruin will be the result of their marriage.

Returning home to Surrey, Cassandra finds her mother dead in her parlor chair. Mrs. Morgeson's death begins the dissolution of the Morgeson household. Now twenty-five, Cassandra is forced to preside over her father's failing business and the dreary domestic duties. When things appear to be on the rebound, Ben marries Veronica, leaving Cassandra isolated and lonely. Shortly before the wedding, Verry has a dream that links Cassandra to a strange man. In a rapid conclusion to the novel, the Somers infant dies (perhaps as a result of Ben and Cassandra's occult meddling), leaving Ben and Desmond to inherit their wealth. At Veronica's wedding, Alice Morgeson impresses Cassandra's father, and Cassandra finds that they wish to be married. After Cassandra explains why she cannot live in the same house with Alice, she becomes aware that Alice and her father are already married. Locke, the young Morgeson Arthur, Aunt Mercy, and the servants remove to Roseville. Alone in Surrey and in sole possession of the house, Cassandra hears of Ben Somers's self-destructive drinking. Desmond, having undergone a strict penance in Spain, returns to claim Cass's love, and Veronica identifies him as the man in her prenuptial dream. Cassandra marries Desmond, and in the final paragraph of the novel we discover that they have returned to Surrey after a two-year stint in Europe. They are joined by Veronica and her baby after Ben dies of delirium tremens.

Cassandra's life is framed by her resistance to a provincial culture haunted by the past.[3] Like Hawthorne's *House of the Seven Gables, The Morgesons* is a family romance that links the destinies of two representative post-Puritan families in a frictional relationship.[4] In each case, the structure of the family is made to bear the consequences of New England history; mired in difficult circumstances, the Maules and the Morgesons are delivered through ambivalent means. In both the Maule and Morgeson families, the deformed and puzzling world of inherited Puritanism wields significant control.

The logic of spiritualism and the implications of witchcraft control the negotiations within *The Morgesons*: Cassandra and Ben are animated by the antinomian and spiritual power of an earlier age; their story is witchcraft brought into the nineteenth century and allowed to roam free. As Barton St. Armand informs us,

> The era of the rapping spirits had been initiated by the mysterious noises visited on, and later through, the Fox sisters of Hydesville, New York, in 1848. Although it was a relatively late manifestation of both the ubiquity and the materiality of the Over-Soul, Spiritualism capitalized on the same occult vogue that had early attracted Sophia Peabody and so horrified her husband, Nathaniel Hawthorne. . . . the veil in all its manifestations, whether it be the cloak of nature, the robe of deity, or the garb of the

spiritualist medium, was a basic metaphor for dealing with the problem of the sublime. (4–5, 21)

It is here, in *The Morgesons*'s intersection of nineteenth-century circumstances with seventeenth-century phenomena, that Stoddard's debt to Mather's *Magnalia* is realized. The popularity of the genre of historical romance is a strong indication that audiences were prepared to read stimulating accounts of the past; and the tendency of popular romancers to hallow rather than criticize certain already famous chapters in the American story (like Salem) only increased Stoddard's power over the genre. Stoddard's novel, in its apprehension of a "historical situation" and in its logical functioning, recasts and extends a vision of events originally brought forward by Cotton Mather. For both, the issues of orthodoxy and subversion combine to make New England a cultural site forever open to subsequent revision. The linkage between these two writers leads us to a significant comparison of their historical narratives. Like Mather, Stoddard locates historical consciousness outside a unified self. *The Morgesons*, like *Magnalia*, is an exercise in semiotic realism, and both writers share the conviction that thought is not an activity within the self but is an external process of sign relations. As Harris notes, "Cassandra's experience encompassed a series of individual choices each contingent on the circumstances of the moment" (166). A certain relationship is brokered with Cotton Mather through the interpretive network of *Magnalia*, in which the conventions of a rational speaking subject are replaced by spectral phenomena.

It is highly appropriate, then, that the dominant narrative voice used in *The Morgesons* is ethnographic. Stoddard's probing of New England is actually a close examination of three cultural centers, each of which, in some capacity, is representative of a whole region. Her oppositional stance to the world that Mather foreshadowed and her own involvement with a culture that generally felt her to be a befuddled writer led her easily to the suggestive power of a narrative based on spiritualism. Behind that fact, however, lies the more pressing issue that Mather took for his subject in *Magnalia*— namely, New England as a cultural site can be defined only in problematic terms, and the writer who attempts to define the cultural significance of the region is always forced to present history in a dispersive mode. Roger Williams and Anne Hutchinson co-opted Mather's own narrative; their stories seemed to be more plausible than Mather's elaborately woven text. Stoddard seemed to have an intuitive grasp that Puritan theory and the practice of piety eventually left dangerous moral vacuums that ordinary human beings filled with their own needs and fears.

Occult Historiography in
The Morgesons and *Magnalia*

The genius of Stoddard's efforts in *The Morgesons* can be appreciated only when we understand her interest in witchcraft and the occult that shapes history parallels Mather's interest: both writers display their learning through the suggestion of the supernatural, and in the process their judiciousness as precise observers is firmly established. On another level, the narration of history by a woman medium is Stoddard's artistic gambit for recapturing the spirit and vitality of Mather's concern with oppositional elements and their determining role in culture. Throughout both texts runs a thread that celebrates the ingenuity not only of Cotton Mather or Elizabeth Stoddard but also of New England. A party to the principle of disorder, Cassandra exhibits "several variations on the idea of possession which enable Stoddard to invert and subvert established codes within the apparent boundaries of a peculiarly New England phenomenon" (Harris 160). Stoddard fits easily into the tradition of Roger Williams, Anne Hutchinson, and Mather himself, who, in attempting to describe the particular circumstances that embroiled them in controversy, made a point of drawing attention to the bases for their representations of social reality.

Stoddard's portrayal of Cassandra as a latter-day witch is engineered to blend romantic notions with aspects of a regional realism. Stoddard's insinuations that a woman's pursuit of her own desires reflects simultaneously both the nineteenth-century aspiration of spiritualist mediums to assert a form of woman's liberation and the weirdness and haunting specter of Puritan history are a daring narrative device. Cassandra, in her role of enacted self for Stoddard, is a significant character because she affirms a connection to a Gothic past. That connection helps differentiate Stoddard's art and suggests a new range of sociohistorical potential. This mimetic duality, as we will see a little later, is also characteristic of Mather; both writers explore the same issue through the adoption of an ethnographic perspective on New England. But if substantial historical consciousness is at play in *The Morgesons*, it is diminished and located outside the scope of the characters themselves. This point, suggested by Mather's strategies, is fully developed in *The*

Morgesons. Though Puritanism has indeed infiltrated Stoddard's world, no one there seems to know its actual significance. Stoddard herself makes this point in her preface to the work:

> If with these characters I have deserved the name of "realist," I have also clothed my skeletons with the robe of romance. "The Morgesons" completed, and no objections made to its publication, it was published. As an author friend happened to be with us, almost on the day it was out, I gave it to him to read, and he returned it to me with the remark that there were a "good many *whiches* in it." That there were, I must own, and that it was difficult to extirpate them. I was annoyed at their fertility. The inhabitants of my ancient dwelling place pounced upon "The Morgesons" because they were convinced it would prove a version of my relations, and my own life. I think one copy passed from hand to hand, but the interest blew over, and I have not been noticed there since. (261)

In a similar vein, despite the technical brilliance of Stoddard's tracing of the trajectory of the past through the mid-nineteenth century, it is the strange cross-patterns of "the Deity of the Illicit" that command her portrait of genteel provincial life in New England.

Spiritualism, from about the time *The Morgesons* was written through the second half of the nineteenth century, preoccupied a broad spectrum of the American public. Originating in upstate New York in 1848, spiritualism quickly attained the status of a new religious movement. It aimed to prove the immortality of the soul by establishing contact with spirits of the dead. Many public citizens became "investigators," who experimented in their homes with planchettes (the precursor of Ouija boards) or turned out in great numbers to hear women give lectures "channeled" from the spirit world. Harriet Beecher Stowe was a serious investigator, as were William Lloyd Garrison, Supreme Court justice John Edmonds, and Ohio congressman Joshua Giddings. For all these people, spiritualism provided a convincing alternative to traditional beliefs, which blocked the individual's access to divine truth. Spiritualism was a natural focal point for anyone in the nineteenth century who wished to oppose temporal authority in one guise or another. Many are familiar with the detailed portrayals of spiritualism made by Henry James in *The Bostonians*, Nathaniel Hawthorne in *The Blithedale Romance*, and William Dean Howells in *The Undiscovered Country*. In *The Morgesons*, however, spiritualism is less a direct subject than it is a manner of seeing events unfold. Spiritualism was well suited to Stoddard's artistry because it gave her an oppositional point from which to examine New England. Spiritualism, in its unconventionality, afforded many literary opportunities that simply did not exist elsewhere.

Ann Braude bases her historical assessment of spiritualism on the understanding that it appeared in a popularized version and a radical form: "though spiritualism contributed to the disestablishment of America's Calvinist heritage, its own doctrines remained permanently outside the pale of acceptable public opinion" (17). Stoddard wished to portray her female exemplar, Cassandra, as inhabiting a space that remained forever outside public opinion. To a lesser degree, that impulse might be called autobiographical, but the main point is that Stoddard enjoyed the exterior position that she held vis-à-vis her culture. Her ethnographic details were sharply defined, and her vantage point on the outside expanded the ideological bases for her explorations of the Puritan past.

Stoddard was a member of an important generation of women who were able to find their voice through alternate channels. We have already discussed how Harriet Beecher Stowe was able to capitalize on a relaxed theology of Christian humanism to enrich the role of women as moral and cultural mediators, but Stowe's particular family ties and republican conservatism gave her a decided advantage over Elizabeth Stoddard. In fact, Stoddard's entrapment in a marriage to the minor poet Richard Henry Stoddard, and her disadvantaged position within a literary legacy that seemed at times bent on excluding her, made her embrace of an oppositional stance all the more important. As Sandra Zagarell is quick to point out, praise for Stoddard's regional, realist, and modernist tendencies has

> actually reinforced prevailing versions of literary history at the expense of illuminating her highly iconoclastic writing. On one level, her work's incompatibility with literary conventions would have given Stoddard a certain ironic satisfaction, for she was bent on challenging reigning conventions of her own day. An outstandingly ambitious woman with a keen sense of her own merits, she wanted equality with male writers in a culture in which most women novelists worked to explore the women's sphere. Though she shared many of the concerns of the American novelists whose work [Nina Baym has reconceived], Stoddard spurned the commercialism and female readership which made women's fiction, in her eyes, inferior to men. ("Repossession of a Heritage" 45)

The qualities of spiritualistic discourse localized in a female medium—a woman's autonomy within public culture, the assertion that a woman's delicate constitution and excitability were virtues that contributed to leadership, the pre-eminence of intuition for reading cryptic texts—gave to Stoddard a means for discarding limitations on her role as a woman writer without questioning accepted ideas about woman's nature.

Trance mediums were understood, by the audiences who gathered to hear them, to be passive vehicles for the expression of unseen intelligences. Mediums presented not their own views but the views of the spirits who spoke through them. Whether we conceive of a medium's voice as inspired by external intelligence or by some remote region of the medium's mind, Stoddard's mediumship liberated Stoddard's voice in the arena of cultural interpretation. In a very real sense, Stoddard's work exhibits Mather's *Magnalia* "speaking out" from the themes and subjects of her novel. The medium's trance provided Stoddard with a connection to Mather's desire for autonomy, and it provided the means for masking her radical narrative from the power of social sanctions.

Cassandra Morgeson is a phenomenon in the mesmeric line, one of those specially endowed, "magnetized" subjects used by the importers of mesmeric lore—Charles Polen and his many imitators—to demonstrate the principles of animal magnetism to the American public after 1836. Richard Brodhead traces the phenomenon with reference to Hawthorne's veiled lady in *The Blithedale Romance*. The figure of the medium, he writes, invoked "a salience of contemporary life, the cultural attraction of . . . the new sciences, those congeries of systems—Swedenborgianism, phrenology, utopian socialism, and Grahamite dietary lore are other examples—that developed into something between fad philosophies and surrogate religions in the 1840s" ("Veiled Ladies" 274). Nathan Hatch, in *The Democratization of American Christianity*, persuasively argues that "the democratic revolution of the early republic sent external religious authority into headlong retreat and elicited from below powerful visions of faith that seemed more authentic and self-evident" (34). Stoddard's cultural logic works on her readers like a form of vernacular preaching: Stoddard's authorship of history proves her to be a communication entrepreneur who opens new avenues into the true-to-life passions and dramatic creativity of Cassandra Morgeson (Hatch 133, 141). The appearance of mesmerism becomes one manifestation of the variously directed energy of social and intellectual reconstruction that touched almost all aspects of American culture in the 1840s under the rubric "reform." And, like Hawthorne's veiled lady, Cassandra Morgeson is a cultural construction of a certain version of woman and of the whole set of social relations built on this figure of domestic life. She leads an "exaggeratedly public life." Behind Cassandra Morgeson

> we could see arrayed the new female celebrities who, first in the 1840s, then more decisively around 1850, began . . . to be known to publics. . . . what [she] registers, we might say, is the historical emergence, at mid-century, of a more massively publicized order of entertainment. . . . She embodies the suggestion that the same contemporary cultural processes that worked in one direction to delimit women to de-physicalized and deactivated domestic privacy also helped open up an enlarged publicity women could inhabit. (Brodhead, "Veiled Ladies" 276–77)

Mediumship and its constructed individuality raise again the specter of Cotton Mather, who in his efforts to combat a spreading antinomianism could merely point out that all individuality is based on the assumption of chaos barely contained through representation.

The impulses of Stoddard's Puritanism are conveyed within a social reality that presupposes a historical context of modernization. Cassandra's negotiations, her presentation of a mediumistic historical narrative, become a way to preserve a premodern sensibility inherited from Cotton Mather, even as the narrative allows us to see the contrast between contemporary social reality and the attenuated source of nineteenth-century culture. The past of the Puritan forefathers was a vision that had become atavistic—that the identity it creates, though somehow always there—must be reactivated by a fairly conscious renewal of antique historical perception. In the world of *The Morgesons* historical associations function as a form of grace. Here as in our other examples of historical romance, readers are forced to maintain a self-questioning attitude that both apprehends the representations made to them and draws attention to the underlying processes that enable the representations in the first place.[5]

In *The Morgesons*, the evocation of Mather's witchcraft theme in *Magnalia* provides the mechanism and resonating power of Stoddard's (re)presentation of the Puritan past. Stoddard's translation of New England history depends on the evocation of witchcraft as a theme. The implication of witchcraft begins early in the novel and runs deep. The novel opens with the suggestion: " 'That child,' said my aunt Mercy, looking at me with indigo-colored eyes, 'is possessed' " (5). In her altercation with Elmira Sawyer, which results in expulsion from school, Cassandra is told by her teacher, " 'You are a bad girl.' . . . 'Miss C. Morgeson is a peculiar case' " (41). Veronica has a sphere that is appropriate to her personality: " 'Home,' father said, 'was her sphere.' " But none exists that can contain Cassandra: " 'Where did I belong?' he asked. I was still 'possessed,' Aunt Merce said, and mother called me 'lawless.' 'What upon earth are you coming to?' asked Temperance. 'You are sowing your wild oats with a vengeance' " (60). Later, during her association with Charles Morgeson in Roseville, strong suggestions are made linking Cassandra with animal magnetism: " 'Mother,' I said afterward, I am afraid I am an animal.' . . . 'These are fine brutes,' he [Charles] said, not taking his eyes from them; 'but they are not equal to my mare, Nell. Alice is afraid of her; but I hope that you, Cassandra, will ride with me sometimes when I drive her.' . . . He struck them, and said, 'Go on now, go on, devils' " (71–72). Indeed, Cassandra's attachment to Charles borders on enchantment:

> An intangible, silent, magnetic feeling existed between us, changing and developing according to its own mysterious law, remaining intact in spite of the contests between us of resistance and defiance. But my feelings died or slumbered when I was beyond the limits of his personal influence. When in his presence I was so pervaded by it that whether I went contrary to the dictates of his will or not I moved as if under a pivot; when away my natural elasticity prevailed, and I held the same relation to others that I should have held if I had not known him. (74)

Earlier, Charles had become aware of Cassandra's mysterious charms when he first met her in Surrey: "He asked me if I knew whether the sea had any influence upon me; I replied that I had not thought of it. 'There are so many things you have not thought of,' he answered, 'that this is not strange' " (62). Alice Morgeson seems well aware of Cassandra's powers, "You are peculiar, then; it may be he [Charles] likes you for being so. He is odd, you know; but his oddity never troubles me." Cassandra's response is a mix of self-recognition and envy of her nemesis sister: " 'Veronica is odd, also,' was my thought; but oddity there runs in a different direction. Her image appeared to me, pale, delicate, unyielding. I seemed to wash like a weed at her base" (85). In an act of self-admission, Cassandra does not deny the claims others have placed upon her: "Of course I was driven from whim to whim, to keep them busy, and to preserve my originality, and at last I became eccentric for eccentricity's sake. All this prepared the way for my Nemesis" (61).

In actuality Cassandra has two nemeses, her sister Veronica and Ben Somers, both of whom spur Cass to perform evil actions. Verry's presence at the Morgeson tea party brings out Cassandra's dark behavior, but it is Ben who acts in concert with her to bring evil to the surface. Verry's communication with Cassandra shows that she knows her sister's secret: "Distant, indifferent, and speculative as the eyes were, a ray of fire shot into them occasionally, which made her gaze powerful and concentrated" (51). Her glib communication with Cass always carries with it oblique references. For instance, when Cass suggests, "Why not have a fire in your room?" Verry utters, "A fire would put me out. One belongs in this room, though. It is the only reality here" (145). With Ben, however, the implication of secret evil becomes more than a mere suggestion. Cass's first encounter with Ben, at a tea hosted by the Bancrofts, indicates their natural affinities:

> I was drawn into speaking of my life at home; my remarks made without premeditation, proved that I possessed ideas and feelings hitherto unknown. I felt no shyness before him, and, although I saw his interest in me, no agitation. Helen was also moved to tell us she was engaged. She rolled up her sleeve to show us a bracelet, printed in ink on her arm with the initials, "L.N." . . . "How could you consent to have your arm so defaced?" I asked. Her eyes flashed as she replied that she had not looked upon the mark in that light before. "We may all be tattooed," said Mr. Somers. "I am," I thought. (97)

Later, the mark on Helen's arm becomes highly charged for Veronica: "The trying on of this dress was the means of her discovering the letters on Helen's arm, which never ceased to be a source of interest. She asked to see them every day afterward, and touched them with her fingers, as if they had some occult power" (150). For both Verry and Cass, Ben holds a Svengali-like power. One day, during Ben's visit to Surrey, Cassandra notes that "his eyes, darting sharp rays, pierced me through; they rested on the thread-like scars which marked my cheek, and which were more visible from the effect of cold" (156). Ben's grasp on Cassandra's soul is continued one day when he leaves a volume of Tennyson. Cass tells us, "It was the book of poems he had spoken of. I lighted on 'Fatima,' read it and copied it." This is a prime manifestation of Stoddard's use of the witchcraft theme, for in Cassandra's attention to a poem about a woman who must "possess" a man or else die, the supernatural is "resolved into a combination of offbeat bohemian charm and scattered instances of hackneyed psychic communication between the Morgeson sisters and their beaux" (Buell, *New England Literary Culture* 364–65).

In their most poignant confrontation in Roseville, Cassandra orders a protesting Ben Somers out of the room, professes her love for her cousin, and enjoins him not to speak of their mutual attraction until their last hell-bound midnight ride together. What she says draws her closer to Ben's influence in spite of her affection for Charles:

> "What on earth has happened to you? Oh!" she [Verry] exclaimed, as I looked at her. "You were out there with Morgeson and Ben Somers," she whispered; "something has occurred; what is it?"
> "You shall never know; never — never — never."
> "Cassandra that man is a devil."
> "I like devils."
> "The same blood rages in both of you." (110)

Ben's home in Belem is an archetypal haunted house. Cass observes, "Ben was not the same in Belem, I saw at once, and no longer wondered at its influence, or at the vacillating nature of his plans and pursuits. Mrs. Somers gave me some tea from a spider-shaped silver teapot, which was related to a spider-shaped cream-jug and a spider-shaped sugar dish" (168). Ben's power over both Cass and Veronica borders on mind control: " 'Cassandra,' said Desmond, 'are you bored?' The accent with which he spoke my name set my pulses striking like a clock. I got up mechanically, as Ben directed" (184). Most of the family in Belem sense that Cassandra is to be an agent in some devilish scheme, but Mrs. Somers feels it acutely: "Did a child of yours ever inflict a blow upon you?" she asks Cass. "He [Ben] has played with such toys as you are, and broken them." Recognizing that both a goblet and a child are endangered treasures in the Somers house, Cassandra "caught up a glass goblet as if to throw it, but only grasped it so tight that it shivered. 'There goes one of the Pickersgill treasures, I am sure,' I thought." Cassandra continues in a mocking Calvinist vein: " 'Madam, I have no plans. If I have a purpose, it is formless yet. If God saves us what can you do?' She made a gesture of contempt. 'You have no soul to thank me for what may be my work,' and I opened the door. Ben stood on the threshold" (194).

This passage, so burdened as it is with implied evil, portrays Cass as a figure whose agency is controlled from outside her moral consciousness. Ben's close proximity to Cass and his "magnetic" influence lead Cass to perform actions of which she is unaware. "This old lady had taught me something," Cass remarks shortly after the Somers infanticide is foreshadowed. "I went to the window, curious to know whether any nerve of association would vibrate again. Nothing stirred me; the machinery which had agitated and controlled me was effete" (196). Cass's complicity with Ben's crime is reinforced by his matter-of-fact presentation when he returns to Cass's home in Surrey: "The child is dead, for the first thing. (Cigar, Manuel.) Second, I was possessed to come home by way of Roseville" (244).

Ben and Cassandra's association is part of a strange cross-pattern of mate-switching and emotional transferences that run throughout the novel. Appropriately, their combination is the articulated nightmare of the culture they inhabit; their power, which in another writer's hands might threaten the credulity of a conventionally "realistic" or "psychological" novel, runs free largely because it is understated and seldom definitively identified. Finally, their complicity ends with a mutual confession just before Cass's marriage to Desmond, during a scene that echoes Dimmesdale and Hester in the forest: " 'Friend,' I said to Ben, who lingered by the door, 'to contend with me was not folly, unless it has kept you from contending with yourself. Tell me how is it with you?' 'Cassandra, the jaws of hell are open. If you are satisfied with the end, I must be' " (252).

When Alice appears to help braid Cassandra's hair, Cassandra becomes the central figure in a dramaturgical scene that defines her status as a woman and the site of a Puritan conceit of evil:

> "Let me braid your hair," she said, "in a different fashion." I assented; the baby was bestowed on a rug, and a chair was put before the glass, that I might witness the operation. "What magnificent hair!" she said, as she unrolled it. "It is a yard long." "It is a regular mane, isn't it?" She began combing it; the baby crawled under the bed, and coming out with the handkerchief in its hand, crept up to her, trying to make her take it. . . . "Do I hurt you Cass?" "No, do I ever hurt you Alice?" . . . "Were any of your family cracked? I have long suspected you of a disposition that way." "The child is choking itself with that handkerchief." (100)

To grasp the precise character of what I have called Stoddard's implication of Puritanism and witchcraft, we might compare the conceit to the mood evoked by this passage. The fact that Cassandra calls her hair a "mane" and that the two women talk in veiled terms about an adulterous situation, as well as the suggestion of infanticide, places Cassandra as a central element in the cosmology of *The Morgesons*. Cassandra's presence explains the existence of death, illness, and personal misfortune, as well as attitudes and behavior antithetical to her culture. Because of her, Charles Morgeson dies a violent death; her father, who has consented to marry Charles's widow, suffers fiscal ruin; the Somers infant dies; and Ben Somers drinks himself into an early grave. Each of these pivotal moments owes its occurrence to the active, precipitating role of Cassandra. Mather's own interest in witchcraft stemmed from the recognition that uncontrollable women posed a great danger to the hierarchical order of Puritan culture, which depended on vigilant self-denial by women. Stoddard toys with this notion of womanhood constantly. Cassandra's portrayal here is designed to resonate with Puritan beliefs that disorderly women posed a threat to the social order. As Karlsen notes, "the witchcraft trials and executions show that only force could ensure such sweeping denial of self. New England witches were women who resisted the new truths [of being a complaisant helpmeet, freeing the man for economic mobility and increased self-importance], either symbolically or in fact. In doing so, they were visible—and profoundly disturbing—reminders of potential resistance in all women" (180–81).

Cassandra's and Ben's story is the tale of witches who have freely exercised their craft and not only lived to witness their handiwork but profited from it. Cassandra is a "half-ingenious, half-deliberate provoker of the emotions from whose intensity she backs away into reserve," remarks Lawrence Buell; "Cassandra's probing yet guarded manner (replicated in the whole style of narration) is the basis of her power as an enchantress, telegraphing to the men around her a tantalizing mixture of audacity and reserve yet also serving as a defense against the advances that her boldness might provoke" (*New England Literary Culture* 361–62). Ben Somers, a kindred spirit "tattooed," as Stoddard phrases it, both encourages and feeds off Cassandra's devilishness. Their lives motivate each other, and their subversiveness, which appears and disappears from the reader's vision like a changeling, is linked "to social and personal derangement in ways that differ sharply but point in each case to a world in need of exorcism" (*New England Literary Culture* 362). Their hidden agendas, like that of Stoddard, both inform the narrative action and rarefy the presentation of historical reality. Cassandra's brazen identity is not obvious to all who see her, however. If she is a demonic figure, her true identity is glimpsed only in flashes of external behavior and in her triggering of spectral phenomena in those around her. In short, she is a woman who symbolically internalizes much of the mysterious force and hidden motivations that so captivate others. She is like Lizzie Doten, a medium figure who mesmerizes and captivates audiences with her apparent access to outside intelligences.[6]

As interesting as Snell or Grand'ther Warren is as a historical curiosity, Stoddard's interest in *Magnalia* is more than a symbolic gesture; it defines her approach to delineating New England as a cultural site. *The Morgesons*'s claim to attention stems from Stoddard's vivid and detailed portrayal of Cassandra's struggles toward maturity in Surrey's latter-day Puritan culture. Her appropriation of that tradition is contained in miniature in the passage cited above. Like Mather, Stoddard delved into the heart of what it means to ask so much of one's region and to be faced with a diminishing reality. By her use of ironic tones ("he was aboriginal in character, not to be moved by antecedent or changed by innovation"), the presentation of absurd details (fingernails like beetles clicking), and a mysterious obsession with a grotesque past (he found his wife dead), Stoddard "defamiliarizes" our grasp of the Puritan past. Like Mather, she questions the notion of a universal *humanitas*: Cassandra says with some remorse, "Was it a pity that my life was not conducted on Nature's plan, who shows us the beautiful, while she conceals the interior? We do not see the roots of her roses, and she hides from us her skeletons" (45).

Where Mather's treatment of Puritan history put forward a history characterized by extreme mystery and opaqueness, *The Morgesons* also depends on a dispersive mode of history where particularity is celebrated as irreducible variety. For both writers, the true concept of Puritanism had less to do with the contemporary significance of the Puritan past than with a recognition that Puritanism is a phenomenon held captive by language itself. Puritanism sought to reduce some area of cognitively problematical experience to a form of comprehension considered to be cognitively secured either by established disciplines or by the ongoing common sense of the culture. This is the whole point underlying Mather's extended treatment of witchcraft in *Magnalia*, and it is why Stoddard borrowed this trope from Mather to create her logic of representation for *The Morgesons*. Mather's belief in the Devil and his interest in witches has less to do with the satanic powers than with biblical, historical, and natural phenomena whose significance may be revealed in history or by means of rational investigation and conjecture. Similarly, Stoddard's interest in spiritualism became an effective rhetorical principle for understanding the effect that a post-Puritan culture has on the sensibilities of an acutely sensitive young woman experiencing a variety of repressive circumstances. In considering these two writers and their shared approach to Puritan history, I am not interested in rehearsing the entire question of witchcraft and other antinomian perversions embedded within Puritanism. Instead, I want to illustrate how each writer encoded New England as a perpetually unstable cultural locus. Three aspects of Mather's *Magnalia* bear directly on this discussion: his location of historical consciousness outside the self, his ethnographic stance toward understanding his subjects, and his reliance on a dispersive mode of historical narrative.

Given the lapse in time between the 1820 publication of the Robbins edition and *The Morgesons*, many of these claims make sense of the ways Mather's text formed New England cultural values. Nevertheless, both authors are trapped by the need to create a sufficient and sympathetic readership. The actual ends accomplished by each of these books depend on the constraints and facilitating choices placed on them by the printing process. The specter of mediumship that underlies both *The Morgesons* and *Magnalia* illustrates that the writer's local relationship to a social governmentality is constituted by an involuntary and predetermined world, on the one hand, and by creative and productive acts, on the other. Thus, Mather's continuing influence for shaping popular conceptions of New England and Stoddard's radical conventions manipulating that legacy converge around an "invisible center" designating (as Robbins had predicted) the local conditions of historical romance. Mather's book initially played to profoundly elite political audiences. Stoddard's immersion in the mid-nineteenth-century literary culture depended on her simultaneous inclusion and exclusion from history. The entrepreneurial impulses that created a reading public for *The Morgesons* had helped transform America from a society in which men and women assumed a fixed place to a fluid society where individuals employed their property and intellectual talents within a liberal environment favoring the clever, the artful, the ambitious, and the capable—those most skilled in the world of market relations.

The Location of Historical Consciousness

Both Mather and Stoddard felt that important aspects of a culture's historical consciousness lay outside the self. In Mather, the historical significance of and responsibility for the Salem delusions were negotiated in synodal meetings, through the procedures of the legal apparatus, and through written accounts. The advantage of this method of arriving at historical conclusions was that no one person could be held accountable for either the wisdom or the errors of any particular case. Consequently, Mather was able to fully interject himself into the events at Salem but was able to dodge any charge of malfeasance. Charles Wentworth Upham's attempt to place Mather as the "man" behind the witchcraft scandals depended on a view that saw Mather as a historically privileged personality. Mather's resistance to Upham's charge depends on his being seen as a product of his culture; any historical significance attached to his singular actions was merely the accidental combination of a collective resolve. Though Stoddard and Mather participate in the negotiations of culture, they do not claim to be the original source of its significance. Elizabeth Stoddard, in the *Alta California* newspaper article "A Village on the Sea Shore" (October 24, 1855), wrote:

> I too am a pilgrim and a sojourner, but not a fashionable one. . . . But to come to the truth and beauty of my surroundings. Here rolls the everlasting sea. On the day of my birth its voice was uplifted; on the day of my death, its song will be the same. The sandy soil of the village grave yard hides generations of my race. The old slate stones level with their mounds, and covered with moss, the upright marble slabs with their names freshly cut have neither age nor date to the deaf and sightless sea. But unpitying as it is, I am drawn to it by a resistless fascination. Ever in motion, yet within impassible [sic] barriers, it seems a type of the soul on earth, fretted by and chained to the body. If it be true that we are in conformity with the configuration of the country and climate, in which we are born, I arrive at the conclusion that I am full of dents; that my disposition is a "norwester," that my intellect is misty, and that I am a queer *cove* generally. (319–20)

Stoddard carefully removes herself from complete conformity with her country and climate, yet the existence of a connection is never fully denied. Posing as a disturbed soul, the author has been battered and shaped by her environment but has never totally freed her self-identity from the culture she inhabits. Stoddard admits that, like her beloved sea, she is a "type of the soul on earth"; her historical consciousness, that "queer cove," is a part of her culture but not the source of it.

Through imaginative invention, Stoddard, like Mather, was able to describe her region in ways that overflow its traditional image. For Mather's ancestors, New England was a place where the elect routinely discerned "sermons in stones" and history was based on typological relationships. The divine mission they embarked on was confirmed by the record of their experiences in the New World. For Mather and Stoddard, however, the world was postcolonial: New England's meaning (where it could be discerned at all) was based on a succession-analogy relationship in which history unfolds in repetitive patterns that draw their significance from the early settlement.

Miss Emily Black, Cassandra's young schoolteacher, is a person engaged in describing the past in terms of succession and analogy:

> She bit her nails when annoyed, and when her superiority made her perceive the mental darkness of others she often laughed. Being pious, she conducted her school after the theologic pattern of the Nipswich Seminary, at which she had been educated. She opened the school each day with a religious exercise, reading something from the bible, and commenting upon it, or questioning us regarding our ideas of what she read. She often selected the character of David, and was persistent in her efforts to explain and reconcile the discrepancies in the history of the royal Son of Israel. (35)

This "discrepancy," of course, is very important to our appreciation of Cassandra's significance as a historical figure; it has an allegorical confusion that readers were invited to ascribe to the protagonist.

In 1 Chronicles 3:5, we learn that Bath-Sheba was originally the wife of Uriah the Hittite, one of David's warriors. During the war against Rabbath-Ammon, David saw Bath-Sheba and ordered her brought to his palace. When David knew that she was pregnant by him, he attempted to return Uriah to his house. Failing to do so, he sought and found a pretext to have Uriah killed in battle; David then married Bath-Sheba. Among biblical scholars, there is considerable difference of opinion about the significance of this tale. Most of the controversy is about the interpretation put forward in the Aggadah, homiletic expositions of the Hebrew Bible found in the Talmud and Midrash. There, Bath-Sheba is claimed to be the granddaughter of Ahithophel, and the prophecies that he believed foretold his own royal destiny in fact applied to her. Bath-Sheba was predestined for David; his sin was that he took her before the appointed time. This interpretation sheds light on the contest among the various men who compete for Cassandra. Like a figure invested with typological significance, Cassandra, as a central negotiator of historical prophecy, is an enchanting figure whose influence creates great disruptions in the male world. Stoddard's portrait of Miss Black depends on seeing Puritan culture as inherently grotesque. Miss Black mistakes form for substance: her attempt to lead a life bathed in religion is merely a disguise for the fact that "her superiority" makes her laugh at the mental darkness of others. This mistaking of form for substance lay at the root of the whole Puritan enterprise: Calvinism leads to pharisaism, which distorts the whole social environment.

Mather's and Stoddard's concerns for representing Puritan history have as their basis the devout Puritan's intense concern for distinguishing authentic from simulated conversions. Consequently, both writers adopted the position that historical consciousness, in order to be a genuine phenomenon, had to be discovered outside mere formalism. Their interpretations of and inventions about the past had to be tested against an accepted paradigm. In *The Morgesons*, as we have seen, this paradigm is the spectral apprehension of witchcraft.

The Morgesons reflects a fundamental split in the Puritan mind. On the one hand, Mather's contemporaries declared in sermon after sermon that nature was awry and that its meaningful potential was destroyed by man's "blasted" faculties. On the other hand, some Puritan intellectuals believed that nature was characterized by a comfortable knowableness. Mather's *Magnalia* bridged these two contradictory notions, so that his position seemed a vacillating one dependent on whom he thought he was addressing. In attempting to preserve a core Calvinist belief, Mather alternately adopts a position defending the validity of mythic identifications and a position that celebrates scientific revelations of law and design in nature.

Cassandra shares this same sensibility. As the appointed historian for a lost community, she describes the Morgesons as a supernatural covenanted community ("The meum and tuum of blood were inextricably mixed and . . . added a still more profound darkness to the anti-heraldic memory of the Morgesons") and as a systematic entity ("Comprehension of life, and comprehension of self, came too late for him [Locke Morgeson] to make either of value. The spirit of progress, however, which prompted his schemes benefited others" [8–9]). With the removal of historical consciousness from the interior to an exterior realm, the influence of supernatural phenomena became loosed in culture.

The Morgesons embodies the ambiguity between two interrelated precepts: the deterioration of man's social connection with nature and the necessity and possibility of his regeneration as natural man. Cassandra's answer to this question (or perhaps the continual re-asking of it that she provokes) puts her ostensibly outside man's law, outside New England's religion, morals, and manners, all of which are seen at times to be repressive at worst, emptied of meaning at best. *The Morgesons* depends on the suggestion that the supernatural may be a constitutive fact of New England life or merely a symbolic aspect of a romanticized history.[7]

Cassandra's "Defamiliarization" of Culture

The remarkable force of spiritualism opens Stoddard's novel in surprising and convincing ways. The fictional world of *The Morgesons* always has a contrived feel to it. As readers, we are barely convinced of its substantiality, and as soon as we recognize an external phenomenon, it becomes telescoped by historical meaning. Lizzie Doten, a celebrated medium, declared "the external phenomenon of Modern Spiritualism . . . compared to the great principles underlying them, are but mere froth and foam on the ocean of truth" (qtd. in Braude 89). Similarly, Stoddard's attachments to physical details are often only coincidental to their more comprehensive but masked role in a larger historical semiology. In one of the most succinct examples of this type of vision, Stoddard shows the entire ancestry of the Morgesons as a capsule container of the New England past and as a signifier for an expanse of meaning locked away in Mather's time: "There was a confusion in the minds of the survivors of the various generations about the degree of their relationship to those who were buried, and whose names and ages simply were cut in the stones which headed their graves. . . . *Morgeson—Born—Lived—Died*—were all their archives" (8–9). Cassandra, Stoddard's enacted self, takes for her role the reapprehension of the Morgeson past. To Cass falls the task of deciphering the riddles bound up in her inheritance and genealogy; she is the "aboriginal [who] reappears to prove the plastic powers of nature" (9). Stoddard, deploying the conventions of the trance speaker, holds herself above the epiphenomenal aspects of New England in order to dwell on the great motivating principles of history that underlie her subject. The essence of "mediumistic history" is captured in Lizzie Doten's description of the trance:

The avenues of external sense, if not closed, were at least disused, in order that the spiritual perception might be quickened to the required degree, and also that the world of causes, of which the earth and its experiences are but the passing effects, might be disclosed to [the medium's vision]. Certain it is that a physical change took place, affecting both my breathing and circulation. (qtd. in Braude 89)

The narration that Cassandra relates in the novel frequently is used to highlight the contingency between her external senses and the substance of her encounters in the world. Stoddard's challenge in *The Morgesons* became how to make the past re-enter the present in a way that continued to portray New England as a vital cultural site whose definition remained irreducibly problematic. As Richard Foster notes in his preface to the 1976 reprint of *The Morgesons*:

the novel is made up of a remarkable variety of departures and returns, conflicts and reconciliations, deaths, births, and marriages, with the rolling on of seasons and years seeming to mark the only certain law within the apparent randomness of existence. Another law gradually suggests itself, however, amid this tangle of events, in the slow convergence, through a succession of crises of passionate attraction. . . . Deeply rooted in the actualities of New England, *The Morgesons* stands both as a kind of diagnosis of that culture's ills and as a prescription for its cure. (17–18)

In order for Cassandra to be an effective diagnostician of New England, she has to take an alien stance vis-à-vis the subjects she describes. Cassandra's analytic capacities stem from her natural disposition to maintain a distance from the important shaping events of her life. When, for instance, she enters school in Surrey, she notices "others who belonged in the category of De-cayed Families, as exclusive as they were shabby. There were parvenus, which included myself. When I entered the school it was divided into clans, each with its spites, jealousies, and emulations." Then, with a sharp recognition that she is a catalytic figure whose standing apart from the rest of humanity has a powerful influence on others, Cassandra notes that "[Surrey's] esprit de corps, however, was developed by my arrival; the girls united against me, and though I perceived, when I compared myself with them, that they were partly right in their opinions, their ridicule stupefied and crushed me. They were trained, intelligent, and adroit; I uncouth, ignorant, and without tact" (35). After her mother's funeral, Cassandra's exclusion from the preparations for the funeral reiterates her separation:

> [Veronica's] course was taken for granted; mine was imposed upon me. I remonstrated with Temperance, but she replied that it was all well meant, and always done. I endured the same annoyances over and over again from relays of people. Bed-time especially was their occasion. I was not to undress alone. I must have drinks, either to compose or stimulate; I must have something read to me; I must be watched while I slept. . . . All the while, like a chorus, they reiterated the character, the peculiarities, the virtues of the mother I had lost, who could never be replaced—who was in a better world. However, I was, in a measure, kept from myself during this interval. (209)

The sense of isolation does more than reflect a daughter's annoyance at being sequestered before her mother's funeral; it indicates a lingering perception that Cassandra's best place is on the margins. The persons who comfort her during a time of great stress are also those who may believe that Cassandra's *malefica* (spectral personality) may have been involved in her mother's death.

Cassandra's ability to remain at a distance from the contexts that attempt to contain her personality makes her an intensely attractive, as well as a fearsome, figure. Her alien stance toward those she loves and toward the places she inhabits makes her the focal point of an elusive exchange between explicit and implicit knowledge in the culture. Her displays of deep passion and unfulfilled desires, which gave her a brush with adultery, and her threat to Surrey's economic order by her inheritance of the Morgeson home implicitly affirmed her dangerous capacities. In a truly Puritan world, Cassandra would have easily fit the typical profile of a witch. In a manner that parallels Mather's treatment of Anne Hutchinson, Stoddard's removal of Cassandra from the center of the world she describes becomes a signal of Cassandra's willful rejection of religious, civil, and ethnic authority in New England.

So potentially destructive is Cass's separation from the social unit that her exiles from Surrey are, like those of Anne Hutchinson and Mary Oliver, fraught with destruction. Her ambiguous stature allows society to hang symbolic significance on Cassandra, and she, in turn, is well suited for describing, reflecting, and masking a world-view predicated on an exchange between the past and present. Ben recognizes this after he has decided to marry the more prosaic Veronica. Ben says to Cassandra:

> "You have been my delight and misery ever since I knew you. I saw you first, so impetuous, yet self-contained! Incapable of insincerity, devoid of affection and courageously naturally beautiful. Then, to my amazement, I saw that unlike most women, you understood your instincts; that you dared to define them, and were impious enough to follow them. You debased my ideal, you confused me also, for I could never affirm that you were wrong; forcing me to confront abstractions, they gave a verdict in your favor, which almost unsexed you in my estimation. I must own that the man who is willing to marry you has more courage than I have. Is it strange that when I found your counterpart, Veronica, that I yielded? Her delicate, pure, ignorant soul suggests to me eternal repose."
>
> "It is not necessary that you should fatigue your mind with abstractions concerning her. It will be the literal you will hunger for, dear Ben." (226)

The conjoining of "eternal repose" and "literal" is Cassandra's death curse on Ben. Cassandra's obvious sexual power over Ben makes it plain that he cannot acquire her directly. Ben's relationship to Cassandra must remain oblique and, like a medium and her stage-man (or like a witch in a protected coven), Cassandra's self-confidence subjects her to deceptions by lesser men like Ben. Ben understands that Cassandra's powerful nature threatens most men, and her unsatisfied desires explain why, in the opinion of those around her, Cassandra would turn to the Devil for satisfaction.

Ben and Cassandra, though kindred spirits, cannot directly marry. Instead, Ben marries Verry, Cass's "lesser twin," and Cassandra marries Desmond, Ben's wayward brother. Although Ben and Cass are both "tattooed" by their secret affections for one another, their surrogate marriages, arranged through a succession of misfortunes, are the only way in which they can connect. If they hold genuine communication with another world, then a temporal marriage would be meaningless.

Premodernity

Stoddard's suggestion of spiritualism at work in *The Morgesons* accomplishes two things simultaneously: it provides a compelling popular basis for her readers to engage her authorship; and, in its implication of a more primitive connection to the past, spiritualism creates a space of premodernity, which in turn becomes the space where New England's past is manipulated. Richard Foster finds that Stoddard's pictures of midcentury life in coastal New England "shaped themselves into patterns suggesting worlds beyond the actual; her characters took on dimensions larger than the 'realistic,' the dynamics of their intense and shifting interrelations acquiring the overtones of myth" (8–9). Cassandra, of course, is the principal figure who acts within this premodern arena, but the presence of a deeper, intuitive, and vital layer that is co-extensive with contemporary social reality is a premise shared and recognized by all in the novel.

After Charles Morgeson's death, the point at which Cassandra's and Ben's lives become forever connected, Cassandra receives a letter that makes plain that she will be suspended between two modes of being. "My youth grew dim; somehow I felt self-pity. I found no chance to embalm those phases of sensation which belonged to my period, and I grew careless. . . . For all this mad longing sometimes seized me to depart into a new world, which should contain no element of the old, least of all a reminiscence of what my experience had made me" (152). Frequently, this more primitive layer of this "new world" purged of contemporary concerns is folded into Stoddard's Gothic preoccupations. During a night walk in Belem, Ben asks Cass, "Are you afraid?" Cassandra says yes, and Ben asks: "Of what?" Cass replies, "The Prince of Darkness." Then, in a passage that is vintage Emily Brontë, Stoddard has Ben interject, " 'The devil lives a little behind us,' 'In you, too, then?' 'In Rash. Look at him; he is bigger than Faust's dog, jumps higher, and is blacker. You can't hear the least sound from him as he gambols with his familiar' " (179). Edmund Stedman, the most lasting, loyal, and indispensable friend of the Stoddards, seized on Elizabeth's affinities to *Wuthering Heights*, saying that she and her husband were "welded iron in their sensitiveness, their pride, their stoicism. . . . Both were Puritan-pagan, each could say of the other: 'I do not love Heathcliff; I am Heathcliff" (Stedman and Gould 533).

Cassandra's special ability to enter and understand the implication of parallel worlds is a common trope in her narration. She was surely a "Puritan-pagan" figure. After her mother's death, Cassandra has this contemplative moment: "Eye-like bubbles rose from among the fronds of the knotted wrack, and sailing on uncertain voyages, broke one by one and were wrecked to nothingness. The last vanished; the pool showed me the motionless shadow of my face again, on which I pondered, till I suddenly became aware of a slow, internal oscillation, which increased till I felt in a strange tumult. I put my hand in the surf and troubled its surface" (214). Cassandra's special nature puts her in command of the mystical influence of the past.

Like the Shaker spiritualists of New Lebanon, Watervliet, and Hancock, Cassandra is entranced by the past, and she frequently is "taken under operations." Her senses appear to be withdrawn from time. Peering into the Somers garden from the summer room (at the vernal equinox), Cassandra notices

> the chestnut had leaved seventy times and more; and the crippled plum, whose fruit was so wormy to eat, was dying with age. As for the elms at the bottom of the garden, for all she knew they were a thousand years old. "The elms are a thousand years old," I repeated and repeated to myself, while she [Mrs. Somers] glided from topic to topic. . . . The garden grew dusk, and the elms began to nod their tops to me. I became silent, listening to the sound of the plummet, which dropped again and again from the topmost height of that lordly domain, over which the shadows had come. Were they sounding its foundations? My eyes roved the garden, seeking the nucleus of an emotion which beset me now — not they, but my senses, formed it — in a garden miles away, where nodded a row of elms, under which *Charles Morgeson* stood. *"I'm glad you're here, my darling, do you smell the roses?"* (189)

In another arresting passage, Cassandra peers into a painting on Veronica's wall and recognizes immediately the fact that the world is constituted through duplicity:

> A large-eyed Saint Cecilia, with white roses in her hair, was pasted on the wall. This frameless picture had a curious effect. Veronica, in some mysterious way, had contrived to dispose of the white margin of the picture, and the saint looked out from the soft ashy tint of the wallpaper. Opposite was an exquisite engraving. . . . At the end of an avenue of old trees, gnarled and twisted into each other a man stood. One hand grasped the stalk of a ragged vine, which ran over the tree near him; the other hung helpless by his side, as if the wrist was broken. His eyes were fixed on some object behind the trees, where nothing was visible but a portion of

the wall of the house. His expression of concentrated fury—his attitude of waiting—testified that he would surely accomplish his intention. (134)

Cassandra's vantage point, between premodern primitivism and nineteenth-century society, reveals the doubled surface of all reality. Further, to her eyes, all that she sees is tinged by evil. Here, in her discernment of Charles Morgeson in Veronica's engraving, Cassandra's occult involvement with Ben Somers emerges as a fantasy of revenge. Cassandra exclaims, "What a picture!" and Verry answers, "The foliage attracted me, and I bought it; but when I unpacked it, the man seemed to come out for the first time. Will you take it?" In a coy recognition of the Gothic humor that this picture implies, Cass responds, "No; I mean to give my room a somnolent aspect. The man is too terribly sleepless" (134). Comparison of Cassandra's behavior with that of other spiritual or primitive sects reveals her as a person with special endowments. *The Morgesons* is replete with allusions that cry out to be identified, repetitions that beg the reader to ask whose story is being told and why.

The mystical experiences of all spiritual fellowships—clairvoyance and clairaudience, speaking in unknown tongues, telepathies, prophecies, and automatisms—are charismatic gifts associated with Cassandra. Her association with the image of the spiritual medium is so revealing that we are tempted to find it definitive. Under Stoddard's logic, the New England past begins to emphasize a complementary point: all moral experience is in a significant sense historical; the spiritual quality of every age is, accordingly, tried in the crucible of its own categories. Audiences that were deeply interested in spiritualism read cryptic behavior as evidence that Cassandra held a unique degree of earnestness and passion, a rare acuteness of conscience. Cass's friend Helen Perkins describes Cass's special knowledge as a form of vision: "You expect to be in a state of beatitude always. What is a mote of dust in another's eye, in yours is a cataract. You are mad at your blindness, and fight the air because you cannot see" (88). Ben does not let Cassandra forget her special election: " 'You have a great power, tall enchantress.' 'Certainly. What a powerful life is mine!' 'You come to these shores often. Are you not different beside them? This colorless picture before us—these value spaces of sea and land—the motion of the one—the stillness of the other—have you no sense that you have a powerful spirit?' 'Is it power?' 'It is pain' " (160). Ben's poignant remarks reveal another facet of Cassandra's personality: her close association with elemental forces in nature. "The desolation of winter sustains our frail hopes," Cass says. "Nature is kindest then; she does not taunt us with fruition. It is the luxury of summer which tantalizes—her long brilliant, blossoming days, her dewy, radiant nights" (155).

A particular trait of witches, Cassandra's alignment with the powerful forces of nature centers on the sea. "A habit grew upon me of consulting the sea as soon as I rose in the morning. Its aspect decided how my day would be spent. I watched it, studying its changes, seeking to understand its effect, ever attracted by an awful materiality and its easy power to drown me." In a flash of self-description, Cassandra associates the tidal process with her supernatural personality: "By the shore at night the vague tumultuous sphere, swayed by an influence mightier than itself, gave voice, which drew my soul to utter speech for speech" (143). Earlier, during her formative years at Roseville, Cass was aware that the elemental forces loose in nature bore down on her: "I found that I was more elastic . . . and more susceptible to sudden impressions; I was conscious of the ebb and flow of blood through my heart, felt it when it eddied up into my face, and touched my brain with its flame-colored wave." Continuing her self-analysis, Cass makes it explicit that in these trancelike excursions into a rudimentary, biologic state, she interprets the significance of history: "I missed nothing that the present unrolled for me, but looked neither to the past nor to the future. In truth there was little that was elevated in me. Could I have perceived it if there had been? Whichever way the circumstances of my life vacillated, I was not yet reached to the quick; whether spiritual or material influences made sinuous the current of being, it still flowed to an undiscovered ocean" (77). Cass, of course, does discover that in some half-conscious way she is a conduit linking the past with the present. At bottom she is a Morgeson, a clan predicated on the significance of the past. Cassandra is an "aboriginal" who "proves the plastic powers of nature" for shaping the course of present events (9).

Cassandra needs a premodern sensibility in order for the Puritan past reflected in her family to resurface. In fact, history has an inevitable quality so that the present seems just a re-enactment of a prior time. Literary critics will find the parallel to Freud almost inevitable, for Cassandra exemplifies what he termed compulsive repetition:

The patient cannot remember the whole of what is repressed in him, and what he cannot remember may be precisely the essential part of it. Thus he acquires no sense of conviction of the correctness of the construction that has been communicated to him. He is obliged to *repeat* the repressed material as a contemporary experience instead of, as the physician would prefer to see, remembering it as something belonging to the past . . . something that seems more primitive, more elementary, more instinctual than the pleasure principle it overrides. (Freud, "Beyond the Pleasure Principle" 18–23)

For Cassandra, ever analyzing her cultural inheritance, the past is keenly associated with destiny: "Father and mother both stopped at the same point with us, but for a different reason; father, because he saw nothing beyond the material, and mother, because her spiritual insight was confused and perplexing. But whatever a household may be, the Destinies spin the web to their will, out of the threads which drop hither and thither, floating in its atmosphere white, black, or gray" (24). As Cassandra's incorrigible behavior seems to prove, she "is one of those people in whose lives the same reactions are perpetually being repeated uncorrected, to their own detriment, who seem to be pursued by a relentless fate, though closer investigation teaches us that they are unwittingly bringing this fate on themselves. In such cases we attribute a 'daemonic' character to the compulsion to repeat" (Freud, "New Introductory Lectures" 106–07). Puritanism in its various disguises is merged with the Gothic apprehension of mysterious power or influence. Cassandra is one of those instruments who has access to its potent power, and, as we see repeatedly in the novel, Cass's close association with Puritan culture brings with it a special burden or curse. It aligns her with powerful taboos in her culture. Cassandra controls a "contagious magic" where, Freud tells us,

> a general overvaluation has come about of all mental processes—an atti-
> tude towards the world, that is, which, in view of our knowledge of the
> relation between reality and thought, cannot fail to strike us as an overval-
> uation of the latter. Things become less important than the ideas of things.
> . . . since distance is of no importance in thinking, since what lies furthest
> apart both in time and space can without difficulty be comprehended in a
> single act of consciousness—so, too, the world of magic has a telepathic
> disregard for spatial distance and treats past situations as though they were
> present. ("Totem and Taboo" 85)

It is much the same in Hawthorne, and both writers write from the suggestive ambiguity of a world that is in fact two parallel realities commingled.

The discourse of spiritualism in antebellum New England offered readers of *The Morgesons* the chance to believe that there was indeed some organic relation between a Puritan tradition and their own times. Stoddard's "resurrection" of the witch controversies forms an important residuum that evokes resonance and wonder among those readers who chance upon it. As Buell contends, Stoddard believed that "American values [were] a nationalized version of what was once the ideology of the tribe that had become dominant in the New England region. In consequence, the Puritan phase of New England history, of which New Englanders were the primary custodians and interpreters, became invested with a special mystique" (*New England Literary Culture* 196). That fact is a vitalizing principle in this novel and one that conveys itself through dark humor or Gothic seriousness. The depth of Stoddard's allusion to the Puritan past comes directly from Mather's treatment of witches and antinomian forces in his own times. Before we consider this connection directly, it would be helpful to review the extent to which witchcraft and a spiritualism of the sort commonly associated with Anne Hutchinson and George Fox color the portrayal of events in the novel.

Cassandra's admission that she never feels fully integrated with her surroundings makes it easier for Stoddard to link her aloofness from her peers with the suggestion that Cass is somehow "possessed." Cass's feelings of separation are not limited to the schoolhouse in Surrey. When she travels to her "grand'ther's" house in Barmouth, Cassandra claims "the atmosphere of my two lives was so different, that when I passed into one, the other ceased to affect me. I forgot all that I had suffered and hated at Miss Black's, as soon as I crossed the threshold, and entered grand'ther's house. The difference kept up a healthy mean; either alone would perhaps have been more than I could then have sustained" (42). Cassandra's connection to the past is well known by all who know her well, but in a characteristic fashion, Cass admits "the name of Morgeson belonged to the early historical time of New England. . . . I never knew it; but bowed, as if not ignorant" (175). That Cassandra sees herself as a figure with two lives associates her with a common understanding in Puritan folk culture, which held that women inhabited by spirits had an "inner weather" that always bore a relation to the outer weather. Puritans believed that the volatility evident in those accused as witches was somehow connected with the woman's manipulation of electrical currents. In the physico-theology of the late seventeenth century, a woman's contradictory nature could be ascribed to her shifting the polarities between the outer and inner weathers. Here, with her admission that her twin lives possess different atmospheres, Cassandra offers a version of femininity in which she understands that she is a balancing point between the worlds represented by her peers in Surrey and her grandfather's stern Puritanism. As she develops into womanhood, Cassandra's remarkable powers flow from this mixed feminine nature. As she matures, Cassandra becomes convinced that she has a right to exist, that the forces of nature created her not as an afterthought and companion but as a mainstay of continuing creation.

Cassandra's alienation often results in sudden disjunctions in the surface realism of the narration. At the Somers house in Belem, where Ben tries to evoke her memory of Charles Morgeson's accident, Cassandra has this exchange with Ben:

> I was in the shadow of the sideboard; Ben stood against it.
> "When have you played whist, Cassandra?" he asked in a low voice. "Do you remember?"
> "Is my name Cassandra?"
> "Have you forgotten that, too?"
> "I remember the rain."
> "It is not October, yet."
> "And the yellow leaves do not stick to the panes." (178)

The trancelike quality of this exchange recurs frequently. The passage, in its solemnity, suggests that Ben and Cassandra's relationship is not unlike that of the medium and her male guide. In another passage that plays off the strange atmospherics of Cassandra and Veronica, we can identify Stoddard's technique of confronting the reader with sudden transitions of mood, disjunctions of mental states, and implications of depravity. Here is a vignette of Cassandra's disruption of her mother's tea party:

> Veronica . . . walked up and down the room in a blue cambric dress. She was twisting her fingers in a fine gold chain, which hung from her neck. I caught her cunning glance as she flourished some tansy leaves before her face, imitating Mrs. Dexter to the life. I laughed and she came to me.
> "See," she said softly, "I have something from heaven." She lifted her white apron, and I saw under it, pinned to her dress, a splendid black butterfly, spotted with red and gold.
> "It is mine," she said, "you shall not touch it. God blew it in through the window, but it has not breathed yet." . . .

"I hate you," she said, in an enraged voice. "I would strike you, if it wasn't for this holy butterfly." . . . She was upstairs putting away her butterfly, in the leaves of her little Bible. . . . "I know," and I flew upstairs, tore the poor butterfly from between the leaves of the Bible, crushed it in my hand, and brought it down to her. She did not cry when she saw it, but choked a little, and turned away her head. . . . A few days after this, sitting near the window at twilight, intent upon a picture in a book . . . of a Hindoo swinging from a high pole with hooks in his flesh, and trying to imagine how much it hurt him, my attention was arrested by a mention of my name in a conversation held between mother and Mr. Park, one of the neighbors. . . . Presently, he began to sing, and I grew lonesome; the life within me seemed a black cave.

"Our nature's totally depraved—
The heart a sink of sin;
Without a change we can't be saved,
Ye must be born again." (17–21)

It is important to quote this passage at length (this is only a small fragment of a complex narrative passage) to convey the elaborateness of Stoddard's suggestion of witchcraft and spiritualism through resonant details. "Cunning glances," a divine butterfly that is awaiting God's breath, and a Hindoo engaged in ritual self-effacement are bizarre details recorded in a child's perception of the world. Stoddard uses the implications of these details to portray Cassandra and her sister as fulfilling their designations as "possessed creatures."

If we accept the contention that Cassandra is in fact a "witch" (a latter-day Anne Hutchinson) and that Ben is a coven leader, then Cass's trancelike behaviors signal the presence of the alien. We know that Cassandra frequently explains her distance from events as awakening from a dream. Listening to her sibling rival Verry play the piano, Cassandra states, "I had no wish to learn to play. I could never perform mechanically what I heard now from Verry. When she ceased, I woke from a dream, chaotic, but not tumultuous, beautiful, but inharmonious" (53). In passages like this one recalling Charles Morgeson's death, the disruption of surface realism is an admission that Cassandra's presence spins enchantments that are subtly masked by the narration. Cassandra's presence "defamiliarizes" the reader's perception of the story, calling into question the larger issue of the novel's underlying logic of representation.

Stoddard's Reconfiguration of Mather

Stoddard connects her novel with Cotton Mather's *Magnalia* directly through the ribald description of the Reverend Dr. Snell—otherwise known as Thomas Robbins, the person responsible for preparing the 1820 edition of Mather's church history.[8]

> I went to Dr. Snell's as soon as I was able. He was in his bedchamber, writing a sermon on fine note-paper, and had disarranged the wide ruffles of his shirt so that he looked like a mildly angry turkey. Thrusting his spectacles up into the roots of his hair, he rose, and led me to a large room adjoining his bedroom, which contained nothing but tall bookcases, threw open the doors of one, pushed up a little ladder before it, for me to mount to a row of volumes bound in calf, whose backs were labelled "British Classics." "There," he said you will find "The Spectator," and trotted back to his sermon, with his pen in his mouth. . . . From that time I grazed with pleasure in his oddly assorted library. (56)

It is in Robbins's library that Stoddard came upon *Magnalia*—one of those "books which I could not digest, and [its] influence located in my mind curious and inconsistent relations between facts and ideas" (56). Thomas Robbins's library was of regional importance, amounting to three thousand volumes in 1832. Robbins, Elizabeth Stoddard's pastor, was an antiquarian with a special interest in Puritan history. This passage both invokes the importance of *Magnalia* and traces its removal from its original context as it has become a volume in a thoroughly genteel, secularized library. Snell's book selection is stereotypical of liberally educated "moderate" Calvinist divines who were being displaced by sectarian, evangelical, and seminary-trained successors during the early part of the nineteenth century. Like Robbins himself, Snell is succeeded by a zealot "red hot from Andover" (255n25).

Snell thus becomes an important bridging figure, linking Cassandra's world to Mather's "authenticated past." She tells us,

> Dr. Snell was no exception to the rule that a minister must not be a native among his own people. His long residence in Surrey had failed to make him appear like one. . . . His library was the only lion in our neighborhood. His taste as a collector made him known abroad, and he had a reputation which was not dreamed of by his parishioners, who thought him queer and simple. He loved old-fashions; wore knee-breeches, and silver buckles in his shoes; brewed metheglin in his closet, and drank it from silver-pegged flagons, and kept diet bread on a salver to offer his visitors. (55)

In short, Snell is a living connection to a prior tradition in much the same way as Stowe's Dr. Hopkins stood in for Jonathan Edwards. Despite its rarefied status, Puritanism is a vital principle in *The Morgesons*. Cassandra's Grandfather Warren is also a Puritan, "a little, lean, leather colored man. His head bent, his eyes cast down."

> He chafed his small, well-shaped hands continually; his long polished nails clicked together with a shelly noise, like that which beetles make flying against the ceiling. . . . All classes in Barmouth treated him with invariable courtesy. He was aboriginal in character, not to be moved by antecedent or changed by innovation—a Puritan, without gentleness or tenderness. He scarcely concealed his contempt for the emollients of life, or for those who needed them. He whined over no misfortune, pined for no pleasure. His two sons, who broke loose from him, went into the world, lived a wild, merry life, and died there never named. He found his wife dead by his side one morning. He did not go frantic, but selected a text for the funeral sermon; and when he stood by the uncovered grave, took off his hat and thanked his friends for their kindness with a loud, steady voice. (28–29)

Mary Warren, Cassandra's mother, was broken by her husband's stern temper and rigid Puritanism. Grand'ther tells Cass, "You are playing over your mother's capers" (36). The duplicity that Puritanism creates in women is a trait of Cass's Aunt Mercy: "she wore a mask before her father. There was a constraint between them; each repressed the other" (32). Cassandra's own duplicity is a product of her tenure in Barmouth. When she returns to Surrey, her understanding of her mother becomes a form of self-knowledge that enables her to secure in her "possession" a degree of freedom that she would not otherwise have had.

The Morgesons: An Artistic Metaphor for Dispersive History

Locating historical reality outside the self heightens a writer's ethnographic stance. Stoddard repeatedly refers to family, friends, and neighbors as "members of her tribe." *The Morgesons* describes New England not as a totality but as a comparative study of three communities. When the book opens, Cassandra tells us directly that her childhood was a curious commingling of theology and ethnographic adventure tales:

> When my aunt said this I was climbing a chest of drawers, by its knobs, in order to reach the book shelves above it, where my favorite work, "The Northern Regions," was kept, together with Baxter's "Saints' Rest," and other volumes of that sort belonging to my mother. . . . To this day Sheridan's Comedies, Sterne's Sentimental Journey, and Captain Cook's Voyages are so mixed up in my remembrance that I am still uncertain whether it was Stern who ate baked dog with Maria, or Sheridan who wept over a dead ass in the Sandwich Islands. (5)

Cassandra's reading material blends accounts of polar explorations with classics of Puritan devotional literature. In contrast to her mother's preferences, Cass's eclectic reading is decidedly secular.

Cassandra's ethnographic description allows her to analyze her family with a great degree of specificity. Stoddard's description of the Morgeson family's involvement in history has important parallels in Mather. For each writer, the identity of the ancestor is a New England antitype of the sort that Mather celebrated in his history. When Mather detailed the life of John Winthrop, he tried to direct the reader's attention to ordinary, temporal, and geographic facts. Mather reminds us of Winthrop's reference to a historical geometry. Cotton Mather, who felt called to measure the progress of the church in the New World, did so figurally by correlating prophecies with contemporary affairs. In like manner, Stoddard portrays the Morgesons figurally; their dignity derives from the fact that they have been connected to the region through an unconventional rhetorical process. And Cassandra, as another version of the exemplar, must negotiate the circumstances that befall her, restoring a meaning to her "line"—a sense of place and soil that inculcates, in turn, a larger destiny.

As in *Magnalia*, witchcraft and spiritualism enhance Stoddard's historical intentions. The image of the witch in the seventeenth century and the image of the medium in the nineteenth provided a symbolic meeting place for old and new traditions. The audiences who attended the witchcraft trials in Salem and the investigators who watched spiritualists on stage shared a simultaneously passive and attentive appreciation of mysterious events. In *The Morgesons*, Stoddard's characters and places are designed to be sanctuaries for ambiguous things. As she describes her family, Cassandra declares,

> there was no accident to reveal, no coincidence to suprize us. Hidden among the Powers That Be, which Rule New England, lurks the Deity of the Illicit. This Deity never obtained sovereignty in the atmosphere where the Morgesons lived. Instead of the impression which my after-experience suggests me to seek, I recall arrivals and departures, an eternal smell of cookery, a perpetual changing of beds, and the small talk of vacant minds. (23)

This Deity, Stoddard suggests, is the "always already" of New England's past, an emblem of the chthonic turbulence that underlies the surface of provincial gentility. In one revealing passage, Stoddard informs us that Cassandra's intuition of events presupposes a distributed intelligence and not an "ideal" faculty:

> I never turned my face up to the sky to watch the passing of a cloud, or mused before the undulating space of sea, or looked down upon the earth with the curiosity of thought, or spiritual aspiration. I was moved and governed by my sensations, which continually changed, and passed away—to come again, and deposit vague ideas which ignorantly haunted me. The literal images of all things which I saw were impressed on my shapeless mind, to be reproduced afterward by faculties then latent. But what satisfaction was that? Doubtless the ideal faculty was active in Veronica from the beginning; in me it was developed by the experience of years . . . and I conclude that my mind, if I had any, existed in so rudimental a state that it had little influence upon my character. (14–15)

Cassandra's and Ben's occult sensibilities and the mysterious threads of communication that exist between characters establish a heterogeneous order within the novel. Around this core representation, Stoddard deploys a dramaturgical cultural dynamic organized around the popular image of spectral evidence and mediumship. In so doing, she plays on the notion that Mather put forward in *Wonders of the Invisible World*: what New England could not contain within the traditional order of things, it licensed to remain on the margins of culture, forever providing commentary on the hegemonic order that excluded it. The significance of history, as it is described through the prosecution of witches or relayed in the hidden communication of mediums, depends on its dispersal away from the powerful center of a culture. For both Mather and Stoddard, telling the significance of New England through an "alien" form of understanding gives their books the advantage of illusionism. Because we as readers are never quite certain that we are reading the story of a woman's growth in the nineteenth century or a tale where witches are running free, Stoddard's novel can, at times, remind us of the peep-show cabinets. These amusing examples of visual deception were wooden compartments that presented a startling image to the viewer's eye by a rigorous application of scientific perspective. These boxes, especially those made by Samuel van Hoogstraaten, were all the more remarkable because their illusory effects were created solely by manipulations of a fixed-eye point. In a metaphorical sense, both Stoddard and Mather, by shifting their readers' attention to a world where alien and extraordinary things are commonplace features of the everyday world, distort their narratives so that a once-familiar scene looks strangely askew.

Stoddard's verisimilitude in representing Cassandra and Ben as witches makes her readers seem to actually see the significance of the occult in New England, or at least the space in which it is represented, even though we, as readers, know that we are looking at a representation and not at the real object. Sandra Zagarell sounds this note when she says, "Cassandra's improbability, the novel's final, unsettling juxtapositions call attention to how many special circumstances have been fashioned, how many conventions of narrative drawn on to endow Cassandra with her ultimate destiny. Women like Cassandra can prevail only because of the energetic good offices of their authors, and they are far from likely to exist except in fiction" ("Repossession of a Heritage" 54). Mather's use of illusionism in his first letter to the Royal Society illustrated "the way he thinks and argues about biblical and scientific subjects. His lifelong habit of playing with words went beyond his irrepressible punning. He loved to tease meanings out of a phrase, to take figurative language literally, to 'open' a text in a spirit that was almost talmudic" (Levin, "Giants in the Earth" 753). In a similar fashion, Stoddard employed the suggestion of a Gothic Puritanism so that we might see New

England's significance as a *trompe l'oeil*; we are tricked into a perception of the reality of the world described in *Magnalia*.[9]

The Morgesons's use of Mather's specialized view of history is a representation that appears to extend the interpretive space of Stoddard's book. *The Morgesons* is an important extension of Mather's church history because it extends his conclusion that New England was an enormously generative, if problematic, cultural site. There is some evidence that Stoddard was a writer impatiently anticipating the critical discernment of her intentions. Like Mather, she wrote for an unborn audience.

Ben and Cassandra's tale is the vindication of a form of subversion that existed in Mather's mind. Stoddard's imitation of Mather's view that the subversive elements in a culture would unexpectedly break free from containment affirms the vitality of a challenging position within Puritanism itself. The antinomianism and spiritualism of the seventeenth century are of primary interest to us because they direct our attention inward toward an understanding of how subjectivity is constituted within the individual. As Mather showed in *Magnalia*, this subjectivity is a realm of the authentic. Its expression in writing is a crafted product of this inner subjectivity, and the modes of its expression, the protection of privacy, are a ritual carefully guarded and performed by the author. Stoddard's use of Cassandra to explain her culture at large is a situation where orthodoxy is described by heresy. Though Stoddard herself may have been convinced that Ben and Cassandra occupy a separate cultural domain, the distinction vanishes when attempts are made to seize and define the intrusion of spiritualism into their daily lives. The distinction between the orthodox and the subversive is removed in *The Morgesons*; what remains is uncertainty that is just strong enough to undermine a confident analysis of orthodoxy. In his description of the supernatural in *Magnalia*, Mather's point was this: New England was founded according to a process of separating itself from and incorporating its opposition. Dominant and oppressed ideologies are mutually constitutive, and the strategies of textuality and historical accountability are available to both. The situation described in *Magnalia* and in *The Morgesons* is essentially the same. Conjectural meaning, whether it is termed orthodox or subversive, is constantly trying to control meaning and, in the process, is constantly captivated by it. If there is a historical importance to the contested meanings of the witch trials, it is the fact that the legacy of those proceedings becomes trapped and permanently fixes the image of the region.

Conclusion

✝

All that I shall add, is this: It hath been seen that "thunders oftener fall upon houses of God, than upon any other houses"; New-England can say so. Our *meeting-houses*, and our *ministers'* houses have had a singular share in the strokes of thunders. . . . The author . . . being at prayer before a sermon in an assembly of Christians, the sudden rise of a thunder-storm was the occasion of his feeling a strong *impression* upon his mind unto this purpose: "Lay aside what you had prepared . . . speak to them in the voice of the glorious God in the thunder. . . ." He could not withstand this *impression*, but ventured upon an *extemporaneous contemplation* of the thunder. Now, the thing which made this digression remarkable was, that at the very same instance when he was thus driven to this theme, the thunder was directed by the God of heaven to fall with very *tearing*, tho' no *killing effects* upon his own house. The *hearers*, I suppose, found a sensible edge given to these meditations, by the wondrous timing of them; and although, no doubt, the author would have digested them with more exactness, had they not been altogether like the accidents that produced them, *sudden*.

—Cotton Mather, "Brontologia Sacra" (2.362–63)

By the time *The Morgesons* was published, New England had been transformed by its political experience. The region experienced a steady decline in population, and the image of New England became progressively rarefied by "summer industry." The local color realism that emerged after the Civil War reflected the isolation and restrictions placed on writers' perceptions of New England's significance. The romantic optimism that Mather's history could fully flower in an atmosphere of literary democracy was attenuated by some of the realistic declension depicted in *The Morgesons*. New England as a concept was less controlling than it was controlled by democratic processes. The fortunes of the East were dictated by the settlement of the West.

New England entrepreneurs were satisfied with profiting from activities conducted elsewhere, and politically the region was not steering the course of national events. The locus of democratic values shifted to the agricultural realm, where the decentralized producer economy best reflected individual choices and self-determination. New England's industrial and centralized economy became ever more ambitious and undemocratic as native values born out of traditional culture were replaced by class and ethnic tensions. New England best represented the notion that the federal Constitution was fundamentally undemocratic. The disorder, perpetual anxiety, and chronic schizophrenia of the antebellum years had proved productive for literary historicism. After the Civil War, however, the sense of grim determinism served to undermine the flexibility of Mather's cultural poetics.

Through the half-decade of the Civil War, there was a massive effort to concentrate the material resources, productive capacity, and spiritual energies of a disparate populace. The vision of New England that Mather had conceived—localized, sectarian, and provincial—was displaced by a systematic program of national consolidation and expansion. As Stoddard's novel shows, a yearning for Puritan sensibility often produced increasingly twisted and contorted isolation. As I have suggested for all the writers in this book, the model for a Puritan historian was put forward by Mather in *Magnalia*. The extent to which Hawthorne, Stowe, and Stoddard fully captured Mather's cultural poetics determined the shape of their careers. Their stress on openness in culture is of interest to anyone interested in reconstituting the particular archive for understanding a region. It is likely that if there had been no widely ranging debate over New England's "original" significance, *Magnalia* with its openness for interpreting the original settlement would have been quietly forgotten.

The fact that these writers, by their concern with alternate frames of reference, were writing for generations to come has been variously noted in the works themselves. In Hawthorne's case it comes in the form of Grandfather's recollection "that when he talked to [the young people around him], it was the past speaking to the present, or rather to the future—for the children were of a generation which had not become actual. Their part in life, thus far, was only to be happy and to draw knowledge from a thousand sources" (51). Mather, and those who appropriated his line of vision, have become newly important in deciding the interpretive foundations for understanding New England. His revisionist historiography is important for decoding the political accents of contemporary American Studies scholarship. The argument of these nineteenth-century writers—that Puritanism and its traces have something substantially significant to contribute to the understanding of national culture—is another way of affirming that cultural difference can solicit our resources not merely as spectators or consumers but as audiences prepared for democratic processes by literature.

The printing considerations that brought *Magnalia* to the public's attention also gave a shape to the life and career of many of the writers whom we associate with the American Renaissance. The trajectory of Hawthorne's, Stowe's, and Stoddard's individual careers after *Magnalia* varies widely; however, the print ideology Robbins negotiated brought to the foreground cultural impulses to be simultaneously self-repudiating and self-validating. This effect is not attributable to any notion of the "New England Mind" or any singular definition of political ideology. It is the result of an editor's need to isolate a "tutor-text" whose form would equate knowledge with power and democracy with the necessity of reading.

Silent reading, as Roger Chartier says, permits a free and secretive intercourse with the written word.[1] However, Robbins's text of *Magnalia* was, from its very inception, designed to highlight the differential uses possible for the same book. Because the volume so evenly split the opinions of readers, *Magnalia* was among the first books in the American canon to uncover the central contradictions necessary in a literate populace:

[The history of reading] is informed by an apparent contradiction: either it affirms the total control of the text in its power to constrain the reader (but then reading can no longer be considered an autonomous practice, and its variations lose their significance) or else it postulates the reader's liberty to produce his own unique sense beyond the text itself. . . . It seeks to identify for each period and each milieu the shared modes of reading that the model individual gestures, and it places the processes by which a reader or group of readers produce their own meaning of a text at the center of its interrogation. The construction of meaning, which varies historically and socially, is thus understood to be at the intersection of, on the one hand, the particularities of readers endowed with specific competencies, identified by their social position and their cultural dispositions (as characterized by their practice of reading), and, on the other hand, the textual and physical forms of those texts appropriated by reading. (Chartier, "Frenchness" 18, 19)

Consequently, those who wished to fully understand Mather's text had to read it as being embedded in and interpenetrating many other discourses in antebellum New England. Mather's original work attempts incompletely to control the centrifugal forces of loyalist and democratic politics, psychological notions of individuality, and obtuse modes of expression. Mather's text demanded, as no other text except the Geneva Bible had, that readers attend to issues of authorship, the permeability of writing to its controlling context, and the various "extensions" coded in the mixture of social events and historical meanings.

The clear message to readers of Mather's volume was this: the governmentality of New England culture was marked by a critical shift in the arena of power from town meetings and market street conversations, familiar to Mather's original readers, to a public realm that in Robbins's time was constituted in writing and print. Mather's cluttered volume signaled that democratic authenticity resided in the plenary meanings of spirituality and texts. Looking upon the "littered landscape" of Puritan identity politics that prevailed after 1820, it is easy to see the hollowness that lies behind every kind of invention. Hawthorne's and Stowe's preoccupations with allegory were natural consequences of a situation where Mather's original signs and markers had become withdrawn from the pressures of social struggle. Voloshinov writes:

> A sign that has been withdrawn from the pressures of the social struggle—which, so to speak, crosses beyond the pale of the class struggle—inevitably loses force, *degenerating into allegory* and becoming the object not of live social intelligibility but of philological comprehension. The historical memory of mankind is full of such worn out ideological signs incapable of serving as arenas for the clash of live social accents. (23, emphasis added)

Robbins's recognition of the textual technologies present in *Magnalia* effectively transformed the contents of *Magnalia* into "literature" and aided the definition of Mather as a profoundly multiple and (dispersed) personality. Nonetheless, like the afterburn of fireworks, Mather as a wounded artifact (the very substance of allegorized historicity) remains capable of Greenblatt's "resonance and wonder"—an oddity struck by new circumstances but perhaps still capable of bearing meaning. At the very least, to judge by the *Columbia Literary History of the United States*, Mather still serves "as the step from Puritan settlers to Franklin, so Franklin can be seen as the step from Mather to the American Romantic writers and to us" (Elliott 106–12). If we are to believe De Prospo, Mather's historicity may assist in the unmooring of early American literature so that it is seen as "no thing other than a signifier [that] begins accordingly, and very vigorously and freely, to float" (258).

In its fully articulated form, democratic political theory assumes that the government of individuals requires the activity and freedom of the governed. The citizens of the republic, in acting and aligning themselves with needs and opportunities made possible by their society, will exercise their particular will in accordance to the ends imposed on them by the culture. Cotton Mather, as the author of *Magnalia*, sought to exchange a perceived limitation in historical circumstances for the opportunity to be held captive by a marketplace that did not exist fully until Robbins's time.

The seventeenth-century desire to construct a sufficient and sympathetic readership, and the actual ends that Robbins's edition accomplished, depended on the constraints and facilitating choices of each aspect of the book's printing. In making this argument, the question then becomes, What conception of democracy is possible and necessary when Mather's work has been targeted by a printing venture whose objective is simultaneously to augment and secure the reputation of the region and the success of its inhabitants? It is clear that Robbins's careful editorial strategies in reissuing Mather were related to vertical lines of dependency. Whether it be the proper means for rendering the history of the Puritans, the cataloguing of texts at the Connecticut Historical Society, or the arrangement of natural specimens in Peale's museum, Robbins seized on the importance of an authentic history in much the same way the Marquis de Condorcet (qtd. in Burchell 132) described the means by which governmentality targets the individual:

How, in this astonishing variety of labors and products, of needs and resources; in this alarming complication of interests, which connects the subsistence and well-being of an isolated individual with the whole system of society; which makes him dependent upon all the accidents of nature and every political event; which extends in a way to the entirety of his capacity to experience either enjoyment or privation; how, in this apparent chaos, do we nonetheless see . . . the common interest requiring that each should be able to understand their own interest and freely pursue it? (Condorcet 209)

In "Governmentality," Foucault characterizes this situation described by Condorcet by explaining that the relationship of the individual to a social governmentality is, in the final analysis, a local situation where the author is fixed in a doubly involuntary world of dependence and productivity. Mather's "power" in his own culture (and perhaps in ours) is generated by his reliance on an extrinsic network of politics, profit, and literacy, as well as by an intrinsic (and perhaps romantic) conceit of "genius," inspiration, or gifted talent. Robbins astutely realized that his culture shared with Mather's a need to reconstitute American works in ways that reinforce our own social and cultural positions.

In their expression of a collective impulse to concern themselves with a wide range of lesser objects that collectively express a tradition, Hawthorne, Stowe, and Stoddard used the evocation of a resonant Puritanism as their primary response to what R. Jackson Wilson terms "the essence of retail, a conception that lies behind the individual ways of figuring the writer, the relations of production, the set of arrangements that make writing and reading possible as social acts in given historical situations" (283). The interest in Puritanism for all of our writers (and for me as well) condensed their investment—both mercenary and imaginative—in the Other and in the increasing instability, even interchangeability, of cultural categories. Acting invisibly, the print ideology of the American Renaissance, described so well by Sacvan Bercovitch, circulates around an "invisible center"[2] designating the local conditions of specific works. Regardless of whether we ultimately celebrate the writers treated in this study as marginal, revolutionary, or conservative representatives of literary tradition, their publication objectives converge only on the condition that their exercise of personal liberty escapes individual knowledge and will.[3] In fact, the very stability of New England culture depended on editors like Robbins who exercised the editorial prerogative of a publisher. At least for the period considered here, the textual technology of the book dictates the simultaneous inclusion and exclusion of readers and writers from the activities of democracy since "entrepreneurial impulses [had] helped transform American society from one in which men and women assumed a fixed place . . . to a fluid one where individuals employed their property and wealth" within a liberal environment favoring "the clever, the artful, the ambitious, and the capable—those most skilled in the newly emerging world of market relations" (Shalhope 124–25). In her description of the cultural function of early American novels in *Revolution and the Word*, Cathy Davidson argues the potency of "minor" texts when she claims that "literature is both an artificially framed world with an organized structure governing its interpretation and a part of a larger structure determined by economic, institutional, and ideological forces that govern its composition, its publication, its circulation, its reading, and the end—canonization or obscurity—to which it is read" (260). Although the analysis I have made here goes a long way toward establishing a resonance between Robbins's text and context, it does not preclude the fact that *Magnalia* may have formed an intimate and possibly subversive shape in the minds of individual readers.

Since *Magnalia* focused readers' attention on the various cultural antinomies surrounding authorship in America, Robbins's edition was a meeting place for critical dissidents. To understand the cultural correlates gestured in *Magnalia*, historicism is a necessary tool because between the lacunae of the volume's publishing history lies the inescapably American conclusion that culture, nature, and the self are granted power only by the limitations and accidents of history. Robbins's *Magnalia* is bounded by and distinguished from its original context by the fact that partial and personal interpretations of Mather polarize into symbolic oppositions such as liberty and equality, freedom and concealment, identity and politics. The symbolic polarities are never a source of oppositional conflict, but they are a dramatic revelation that, in the antebellum era, fragmentation is a necessary consequence of consensus. The text and context of *Magnalia* were, in the Robbins edition, fully reciprocal concepts that were culturally imaged not at the level of symbolism but in the governmentality of the printing trade. Robbins brought attention to the issue of the "ownership" of history and the deceptions of individual liberty.

More important, however, is the realization that historical forces in 1820 demanded that *Magnalia* happen in the way it did because New England was one significant place in American society where the issue of history and national destiny was fundamentally unresolved. Robbins's text bridged the interstices between public rhetoric and private expression and invited "forays into alternative possibilities of meaning where readers might not willingly venture on their own" (Davidson 260). If we view Mather in this way, his history, whatever its literary merit might be for us, was profoundly important because it had been isolated and "marketed" for an anxious generation.

Christology, which provided Mather with a magnificent rhetoric for concealing his political attachments, relies on such language to erase the perceived importance of his authorship. When, as critics, we are constantly drawn to the impossibility of adequately summarizing an "original" literature such as the works that have commonly been lumped under the rubric American Renaissance, it is necessary to remember that Robbins's *Magnalia* was meant to frustrate, at the very outset, any notion that "America" could be considered a relational or corporate event. To suggest otherwise betrays a pervasive weakness for American exceptionalism and a naive historicizing of early American literature. Although many of my readers will no doubt see traces of exceptionalism in isolating Mather, the important thing to bear in mind is the precariousness that surrounded Thomas Robbins's desire to introduce a standard text for evaluating the most important issues of his day. Throughout, I have avoided categorizing my study as a study of the influence of Mather on a generation of highly accomplished writers. Instead, my aim has been to argue, from the level of *Magnalia* as "book," that the Robbins edition framed a peculiarly poignant moment when the radically destabilizing anxieties that constitute American culture seemed, briefly, to offer a rationale for many sorts of cultural "invention." By this point, it should be obvious to many that theories of continuity (especially in politics and democracy but also in literature) are irrepressibly pernicious lies that we tell ourselves in the hope that we, like Emerson, Miller, or Bercovitch, can stand "alone with America."

As Bercovitch has so admirably shown, the essence of renewing a correspondence with the "Puritan Imagination" depends on repeatedly advancing the clock that we use to identify our literary-historical progenitors. If Mather considered the first generation of Puritan settlers to be the original, and Bercovitch and Miller claim the second generation, then I am undoubtedly liable for claiming the third. The more important observation, however, is that the progress of our history has always and everywhere been punctuated by a limitless world-alienation, so that, as Hannah Arendt has said, man, wherever he goes, encounters only himself. In truth, we have always been understandably afraid of our self-image, so it seems only reasonable that our sentimentality has now been reserved for the prospect of a world *sans l'homme*: a stirring of indifference, the anonymity of a murmur, the man who would be erased, as Foucault suggested in *The Archaeology of Knowledge*. And little wonder, for even our recent attachments to understanding the history of the book and the machinations of textual technologies appear to be consigned to the brink of erasure by a radically redefined sense of literacy and the conditions of its expression.

Whether we are concerned with 1693 or 1993 or the next millenium, Mather's politically inflected typology, which equated the writer's life with the rumblings of scriptural history, is a constant reminder that the story has already been written; our claims to originality will always by necessity rest with our capacity for rearrangement and invention. Although *figura* remains rooted in history, the close attention to history shows that what Gura, in "Baring the New England Soul," calls the "glamor" that attaches to continuity can be bought only at the expense and sophistication of early American literature and the publication process that contrived its importance. It is true that in *Magnalia*—at those points when Mather contends he stands in a special relationship with the providential wonders near the center of the *miracula apocalypsis*—attempts are made to link the author's career and the progress of New England at large to the history of redemption. More important, however, are those moments, which are just as obvious, that show Mather recoiling from the compulsion to establish origins and to trace continuities for fear of mutilating the anxiety that America needed (and needs) to embrace.

On the basis of these and similar observations, critical debates will continue with or without the assistance of Mather's redemptive history. What will be understood as the need for a federal identity (be it resolved in notions of ideology, in antique or newly fashioned historicism, or in a compulsive desire to "speak with the dead") will continue unabated with ourselves as the author of texts limited by conditions of historicity and technology. Perhaps we will be better able to grapple with the deceptions and censorious selectivity that awaits us all if we prepare to meet the image of ourselves that surely awaits us (no matter how the dialogue is managed) by recalling that we typically have succumbed to the hunter of souls and, having stuck the darts of some extreme disorder into poor hearts, have seduced a great part of ourselves into our bewildering errors, which being unrecoverable force our wandering removal.[4] I am sure that my own recent possession with Puritan conceits accords with a rather simple complication: "They mate not well; they sit not on one seat."

Appendix

Declaration of the Gentlemen, Merchants, and Inhabitants of Boston, and the Country Adjacent, April 18, 1689

§ I. We have seen more than a decad of Years rolled away, since the *English* World had the Discovery of an horrid *Popish Plot*; wherein the bloody *Devotoes* of *Rome* had in their Design and Prospect no less than the Extinction of the *Protestant Religion*: which mighty Work they called *the utter subduing of a Pestilent Heresy*; wherein (they said) there never were such hopes of Success since the Death of Queen *Mary*, as now in our days. And we were of all men the most insensible, if we should apprehend a Countrey so remarkable for the true Profession and pure Exercise of the Protestant Religion as *New-England* is, wholly unconcerned in the Infamous Plot. To crush and break a Countrey so entirely and signally made up of *Reformed Churches*, and at length to involve it in the miseries of an utter Extirpation, must needs carry even a Supererogation of merit with it among such as were intoxicated with a Bigotry inspired into them by the great *Scarlet Whore*.

§ II. To get us within the reach of the desolation desired for us, it was no improper thing that we should first have our *Charter* Vacated, and the hedge which kept us from the wild Beasts of the field, effectually broken down. The accomplishment of this was hastened by the unwearied solicitations, and slanderous accusations of a man, for his *Malice* and *Falshood*, well known unto us all. Our *Charter* was with a most injurious pretence (and scarce that) of Law, condemned before it was possible for us to appear at *Westminster* in the legal defence of it; and without a fair leave to answer for our selves, concerning the Crimes falsly laid to our charge, we were put under a *President* and *Council*, without any liberty for an Assembly, which the other *American Plantations* have, by a Commission from His *Majesty*.

§ III. The Commission was as *Illegal* for the form of it, as the way of obtaining it was *Malicious* and *unreasonable*: yet we made no Resistance thereunto as we could easily have done; but chose to give all *Mankind* a Demonstration of our being a people sufficiently dutiful and loyal to our King: and this with yet more Satisfaction, because we took pains to make our selves believe as much as ever we could of the Whedle then offer'd unto us; That his *Majesty's* Desire was no other than the happy encrease and advance of these *Provinces* by their more immediate Dependance on the *Crown of England.* And we were convinced of it by the Courses immediately taken to damp and spoyl our *Trade*; whereof decayes and complaints presently filled all the Country; while in the mean time neither the Honour nor the Treasure of the King was at all advanced by this new Model of our Affairs, but a considerable Charge added unto the Crown.

§ IV. In little more than half a Year we saw this Commission superseded by another yet more Absolute and Arbitrary, with which Sir *Edmond Andross* arrived as our Governour; who besides his Power, with the Advice and Consent of his Council, to make Laws and raise Taxes as he pleased; had also Authority by himself to Muster and Imploy all Persons residing in the Territory as occasion shall serve; and to transfer such Forces to any English Plantation in *America*, as occasion shall require. And several Companies of Souldiers were now brought from *Europe*, to support what was to be imposed upon us, not without repeated Menaces that some hundreds more were intended for us.

§ V. The Government was no sooner in these Hands, but care was taken to load Preferments principally upon such Men as were strangers to and haters of the People: and every ones Observation hath noted, what Qualifications recommended a Man to publick Offices and Employments, only here and there a *good Man* was used, where others could not easily be had; the Governour himself, with Assertions now and then falling from him, made us jealous that it would be thought for his Majesties Interest, if this People were removed and another succeeded in their room: And his far-fetch'd Instruments that were growing rich among us, would gravely inform us, that it was not for his Majesties Interest that we should thrive. But of all our Oppressors we were chiefly *squeez'd* by a Crew of abject Persons fetched from *New York*, to be the Tools of the Adversary, standing at our right hand; by these were extraordinary and intollerable Fees extorted from every one upon all occasions, without any Rules but those of their own insatiable Avarice and Beggary; and even the probate of a Will must now cost as many *Pounds* perhaps as it did *Shillings* heretofore; nor could a small Volume contain the other Illegalities done by these *Horse-leeches* in the two or three Years that they have been sucking on us; and what Laws they made it was as impossible for us to know, as dangerous for us to break; but we shall leave the Men of *Ipswich* and of *Plimouth* (among others) to tell the story of the kindness which has been shown them upon this account. Doubtless a Land so ruled as once *New-England* was, has not without many fears and sighs beheld the wicked walking on every side, and the vilest Men exalted.

§ VI. It was now plainly affirmed, both by some in open Council, and by the same in private converse, that the people in *New-England* were all *Slaves*, and the only difference between them and *Slaves* is their not being bought and sold; and it was a maxim delivered in open Court unto us by one of the Council, *that we must not think the Priviledges of English men would follow us to the end of the World*: Accordingly we have been treated with multiplied contradictions to *Magna Charta*, the rights of which we laid claim unto. Persons who did but peaceably object against the raising of Taxes without an Assembly, have been for it fined, some twenty, some thirty, and others fifty Pounds. Packt and pickt Juries have been very common things among us, when, under a pretended form of Law, the trouble of some honest and worthy Men has been aimed at: but when some of this Gang have been brought upon the Stage, for the most detestable Enormities that ever the Sun beheld, all Men have with Admiration seen what methods have been taken that they might not be treated according to their Crimes. Without a Verdict, yea, without a Jury sometimes have People been fined most unrighteously; and some not of the meanest Quality have been kept in long and close Imprisonment without any the least Information appearing against them, or an *Habeas Corpus* allowed unto them. In short, when our Oppressors have been a little out of Mony, 'twas but pretending some Offence to be enquired into, and the most innocent of Men were continually put into no small Expence to answer the Demands of the Officers, who must have money of them, or a Prison for them, tho none could accuse them of any Misdemeanour.

§ VII. To plunge the poor People every where into deeper Incapacities, there was one very comprehensive Abuse given to us; Multitudes of pious and sober Men through the Land, scrupled the Mode of Swearing on the Book, desiring that they might Swear with an uplifted Hand, agreeable to the ancient Custom of the Colony; and though we think we can prove that the Common Law amongst us (as well as in some other places under the *English Crown*) not only indulges, but even commands and enjoins the Rite of lifting the Hand in *Swearing*; yet they that had this Doubt, were still put by from serving upon any Juries; and many of them were most unaccountably Fined and Imprisoned. Thus one Grievance is a *Trojan Horse*, in the Belly of which it is not easy to recount how many insufferable Vexations have been contained.

§ VIII. Because these Things could not make us miserable fast enough, there was a notable Discovery made of we know not what *flaw* in all our *Titles to our Lands*; and, tho *besides* our purchase of them from the Natives; and, *besides* our actual peaceable unquestioned possession of them for near threescore Years, and besides the Promise of K. *Charles* II. in his Proclamation sent over to us in the Year 1683, That *no Man here shall receive any Prejudice in his Freehold or Estate*: We had the Grant of our Lands, under the Seal of the Council of Plimouth: which Grant was Renewed and Confirmed unto us by King *Charles* I. under the Great Seal of England; and the General Court which consisted of the Patentees and their Associates, had made particular Grants hereof to the several *Towns* (though 'twas now deny'd by the Governour, that there was any such Thing as a *Town*) among us; to all which Grants the General Court annexed for the further securing of them, *A General Act*, published under the Seal of the Colony, in the Year 1684. Yet we were every day told, *That no Man was owner of a Foot of Land in all the Colony*. Accordingly, *Writs of Intrusion* began every where to be served on People, that after all their Sweat and their Cost upon their formerly purchased Lands, thought themselves *Free-holders* of what they had. And the Governor caused the Lands pertaining to these and those *particular Men*, to be measured out for his Creatures to take possession of; and the *Right Owners*, for pulling up the Stakes, have passed through Molestations enough to tire all the patience in the World. They are more than a few, that were by Terrors driven to take *Patents* for their Lands at excessive rates, to save them from the next that might petition for them: and we fear that the forcing of the People at the *Eastward* hereunto, gave too much Rise to the late unhappy Invasion made by the *Indians* on them. *Blanck Patents* were got ready for the rest of us, to be sold, at a Price, that all the Mony and Movables in the Territory could scarce have paid. And several *Towns* in the Country had their *Commons* begg'd by Persons (even by some of the Council themselves) who have been privately encouraged thereunto, by those that sought for Occasions to impoverish a Land already *Peeled, Meeted out and Trodden down*.

§ IX. All the Council were not ingaged in these ill Actions, but those of them which were true Lovers of *their Country*, were seldom admitted to, and seldomer consulted at the Debates which produced these unrighteous Things: Care was taken to keep them under Disadvantages; and the Governor, with five or six more, did what they would. We bore all these, and many more such Things, without making any attempt for any Relief; only Mr. *Mather*, purely out of respect unto the Good of his Afflicted Country, undertook a Voyage into *England*; which when these Men suspected him to be preparing for, they used all manner of Craft and Rage, not only to interrupt his *Voyage*, but to ruin his *Person* too. God having through many Difficulties given him to arrive at *White-hall*, the King, more than once or twice, promised him a certain *Magna Charta* for a speedy Redress of many things which we were groaning under: and in the mean time said, *That our Governor should be written unto, to forbear the Measures that he was upon.* However, after this, we were injured in those very Things which were complained of; and besides what Wrong hath been done in our Civil Concerns, we suppose the *Ministers* and the *Churches* every where have seen our Sacred Concerns apace going after them: How they have been Discountenanced, has had a room in the reflections of every man, that is not a stranger *in our Israel*.

§ X. And yet that our Calamity might not be terminated here, we are again Briar'd in the Perplexities of another *Indian War*; how, or why, is a mystery too deep to us to unfold. And tho' 'tis judged that our *Indian* Enemies are not above 100. in number, yet an Army of *One thousand* English hath been raised for the Conquering of them; which Army of our poor Friends and Brethren now under *Popish Commanders* (for in the Army as well as in the Council, Papists are in Commission) has been under such a conduct, that not one *Indian* hath been kill'd, but more English are supposed to have died through sickness and hardship, than we have adversaries there alive; and the whole War hath been so managed, that we cannot but suspect in it, a branch of the Plot *to bring us low*; which we leave to be further enquir'd into in due time.

§ XI. We did nothing against these Proceedings, but only cry to our God; they *have caused the cry of the Poor to come unto him, and he bears the cry of the Afflicted*. We have been quiet hitherto, and so still we should have been, had not the Great God at this time laid us under a *double engagement* to do something for our security; besides, what we have in the strangely unanimous inclination which our Countrymen by extreamest necessities are driven unto. For first, we are informed that the rest of the English *America* is alarmed with just and great fears, that they may be attaqu'd by the *French*, who have lately ('tis said) already treated many of the English with worse then *Turkish* Cruelties; and while we are in equal danger of being surprised by them, it is high time we should be better guarded, than we are like to be while the Government remains in the hands by which it hath been held of late. Moreover, we have understood, (though the *Governour* has taken all imaginable care to keep us all ignorant thereof) that the Almighty God hath been pleased to prosper the noble undertaking of the Prince of *Orange*, to preserve the three Kingdoms from the horrible brinks of Popery and Slavery, and to bring to a Condign punishment those *worst of men*, by whom *English Liberties* have been destroy'd; in compliance with which Glorious Action we ought surely to follow the Patterns which the Nobility, Gentry and Commonality in several parts of those Kingdoms have set before us, though *they* therein chiefly proposed to prevent what *we* already endure.

§ XII. We do therefore seize upon the Persons of those few *Ill Men* which have been (next to our Sins) the grand Authors of our Miseries; resolving to secure them, for what Justice, Orders from his Highness, with the *English Parliament* shall direct, lest, ere we are aware, we *find* (what we may *fear*, being on all sides in danger) our selves to be by them given away to a Forreign *Power*, before such Orders can reach unto us; for which Orders we now humbly wait. In the mean time firmly believing, that we have endeavoured nothing but what meer Duty to God and our *Country* calls for at our Hands: We commit our *Enterprise* unto the Blessing of Him, *who hears the cry of the Oppressed*, and advise all our Neighbours, for whom we have thus ventured our selves, to joyn with us in Prayers and all just Actions, for the Defence of the Land.

At the *Town-House* in *Boston, April* 18. 1689.

SIR,

Our Selves and many others the Inhabitants of this Town, and the Places adjacent, being surprized with the Peoples sudden taking of Arms; in the first motion whereof we were wholly ignorant, being driven by the present Accident, are necessitated to acquaint your Excellency, that for the quieting and securing of the People inhabiting in this Country from the imminent Dangers they many ways lie open and exposed to, and tendring your own Safety, We judge it necessary you forthwith surrender and deliver up the Government and Fortification to be preserved and disposed according to Order and Direction from the Crown of England, which suddenly is expected may arrive; promising all security from violence to your Self or any of your Gentlemen or Souldiers in Person and Estate: Otherwise we are assured they will endeavour the taking of the Fortification by Storm, if any Opposition be made.

To Sir Edmond Andross *Kt.*

Waite Winthrop.	Elisha Cook.
Simon Bradstreet.	Isaac Addington.
William Stoughton.	John Nelson.
Samuel Shrimpton.	Adam Winthrop.
Bartholomew Gidney.	Peter Sergeant.
William Brown.	John Foster.
Thomas Danforth.	David Waterhouse.
John Richards.	

FINIS.

Notes

+

Notes to the Preface

1. Throughout this study, I have quoted from the 1852 two-volume edition of *Magnalia Christi Americana* reissued in 1967 by Russell & Russell (New York). That edition reprints the original 1820 edition of Thomas Robbins with only minor modifications and includes both of Robbins's prefaces.

2. See David Harlan, "A People Blinded from Birth: American History According to Sacvan Bercovitch," *Journal of American History* 78.3 (December 1991): 955.

3. Bercovitch has assumed Miller's place at Harvard University and, along with a cadre of scholars whose work dominated the field in the 1970s—Emory Elliott, Larzer Ziff, Ursula Brumm, Mason Lowance, and others—has brought about what David Hall terms, in "On Common Ground," "a veritable revolution in our under standing of the 'Puritan imagination' " (195). For a review of the salient discussions of this point, see Edmund Morgan, "The Chosen People," *New York Review of Books* (July 19, 1979): 33; Norman Fiering, "The First American: Cotton Mather," *Reviews in American History* 12 (December 1984): 479; Nina Baym, rev. of *The American Jeremiad* and *The Puritan Origins of the American Self*, by Sacvan Bercovitch, *Nineteenth Century Fiction* 34 (December 1979): 350; Leo Marx, rev. of *The Puritan Origins of the American Self*, by Sacvan Bercovitch, *New York Times Book Review* (February 1, 1976): 21; Alan Trachtenberg, "The Writer as America," *Partisan Review* 44.3 (1977): 468; Cushing Strout, "Paradoxical Puritans," *American Scholar* 45 (Autumn 1976): 602; David Hall, "On Common Ground: The Coherence of American Puritan Studies," *William and Mary Quarterly* 64.2 (April 1987): 193–229; Norman Pettit, "The Puritan Legacy," *New England Quarterly* 48.2 (1975): 283–94; and Donald Weber, "Historicizing the Errand," *American Literary History* 2.1 (1990): 102.

4. The exceptional critical bickering that has surrounded this issue (largely as the result of critical tensions among new historicists and New Americanists) may be traced in Michael J. Colacurcio, "The American-Renaissance Renaissance," *New England Quarterly* 64.3 (September 1991): 445–93; R. C. De Prospo, "Marginalizing Early American Literature," *New Literary History* 23 (Spring 1992): 233–65; Earl N. Harbert, rev. of *The Office of the Scarlet Letter*, by Sacvan Bercovitch, *New England Quarterly* 65.2 (March 1992): 168–70; Eric Cheyfitz, "Matthiessen's American Renaissance: Circumscribing the Revolution," *American Quarterly* 41.2 (1989): 341–61;

Douglas Anderson, rev. of *The Office of the Scarlet Letter,* by Sacvan Bercovitch, *Nineteenth Century Literature* 47.1 (June 1992): 105–08; Joseph G. Kronick, rev. of *The Office of the Scarlet Letter,* by Sacvan Bercovitch, and *The Anatomy of National Fantasy: Hawthorne, Utopia and Everyday Life,* by Lauren Berlaut, *Criticism* 34.4 (Fall 1992): 624–28; Philip F. Gura, *The Wisdom of Words* (1981); Robert D. Richardson, *Myth and Literature in the American Renaissance* (1978); John T. Irwin, *American Hieroglyphics* (1980); Larzer Ziff, *Literary Democracy* (1981); Walter Benn Michaels and Donald Pease, eds., *The American Renaissance Reconsidered* (1985); Lawrence Buell, *New England Literary Culture* (1986); Donald Pease, *Visionary Compacts* (1987); Jeffrey Steele, *The Representation of the Self in the American Renaissance* (1987); Larry J. Reynolds, *European Revolutions and the American Literary Renaissance* (1988); Leon Chai, *The Romantic Foundations of the American Renaissance* (1987); David S. Reynolds, *Beneath the American Renaissance* (1988); David Leverenz, *Manhood and the American Renaissance* (1989); Sacvan Bercovitch, *The Office of the Scarlet Letter* (1991), and Bercovitch, *The Rites of Assent* (1993).

Notes to the Introduction

1. Cotton Mather was fond of addressing sermons to young ministers, instructing them on presentation style in the pulpit that relied on stereotypes of the preacher as weeping prophet and as angel of light. See William Henry Roen, *Prophets and Angels: A Study of the Self-Presentation of Selected American Puritan Preachers,* PhD diss., Catholic University of America, 1987.

2. For useful interpretations of new historicism, see Edward Pechter, "The New Historicism and Its Discontents: Politicizing Renaissance Drama," *PMLA* 102 (May 1987): 292–303; and Peter Nicholls, "Old Problems and the New Historicism," *Journal of American Studies* 23.3 (1989): 423–34.

3. "Eventalization" as a possible mode of historical inquiry is described in a roundtable debate between Michel Foucault and a number of French historians on complementary aspects of nineteenth-century penal history. The discussion was published in a volume edited by Michelle Perrot, *L'impossible prison: Recherches sur le système pénitentiaire au XIXe siècle.* It is translated in Graham Burchell, Colin Gordon, and Peter Miller, eds., *The Foucault Effect* 73–86. Before publication, Foucault revised his own contributions, and the questions of the several historians were rearranged into a series of questions posed by a "collective Historian."

4. The term *accents* is borrowed from the linguistic theories of V. N. Voloshinov (see *Marxism and the Philosophy of Language*). By focusing on political accents in the works I discuss, I am saying that these accents are codes that convey meanings; there are "accents" in the way a writer like Mather understands his relation to the material of New England history and political experience, and there are "accents" placed on his work by readers who actively read. Voloshinov's notion of *accent* and the *word* helps us to understand Mather's way of writing history:

> The word is implicated in literally each and every act or contact between people —
> in collaboration on the job, in ideological exchanges, in the chance contacts of

ordinary life, in political relationships, and so on. Countless ideological threads running through all areas of social intercourse register effect in the word. It stands to reason, then, that the word is the most sensitive *index of social changes*, and what is more, of changes still in the process of growth, still without definitive shape and not as yet accommodated into already regularized and fully defined ideological systems. The word is the medium in which occur the slow quantitative changes which have not yet achieved the status of a new ideological quality, not yet produced a new and fully ideological form. The word has the capacity to register all the transitory, delicate, momentary phases of social change. (19)

Voloshinov develops his theory that "an ideological theme is always socially accentuated" (22) in order to understand the kind of causality (specifically not mechanical causality) that exists between base (or basis) and superstructure, or between material conditions and "ideology" in what Voloshinov calls the "strict" sense of ideology.

5. See Denning, *Mechanic Accents*.

6. See ibid.

7. It will be obvious to some of my readers that I have drawn from a variety of prior sources on Mather and his public and private anxieties. David Levin's *Cotton Mather: The Young Life of the Lord's Remembrancer* is a meticulous consideration of Mather's life and work. Kenneth Silverman's biography, *The Life and Times of Cotton Mather*, stresses Mather's reactions to rapid political and social exigencies and thus is more important to this study, for it looks at Mather's complex postures as evidence of an "ambidexter" opportunism. See also Richard Lovelace, *The American Pietism of Cotton Mather: Origins of American Evangelicalism*; Sacvan Bercovitch, *The Puritan Origins of the American Self*, and Bercovitch, "Cotton Mather," in *Major Writers of Early American Literature*, ed. Everett Emerson, which was the first study to suggest that Mather's literary persona, producing an array of narrative modes, was a function of Puritanism's loss of external controls; Robert Middlekauff, *The Mathers: Three Generations of Puritan Intellectuals*; and Peter Gay, *A Loss of Mastery: Puritan Historians in Colonial America*.

8. I borrow this reference to cultural "dreamwork" (a concept put forward by Freud) from *Mechanic Accents*, Michael Denning's book on dime novels and working-class culture. It describes a form of literature and a social environment far different from Mather's but has great usefulness for describing the specific ways in which texts like *Magnalia*, which depend on "open" interpretations of ideological struggle, function in acts of reading.

9. In what follows, I ask two principal questions: (1) What are *Magnalia*'s textual traces or accents of a struggle for meaning in colonial politics? (2) How are these markers redeployed in the work of other writers treating the interplay of cultural identity and political ideology? To answer the first question, I address theoretical aspects of how Mather "fashions" a representation of the political culture in Massachusetts between 1684 and 1691 and how he insinuates his personality into that account. The first two chapters are meant to provide the context for understanding what political conditions were being marked by Mather's text and to suggest a critical reading of this book in light of those circumstances. The answer to the second

question depends on our seeing Mather's text not as an expression of any denotative historical reality. Rather, I see *Magnalia* of 1820 as an important terrain of negotiation and conflict among writers of the antebellum period over the proper means for rendering popular politics. The cultural importance of Thomas Robbins's 1820 edition lies in the way in which it enabled the three writers I discuss to address a need for greater pluralism in Puritan history. The text allowed writers to frame more precise paradigms for managing social conflicts in a democratic society. The literature that emerges from Stowe's, Stoddard's, and Hawthorne's readings of Mather's text makes apparent how much social "scrimmaging" can take place *in* and *around* texts. The study I offer gives a new basis for understanding the importance of *Magnalia* in describing social reality in colonial New England. My work complicates assumptions of realism's unproblematic reflection of cultural milieu by critics who practiced a "myth-symbol" method for American Studies scholarship. Earlier approaches to Puritanism generally have been faulted on many grounds: for their holistic, consensual, and ideational model of culture, which often conflated humanistic and anthropological definitions of the term; for their neglect of American race, gender, and class conflict; for relying on canonical texts and justifying that reliance by employing New Critical notions of "intrinsic" literary power, rather than a historically reconstructed sense of cultural production and reception; for equating textual meaning, audience reception, and popular belief; and for employing tautological reasoning that reduced literary texts to redundant reflections of other historical documents.

10. See Mitchell Breitwieser, *American Puritanism and the Defense of Mourning* 79–83, 104–07.

11. See Denning, *Mechanic Accents* 82–84.

12. I am paraphrasing E. D. Hirsh, who in *Validity in Interpretation* writes, "to reproduce in himself the author's logic, his attitudes, his cultural givens, in short his world thus achieving the imaginative reconstruction of the speaking subject" (242).

13. See Denning, *Mechanic Accents* 105.

14. See Lawrence Buell, *New England Literary Culture* 69.

15. Quite often, the genre of historical romance is transformed by the weaving together of Mather's poetics and the political conditions addressed by nineteenth-century writers. Each of the principal works discussed in later chapters—*The Minister's Wooing, The Morgesons,* and *Grandfather's Chair*—incorporates ironic narrative formulas that involve real ideological contradictions that it was the task of the story to resolve. In Stowe's case, the resolution is fairly complete, but in Stoddard's and Hawthorne's work the anxiety induced by the contradictory formulas generally persists indefinitely in the reader's imagination. The intrinsic textual power or "designs" of the three principal texts I examine do not contain, in themselves, an entire culture's conflict over the political atmosphere of democracy; nor do I claim that the genre of historical romance is particularly useful for measuring the potency of these individual texts for executing such a generalized function. Rather, my main interest, like Denning's claims for the significance of dime novels, is in uncovering some of the ruses of the representation of political cleavages that are found in the plots, characterizations, and arrangement of subjects in these works.

16. The literary efforts of the three writers I discuss helped to show to their audiences the importance of politically decoding the historical (re)presentations made in their literature. All three of these writers calculated their rehearsals of Mather's original text with an eye toward helping their readers to penetrate the disguises of their own representations.

17. See Christopher Felker, "Roger Williams's Uses of Legal Discourse: Testing Authority in Early New England," *New England Quarterly* 63.4 (December 1990): 624–48.

18. History and the practice of fiction poignantly delineate "an area of plausibility which reveals the possible in the very act of unmasking it as false" (Roland Barthes, *Degree Zero* 32). Each of the writers considered in this study (including Cotton Mather) used specific reading situations to encourage their audiences to modify, sometimes decisively, the cultural work done by their texts. The reworking of the canonical archive that Mather provided in *Magnalia* presented writers like Hawthorne, Stoddard, and Stowe with the opportunity to reverse a hypostasis of Puritanism typical of amateur historical fictionalists. Hawthorne's attraction to a cluttered Puritanism represented in a form derivative of Peale's museology, Stowe's presentation of Aaron Burr courting a Republican Puritan maiden, and Stoddard's suggestion of historical mediumship and spiritualism, all seriously challenged the genteel amateurism of New England's early national years. All attempted to qualify (as Mather had done in his examination of the limitations that Puritanism placed on social formations in Massachusetts) the notion that New England history could participate in a program of generalized cultural coherence.

Notes to Chapter One

1. One of the more significant early attempts to retune Mather's image was Susan Cherry Bell, *History and Artistry in Cotton Mather's "Magnalia Christi Americana,"* PhD diss., State University of New York at Binghamton, 1981. Bell's study presents a fresh understanding of *Magnalia Christi Americana* by attending to its rhetorical medium as the expression of a complex and sophisticated sensibility. It argues that a cluster of derogatory assumptions about Mather (and his place in the history of the Puritan consciousness in New England) has colored even the most distinguished readings of the work, lending a special urgency to the problem of hearing Mather aright. Her account eschews (as mine does) a straightforward chronological reading to engage more immediately the dynamics of New English history and the pressure of its shaping voice. Mather's apparently odd conjunction of urbane sophistication and a peculiarly intense piety is first heard and clarified in the "General Introduction," which complicates the design of *Magnalia*'s seven-book organization. Mather is seen by Bell to be very aware, especially in the account of Phips's governorship, of the problems of the recent past.

2. See Terry Odell Engebretsen, *Pillars of the House: Puritan Funeral Sermons Through the "Magnalia Christi Americana,"* PhD diss., Washington State University, 1982.

3. For example, see Ursula Brumm, *American Thought and Religious Typology*; Jesper Rosenmeier, *The Image of Christ: The Typology of John Cotton*, PhD diss., Harvard University, 1966; Sacvan Bercovitch, ed., *Typology and Early American Literature*, and Bercovitch, "Typology in Puritan New England: The Williams-Cotton Controversy Reassessed," *American Quarterly* 19 (1967): 166–91; Earl Miner, ed., *Literary Uses of Typology*; Mason Lowance, *The Language of Canaan*, and Lowance, *Images and Shadows of Divine Things: Puritan Typology in New England from 1660–1750*," PhD diss., Emory University, 1967; Thomas Davis, *Typology in New England Puritanism*, PhD diss., University of Missouri, 1969; Stephen Manning, *Scriptural Exegesis and Literary Criticism*.

4. Breen, in *Puritans and Adventurers*, seizes on the image of the meetinghouse and uses it to explain, as Mather seems to want to do in his map, the strength of localism in New England. Breen's description will be familiar to most readers as perhaps the archetypal stereotype of New England cultural organization: "Almost as soon as they arrived in the New World, the migrants succeeded in constructing a physical embodiment of their commitment to localism. Each community built a meetinghouse that served both civil and ecclesiastical functions. It provided a central place where men and women regularly assembled to shape and define their society. . . . The buildings took on a symbolic significance—much as cathedrals did in medieval towns or smaller churches still do in Latin American peasant villages" (18).

5. The provocation of Mather's map (especially in contrast to Wells's map) is, to use terminology coined by Roland Barthes in *S/Z*, "writerly" ("because the goal of literary work . . . is to make the reader no longer a consumer, but a producer of text" [4]) because a plurality of interpretations is expected and rewarded by the methodology perhaps employed by Mather, for his 1690 map repeats the cartographic conventions of a typical map of 1630.

6. During the 1640s, Massachusetts extended its jurisdiction to four towns in this region, although their charter ran only to the southern bank of the Merrimack.

7. Andrew Delbanco, in *The Puritan Ordeal*, points to Increase's willingness to go to and remain in England as being particularly hard for Cotton to accept. It served to fuel an "ironic panic" "because the utility and devotion of New England to Old had been the Mathers' theme for decades" (185). It may be that Increase's apparent desertion and his already documented unwillingness to accept his son into his pulpit were strong motivations for Cotton to fashion a public identity that executed a cultural agenda that was quite different from his father's tradition but that still seemed respectful to the order he (potentially) represented. Something like this difference in aims and political allegiances may indeed be reflected in Mather's complicity with the scandal sheet accounts of the actions in Quebec found in the *Publick Occurrences*.

8. *Andros Tracts* 1:71–72, 2:206, 3:226; 3 Massachusetts Historical Society, *Collections* I:100; Hutchinson, *History of Massachusetts*, I:380, note 381; *Calendar of State Papers*, Colonial Series, 1689–92, §§152, 285. Edward Randolph maintained that "the revolt here [in Boston] was pushed on by the agent in England, Mr. [Increase] Mather, who sent a letter to Mr. Bradstreet encouraging him to go cheerfully to so

acceptable a piece of service to all good people" (*Calendar of State Papers*, Colonial Series, 1689–92, §407). That Increase may indeed have sown the seeds of revolution in the minds of the American Puritan leadership is indicated in a revolutionary pamphlet directed against Edmund Andros, "Whether common cursing and Swearing and Sabbath breaking be not admirable qualities in a Governor, and such as may make any New-Englanders dote upon him, or endeavor his re-establishment, when we have all the assurance in the world that we shall be commended by the Authority of England for our deposing him" (*Andros Tracts* 3:194). Gershom Bulkeley in his *Will and Doom* asserts that the theocrats of Connecticut in 1689 received "encouragement by letter from England, to take their Charter Government again, telling them, they were a company of *hens* if they did not do it" (New England Colonial Records III:456).

9. According to David Levin, "except for Mather's refusal to deny authorship of the *Declaration* when it was attributed to him later on, none of the conspirators ever admitted to planning the revolution. Their shrewd emphasis in the document itself, and in all the subsequent reports that survive, fell on the outrages committed by the 'crew of abject wretches' that Andros had 'fetched from New York' " (*Cotton Mather* 165).

10. The *Declaration* begins with an elaborate allusion to a popish plot that New Englanders have patiently borne. The people of New England, Mather claimed, were a people of law who wanted to retain their ancient liberties. Disputing the arbitrary authority of the Andros administration, Mather cloaked his criticisms with the moral force of middle-class Puritanism. The "accidental" happenings in Boston not only generated Cotton Mather's own sense of authorship but set in place the template for public documentation of the American Revolution eighty-six years later.

11. Mather's appeal to "design" is not accidental because at one basic level *Magnalia* tries to be an epochal treatment of the material difference between "America" and "American." For examples of the ways in which Puritan ideology confronted the hostile geography of American history, see Myra Jehlen, *American Incarnation*.

12. The historical precedents cited in the "General Introduction" include Herodotus, Thucydides, Xenophon, Cyrus, Diodorus, Siculus, Arianus, Justin, Curtius, Polybius, Lucius Florus, Dionysius of Halicarnassus, Livy, Suetonius, Tacitus, Herodian, Plutarch, and Polyhistor.

13. The recognition of these cultural processes, made in the context of republicanism by Michael Warner—see "Franklin and the Letters of the Republic" in Fisher, 3–24—is usefully extended to Cotton Mather's print activities.

14. *Andros Tracts* 2:209, 210, 211–12, 3:145, note 234; *Calendar of State Papers*, Colonial Series, 1689–92, §§181, 285, 510, 901; Hutchinson, *History of Massachusetts* I:380–81, note; 4 Massachusetts Historical Society, *Collections* V:190, 198.

15. The Glorious Revolution, Mather intuited, could not sustain itself for long. His analysis therefore aims to describe the curve of motion that goes from his public statements at the Town House to a statement of his "worth" as a historical variation within Puritan discourse. The order of this discourse, Mather knew, was maintained by legislated accident as the letters his father sent from Whitehall continually at-

tested. The odd, distinctive quality of *Magnalia* is that Mather's general narrative is designed to illuminate a large number of repetitive phenomena that are continuously appearing with such disconcerting randomness as to seem chaotic.

16. *Andros Tracts* 1:62.

17. The contingency with which Cotton addressed the story of his father's role in the region is a textbook illustration of the "anxiety of influence," defined by Harold Bloom in *The Anxiety of Influence* as *apophrades*: "the obvious achievement and excellence of insight in the successor's work makes the predecessor's work seem like a faulty and imperfect adumbration" (139–55). Mather labored under this anxiety when writing *Magnalia*:

> Reader, the interest and figure which the world knows this my *parent* hath had, in the ecclesiastical concerns of this country, ever since his first return from England in the twenty-second, until his next return from England in the fifty-third year of his age; makes it a difficult thing for *me* to write the church-history of the country. Should I insert every where the relation which he hath had unto the public matters, it will be thought by the *envious* that I had undertaken this work with an eye to such a *motto* as . . . *patriæque patrique* [my country and my sire]: should I, on the other side, bury in utter silence all the effects of that care and zeal wherewith he hath employed in his peculiar opportunities . . . I must cut off some *essentials* of my story. I will, however, bowle nearer to the *latter* mark than the *former.* (2.18)

As Kenneth Silverman points out in *The Life and Times of Cotton Mather*, "Increase did not want the North Church to have them both. He antagonized his flock, many of whom, he noticed, 'seemed to be troubled' at his opposition to Cotton's settlement. . . . Considering that he felt mistreated by his congregation, he may have been galled by their enthusiasm for his son; or he may have feared Cotton's rivalry and possible dissent. . . . When one of his illnesses led him to advise the brethren to seek his replacement, they unanimously elected Cotton" (27).

18. *Calendar of State Papers*, Colonial Series, 1693–96, 5–6, 63–64, 67–68, 209–10, 246, 250.

19. Mitchell Breitwieser, in his corrective to Eberwein and Gura, states, "As the book of the governors proceeds, Mather's desire for an independent modernity gains increasingly direct expression in the form of admiration. He uses the formal tension between pattern and experience that is innate to the book as a vehicle for his own characteristic affective tension; and his desire emerges fully articulate" (*Cotton Mather and Benjamin Franklin* 155).

20. See Kaja Silverman, *The Subject of Semiotics*, ch. 5.

21. As John Demos puts it in *Entertaining Satan*: "Witchcraft beliefs are thought to perform functions, confer advantages, impart strength and resiliency to the social fabric as a whole. . . . Witchcraft charges bring to a head the tensions and strains of a difficult relationship. They furnish a pretext for quarreling, which in turn may yield a new balance of social forces" (277).

22. On the "The Life of Phips," see also Jane Eberwein, " 'In a Book, as in a Glass': Literary Sorcery in Mather's Life of Phips," *Early American Literature* 10

(1976): 293–98; and Philip Gura, "Cotton Mather's *Life of Phips*: 'A Vice with the Vizard of Vertue upon It,' " *New England Quarterly* 50.3 (September 1977): 447–57.

23. According to Ann Kibbey, John Cotton's *A Brief Exposition of the Whole Book of Canticles, or, Song of Solomon* (1642) relies on

> non-representational imagery, the visual absurdity of absence "marks" the presence of supernatural power. For the faithful, the mental picture is a mental blank. . . . its reality [is] marked by figures but its integral shape [is] unknown. Within this system of thought, the pressure to believe is intense because, for the faithless literalist who insists on his idolatrous "mental picture," the visualized mystical body is a phantasmagoric horror, a grotesque image of things and people assembled to substitute for human bodily parts. . . . figural realism enables [one] to move with ease and indifference between type and poetic image—between historical things, people, and events, on the one hand, and the imagery of the text, on the other. (*The Interpretation of Material Shapes* 84–85)

24. Mather was fully cognizant of the implicit "madness" that circumscribed man's view of himself as a unitary being. As Mary Ann Jimenez argues, "Cotton Mather's model of madness was not idiosyncratic, for it was the only logical one that could have existed within the Puritan symbolic world" (*Changing Faces of Madness* 17; see also 12–19).

25. See Jonathan Crewe, who discusses Tudor biographies in *Trials of Authorship*—especially the sections about William Roper on Sir Thomas More and George Cavendish on Cardinal Wolsey.

26. Here Mather is referring to the Greek legend in which Jason, convinced that his son Phryxus is the cause of a famine in their blighted land, orders him to be sacrificed.

27. In Jeffrey Jeske's opinion, Mather's persona during shifts in the text's mode of explanation "consists of three interrelated elements, each running counter to the founders' orthodoxy"—an Enlightenment-like regard for reason, a mechanistic interpretation of the universe, and a lessening of sacerdotal and affective preoccupations ("Cotton Mather: Physico-Theologian" 587–89 and 591).

28. Here it is important to note David Scobey's observation that

> What lay at the source of New England's crisis was less the particular contradictions of Puritan orthodoxy than the nature of orthodoxy itself. Almost invariably orthodoxy looks to its history for the "Rule" by which it guides action and erases ambiguity. Either it locates this rule in a scriptural text or it [as in the case of Mather] turns history into a kind of scripture, endowing the past with interpretative authority. . . . the orthodox tend to ignore their own agency in recreating the traditions to which they submit themselves. Social memory . . . is itself the product of present-day needs, codes, and conflicts. It is transformed by precisely those forces of change that an orthodoxy like Puritanism looks to history to deny. . . . Indeed, because the past is usually invoked as a way of resolving struggles over cultural authority, mirroring conflict is what it does best. ("Revising the Errand" 30)

29. See Michel Foucault, "Governmentality."

30. See Dennis Perry, *Autobiographical Structures in Seventeenth-Century Puritan Histories*, PhD diss., University of Wisconsin, Madison, 1986.

31. See Richard Boyd, *Three Generations of Puritan Spiritual Autobiography: Problems of Self-Definition in a Time of Declension*, PhD diss., University of California, San Diego, 1985.

Notes to Chapter Two

1. Rivington began to advertise his intention to enter the field of book publishing on May 27, 1773, by placing the first of many columns in the most widely distributed newspaper at the time, Rivington's *New-York Gazetter; or the Connecticut, New Jersey, Hudson's River, and Quebec Weekly Advertiser*. See John Tebbel, *A History of Book Publishing in the United States* 87.

2. As Sacvan Bercovitch has pointed out, "Thomas Robbins reissued *Magnalia* to an audience for whom, as for Mather, the events of national history seemed indistinguishable from the spiritual patterns of scripture" (*Puritan Origins* 149).

3. For a fuller treatment of Taylor's sermonizing, see Richard Rabinowitz, *The Spiritual Self in Everyday Life* 89–90 and 92–93 (Taylor) and 142–43 and 147–49 (Beecher).

4. For the most thorough discussion of Mather's symbolic importance to nineteenth-century New England historiography, see Lawrence Buell, *New England Literary Culture* 218–24.

5. See Elizabeth Stoddard, *The Morgesons and Other Writings, Published and Unpublished*, ed. Lawrence Buell and Sandra Zagarell, 255 n25.

6. See Page Smith, *The Nation Comes of Age* 9.

7. Erving Goffman suggests in *Behavior in Public Places* that

> a shared definition of the situation comes to prevail. This includes agreement concerning perceptual relevances and irrelevancies, and a "working consensus" involving a degree of mutual considerateness, sympathy, and a muting of opinion differences. . . . At the same time a heightened sense of moral responsibility for one's acts also seems to develop. A "we-rationale" develops, being a sense of a single thing that we the participants are avowedly doing at the same time. (96–98)

8. See Michael Denning, *Mechanic Accents* 82–83.

9. The principal unit in the virtual reality of Mather's text was the anecdote, which perfectly conveyed Mather's feelings for contingency in relation to history. Joel Fineman has identified the anecdote "as the literary form that uniquely *lets history happen* by virtue of the way it introduces an opening into the teleological . . . narration of the beginning, middle, and end. The anecdote produces the effect of the real, the occurrence of contingency, by establishing an event as an event within and yet without the framing context of historical successivity" (61).

10. The trait I refer to here shares with Roland Barthes a sense of how both the

work and the author can be broken and reconstituted within the metaphor of the network:

> The metaphor of the Text is that of the network; if the Text extends itself, it is as a result of a combinatory systematic. . . . Hence no vital respect is due the Text: it can be broken . . . ; it can be read without the guarantee of its father, the restitution of the inter-text paradoxically abolishing any legacy. It is not that the author may not come back in the Text, in his text, but he then does so as a "guest." If he is a novelist, he is inscribed in the novel like one of his characters, figured in the carpet; no longer privileged, paternal, aletheological, his inscription is ludic. He becomes, as it were, a paper-author: his life is no longer the origin of his fictions but a fiction contributing to his work. ("From Work to Text" 161)

Notes to Chapter Three

1. The source of this myth, which is alluded to by Colacurcio in *The Province of Piety* (207–08), is the famous passage in volume 1 of Bancroft's *History of the United States*:

> To cover his confusion, Cotton Mather got up a case of witchcraft in his own parish. . . . Believe his statements, and you must believe that his prayers healed diseases. But he was not bloodthirsty; he wished his vanity protected, not his parishioners hanged; and his bewitched neophyte, profiting by his cautions, was afflicted by veiled specters. The imposture was promptly exposed to ridicule by a "malignant, calumnious, and reproachful man," "a coal from hell," the unlettered but rational and intelligent Robert Calef. Was Cotton Mather honestly credulous? Ever ready to dupe himself, he limited his credulity only by the probable credulity of others. He changes, or omits to repeat, his statements, without acknowledging error, and with a clear intention of conveying false impressions. . . . His self-righteousness was complete, till he was resisted. . . . Cotton Mather endeavored to shield himself by calling his adversaries the adversaries of religion. . . . Denying the jurisdiction of popular opinion, he claimed the subject [of witchcraft] as "too dark and deep for ordinary comprehension." . . . The common mind of New England was more wise. . . . In the west of Massachusetts, and in Connecticut, to which the influence of Cotton Mather . . . did not extend, we must look for the unmixed development of the essential character of New England; there faith and "common sense" were reconciled. (266–67)

2. It bears mentioning that the evocation of attics appears in all three novels by Hawthorne, Stoddard (if one considers a library a form of attic), and Stowe. This is not accidental, for the image of the archive has a duplicitous meaning that is a function of both reading and writing. Historical activity is presumed by these writers to be implicated in the tasks of preserving and manipulating power within the cultural "archive." "Like a treasure hunter or a literary archaeologist . . . Hawthorne wished

to recycle public records and early American histories, to put them back out before the public in order both to set the historical record straight and to preserve documents that, in a culture increasingly devoted to the 'new' were threatened with extinction" (Keil 247–48).

3. A. H. Everett to Bancroft, March 26 and July 6, 1831, *Bancroft Papers*.

4. Lawrence Levine, in *Highbrow/Lowbrow* (1988), says (in reference to the nineteenth century), "because the primary categories of culture have been the products of ideologies which were always subject to modifications and transformations, the perimeters of our cultural divisions have been permeable and shifting rather than fixed and immutable" (8). David Hall, in *Worlds of Wonder, Days of Judgment* (1989), calls seventeenth-century culture both ordered and disordered, "where learning how to read and becoming 'religious' were perceived as one and the same thing" (3, 18). Janice Radway's (*Reading the Romance*, 1984) methodology for analyzing the popular romance accepts "that literary meaning is not something to be found in a text. It is, rather, an entity produced by a reader in conjunction with the text's verbal structure" (11). Michael Denning, in *Mechanic Accents* (1987), suggests that story papers "were not an expression of any one class so much as a terrain of negotiation and conflict over the proper accents of the popular" (136). Richard Brodhead, in *Hawthorne, Melville, and the Novel* (1976), argues that narrative frames are not simply "imposed necessities," they are instead a "hostage offered to the novel-reading public" (14). Jane Tompkins, in *Sensational Designs* (1985), argues for a way of reading that sees texts as "nodes within a network, expressing what lay in the minds of many or most of their contemporaries" (16).

5. See Tompkins, *Sensational Designs* 122–46.

6. Cotton Mather was a connoisseur in the sense that he collected natural objects and curiosities reflecting the prestige of the individual. In 1716, he communicated his "Curiosa Americana" to the Royal Society in London, saying that he had "made agreeable collections of such things in the countrey, as may give some entertainment unto men of ingenuity" (qtd. in Charles Goodspeed, *Nathaniel Hawthorne and the Museum of the Salem East India Marine Society* 12–13).

7. Note that Jane Tompkins makes an alternate argument, showing that Hawthorne's reputation is a highly political matter. See *Sensational Designs* 3–39.

8. Peale was deeply committed to popular education. A member of Philadelphia's radical artisan culture, he had great confidence in the importance of self-education for supporting democratic aims. "This is an age of discovery," Peale declared, "every experiment that brings to light the properties of any natural substance, helps to expand the mind and makes men better, more virtuous and liberal" (Charles Willson Peale, Autobiography, American Philosophical Society). In its equalizing the pressure between the general and the specific, Peale's museum was America's first serious attempt to accomplish the aims of a great public museum, one where the visitor's ideas on art and nature might routinely exceed the visitor's "station" in life.

9. According to Gary Kulik, the museum existed in Peale's mind from the beginning as a hybrid institution. He wanted to provide a visual experience that would bring his visitors "nearer to the Great-First-Cause," and he wanted the museum to

serve the public as a "school of useful knowledge," a point he emphasized by lecturing and publishing guides to accompany his exhibitions. The museum, for all its scholastic standards and dedication, was in fact the consummate creation of the artist (see Kulik, "Designing the Past: History-Museum Exhibitions from Peale to the Present," 4–5). An equally important model for Hawthorne was the Marine Museum of the Salem East India Company on Essex Street in Salem, Massachusetts. That museum was founded in 1799. See Goodspeed, *Nathaniel Hawthorne and the Museum of the Salem East India Marine Society* 7–9. See also Lawrence Jenkins and Walter Whitehill, "The Restoration of East India Marine Hall," *American Neptune* 4 (1944): 5–7.

10. Characteristically, both Peale and Hawthorne were skeptical about where the line was between democracy and corrupt entertainments. For a discussion of how Peale's museum framed issues of collection, display, and pedagogy for all subsequent American history museums, see Kulik, "Designing the Past." Kulik also treats the Smithsonian Institution, the American Wing of the Metropolitan Museum of Art, and the New York State Historical Association at Cooperstown.

11. Sacvan Bercovitch argues in "Hawthorne's A-Morality of Compromise" that *The Scarlet Letter* deploys power through long-preserved cultural artifacts that "reveal the variety of tactics available to the culture at a certain historical moment" (8). And as Christine Brooke-Rose suggests in "A for But: 'The Custom House' in Hawthorne's *The Scarlet Letter*," the very conceit of the Custom House implies "a public institutional place . . . a threshold of the narrative" (143).

12. The first *wunderkammer* was established in Vienna in 1550 and flourished in Europe for approximately one hundred years. By 1605, Sir Francis Bacon noted such displays as a "substantial and severe collection of the Heteroclites or Irregulars of nature" and derided wonder-cabinets were "frivolous impostures for pleasure and strangeness" (Bacon, *Works*, 3:330–31). Steven Mullaney, in "Strange Things, Gross Terms, Curious Customs: The Rehearsal of Custom in the Renaissance," notes that

> the museum as an institution rises from the ruins of such collections, rising like country houses from the dismantled stone work of dissolved monasteries; it organizes the wonder-cabinet by breaking it down—that is to say, by analyzing it, regrouping the random and the strange into recognizable categories that are systematic, discrete, and exemplary. The museum represents an order and a categorical will to knowledge whose absence—or suspension—is precisely what is on display in renaissance wonder-cabinets. (66)

13. Gordon Hutner, in *Secrets and Sympathy*, has alluded to this effect in his reading of *The House of the Seven Gables*: "Split between its aspirations to cultural prophecy and commercial appeal . . . [the novel] collapses under the weight of its unresolved contradictions" (65).

14. These terms are defined by Stephen Greenblatt in "Resonance and Wonder."

15. We know that Hawthorne read *Magnalia* as early as 1827, and Michael J. Colacurcio states in "Visible Sanctity" that Hawthorne's literary impressions were augmented by two works: Daniel Neal's *History of New England* (1719), which derives from *Magnalia*, and Benjamin Trumbull's *History of Connecticut* (1713), which

"parallels" Mather's text. All three of these related texts, but most particularly *Magnalia* itself with its "diagnosis and prescriptions for the maladies of the third-generation Puritans," gave Hawthorne all he needed to know about historical Puritanism and its perceived effects on the theory and practice of New English culture. See 266n11. As Richard Brodhead writes in *The School of Hawthorne*, "Hawthorne's authenticity derives in part from his exploitation of Mather's literary form" (12).

16. According to Philip Gura in "Baring the New England Soul," Hawthorne shared with Melville a knowledge that men "are deceived not only by their inordinate regard for personal interests but also by their thoughtless susceptibility to the confidence man's rhetoric addressing such supposedly worthwhile causes as 'charity,' 'benevolence,' and 'investment' " (151).

17. A very interesting play, William Crafts's *The Sea Serpent; or, Gloucester Hoax: A Dramatic jeu d'esprit in Three Acts* (1819), that illuminates this cultural moment is described by Chandos Brown in "A Natural History of the Gloucester Sea Serpent." The image of the natural history museum symbolized the intellectual state of the time, and the play that Brown describes satirizes the "American penchant for discovering giantism in nature and the triviality of such claims of exceptionalism" (430). Hawthorne, in a highly ironic gesture, could see that Peale's museum, with its democratic possibility, was also an institution driven by cultural chauvinism and misdirected national pride. In Mather's own time, his glorification of the New England Way would have been roundly criticized by William Berkeley and members of the Virginia gentry as an egregious act of misdirected chauvinism against the Stuart authority in England.

18. Hyatt Waggoner refers to this impulse in *The Presence of Hawthorne* 21–22. Allan Lloyd-Smith asserts in *Eve Tempted* that "Hawthorne remained obsessed by the borderline between the registration of an action and its effacement, so that his encounters with 'trace' are always informed by his insistence upon unreadability" (150). As in "The Old Apple Dealer," Hawthorne resorts to negative comparisons to drive home to his readers that he, as an artist, can describe a figure like the civil servant, but he cannot finally be said to "have" him totally. Waggoner says, "Knowledge brings with it the possibility of control . . . but [the artist] will falsify reality if he omits the element of mystery and assumes he knows the unknowable" (24). In this way, Mather's and Hawthorne's interests in the pneumatic realities of culture aim at preserving a degree of historical contingency.

19. Hawthorne's imaging effects are used both to establish in his readership a sense of "taste" with regard to exhibition techniques and to show that imaging produces one of two possible outcomes: (1) the arrangement of objects will create a visual confusion that can clarify the incompleteness of the thing being displayed; or (2) imaging will, by presenting a pristine image, create a silent testimony to the efficacy of a philosophical perspective manifested physically. The classic formulation of imaging as the principal activity of the romancer is, of course, Joel Porte, *The Romance in America*; see especially 98–114.

20. As Donald Pease points out in *Visionary Compacts* with reference to Melville, Hawthorne "reminded his readers of their continuing relationship with the ancestral

agreements upon which the nation was founded. Hawthorne was acutely aware that *Magnalia* constituted one of the richest collections in the cultural reserve" (46). Although I disagree with Pease's psychologism, he is right to point out that in the prefaces (and other secondary narration) Hawthorne and the other writers I have considered sought to manage the cultural possibilities of history in their works (see *Visionary Compacts* 46). Hawthorne's historical insights recognized the nineteenth century's prevailing concern with the instrumental, political uses of history writing. Most of the historians of this period were politicians or campaign biographers (Bancroft, Richard Hildreth, and Calcott, for example); Hawthorne's rigorous antiquarianism was calculated to expose the unrelenting irony within historians' attempts to manufacture flattering accounts of America's present circumstances.

21. Neal Doubleday, in *Hawthorne's Early Tales*, frames Hawthorne's projected collections and experiments in terms of an anxious tension between a deference to nationalistic critical prescription and skeptical irony. *Grandfather's Chair* may well have been Hawthorne's ideal antiquarian laboratory for testing the combinatorial possibilities of fragments in an arrangement that mimics the intention and poetics of *Magnalia*. Note the parallel conclusion that Susan Mizruchi makes in regard to Hawthorne's historical understanding in *The House of the Seven Gables*. Mizruchi, in *The Power of Historical Knowledge*, contends "that history is only available to consciousness in reified form, which helps explain how [Hawthorne's] characters can be obsessed with theories of temporality and history, but deny their own relationships to their particular historical moment" (88). Diffuseness in Hawthorne, according to Mizruchi, comes from his conscientious opposition of different conceptions of history. Those same traces and impulses emerge clearly from Hawthorne's balancing, in the texts I treat here, of materials evocative of resonance and wonder.

22. To use terminology borrowed from Christopher Wilson's *The Labor of Words*, both Mather and Hawthorne were aware that the market was more than a medium; it "was also a crucible of a new cultural style" (2). Their project, in narrowly artistic terms, was to capture a sense of the hermeneutic potential that New England history afforded American culture within the energy of print. The occupational and ideological consequences of the "new marketplace" brought for Hawthorne the possibility of constructing Brodhead's "School of Hawthorne" and for Mather an unprecedented surplus of marketable personality. According to Michael Gilmore, Hawthorne was deeply "concerned with his relation to the public and with his priorities as a writer who craved both fame and money" (*American Romanticism and the Marketplace* 96).

23. For the use Christopher Columbus made of Marco Polo and *Mandeville's Travels*, see Stephen Greenblatt's *Marvelous Possessions*, especially 26–51. *Mandeville's Travels* in this connection is particularly interesting because it participates in the traditions of aliases, unknown authorship, and nation building.

24. As Alice McNeill Donohue suggests in *Hawthorne: Calvin's Ironic Stepchild*, the Old Manse frames a signal ambiguity in Hawthorne and his attitude toward humanity's moral nature. He demonstrates an apparent, not real, vacillation between trusting the human heart's intuitions as good and advancing his conviction that the heart is a "foul-cavern" that must be destroyed in order to be purified.

25. *Grandfather's Chair* was written in 1839 and first published by Elizabeth Peabody in 1840 as the first volume in a three-volume series. It was republished in 1842 and, after the success of *The Scarlet Letter*, in 1850 and 1854. Nine printings of the work brought Hawthorne $667.50 in royalties by 1863.

Publication History of *Grandfather's Chair*

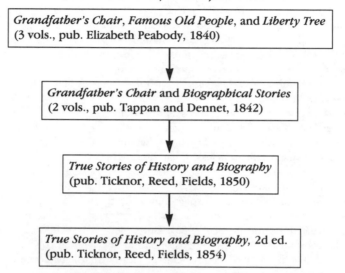

Grandfather's Chair, Famous Old People, and *Liberty Tree*
(3 vols., pub. Elizabeth Peabody, 1840)

Grandfather's Chair and *Biographical Stories*
(2 vols., pub. Tappan and Dennet, 1842)

True Stories of History and Biography
(pub. Ticknor, Reed, Fields, 1850)

True Stories of History and Biography, 2d ed.
(pub. Ticknor, Reed, Fields, 1854)

26. Hawthorne considers two other episodes that relate the chair to its specifically Puritan origin. The first, where Grandfather relates the tale of Governor Pownall, ties the chair's destiny to the sole destiny of Massachusetts. Laurence tells his Grandfather, " 'If Governor Pownall had put it aboard the vessel in which he sailed for South Carolina, she would probably have lain wind-bound in Boston harbor. It was ordained that the chair should not be taken away' " (136). The second episode equates the material substance of the chair as playing a role in the preservation of Puritanism's "king-resisting" tendencies among the colony's leaders and people. This is referred to in a portion of the text dealing with the passage of the Stamp Act. Grandfather says, " '[at that time] it had seemed as if these [Puritan] characteristics were disappearing. But no sooner did England offer wrong to the colonies, than the descendants of the early settlers proved that they had the same kind of temper as their forefathers' " (151).

27. We know that Hawthorne parodied this idea of himself as a curious museum piece in his *American Notebooks*:

Here I am, in my old chamber where I produced those stupendous works of fiction which have since impressed the universe with wonderment and awe! To this chamber, doubtless, in all succeeding ages, pilgrims will come to pay their tribute of reverence. . . . "There," they will exclaim, "is the very bed in which he slumbered, and where he was visited by those ethereal visions. . . . There is the wash-stand at which this exalted personage cleansed himself. . . . There, in its mahogany frame, is the dressing-glass, which often reflected that noble brow. . . . There is the pine table,—there the old flag-bottomed chair on which he sat. . . . There is the old chest of drawers. . . . There is the closet. . . . There is the worn-out shoe-brush with which this polished writer polished his boots—but I believe this will be pretty much all, so here I close the catalogue. (334–35)

The reference to the museum, according to Robert Shulman, underscores Hawthorne's belief that he was "imprisoned" by Jacksonian culture: "Hawthorne had special reasons for simultaneously communicating and concealing the manner both of the symbolic artist and of the prisoner" (195).

28. For a counterargument that sees Hawthorne and transcendentalism as being more closely related, see Lloyd-Smith's *Eve Tempted*, especially 3–4 and 33–34.

29. Hyatt Waggoner, for instance, claims that Hawthorne desired to evoke "wonder," operating as he did from "essentials" of human experience, which he distilled into the timelessness of "classic art" (*Hawthorne* 8).

30. Many other examples of the chair's importance for circulating social energies and the sources that captured them can be drawn from the text. Some of the most important are the library of the Boston Athenaeum and Eliot's Indian Bible (470); the chair's association with the development of democracies in the New World (456); Dr. Francis's *Life of Eliot* (476); Longfellow's poem "Evangeline" and the Acadian migration (552); and Samuel Adams and the discourse of Revolutionary Boston, an episode that features Adams in an antiquarian role rummaging through "a vast collection of ancient letters and other documents in the tower of Old South church" (630).

31. Further examples include the connection of Roger Williams's name to banking in Rhode Island; Eliot's mastery over the pride of his ministerial colleagues by exposing them to the unexpected beauty of the Indian language spoken by a boy; Phips's rise to power because of his discovery of treasure remaining underwater after several hundred years.

32. Hawthorne is recasting an anecdote about Peale's illusionistic painting *Staircase Group*, which showed Peale's sons Raphael and Titian climbing a staircase within a frame constructed to look like a door frame, complete with a three-dimensional step built out into the room from the bottom of the canvas. Looby claims that Peale's image "fooled even such a reality-tested visitor as George Washington, who saluted it mistakenly" (365).

33. The Grandfather's chair feels that Hawthorne's Grandfather has so succeeded in his essentially "correct" telling of the narrative adventures that "it must be owned, that your correctness entitles you to be held up as a pattern to biographers" (208).

34. As many critics, notably Dennis Pahl, have pointed out, much of what passes for interpretation in Hawthorne's fiction is meaningful because it is primarily ironic (*Architects of the Abyss* 15–16).

35. See Davidson, *Revolution and the Word* 260.

Notes to Chapter Four

1. *The Minister's Wooing* is an early example of the consequences that result when the image of Mather becomes shopworn by excessive invocation. In all, eight nineteenth-century anti-Calvinist novels had disillusionment with orthodoxy and its ministers and the desire to discover some new means of salvation as themes. Further, religious problems are treated in the novels by depicting women as sufferers who are trying to find salvific alternatives. Some fail. Others win salvation by embracing a series of democratic alternatives: another sect or the substitution of something else for the old religion—the love of Jesus, the altruism of the Social Gospel. These themes are traced in Nathaniel Hawthorne's *The Scarlet Letter*; Harriet Beecher Stowe's *The Minister's Wooing* and *Oldtown Folks*; Mary Wilkins Freeman's *Pembroke*; Harold Frederic's *The Damnation of Theron Ware*; Margaret Deland's *John Ward, Preacher*; W. D. Howells's *Annie Kilburn*; and Sarah Orne Jewett's *The Country of the Pointed Firs*. In all these works but two—*Pembroke* and *Pointed Firs*—significant minister-woman relationships bring into focus the problem of weak Calvinism and the need for change.

2. See Page Smith, *The Nation Comes of Age* 9.

3. See Dolores Hayden, *The Grand Domestic Revolution*; Beverly Voloshin, "The Limits of Domesticity: The Female Bildungsroman in America, 1820–1870," *Women's Studies* 10 (1984): 283–302; Maxine Vandewetering, "The Popular Concept of 'Home' in Nineteenth-Century America," *Journal of American Studies* 18 (1984): 2–28; and Lisa MacFarlane, "The New England Kitchen Goes Uptown: Domestic Displacements in Harriet Beecher Stowe's New York," *New England Quarterly* 64.2 (June 1991): 272–91.

4. Most of the critical work about *The Minister's Wooing* has understandably centered on its explicit religious agenda and the autobiographical connection between James Marvyn and the drowning of Stowe's fiancé, the unconverted Alexander Fisher, in 1822, and the drowning of her unredeemed son Henry in 1857. Two of the more important articles on *The Minister's Wooing* are pieces written by Christopher Wilson and Lawrence Buell. Wilson, in "Tempests and Teapots: Harriet Beecher Stowe's *The Minister's Wooing*," *New England Quarterly* 58.4 (December 1985): 554–77, carefully examines Stowe's emphasis on aesthetic ideology in order to show that Mary Scudder is not "a static symbol of influence but a character who must undergo a traceable process of maturation" and insists that we view *The Minister's Wooing* not as rational theology but as a romance refiguring Puritanism (558). Buell, in a seminal article, "Calvinism Romanticized: Harriet Beecher Stowe, Samuel Hopkins, and *The Minister's Wooing*," *Emerson Society Quarterly* 24.3 (Fall 1978): 119–32, uses Stowe's novel to describe an important but neglected tradition in American literature: "the gradual secularization of Edwardseanism is, in its own way, just as important to the history of American literature as the earlier, better understood process of secularization in the liberal ranks" (119).

5. In *The Rungless Ladder* Charles Foster tells us that Stowe wrote a letter to her sister Catherine on the subject of the halfway covenant and the exclusivity of church membership. According to Foster, Harriet consulted Book Five of *Magnalia* and

found passages where Cotton Mather muffled the original Puritan exclusiveness concerning membership and baptism. She stated to Catherine, "Old Cotton waxes warm in arguing this subject." From *Magnalia* she copied passage after passage that apparently established the warm liberalism of the seventeenth-century Puritan church. Foster is willing to admit that Stowe could be studious of sources in this way, but he feels that Stowe actually understood little of what she read and copied. I think that is an unfortunate, paternalistic conclusion. Unlike Foster, I think Stowe was highly conscious of Mather's intentional obscuring of the background facts leading to the halfway covenant. Because their projects share a fundamental goal—to project a unified society constructed out of disunited materials—Stowe's exploitation of an aspect of Mather's cultural mechanics assists her own artful ambiguities. If we grant that Stowe's representational logic is managed according to Mather's historicism (and there are no facts to prove otherwise), then Stowe's rejection of Edwards seems not anomalous but deconstructively precise. See Foster, *The Rungless Ladder* 227ff.

6. Mather was clearly one of Stowe's most cherished "soul-artists"—that good *motherly* Cotton Mather. Dorothy Berkson, in "Millennial Politics and the Feminine Fiction of Harriet Beecher Stowe," claims that Stowe's association of Cotton Mather with pleasurable hours she spent reading in the garret of her Litchfield house may account for "the surprisingly warm and gentle image of Mather she carried throughout her life. Given her generally hostile attitude toward Edwards, whom all accounts suggest was a much gentler person than Mather, nothing else seems to account for her somewhat eccentric fondness for Mather" (258n11). Vernon Parrington, in *Main Currents in American Thought*, claims that Harriet's "imagination was awakened by *Magnalia Christi Americana*. Theocratic New England lay enveloped for her in a haze of romance, more fascinating than any Sir Walter had written about the Scottish Highlands; she had discovered there noble figures and heroic deeds to kindle an ardent hero worship" (2:371). Placing *The Minister's Wooing* in context, Charles Foster remarks, "in 1852 the last vestiges of seventeenth-century Puritan theocracy had faded from sight; but in the heart and mind of a Puritan like Harriet, who had been nourished on Cotton Mather's *Magnalia Christi Americana*, patterns of feeling and thought fundamental to the Massachusetts Bay Colony persisted. For her, America, like 17th-century New England in the eyes of Cotton Mather, was a covenanted society" (*Rungless Ladder* 56). Stowe, in *Oldtown Folks*, recapitulates her life-long admiration for Mather's nativist historicism: "No Jewish maiden ever grew up with a more earnest faith that she belonged to a consecrated race. . . . her faith in every word of the marvels related in this book [*Magnalia*] was fully as great as the dear old credulous Dr. Mather could have desired" (7–8).

7. In considering the large issue of exemplaristic representation in Puritan ideology, I have been influenced here, as elsewhere in this study, by Mitchell Breitwieser's consideration of these issues with respect to Mary Rowlandson in *American Puritanism and the Defense of Mourning*.

8. If, as some critics have suggested, *The Minister's Wooing* is a search for paternal figures who give shape to neo-Puritan theology, then perhaps the predominant influence is not the image of Jonathan Edwards but rather the longer shadow of

Cotton Mather, whose conspicuous absence nevertheless controls events. To be sure, Mather's personality is distributed among all the characters, and the rehearsal enacted by Stowe's character lends itself to the antitypic posture that what is valuable is the notion not of a representative "man" but of representative "women." Mather may well be the spirit of Mr. Scudder, whose heavy influence is most strongly perceived in Katy's life: "To say the truth, there lay at the bottom of her doctrinal system this stable corner-stone,—'Mr. Scudder used to believe it,—I will.' And after all that is said about independent thought, isn't the fact, that a just and good soul has thus or thus believed, a more respectable argument than many that often are adduced? If it be not, more's the pity,—since two thirds of the faith in the world is built on no better foundation" (534). In a symbolic gambit, Stowe "weds" Katy Scudder to Mather's world by conflating the figure of her departed husband and the icon of William Phips as a sea-adventurer. Phips's life became one means for Cotton Mather to "enact" his historicism, and Phips's experiences as related in *Magnalia* (the swashbuckling Anglican converted into heroic sainthood by his acceptance of Congregational sympathies) seem ironically to prefigure the significance of James Marvyn's voyages: "It is true that [Mrs. Scudder] yet wore on her third finger the marriage-ring of a sailor lover, and his memory was yet fresh in her heart. . . . As we have said before, it is almost impossible to make our light-minded times comprehend the earnestness with which these people lived" (850). It may try the patience of some readers to see Mather in sidelong glances, but we must remember that this is the intellectual matrix that binds Stowe's appreciation of the past: "The innocent credulities, the subtle deceptions . . . were exactly of the kind that have beguiled man in all ages" (602).

9. It is important to state at this point that I hold all essentialist distinctions that suggest that femininity and masculinity operate according to clearly different sets of assumptions to be inherently misleading and historically naive. Personally, I see such distinctions as constructed categories that have to do with the convenience of elaborating a wide range of human activities and attitudes that are hard to describe. However, Stowe's belief in gender-marked distinctions is a persistent feature of her narration in *The Minister's Wooing*, as this passage illustrates: "Spite of all the treatises that have lately appeared, to demonstrate that there are no particular inherent diversities between men and women, we hold to the opinion that one thorough season of house-cleaning is sufficient to prove the existence of awful and mysterious difference between the sexes, and of subtle and reserved forces in the female line" (824). The positing of an essential sphere where women reign supreme and men are largely excluded I take to be a necessary doctrine if Stowe's portrayal of Mary Scudder is to have a logical basis.

10. Other places in the text where Mary's sexuality is linked to her association with power include James's contention that he "is not worthy to touch the hem [referring to Christ] of your garment" in his letter to her (569); her appearance to the Doctor in a clean white dress (583); and her attractiveness to Virginie de Frontignac (757).

11. Notice, for instance, the many poses Stowe assumes in her narration of the

novel. At various points she portrays herself as a literary critic, citing for authority *The Atlantic* magazine. She takes on the role of a director staging a play. She assumes an anthropological stance, relaying ethnographic details as if New England were some exotic or unique culture that needed "deciphering." She plays the role of moral censor, showing the reader only those things appropriate to be seen, though the reader knows full well that other activities are transpiring "behind closed doors."

12. Here, as elsewhere in this chapter, when I refer to Penelope, I do so not because I am practicing a form of myth criticism; instead, I want to invoke a suggestive metaphor in Mary Scudder's complex interactions with the residents of Newport. The metaphor most often used to explain Stowe's narrative technique is that of quilting. In her weaving together (and consequent unweaving) of anti-Catholicism, mercantile capitalism, and theological accommodation, Mary becomes emblematic of Stowe's historical understanding as she illustrates both the potent influence of a creative explanation of events and the problematic nature of taking anything so fantastic at face value. History, as Mary becomes involved with it, is both a claim to remain true to prior traditions (as Penelope stayed faithful to her husband) and also a means of avoiding commitment to others. As was the case with Penelope, remembrance has both its conservative and its defensive aspects.

13. Other important instances where this theme is sounded in the novel include James's farewell letter to Mary (570); Hopkins's place within the Calvinist tradition (579); the description of Mrs. Marvyn (590); Mrs. Scudder's social admiration for Hopkins (585); the account of Mrs. Marvyn's grief (731–32); Virginie's confession to the Abbé (761); and Virginie's education of Mary on earthly love (809–10).

14. Behind this reading of Stowe's intention lies some precedent among liberal Protestant theologians like Thomas Lathrop, who wrote in an 1854 sermon, "It is a low and gross estimate of woman to fix her distinction in the senses. Rightly developed, she is not sensual, but ideal and hopeful. [Woman's] natural life is not positive, but in the conceivable; and, for all her undefined, sensitive activity, the ordinary world has no sphere, no vocabulary. She looks into a higher world than ordinary experience" (*Individualism in the Forms of Life and in the Culture of the Soul* 22). Perry Westbrook, in *A Literary History of New England*, claims that Stowe had unique and precise insights: "Stowe came much closer to an understanding of Puritanism than most authors in the nineteenth century" (213).

15. Stowe's attempted exclusions include Arminian heresy (565); the fact that Burr's parental influences may have been less than ideal (656); Mary's desire to be seduced by Burr (709); Mary's growing acceptance of Candace's theosophy (742); and the reader's firsthand knowledge of the Doctor's marriage proposal to Mary (785). Her role as an author is largely defined in these passages: her offering the reader theological tea (566); her repeated use of epistolary evidence for creating intertextual connections to the commerce of the society at large (568 and elsewhere); as a Penelopean figure who ravels and unravels the lives of men (638–39); and her mingling of two disparate modes of understanding (650). Her governance of the social appropriation of her work is indicated by organic metaphors drawn from natural philosophy (584 and elsewhere); her romantic deflation of male authority figures

like the banker Mr. Smith (598); her alliance of Candace and the militant woman's rights movement (635); the equation of the New England home with Arcadian romance (688); the resuscitation of the image of Anne Hutchinson and the trope of the woman priestess (747); her depiction of love among Puritans as caloric (784); the belief in Mather's concept of particular faiths (855); the assertion of a democratic network of feminine influences (864); and the image of a stable, domesticated Christianity (870). To one degree or another, each of these fictional tropes for reading the culture is counterfactual to the documented historical trends of the 1850s. This fictionality, I have claimed, is important not just because it regulates our reception of the novel but also because it draws attention to itself as a historical construct enabled by specific negotiations between the author and her subject.

16. There are several examples in *The Minister's Wooing* where this statement is dramatized: where Candace, while performing her domestic duties, helps train James for his future years of wanderlust (594–95); where the labors of the Scudder house are seen to be the foundation of Hopkins's public status (628); where Hopkins's choice of a patterned brocade is viewed with knowing looks among all the women present at Mary's house prior to their planned wedding (825); and where Candace warns Prissy against telling Mary about James's reappearance in the confines of the kitchen: "not to spoil a novel before it got halfway through the first volume, by blurting out some of those things that they let go trailing on so, till everybody gets so mixed up they don't know what they're doing" (856).

17. Stowe could look to Newport in 1841 for confirmation that her version of New England faced an invasion of subversive ideology, particularly from the South. George Noble Jones, a Georgian, built the first prestigious mansion, Kingscote, along Bellevue Avenue. This house and its owner were representative of New England's decline. During the 1840s and 1850s, Newport's atmosphere was decidedly southern despite the seasonal influx of Bostonians.

18. In *The Rungless Ladder*, Foster says that embedded within Miss Roxy's story about Mrs. Titcom in *Oldtown Folks*, Stowe carefully uses the passage from *Magnalia* (2.407) in which the son of J. C. Deacon dies on a ship at sea at precisely the same time his mother passes away in Charlestown (149). We see echoes of this tale in James Marvyn's apparent death and its effect on his mother and Mary Scudder.

19. At this point, Stowe is echoing the popular sentiments that, in the words of Daniel Eddy, "Home is woman's throne, where she maintains her royal court, and surveys her queenly authority. It is there that man learns to appreciate her worth, and to realize the sweet and tender influences which she casts around her" (*The Young Woman's Friend* 23).

20. For other instances of the same counterfactual process, whereby a historically contingent figure expresses a cultural phenomenon yet acts at variance with that notion, consider Mary's apparent belief in self-renunciation and her contention that "a thousand intoxicating influences combine to cheat the victims from the thought that their next step might be into a abyss of horrors without end" (542); Stowe's claim that history must be concealed in the guise of imagination because "if things were said out, they might not be said wisely, — they might repel by their freedom, or

disturb by their unfitness; but what is only looked is sent into the soul through the imagination, which makes of it all that the ideal faculties desire" (605); Mrs. Scudder's initial reaction to Hopkins's antislavery position (615); Stowe's contention that gossip is an important narrative form for presenting a local color narrative (643); Burr's contradictory constitution as a man of gallantry (667–68); the social status of First Families (671); James's conversion letter (841); Stowe's account of "celestial gardening" (745); and the connection between moral effects and music (765). In each of these cases, some oblique notion that is beyond the level of surface appearance is infolded into the iconic meaning of the region that Stowe expects her readers to perceive.

21. Most of Stowe's principal characters—Hopkins, Burr, Mary, Virginie, and Katy (and the ever absent husband who is essentially Katy)—are loci for the multiple discourse communities being accommodated in or excluded from Newport society in the late 1700s. In the arena of wealth and force that is Newport, Mary's doubleness, which is determined by her culture, leads to her ready acceptance of variety in those around her. In the realm of romantic love, Mary is mollified by Virginie's dramatic feats of Christian kindness and class-blindness. As defender of New England values, Mary is the Puritan wrath that roots out the corruptions of Burr. As the product of maternal training, she is her mother's icon of pietistic fidelity to the New England Way. As a typological figure, she is Hopkins's domestic ideal "helpmeet," and as a practitioner of a religion of the heart, she is her cousin's salvation. The very recognition of these facts (without which no identifiable New England exists), Stowe suggests, might somehow enable the present generation—not by full liberation or full empowerment—to create a new workable hypothesis by reducing the binding power of the past to realistic and manageable negotiations. Hopkins is either Puritanism's last hope as he decides from his heart to allow James and Mary to wed or the personification of an impotent and sterile region whose vitality has been constantly sapped since the Revolution. All the figures who come from outside New England—most notably Burr, Madame de Frontignac, and James (but also the resident blacks)—are utterly transformed by their re-entry to the region. That transformation happens because their involvement in the negotiations of culture is complete; with Stowe, the practice of storytelling is co-extensive with the practice of forceful changes in personality. In the end, Puritanism's potential containment of an unbridled individualism is Stowe's bass note. The eventual isolation of Virginie (and the tendencies in women that she represents) in France indicates that the social order has been preserved; she has found new inspiration in a previously unhappy marriage. Mary, too, is liberated from a marriage that would have satisfied the community and her mother but not her own personal desires. She has tamed James, and he has acquired her "authenticity."

Notes to Chapter Five

1. For recent criticism that respectfully addresses Stoddard's anomalous position in nineteenth-century women's fiction, see Sybil Weir, "*The Morgesons*: A Neglected

Feminist *Bildungsroman*," *New England Quarterly* 49.3 (September 1976): 427–39; Elizabeth Stoddard, *The Morgesons and Other Writings, Published and Unpublished*, ed. Lawrence Buell and Sandra Zagarell; Sandra Zagarell, "The Repossession of a Heritage: Elizabeth Stoddard's *The Morgesons*," *Studies in American Fiction* 13.1 (1985): 45–56; and, most significant, Susan K. Harris, "Projecting the "I"/Conoclast: First Person Narration in *The Morgesons*," *19th-Century American Women's Novels: Interpretative Strategies*, which views Cassandra's radical possibilities as a function of her historical heritage.

2. See Kate Field, *Planchette's Diary*, and Epes Sargent, *Planchette, or the Despair of Science*.

3. *The Morgesons* identifies the source of female creativity within the Puritan past. Thus, it is interesting to note the reaction of Thomas Wentworth Higginson to the novel's power to make plain the cryptic femininity of Emily Dickinson. After meeting Dickinson in Amherst, Higginson wrote to his wife that she would understand the Dickinson household if she read Mrs. Stoddard's novels (Dickinson, *Letters* 2:473). This comment—from a man whose cosmopolitan biases and uncomfortableness with generic improvisation did much to obscure Dickinson's work—could be said to be symptomatic of the views of a reading audience that willingly excluded women as authorities on "serious" topics like Puritanism's enduring legacy.

4. Hawthorne greatly admired *The Morgesons*. He received and read the novel at Wayside in June 1862. In January 1863, he wrote to Richard Henry Stoddard (Elizabeth's husband):

> I read *The Morgesons* at the time of publication, and thought it a remarkable and powerful book, though not without a painful element mixed up in it. It interested me very much, because I thought I could recognize a sort of misty representation of my native town, and likewise the half-revealed features of peoples whom I have known—some of my own relatives, in fact. Old Simon Forrester was brought to this country from Ireland by a progenitor of mine, whose beautiful daughter he afterwards married; so that those respectable individuals in the novel were my cousins. As for their pride of lineage, I know not what may have been its foundations. (N. Hawthorne to RHS, January 8, 1863, Berg Collection)

Simon Forrester, a prominent figure in Salem history, was the model for Stoddard's Desmond Pickersgill in *The Morgesons*. As James Matlack notes, not only was Hawthorne closely related to the Forresters, but so was Elizabeth Stoddard, through a Barstow uncle (Barstow was Elizabeth's maiden name). She and Hawthorne were distant cousins. Although Hawthorne was never aware of the connection, it is of enormous value in our positing a linkage of these two writers not only through their appropriation of source material but through genealogy. For an exhaustive discussion of the Barstow-Forrester connection see Matlack, "Hawthorne and Elizabeth Barstow Stoddard," *New England Quarterly* 50.3 (1977): 278–302.

5. This self-referentiality is of enormous importance in Sandra Zagarell's analysis of *The Morgesons*. In "The Repossession of a Heritage: Elizabeth Stoddard's *The Morgesons*," she states, "Because Stoddard recognized that gender and genre hindered female character and female author alike, *The Morgesons* also engages in a

continual commentary on the traditions it seeks to synthesize" (46). Stoddard's strategy is essentially the same as Amy Schrager Lang's notion, in *Prophetic Women*, that "the antinomian and the sentimentalist, both of whom appeal to an inner voice to rationalize their intrusion into the public arena, cast the critic [and reader] alike in the role of the Puritan magistrate. . . . the act of female authorship constitutes an assertion of autonomy and, thus, a challenge to authority as dramatic as Hutchinson's antinomianism. . . . the antinomian lays claim to an unassailable inner knowledge" (2–3, 13). Stoddard's narrative strategy, because it originates in an "inward voice," testifies in unseemly public expression, and prefigures radical social effects, capitalizes on the conjunction of witchcraft, antinomianism, and the writing of historical romance.

6. Stoddard's tale, when seen as a mystical text, transforms itself in many ways into a tale of "passions" *of* and *in* history. The array of trends that Cassandra must make sense of, her confrontations with Ben's hidden truths, the opaque authority of her grandfather Warren and her father Locke Morgeson, and the divided and ailing institutions of the Snells and the Warrens do not cause her to pioneer new systems of knowledge, topographies, or complementary powers; rather they define a different treatment of the Matherian tradition of the seventeenth century. Stoddard is one of Barton St. Armand's consummate "veiled ladies" who don the veil of the medium in order to seek "an outlet for their stifled sensitivity and longing for acclaim" ("Veiled Ladies: Dickinson, Bettine, and Transcendental Mediumship" 18). Under the veil of mediumship, the act of narration becomes not so much the discovery of a body of doctrines but rather a discovery of an epistemic foundation of a domain in which new spaces, new mechanisms, effect a reinterpretation of tradition. Cassandra's deep association with the sea, for instance, has a significant parallel in Puritan ideology. Roger Stein notes, "for the Puritan the experience of the voyage itself was by its very nature dislocating, alienating man from the familiar and projecting him into a hazardous unknown. . . . The study of Puritan seascape illuminates the particular ways in which men and women came to terms imaginatively with the various psychological and social pressures upon them" ("Seascape and the American Imagination: The Puritan Seventeenth Century" 26).

7. As Carol Karlsen explains in *The Devil in the Shape of a Woman*: "witches [in Puritan culture] are generally portrayed as disagreeable women, at best aggressive and abrasive, at worst ill-tempered, quarrelsome, and spiteful. They are almost always described as deviants—disorderly women who failed to, or refused to, abide by the behavioral norms of their society" (118).

8. See Stoddard, *The Morgesons and Other Writings, Published and Unpublished* 255n25.

9. Stoddard's work exemplified the conclusion that a reviewer made in the *Mirror* of July 7, 1839: "People will not read history with sufficient attention to make it familiar, but when the naked truth is clothed in a 'coat of many colors,' all are ready to admire."

Notes to the Conclusion

1. "Silent reading does in fact establish a freer, more secret, and totally private intercourse with the written word. It permits more rapid reading, which is not im-

peded by the complexities of the book's organization and the relationships established between the discourse and the glosses, the quotations and the comments, the text and the index. It also permits differential uses of the same book: given the social or ritual context, it can be read aloud for others or with others, or else it can be silently read for oneself in the retreat of the study, the library, or the oratory" (Roger Chartier, "Frenchness in the History of the Book" 18–19).

2. I borrow freely the term "invisible center" from Russell Ferguson, who uses it to describe the process by which historically marginalized groups challenge the hegemony of a dominant ideology. In Ferguson's view, "the power of a center," such as republican notions about personal liberty, depends on a relatively unchallenged authority. Mainstream culture exists because of this omnipresent center, "which claims universality without ever defining itself, and which exiles to its margins those who cannot or will not pay allegiance to the standards which it sets or the limits it imposes" ("Introduction: The Invisible Center" 10–13).

3. Although I have not taken it as a direct subject, the details of Phillis Wheatley's biography, after its publication, were probably viewed in Wheatley's own time as a perfect unfolding of republican notions of personal liberty. Wheatley, because of her unusual connection with Anglo-American society, presented the citizens of Boston with the practical problem of integrating persons with different particular interests, needs, aptitudes, and abilities. Republicans presupposed that a person like Phillis Wheatley would consistently act in her own best interest as a rational, interest-motivated economic agent. Consequently, her failure to succeed in a harsh marriage and to rise above her poverty is a secondary effect of her release from slavery, which rendered her governable. In the few glimpses of anxiety that we see in her letters and occasional writings, Wheatley's situation reflects the sea change brought about by those who are made examples of liberal political thought: "it is when we are called upon to change our relation to government that we are also required to change our relation to ourselves, to change our subjective self-identity, and it is then that we become aware of the ways in which the political power of the state impinges on our individual lives, that we *feel* it" (Foucault, "Social Security" 163).

4. A paraphrase of Mather in Book Three of *Magnalia*, 2.242–43.

Bibliography

✢

Abel, Darrel. *The Moral Picturesque.* 1988.

Adams, Robert M. Rev. of *Columbia Literary History of the United States,* Emory Elliott, general editor. *New York Times Book Review* (January 24, 1988): 6.

Anderson, Douglas, Rev. of *The Office of the Scarlet Letter,* by Sacvan Bercovitch. *Nineteenth Century Literature* 47.1 (June 1992): 105–08.

Andros Tracts. Ed. W. H. Whitmore. 3 vols. 1868–74.

Arch, Stephen. *Mastering History: Puritan Historians in Colonial America.* PhD diss. University of Virginia, 1989.

Bacon, Sir Francis. *The Works of Sir Francis Bacon.* Ed. James Spedding. 1863.

Bancroft, George. *The George Bancroft Papers at Cornell University, 1811–1901.* Microfilm. Ed. Herbert Finch. Collection of Regional History and University Archives, John M. Olin Library. 1965.

———. *History of the United States.* 3 vols. 1876.

Barthes, Roland. "From Work to Text." *Image-Music-Text.* Trans. Stephen Heath. 1977.

———. *S/Z.* Trans. Richard Miller. 1974.

———. *Writing Degree Zero.* Preface by Susan Sontag. Trans. Annette Lavers and Colin Smith. 1968.

Bayle, Pierre. *Dictionnaire historique et critique.* 1697.

Baym, Nina. Rev. of *The American Jeremiad* and *The Puritan Origins of the American Self,* by Sacvan Bercovitch. *Nineteenth Century Fiction* 34 (December 1979): 350.

———. *The Shape of Hawthorne's Career.* 1976.

Bell, Michael. *Hawthorne and the Historical Romance of New England.* 1971.

Bell, Millicent. *Hawthorne's View of the Artist.* 1962.

Bell, Susan Cherry. *History and Artistry in Cotton Mather's "Magnalia Christi Americana."* PhD diss. State University of New York at Binghamton, 1981.

Bercovitch, Sacvan. "A-Morality of Compromise." *Representations* 24.3 (Fall 1988): 1–27.

———. "Cotton Mather." *Major Writers of Early American Literature.* Ed. Everett Emerson. 1972.

———. " 'Nehemias Americanus': Cotton Mather and the Concept of the Representative American." *Early American Literature* 8 (1974): 220–38.

———. *New England Epic: A Literary Study of Cotton Mather's "Magnalia Christi Americana."* PhD diss. Claremont Graduate School, 1965.

———. *The Office of the Scarlet Letter.* 1991.

———. *The Puritan Origins of the American Self.* 1975.

———. *The Rites of Assent.* 1993.

———. "Typology in Puritan New England: The Williams-Cotton Controversy Reassessed." *American Quarterly* 19 (1967): 166–91.

———, ed. *The American Puritan Imagination.* 1974.

———, ed. *Typology and Early American Literature.* 1972.

Berg, Henry W. and Albert, Collection. New York Public Library, New York.

Berkeley, William. *Discourse and View of Virginia.* 1663.

Berkson, Dorothy. "Millennial Politics and the Feminine Fiction of Harriet Beecher Stowe." *Critical Essays on Harriet Beecher Stowe.* Ed. Elizabeth Ammons. 1980.

Bloom, Harold. *The Anxiety of Influence.* 1973.

Bloom, James D. "Reconstructing American Literary History." *American Quarterly* 39.2 (Summer 1987): 313.

Bossuet, Jacques. *Histoire des Variations des Eglises Protestantes.* 1688.

Boyd, Richard. *Three Generations of Puritan Spiritual Autobiography: Problems of Self-Definition in a Time of Declension.* PhD diss. University of California, San Diego, 1985.

Bradford, William. *The History of Plimouth Plantation.* 1642. Ed. W. T. Davis. 1964.

Braude, Ann. *Radical Spirits.* 1989.

Breen, T. H. *Puritans and Adventurers: Change and Persistence in Early America.* 1980.

Breen, Timothy, and Stephen Foster. "The Puritans' Greatest Achievement: A Study in Social Cohesion in Seventeenth-Century Massachusetts." *New England Rediscovered.* Ed. Peter Hoffer. 1988. 335–52.

Breitwieser, Mitchell. *American Puritanism and the Defense of Mourning.* 1990.

———. *Cotton Mather and Benjamin Franklin.* 1984.

Brodhead, Richard. *Hawthorne, Melville, and the Novel.* 1976.

———. *The School of Hawthorne.* 1986.

———. " 'Veiled Ladies': Toward a History of Antebellum Entertainment." *American Literary History* 1.3 (Summer 1989): 273–94.

Brooke-Rose, Christine. "A for But: 'The Custom House' in Hawthorne's *The Scarlet Letter.*" *Word & Image* 3.2 (1987): 143–55.

Brown, Chandos. "A Natural History of the Gloucester Sea Serpent: Knowledge, Power, and the Culture of Science in Antebellum America." *American Quarterly* 42.3 (September 1990): 402–36.

Brumm, Ursula. *American Thought and Religious Typology.* 1970.

Budick, Emily Miller. "Sacvan Bercovitch, Stanley Cavell, and the American Romance Theory of American Fiction." *PMLA* 107.1 (January 1992): 78–91.

Buell, Lawrence. "Calvinism Romanticized: Harriet Beecher Stowe, Samuel Hopkins, and *The Minister's Wooing.*" *Emerson Society Quarterly* 24.3 (Fall 1978): 119–32.

——. "It's Good, but Is It History?" *American Quarterly* 41.3 (September 1989): 496–500.

——. *New England Literary Culture*. 1986.

——. "Reconstructing American Literary History." *Journal of American History* 74.4 (March 1988): 1315.

Burchell, Graham. "Peculiar Interests: Civil Society and Governing 'The System of Natural Liberty.'" Burchell, Gordon, and Miller 119–50.

Burchell, Graham, Colin Gordon, and Peter Miller, eds. *The Foucault Effect*. 1991.

Byfield, Nathaniel. "An Account of the Late Revolution in New England." *Andros Tracts* 1:1 (1868): 3–17.

Calendar of State Papers. Microform. Colonial Series. 1860–1926.

Calvin, John. *Institutes of the Christian Religion*. Ed. John T. McNeill. Trans. Ford Lewis Battles. 1536. 1960.

Chai, Leon. *The Romantic Foundations of the American Renaissance*. 1987.

Chartier, Roger. *The Cultural Uses of Print in Early Modern France*. Trans. Lydia G. Cochrane. 1987.

——. "Frenchness in the History of the Book." James Russell Wiggins Lecture. 1987.

Cheyfitz, Eric. "Matthiessen's American Renaissance: Circumscribing the Revolution." *American Quarterly* 41.2 (1989): 341–61.

Colacurcio, Michael J. "The American-Renaissance Renaissance." *New England Quarterly* 64.3 (September 1991): 445–93.

——. *The Province of Piety*. 1984.

——. "Visible Sanctity." *Essex Institute Historical Collections*. 110.4 (1974): 263–78.

Condorcet, Marquis de. *Esquisse d'un Tableau Historique des Progres de l'Espirit Humain*. 1788. 1971.

Cooper, James Fenimore. *The American Democrat*. 1838. 1984.

Crewe, Jonathan. *Trials of Authorship: Anterior Forms and Poetic Reconstruction from Wyatt to Shakespeare*. 1990.

Cutler, Manasseh. *Life, Journals, and Correspondence of Rev. M. Cutler, L.L.D.* 1888.

Davidson, Cathy. *Revolution and the Word*. 1986.

Davis, Thomas. *Typology in New England Puritanism*. PhD diss. University of Missouri, 1969.

Dekker, George. *The American Historical Romance*. 1987.

Deland, Margaret. *John Ward, Preacher*. 1888.

Delbanco, Andrew. *The Puritan Ordeal*. 1989.

Demos, John. *Entertaining Satan*. 1982.

Denning, Michael. *Mechanic Accents*. 1987.

De Prospo, R. C. "Marginalizing Early American Literature." *New Literary History* 23 (Spring 1992): 233–65.

Dickinson, Emily. *The Letters of Emily Dickinson*. 2 vols. Ed. Thomas Johnson. 1958.

Donohue, Alice McNeill. *Hawthorne: Calvin's Ironic Stepchild*. 1985.

Doubleday, Neal. *Hawthorne's Early Tales*. 1972.

Douglas, Ann. *The Feminization of American Culture.* 1978.

Eberwein, Jane. " 'In a Book, as in a Glass': Literary Sorcery in Mather's Life of Phips." *Early American Literature* 10 (1976): 293–98.

———. "Indistinct Lustre: Biographical Miniatures in Cotton Mather's *Magnalia Christi Americana.*" *Biography* 4.3 (Summer 1981): 195–207.

Eddy, Daniel C. *The Young Woman's Friend; or the Duties, Trials, Loves, and Hopes of Woman.* 1860.

Edwards, Jonathan. *The Nature of True Virtue.* 1754. 1960.

Elliott, Emory, ed. *Columbia Literary History of the United States.* 1988.

Emerson, Ellen Tucker. *The Life of Lidian Jackson Emerson.* 1880.

Emerson, Everett. Rev. of *Forms of Uncertainty*, by David Levin. *New England Quarterly* 66.1 (March 1993): 131–33.

———, ed. *Major Writers of Early American Literature.* 1972.

Engebretsen, Terry Odell. *Pillars of the House: Puritan Funeral Sermons Through the "Magnalia Christi Americana."* PhD diss. Washington State University, 1982.

Febvre, Lucien, and Henri-Jean Martin. *The Coming of the Book.* Trans. David Gerard. 1976.

Felker, Christopher. "Roger Williams's Uses of Legal Discourse: Testing Authority in Early New England." *New England Quarterly* 63.4 (December 1990): 624–48.

Ferguson, Russell. "Introduction: The Invisible Center." *Out There: Marginalization and Contemporary Cultures.* 1990.

Field, Kate. *Planchette's Diary.* 1868.

Fiering, Norman. "The First American: Cotton Mather." *Reviews in American History* 12 (December 1984): 479.

Fineman, Joel. "The History of the Anecdote: Fiction and Fiction." *The New Historicism.* Ed. H. Aram Veeser. 1989.

Fisher, Philip, ed. *The New American Studies.* 1991.

Folsom, James. *Man's Accidents and God's Purposes.* 1963.

Foster, Charles. *The Rungless Ladder.* 1954.

Foster, Richard, ed. Introduction. *The Morgesons.* 1971.

Foster, Stephen. *The Long Argument.* 1991.

Foucault, Michel. *The Archaeology of Knowledge.* 1972.

———. "Governmentality." Burchell, Gordon, and Miller 87–107.

———. *The Order of Things.* 1973.

———. "Social Security." *Politics, Philosophy, Culture.* Trans. Alan Sheridan et al. 1988.

Frederic, Harold. *The Damnation of Theron Ware.* 1896. 1988.

Freeman, Mary Wilkins. *Pembroke.* 1894. 1971.

Freud, Sigmund. "Beyond the Pleasure Principle." *The Standard Edition of the Complete Psychological Works.* Vol. 18. Trans. James Strachey. 1964.

———. "New Introductory Lectures." *The Standard Edition of the Complete Psychological Works.* Vol. 22. Trans. James Strachey. 1964.

———. "Totem and Taboo." *The Standard Edition of the Complete Psychological Works.* Vol. 12. Trans. James Strachey. 1964.

Friedman, Rachelle Elaine. *Writing the Wonders: Puritan Historians in Colonial New England.* PhD diss. UCLA, 1991.

Fuller, Thomas. *Church-History of Britain.* 1655.

Gardner, Henry. *Acts and Resolves Passed by the General Court of Massachusetts in the Years 1856–7.* 1857.

Gay, Peter. *A Loss of Mastery: Puritan Historians in Colonial America.* 1968.

Geertz, Clifford. "Thick Description: Toward an Interpretive Theory of Culture." *The Interpretation of Cultures.* 1973.

Gilbert, Sandra, and Susan Gubar. *Madwoman in the Attic.* 1979.

Gilmore, Michael. *American Romanticism and the Marketplace.* 1988.

Gilmore, William J. *Reading Becomes a Necessity of Life.* 1989.

Glassie, Henry. "Meaningful Things and Appropriate Myths: The Artifact's Place in American Studies." *Material Life in America, 1600–1860.* Ed. Robert St. George. 1987. 63–94.

Goffman, Erving. *Behavior in Public Places: Notes on the Social Organizations of Gatherings.* 1963.

Goodspeed, Charles. *Nathaniel Hawthorne and the Museum of the Salem East India Marine Society; or, The gathering of a virtuoso's collection.* 1946.

Greenblatt, Stephen. *Marvelous Possessions.* 1991.

———. *Renaissance Self-Fashioning.* 1980.

———. "Resonance and Wonder." *Literary Theory Today.* Ed. Peter Collier and Helga Geyer-Ryan. 1990.

———. *Shakespearean Negotiations.* 1988.

Gunn, Giles. "Beyond Transcendence or Beyond Ideology: The New Problematics of Cultural Criticism in America." *American Literary History* 2.1 (Spring 1990): 1–18.

Gura, Philip F. "Baring the New England Soul." *American Quarterly* 38.4 (1986): 653–60.

———. "Cotton Mather's *Life of Phips*: 'A Vice with the Vizard of Vertue upon It.' " *New England Quarterly* 50.3 (September 1977): 447–57.

———. *The Wisdom of Words.* 1981.

Haffenden, Phillip. *New England in the English Nation.* 1974.

Haims, Lynn. "The Face of God: Puritan Iconography in Early American Poetry, Sermons, and Tombstone Carving." *Early American Literature* 14.1 (1979): 15–47.

Hall, David. *Needs and Opportunities in the History of the Book.* 1987.

———. "On Common Ground: The Coherence of American Puritan Studies." *William and Mary Quarterly* 64.2 (April 1987): 193–229.

———. *Worlds of Wonder, Days of Judgment.* 1989.

Hall, Michael G. *The Last American Puritan: The Life of Increase Mather, 1639–1723.* 1988.

Harbert, Earl N. Rev. of *The Office of the Scarlet Letter*, by Sacvan Bercovitch. *New England Quarterly* 65.2 (March 1992): 168–70.

Harlan, David. "A People Blinded from Birth: American History According to Sacvan Bercovitch." *Journal of American History* 78.3 (December 1991): 949.

Harlow, Thompson. "Thomas Robbins, Clergyman, Book Collector, and Librarian," *Papers of the Bibliographical Society of America* 61 (First Quarter 1967): 1–11.

Harris, Susan K. *9th-Century American Women's Novels: Interpretive Strategies.* 1990.

Hatch, Nathan. *The Democratization of American Christianity.* 1989.

Hawthorne, Nathaniel. *The American Notebooks.* Centenary Edition. 1972.

———. *Biographical Sketches.* 1876.

———. *The Blithedale Romance.* Centenary Edition. 1964.

———. "The Custom House." In *The Scarlet Letter.* Centenary Edition. 1962.

———. *The House of the Seven Gables.* Centenary Edition. 1965.

———. *The Marble Faun.* Centenary Edition. 1974.

———. "The Minister's Black Veil." In *Twice-told Tales.* Centenary Edition. 1974.

———. *Mosses from an Old Manse.* Centenary Edition. 1974.

———. "The Old Apple Dealer." In *Twice-told Tales.* Centenary Edition. 1974.

———. "The Old Manse." In *Mosses from an Old Manse.* Centenary Edition. 1974.

———. "Old News." In *The Snow Image.* Centenary Edition. 1974.

———. "Passages from a Relinquished Work." In *Mosses from an Old Manse.* Centenary Edition. 1974.

———. "Portrait of Phips." In *Biographical Sketches.* Centenary Edition. 1974.

———. *The Scarlet Letter.* Centenary Edition. 1972.

———. *The Story-Teller.* Centenary Edition. 1974.

———. "The Virtuoso's Collection." In *Mosses from an Old Manse.* Centenary Edition. 1974.

———. *The Whole History of Grandfather's Chair.* Centenary Edition. 1972.

———. "Young Goodman Brown." In *Twice-told Tales.* Centenary Edition. 1974.

Hayden, Dolores. *The Grand Domestic Revolution.* 1982.

Hedrick, Joan. " 'Peaceable Fruits': The Ministry of Harriet Beecher Stowe." *American Quarterly* 40.3 (September 1988): 307–32.

Hirsh, E. D. *Validity in Interpretation.* 1967.

Holmes, Thomas James. *Cotton Mather, a Bibliography of His Works.* 1940.

Howells, William Dean. *Annie Kilburn.* 1888. 1992.

———. *The Undiscovered Country.* 1880.

Hubbard, William. *General History of New England.* 1682.

Hutner, Gordon. *Secrets and Sympathy.* 1988.

Irwin, John T. *American Hieroglyphics.* 1980.

James, Henry. *The Bostonians.* 1886. 1974.

Jauss, Hans Robert. *Towards an Aesthetic of Reception.* Trans. Timothy Bahti. 1982.

Jehlen, Myra. *American Incarnation.* 1986.

Jenkins, Lawrence, and Walter Whitehill. "The Restoration of East India Marine Hall," *American Neptune* 4 (1944): 5–17.

Jerome, Saint. *De viris illustribus.* A.D. 393.

Jeske, Jeffrey. "Cotton Mather: Physico-Theologian." *Journal of the History of Ideas* 47 (October–December 1986): 583–94.

Jewett, Sarah Orne. *The Country of the Pointed Firs.* 1896. 1982.

Jimenez, Mary Ann. *Changing Faces of Madness.* 1987.

Johnson, Edward. *The Wonder-Working Providence of Sion's Saviour in New England.* 1650. 1910.

Johnson, Parker. "Humiliation Followed by Deliverance: Metaphor and Plot in Cotton Mather's *Magnalia*." *Early American Literature* 15.3 (1980): 237–46.

Johnson, Richard. *Adjustment to Empire*. 1981.

Kamuf, Peggy. "Penelope at Work: Interruptions in *A Room of One's Own*." *Feminism and Foucault*. Ed. Irene Diamond and Lee Quinby. 1988.

Karlsen, Carol F. *The Devil in the Shape of a Woman*. 1987.

Keil, James C. "Reading, Writing, and Recycling: Literary Archaeology and the Shape of Hawthorne's Career." *New England Quarterly* 65.2 (June 1992): 238–64.

Kelley, Mary. *Private Woman, Public Stage*. 1954.

Kerber, Linda. "Separate Spheres, Female Worlds, Woman's Place: The Rhetoric of Women's History." *Journal of American History* 75 (June 1988): 9–39.

Kibbey, Ann. *The Interpretation of Material Shapes in Puritanism*. 1986.

Kronick, Joseph G. Rev. of *The Office of the Scarlet Letter*, by Sacvan Bercovitch, and *The Anatomy of National Fantasy: Hawthorne, Utopia and Everyday Life*, by Lauren Berlaut. *Criticism* 34.4 (Fall 1992): 624–28.

Kulik, Gary. "Designing the Past: History-Museum Exhibitions from Peale to the Present." *History Museums in the United States*. Ed. Leon Warren and Roy Rosenzweig. 1989. 3–37.

Lang, Amy Schrager. *Prophetic Woman*. 1987.

Lathrop, Thomas. *Individualism in the Forms of Life and in the Culture of the Soul*. 1854.

Lawrence, D. H. *Studies in Classic American Literature*. 1923. 1955.

Lentricchia, Frank. *After the New Criticism*. 1980.

Leverenz, David. *The Language of Puritan Feeling*. 1980.

———. *Manhood and the American Renaissance*. 1989.

Levin, David. *Cotton Mather: The Young Life of the Lord's Remembrancer*. 1978.

———. *Forms of Uncertainty*. 1992.

———. "Giants in the Earth: Science and the Occult in Cotton Mather's Letters to the Royal Society." *William and Mary Quarterly* 45 (October 1988): 751–70.

———. "The Hazing of Cotton Mather: The Creation of a Biographical Personality." *In Defense of Historical Literature*. 1967. 34–57.

———. "Trying to Make a Monster Human: Judgment in the Biography of Cotton Mather." *Yale Review* 73.2 (Winter 1984): 210–29.

Levine, Lawrence. *Highbrow/Lowbrow*. 1988.

Lloyd-Smith, Allan Gardner. *Eve Tempted*. 1983.

Longfellow, Samuel, ed. *Life of Henry Wadsworth Longfellow with Extracts from His Journals and Correspondence*. 3 vols. 1891.

Looby, Christopher. "Charles Willson Peale and the Labor of Representation." *American Quarterly* 41.2 (1989): 362–66.

Lovelace, Richard. *The American Pietism of Cotton Mather: Origins of American Evangelicalism*. 1979.

Lowance, Mason. *Images and Shadows of Divine Things: Puritan Typology in New England from 660– 750*. PhD diss. Emory University, 1967.

—————. *The Language of Canaan.* 1980.

Lukács, Georg. *Studies in European Realism.* 1964.

Luther, Martin. *Luther's Ninety-five Theses.* Trans. C. M. Jacobs. Revised by Harold J. Grimm. 1957.

MacFarlane, Lisa. "The New England Kitchen Goes Uptown: Domestic Displacements in Harriet Beecher Stowe's New York." *New England Quarterly* 64.2 (June 1991): 272–91.

Manning, Stephen. *Scriptural Exegesis and Literary Criticism.* 1972.

Marx, Leo. Rev. of *The Puritan Origins of the American Self,* by Sacvan Bercovitch. *New York Times Book Review* (February 1, 1976): 21.

Mather, Cotton. "Biblia Americana." In *Mather Papers.* Massachusetts Historical Society, *Collections.* 4th series. 8. 1866.

—————. *The Diary of Cotton Mather.* Ed. Worthington Ford. 1912.

—————. *Johannes in Eremo.* 1695.

—————. *Magnalia Christi Americana; or, The Ecclesiastical History of New-England, from its First Planting in the Year 1620, unto the Year of Our Lord 1698.* Introduction and occasional notes by Thomas Robbins. 1852 ed. 2 vols. Reproduction of 1820 edition. 1967.

—————. *Magnalia Christi Americana; or, The Ecclesiastical History of New-England, from its First Planting in the Year 1620, unto the Year of Our Lord 1698.* 1820.

—————. *Magnalia Christi Americana; or, The Ecclesiastical History of New-England, from its First Planting in the Year 1620, unto the Year of Our Lord 1698.* Edited by Kenneth Murdock, with the assistance of Elizabeth W. Miller. 1976.

—————. (authorship uncertain). *Publick Occurrences.* 1690.

—————. *Selected Letters of Cotton Mather.* Ed. Kenneth S. Silverman. 1971.

—————. *Selections.* Ed. Kenneth Murdock. 1960.

—————. *Wonders of the Invisible World.* 1692.

Mather, Increase. *A Brief Discourse Concerning the Unlawfulness of the Common Prayer Worship.* 1686.

—————. *A Further Account of the Tryals of the New England Witches.* 1693.

—————. *A Narrative of the Miseries of New England by Reason of an Arbitrary Government Erected There Under Sir Edmond Andros.* 1884.

—————. *Practical Truths Tending to Promote the Power of Godliness.* 1682.

—————. *The Revolution in New England Justified and the People There Vindicated from the Aspersions Cast upon Them by Mr. John Palmer in His Pretended Answer to the Declaration Published by the Inhabitants of Boston and the County Adjacent, on the Day When They Secured Their Late Oppressors, Who Acted by an Illegal and Arbitrary Commission of the Late King James.* 1691.

—————. *A Testimony Against Several Prophane and Superstitious Customs.* 1687.

Mather, Richard. *A Heart Melting Exhortation.* 1653.

Mather, Samuel. *The Figures or Types of the Old Testament.* 1683. Rpt. 1705.

Mather Papers. Massachusetts Historical Society, *Collections.* 4th series. 8. 1866.

Matlack, James. "Hawthorne and Elizabeth Barstow Stoddard." *New England Quarterly* 50.3 (1977): 278–302.

Matthiessen, F. O. *American Renaissance: Art and Expression in the Age of Emerson and Whitman.* 1941. 1968.

Michaels, Walter Benn. *The Gold Standard and the Logic of Naturalism.* 1987.

Michaels, Walter Benn, and Donald Pease, eds. *The American Renaissance Reconsidered.* 1985.

Middlekauff, Robert. *The Mathers: Three Generations of Puritan Intellectuals, 596–728.* 1971.

Miller, Perry. *The American Puritans.* 1956.

———. *Errand into the Wilderness.* 1981.

———. *The New England Mind: From Colony to Province.* 1983.

———. *The New England Mind: The Seventeenth-Century.* 1961.

Miner, Earl, ed. *Literary Uses of Typology.* 1977.

Mizruchi, Susan. *The Power of Historical Knowledge.* 1988.

Montrose, Louis, " 'Shaping Fantasies': Figurations of Gender and Power in Elizabethan Culture." *Representing the English Renaissance.* Ed. Stephen Greenblatt. 1988. 31–64.

Moody, Robert E. and Richard C. Simmons. *The Glorious Revolution in Massachusetts Selected Documents, 1689–1692.* 1988.

Morgan, Edwin. "The Chosen People." *New York Review of Books* (July 19, 1979): 33.

Morton, Nathaniel. *New Englands Memoriall.* 1669.

Mullaney, Steven. "Strange Things, Gross Terms, Curious Customs: The Rehearsal of Cultures in the Late Renaissance." *Representing the English Renaissance.* Ed. Stephen Greenblatt. 1988. 65–92.

Murdock, Kenneth. "Clio in the Wilderness: History and Biography in Puritan New England." *Church History* 24 (1955): 221–38.

———. "Cotton Mather." In *Magnalia Christi Americana.* 1976, 1–25.

Neal, Daniel. *History of New England.* 1719.

New England Colonial Records. Connecticut State Library, Hartford.

Nicholls, Peter. "Old Problems and the New Historicism." *Journal of American Studies* 23.3 (December 1989): 423.

Oakes, Urian. *New England Pleaded With.* 1683.

Osgood, Russell K. *The History of the Law in Massachusetts, 1692–1992.* 1992.

Pahl, Dennis. *Architects of the Abyss.* 1989.

Parker, Theodore. *The Collected Works of Theodore Parker.* Ed. Frances Cobbe. 1864.

Parrington, Vernon. *Main Currents in American Thought.* 2 vols. 1939.

Pearce, Roy Harvey. *Historicism Once More.* 1969.

Pease, Donald. *Visionary Compacts.* 1987.

Pechter, Edward. "The New Historicism and Its Discontents: Politicizing Renaissance Drama." *PMLA* 102 (May 1987): 292–303.

Perrot, Michelle, ed. *L'impossible prison: Recherches sur le système pénitentiaire au XIXe siècle.* 1980.

Perry, Dennis. *Autobiographical Structures in Seventeenth-Century Puritan Histories.* PhD diss. University of Wisconsin, Madison, 1986.

Pettit, Norman. "The Puritan Legacy." *New England Quarterly* 48.2 (1975): 283–94.
Porte, Joel. *The Romance in America.* 1969.
Rabinowitz, Richard. *The Spiritual Self in Everyday Life.* 1989.
Radway, Janice. *Reading the Romance.* 1984.
Raleigh, Sir Walter. *History of the World.* 1614.
Reynolds, David S. *Beneath the American Renaissance.* 1988.
Reynolds, Larry J. *European Revolutions and the American Literary Renaissance.* 1988.
Richards, Jeffrey. *Theater Enough.* 1991.
Richardson, Robert D. *Myth and Literature in the American Renaissance.* 1978.
Robbins, Thomas. *Diary of Thomas Robbins, D.D., 1796–1854.* Ed. Increase N. Tarbox. 1886–87.
Robertson, Eric S. *Life of Henry Wadsworth Longfellow.* 1887.
Roen, William Henry. *Prophets and Angels: A Study of the Self-Presentation of Selected American Puritan Preachers.* PhD diss. Catholic University of America, 1987.
Rosenmeier, Jesper. *The Image of Christ: The Typology of John Cotton.* PhD diss. Harvard University, 1966.
———. "The Teacher and the Witness: John Cotton and Roger Williams." *William and Mary Quarterly* 25 (1968): 408–31.
———. " 'With My Owne Eyes': William Bradford's *Of Plymouth Plantation*." *Typology and Early American Literature.* Ed. Sacvan Bercovitch. 1972. 69–105.
Rowlandson, Mary White. *A Narrative of the Captivity, Suffering, and Removes of Mrs. Mary Rowlandson.* 1856.
Rugoff, Milton. *The Beechers: An American Family in the Nineteenth Century.* 1981.
Rutman, Darrett. "New England as Idea and Society Revisited." *William and Mary Quarterly* 61.1 (1984): 56–61.
Ryan, Mary P. *The Empire of Mother.* 1982.
Sargent, Epes. *Planchette, or the Despair of Science.* 1869.
Schlesinger, Arthur M., Jr. *The Age of Jackson.* 1948.
Scobey, David. "Revising the Errand." *William and Mary Quarterly* 41.1 (1984): 3–31.
Shalhope, Robert. *The Roots of Democracy.* 1990.
Shulman, Robert. *Social Criticism and Nineteenth-Century American Fictions.* 1987.
Silverman, Kaja. *The Subject of Semiotics.* 1983.
Silverman, Kenneth. *The Life and Times of Cotton Mather.* 1984.
Sklar, Kathryn Kish. *Catherine Beecher: A Study in American Domesticity.* 1976.
Smith, Page. *The Nation Comes of Age.* 1990.
St. Armand, Barton. "Veiled Ladies: Dickinson, Bettine, and Transcendental Mediumship." *Studies in the American Renaissance.* Ed. Joel Myerson. 1987. 1–52.
Stedman, Laura, and George Gould. *Life and Letters of E. C. Stedman.* 1910.
Steele, Jeffrey. *The Representation of the Self in the American Renaissance.* 1987.
Stein, Roger. "Seascape and the American Imagination: The Puritan Seventeenth Century." *Early American Literature* 7 (Spring 1972): 17–37.

Stoddard, Elizabeth. *The Morgesons and Other Writings, Published and Unpublished.* Ed. Lawrence Buell and Sandra Zagarell. 1984.

Stoughton, William. *A Narrative of the Proceedings of Sir Edmond Androsse and His Accomplices.* 1691.

Stowe, Harriet Beecher. *The Minister's Wooing.* 1859. 1982.

———. *Oldtown Folks.* 1869. 1982.

Strong, George Templeton. *The Diary of George Templeton Strong.* Ed. Allan Nevins and Milton Halsey Thomas. Abridged by Thomas J. Pressly. 1988.

Strout, Cushing. "Paradoxical Puritans." *American Scholar* 45 (Autumn 1976): 602.

Taylor, Francis. *Babel's Tower.* 1945.

Tebbel, John. *A History of Book Publishing in the United States.* 1972.

Thoreau, Henry D. *A Week on the Concord and Merrimack Rivers.* Ed. Carl F. Houde, William L. Howarth, and Elizabeth Hall Witherell. 1980.

Tichi, Cecelia. "The Puritan Historians and Their New Jerusalem." *Early American Literature* 6 (1971): 143–55.

Tompkins, Jane. *Sensational Designs.* 1985.

Trachtenberg, Alan. "The Writer as America." *Partisan Review* 44.3 (1977): 468.

Trefz, Edward. "The Puritans' View of History." *Boston Public Library Quarterly* 9 (1957): 115–36.

Trumbull, Benjamin. *History of Connecticut.* 1713.

Vandewetering, Maxine. "The Popular Concept of 'Home' in Nineteenth-Century America." *Journal of American Studies* 18 (1984): 2–28.

Vicars, John. *Magnalia Dei Anglicana.* 1646.

Voloshin, Beverly. "The Limits of Domesticity: The Female Bildungsroman in America, 1820–1870." *Women's Studies* 10 (1984): 283–302.

Voloshinov, V. N. *Marxism and the Philosophy of Language.* 1986.

von Abele, Rudolph. *The Death of the Artist.* 1955.

Wade, Melvin. " 'Shining in Borrowed Plumage': Affirmation of Community in the Black Coronation Festivals of New England, ca. 1750–1850." *Material Life in America, 1600–1860.* 1987. 171–84.

Waggoner, Hyatt. *Hawthorne.* 1955.

———. *The Presence of Hawthorne.* 1979.

Wallace, James. *Early Cooper and His Audience.* 1986.

Warhol, Robyn. "Towards a Theory of the Engaging Narrator: Earnest Interventions in Gaskell, Stowe, and Eliot." *PMLA* 101.5 (October 1986): 811–17.

Warner, Michael. "Franklin and the Letters of the Republic." Fisher 3–24.

Watters, David. "Hawthorne Possessed: Material Culture and the Familiar Spirit of *The House of the Seven Gables.*" *Essex Institute Historical Collections* 125.1 (January 1989): 25–44.

———. "The Spectral Identity of Sir William Phips." *Early American Literature* 18.3 (Winter 1983): 219–32.

Weber, Donald. "Historicizing the Errand." *American Literary History* 2.1 (1990): 101–18.

Weir, Sybil. "*The Morgesons*: A Neglected Feminist *Bildungsroman*," *New England Quarterly* 49.1 (September 1976): 427–39.

Westbrook, Perry. *A Literary History of New England*. 1988.

Wiebe, Robert. *The Opening of American Society*. 1984.

Wilburn, Cora. *Banner of Light*. March 19, 1870. 3.

———. *Banner of Light*. July 16, 1870. 4.

William of Orange. *Declarations of the Hague*. 1691.

Williams, Roger. *Key into the Language of America*. 1643.

Wilson, Christopher. "Containing Multitudes: Realism, Historicism, American Studies." *American Quarterly* 41.3 (September 1989): 466–95.

———. *The Labor of Words*. 1985.

———. "Tempests and Teapots: Harriet Beecher Stowe's *The Minister's Wooing*." *New England Quarterly* 58.4 (December 1985): 554–77.

Wilson, Edmund. "Harriet Beecher Stowe." *Critical Essays on Harriet Beecher Stowe*. 1980. 117–21.

Wilson, Forrest. *Crusader in Crinoline: The Life of Harriet Beecher Stowe*. 1941.

Wilson, R. Jackson. *Figures of Speech*. 1989.

Winship, Michael. "Cotton Mather, Astrologer." *New England Quarterly* 63.2 (1990): 308–14.

Winters, Yvor. *Maule's Curse*. 1938.

Winthrop Papers, 1498–1649. Ed. Allyn Forbes. 5 vols. 1929–47.

Zagarell, Sandra. "The Repossession of a Heritage: Elizabeth Stoddard's *The Morgesons*." *Studies in American Fiction* 13.1 (1985): 45–56.

Ziff, Larzer. *Literary Democracy*. 1981.

———. *Puritanism in America: New Culture in a New World*. 1973.

Index

✢

Index

Richlieu, Cardinal, 71
Richmond Enquirer, 158
Richmond Junto, 158
Ripley, Ezra, 130
Rivington, James, 90
Robbins, Ammi Ruhamah, 88
Robbins, Philemon, 89
Robbins, Thomas: as Calvinist icon, 238;
    characterization by Stoddard, 237–38;
    as cultural worker, 248; and departure
    from ministry, 95; editorial strategies,
    247; and 1820 edition of *Magnalia,* xii,
    xiv, 12; library, 89; and Mather's map,
    27; and ownership of history, 249; and
    project of national self-definition, 87;
    republicanism, 91
Rochester, Massachusetts, 94
romance, 190
romanticism, 210
Rome, 91, 160
Rose, 32, 33, 51
Rowlandson, Mary, 21, 43
Royal Society, 153

sacred history, 20, 40–41
Saint Jerome, 46; *De viris illustribus,* 49
Salem, Massachusetts, 31, 62, 92, 98,
    131–32, 142, 207; material legacy, 120–
    21
Salem witchcraft delusion, 57, 137, 222,
    240, 242
school of Hawthorne, 108, 201
Scott, James, 32
scriptural history, 251
second charter, 19
sectionalism, 192
secular politics, as Puritanized history,
    197
self-fashioning, 114
semiotic realism, 209
Shaker spiritualists, 230
Shepard, Thomas, 41
Sheridan, Comedies, 239
Shrimpton, Samuel, 51
slave trade, 196

spectral evidence, 241
spectral identity, 66
spectral personality, 227
spectral phenomenon, 220
spiritualism, 202, 203, 208, 209, 211, 212,
    242, 265n.18
Sterne, Laurence, *Sentimental Journey,*
    239
Stoddard, Elizabeth, xi, xii, 13, 16, 19;
    alien stance, 205, 222, 226; criticisms
    of Nathaniel Hawthorne, 108; defami-
    liarization of Puritanism, 220; entre-
    preneurial impulse, 22; ethnographic
    narration, 209; figural portrayal, 239;
    friendship with Thomas Robbins, 94;
    historical fiction, 97, 210; iconoclasm,
    212; identity of ancestor, 239; liberated
    by mediumship, 213, 225–27; occult
    interests, 210–11; oppositional stance,
    209; parallels to Hawthorne, 208; as
    realist, 211; recasting of *Magnalia,* 209;
    recollection of Salem, 132; reliance on
    openness, 244; shape of career, 245;
    and spiritualism, 98–99, 228–29: as a
    rhetorical principle, 221; use of politi-
    cal accents, 101; vernacular preaching,
    213; and women, 5
    Works: *The Morgesons,* 13, 15: and
    Mather's discussion of aliases and
    specters, xvi; narrative device of the
    planchette, 99; and radical histori-
    cism, xvi; witchcraft theme, 214–19,
    "A Village on the Sea Shore," 222
Stoddard, Richard Henry, 212
Stoughton, William, 30, 51
Stowe, Harriett Beecher, xi, xii, 13, 16,
    19; aesthetic ideology, 278n.4; basis of
    historical analysis, 190–91; conception
    of government, 158, 159–60, 164; dem-
    ocratic literacy, 170; domesticity in
    narration and history, 162, 186–90;
    eastward retreat, 193; exemplaristic
    characterization, 160, 166–67; as a his-
    torian, 180–81, 198; historical fiction,
    97; impatient readers, 168; interest in